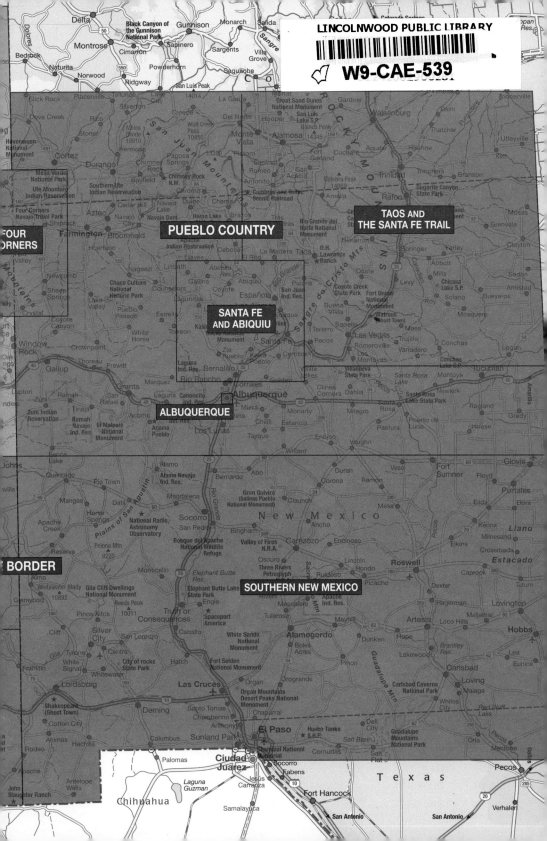

INSIGHT ⦿ GUIDES

USA SOUTHWEST

◉ Walking Eye App

YOUR FREE DESTINATION CONTENT AND EBOOK AVAILABLE THROUGH THE WALKING EYE APP

Your guide now includes a free eBook and destination content for your chosen destination, all for the same great price as before. Simply download the Walking Eye App from the App Store or Google Play to access your free eBook and destination content.

HOW THE WALKING EYE APP WORKS

Through the Walking Eye App, you can purchase a range of eBooks and destination content. However, when you buy this book, you can download the corresponding eBook and destination content for free. Just see below in the grey panels where to find your free content and then scan the QR code at the bottom of this page.

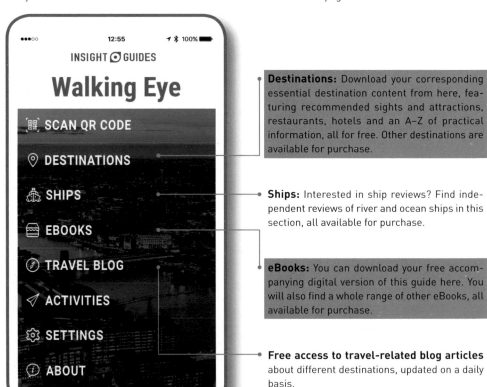

Destinations: Download your corresponding essential destination content from here, featuring recommended sights and attractions, restaurants, hotels and an A–Z of practical information, all for free. Other destinations are available for purchase.

Ships: Interested in ship reviews? Find independent reviews of river and ocean ships in this section, all available for purchase.

eBooks: You can download your free accompanying digital version of this guide here. You will also find a whole range of other eBooks, all available for purchase.

Free access to travel-related blog articles about different destinations, updated on a daily basis.

HOW THE DESTINATION CONTENT WORKS

Each destination includes a short introduction, an A–Z of practical information and recommended points of interest, split into 4 different categories:

- Highlights
- Accommodation
- Eating out
- What to do

You can view the location of every point of interest and save it by adding it to your Favourites. In the 'Around Me' section you can view all the points of interest within 5km.

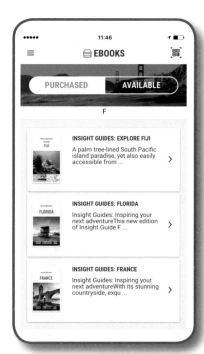

HOW THE EBOOKS WORK

The eBooks are provided in EPUB file format. Please note that you will need an eBook reader installed on your device to open the file. Many devices come with this as standard, but you may still need to install one manually from Google Play.

The eBook content is identical to the content in the printed guide.

HOW TO DOWNLOAD THE WALKING EYE APP

1. Download the Walking Eye App from the App Store or Google Play.
2. Open the app and select the scanning function from the main menu.
3. Scan the QR code on this page – you will then be asked a security question to verify ownership of the book.
4. Once this has been verified, you will see your eBook and destination content in the purchased ebook and destination sections, where you will be able to download them.

Other destination apps and eBooks are available for purchase separately or are free with the purchase of the Insight Guide book.

CONTENTS

Travel Tips

TRANSPORTATION

A – Z

FURTHER READING

Maps

Inside front cover American Southwest
Inside back cover Canyonlands National Park
  and Zion National Park

LEGEND
◯ Insight on
◉ Photo Story

THE BEST OF THE AMERICAN SOUTHWEST: TOP ATTRACTIONS

△ **The Grand Canyon**. Words cannot easily express the scale and grandeur of one of the world's greatest natural wonders, millions of years in the making. See page 305.

▽ **Monument Valley**. The backdrop of countless Western movies, this is one of the iconic landscapes of the American West and an epicenter of traditional Navajo culture. See page 294.

△ **Santa Fe**. Lovely old adobe homes, intriguing museums, and world-class cuisine and art markets make Santa Fe, the country's oldest state capital and first designated American Unesco Creative City, a must. See page 239.

△ **Taos Pueblo**. Iconic and inspiring, this thousand-year-old pueblo is one of the country's oldest continuously occupied villages. See page 259.

△ **Sedona**. Set within stunning red-rock formations, this town has a lively arts scene, lots of shopping and dining, and a reputation for New Age vibrations. See page 322.

◁ **Kartchner Caverns**. A rare wet, living-cave system in the Whetstone Mountains, the beautiful caverns below this former ranch make it Arizona's top state park. See page 190.

▷ **Mesa Verde National Park**. Cliff Palace is one of the most magical Ancestral Pueblo cliff dwellings at the nation's favorite archeological park, near Durango in the Four Corners region of southwestern Colorado. See page 276.

△ **Utah's Grand Circle of Parks**. Carved into labyrinthine canyons by the Colorado and Green rivers, Canyonlands is a highlight of a park circuit that includes visits to Arches, Capitol Reef, Bryce, and Zion national parks. See page 285.

▽ **Chaco Culture National Park**. Haunting great house and kiva ruins in a remote canyon in northwestern New Mexico are still revealing the extraordinary story of the ancient world's most powerful civilization. See page 274.

△ **The Sonoran Desert**. Symbolized by the endemic saguaro cactus, an iconic presence, and "sky island" mountains harboring unique wildlife, the sweeping Sonoran Desert surrounds the cities of Phoenix and Tucson and invites exploration. See page 183.

THE BEST OF THE AMERICAN SOUTHWEST: EDITOR'S CHOICE

Tombstone actors.

BEST FOR FAMILIES

Meow Wolf. Santa Fe's top visitor attraction is a mind-altering Victorian haunted house with experiential rooms envisioned and created by an imaginative artists collective. See page 247.

Arizona-Sonora Desert Museum. Not really a museum but a huge zoo in Tucson celebrating animals of the Sonoran Desert, which are housed in naturalistic enclosures and star in well-conceived presentations. See page 177.

Tombstone. "The Town Too Tough to Die" now offers staged gunfights, stage coach and wagon rides, live music in some of the saloons, Boot Hill Cemetery, and a museum with exhibits on the Shootout at the OK Corral. See page 191.

New Mexico Museum of Natural History. Exploding volcanoes, towering dinosaur skeletons, and other experiential exhibits attract kids of all ages to this popular downtown Albuquerque museum adjoining the children's museum, Explora! See page 225.

Durango & Silverton Narrow Gauge Railroad. Ride to Silverton and enjoy views of Mount Sneffels and the glorious Animal River valley, preferably during the fall when the aspens turn golden. See page 277.

BEST SCENERY

Grand Canyon National Park. One of the must-see wonders of the world, the "Big Ditch" delivers sublime scenery and glimpses of 2 billion years of earth history. See page 305.

Canyonlands National Park. A 100-mile bird's-eye view of mountain ranges, buttes, canyons, and human history awaits visitors to Canyonlands' spectacular Island in the Sky near Moab. See page 288.

Rio Grande Gorge. Protected within one of New Mexico's newest national monuments, the gorge cut by the Rio Grande through a dark lava escarpment north of Taos is an awesome sight. See page 260.

Monument Valley. Its iconic redrock landmarks set against a sandy valley deep in the Navajo Nation not far from Canyon de Chelly are the epitome of the Wild West. See page 294.

Zion Canyon. The Virgin River, a tributary of the Colorado, has carved through sedimentary rocks to create a deep, narrow canyon hemmed in by sheer redrocks at this scenic Utah park. See page 300.

San Luis Valley. Combining traditional Hispanic culture, New Age retreats, hot springs, high peaks, America's tallest sand dunes, and over-wintering sandhill cranes, the San Luis Valley surrounding Alamosa is a unique destination. See page 262.

BEST HISTORIC SITES

Pecos Pueblo National Historical Park. Ruins of an important prehistoric pueblo and Spanish Colonial church are protected at this Pecos Valley site, alongside a Civil War battlefield. See page 248.

Bandelier National Monument. Cavelike cliff dwellings and a large pueblo ruin are protected deep in Frijoles Canyon in this Jemez Mountains park, along with WPA-era art. See page 250.

Pipe Spring National Monument. A restored 19th-century fortified Mormon pioneer dairy ranch and ancient pueblo ruins sit on permanent springs on Paiute Indian land. See page 302.

San Xavier del Bac Mission. A stunning 18th-century Spanish Catholic mission church built to serve Tohono O'odham Indians near Tucson, the "White Dove of the Desert" still serves the reservation. See page 181.

El Presidio Historical District. The Old Pueblo of Tucson's historic adobes are clustered around the old Spanish presidio and include modest pioneer homes and Nob Hill mansions. See page 173.

Taliesin West. Frank Lloyd Wright's low-slung Southwest home and school in the Scottsdale hills offers daily tours and fascinating insights into Wright's work in Phoenix. See page 168.

BEST WILDLIFE VIEWING

Bosque del Apache NWR. Overwintering snow geese and sandhill cranes making mass ascensions at dawn are the draw at this famous viewing spot on the Rio Grande. See page 214.

Willcox Playa. A flooded desert playa forms a wetland for overwintering migratory waterfowl in southeastern Arizona that attracts birders all winter long. See page 195.

San Pedro Riparian National Conservation Area. An international flyover river for numerous bird species, the San

Pedro River has been used by ancient humans as far back as Paleo-Indian times. See page 191.

Ramsey Canyon. Seven species of migratory hummingbirds are the big attraction for birders in summer at this Nature Conservancy site in the Huachuca Mountains. See page 188.

Grand Canyon South Rim. Visitors to the South Rim can view released endangered condors at an overlook near the Kolb Studio, as well as upriver at Marble Canyon. See page 307.

BEST MUSEUMS AND GALLERIES

Museum of New Mexico Palace of the Governors. Overlooking Santa Fe Plaza, this venerable adobe has seen over four centuries of New Mexico history and is part of the History Museum. See page 240.

International Museum of Folk Art. Santa Fe's most popular museum displays a large and unusual collection of folk art from all over the world in dioramas and special exhibits. See page 247.

Heard Museum. The perfect introduction to Arizona's Indian cultures through an award-winning multimedia presentation, special collections, contemporary exhibits, and Indian arts and crafts festivals, all in historic downtown Phoenix. See page 163.

Museum of Northern Arizona. Founded in Flagstaff by archeologist Harold Cotton, MNA is the major repository for artifacts unearthed at nearby

Wupatki Pueblo and other digs and has exhibits on northern Arizona's geology, history, and cultures. See page 326.

Phoenix Art Museum. After a major expansion, PAM's own excellent collections have been augmented by international traveling art exhibits. See page 162.

Georgia O'Keeffe Museum. The only museum dedicated to an American woman artist, this delightful museum displays revolving selections of O'Keeffe's work and offers lectures and special tours to the artist's home in Abiquiu. See page 242.

Western Spirit: Scottsdale's Museum of the West. Private collections of extraordinary cowboy and Indian art tell the story of the Western states in a beautifully designed, sustainable museum building in Old Town Scottsdale. See page 166.

Snow geese take flight in Bosque del Apache NWR.

The Wave is a unique sandstone formation shaped by wind and rain in the Coyote Buttes area of Arizona.

White Mountain Apache dancers at Indian Pueblo Cultural Center, Albuquerque, New Mexico.

Horses at Rancho de los
Caballeros, Wickenburg, Arizona.

Antelope House ruins, Canyon de Chelly National Monument.

AN ANCIENT LAND

Numerous Indian cultures mingle with a rich Spanish Colonial legacy to create an alluring experience in the American Southwest.

Makers of maps like to keep things orderly and will define the American Southwest in terms of state boundaries. But those who live there know that another boundary must be applied. The Southwest begins where the land rises out of that vast ocean of humid air that covers the American Midwest and makes it the fertile breadbasket it is. And it ends along that vague line where winter cold wins out over sun and even the valleys are buried under snow. There is one ever more essential requirement. Wherever you stand in the Southwest there must be, on one horizon or another, the spirit-healing blue shape of mountains. Thus you have Arizona and New Mexico, a slice of southern Colorado, much of southern Utah, and parts of Nevada and Texas.

The Southwest is high – an immense tableland broken by the high ridges of the southern Rocky Mountains – and dry, with annual precipitation varying drastically with altitude. This highness and dryness affects the air, making it exceptionally transparent and adding clarity to everything one sees. The few minutes required to travel from the Rio Grande to the top of the ski basin in Albuquerque's Sandia Mountains traverses five of North America's biological life zones, from the Upper Sonoran Desert to the cool spruce forests of the Arctic-Alpine zone.

In northern New Mexico, culture as well as beauty attracted scores of artists to Taos. This is Indian Country. The complex culture of the Pueblo Indians has survived in centuries-old adobe villages scattered along the Rio Grande and inland at Zuni and the Hopi Mesas. And so has America's largest tribe, the Navajo Nation, or as they call themselves, the Dineh. Some 200,000 strong, they occupy a vast reservation that sprawls across the heart of the Southwest in Arizona, New Mexico, and Utah. These first Americans occupy a sacred land of shrines and holy mountains.

A Navajo man tries to explain why he has returned to this empty land from a lonely, crowded California city. He looks down into the immense valley that spreads below the southwest slope of the Chuska Mountains and surveys a harsh but hauntingly beautiful land of sun-baked stone stretching into the distance. Gray caliche, wind-cut clay as red as barn paint, great bluish outcrops of shale, and cracked salt flats where mud formed by the violent "male rains" of summer tastes as bitter as alum. Everything is worn, eroded, and tortured. The desert teems with life, but to the naked eye, nothing seems to be alive. European map-makers might call it Desolation Sink, but this prodigal son returning home smiles affectionately. "The Navajo name for this place," he says, "is Beautiful Valley."

The iconic landsape of
Monument Valley.

A GEOLOGIST'S PARADISE

Don't discount the desert as an empty, boring place.
The geology of the American Southwest is highly complex,
both mesmerizing and enriching in what it reveals.

Few places in the world can rival the desert of the American Southwest for its striking geological structures. It is a geologist's paradise, but it is also a fine place for non-geologists to make a foray into the subject. The rocks are beautiful, and the stories they tell are easy to learn. In addition, there is no need to contend with those intrusive green things called trees, which so often prevent an observer from seeing rocks.

As the great explorer of the Grand Canyon, John Wesley Powell, wrote more than a century ago, "Wherever we look there is but a wilderness of rocks, deep gorges where the rivers are lost below cliffs and towers and pinnacles and ten thousand strangely carved forms in every direction, and beyond them mountains blending with the clouds."

John Wesley Powell also was the first person to compare the geology of the Southwest to a vast book waiting to be read. Like all good stories, this one is best told from the beginning.

BEGINNINGS

The oldest rocks in the Southwest, and some of the oldest rocks on the planet, rest in the depths of the Grand Canyon. The 2-billion-year-old rocks are known as the Vishnu Schist and consist of sediments originally deposited into a sea that washed onto a shore at the edge of a continent. These rocks were then uplifted and folded into a mountain chain, injected with veins of molten rock and then uplifted and folded again. And possibly yet again. This created a rock that today is banded and contorted in some places, and platy and shiny in others.

The next oldest rocks in the Grand Canyon, which rest directly on top of the Vishnu Schist,

Antelope Canyon, Arizona.

⊘ A BRIEF HISTORY OF EARTH

Years Ago: Event of Some Significance
4.6 billion: Formation of Earth
4.3 billion: The crust, ocean, and atmosphere form
3.96 billion: The oldest known rocks (Yukon, Canada)
3.9 billion: End of the major meteorite impacts
2.4 billion: Large continents develop
2.0 billion: The atmosphere becomes oxygen-rich
1.45 billion: Single-cell organisms develop
680 million: Multi-celled animals develop
290 million: Dinosaurs begin their dominance
100 million: Flowering plants take root

are only 545 million years old. Did no deposition occur in the intervening 1.2 billion years? Or were rocks deposited and then beveled away by erosion? No one knows. Geologists call a feature like this, where two rocks of vastly different ages are in contact, an unconformity. Unconformities are more the norm in geology than the exception to the rule. No matter where one looks in the rock record, more pieces are missing than are present. Erosion sometimes complicates the matter.

The 500-million-year-old sandstones of the

Glen Canyon National Recreation Area.

Grand Canyon were deposited at the edge of another sea that left behind sediments from Arizona to Canada. It remained in the region for many millions of years, depositing additional sediments. Geologists find fine examples of fossil trilobites intriguing because they were one of the first organisms on the planet to contain a skeleton. The Grand Canyon trilobite fossils range in size from 0.25in (0.6cm) to around 3ins (7.5cm) in length.

A TIME OF FISH AND TROPICAL SEAS

Trilobites became extinct 220 million years ago, followed by yet another period of missing time, but only the small amount of just 100 million

years. At this point in time, the North American continent, which was slowly moving northward, straddled the equator.

A warm, tropical sea covered much of the Southwest and a new group of creatures had begun to make their appearance – fish – although we might not recognize their profile, since a hard coat of bony armor protected their heads. Fossilized scales from these fish occur in a few places in the Grand Canyon.

This span of time, known as the Devonian Period (408–360 million years ago), is often

---

Trilobites, an extinct order of woodlouse-like animals, were one of the first animals to form a protective casing. Nowadays, fossils of trilobites are common.

---

called the Age of Fish. In the next period, the Mississippian (360–320 million years ago), another sea spread over the Southwest and deposited a thick blanket of limestone from Canada to Mexico. Small and poker-chip shaped discs, known as crinoid stems, are one of the most commonly recognizable fossils in the aquatic graveyard of this rock layer, known as the Redwall Limestone. Crinoids were small invertebrates related to sand dollars and sea urchins. They resembled plants, with a base, a stem, and a flowerlike top. Other fossils are solitary corals, looking like a horn or ice cream cone.

Although this fossil-rich period has a red face in the Grand Canyon, it is actually a gray rock covered by coat of red. The red comes from red sediments washing out of the rock layer directly above the Redwall.

Iron is the principal coloring agent of sedimentary rocks in the Southwest. Oxidized iron, which is similar to rust produced on a nail left out in the rain, gives rock its characteristic red color. Sandstone consists of approximately 3 percent iron, mostly as a surface coating on individual grains of sand.

Green layers of rock, especially the ones found in Utah's Arches National Park, contain iron that was altered in a low oxygen environment, such as a shallow lake or mud flat.

Dark brown to black streaks, known as desert varnish, cover many southwestern rock surfaces. This micro-thin coating receives its color from manganese oxides (black) and iron oxides (reddish brown). Geologists argue about how the manganese and iron, which are derived from sources outside the rock, are bonded to the rock surface. Some believe the process involves bacteria that oxidizes the minerals and cements them to the rock, while others believe that a purely chemical reaction occurs among iron, manganese, and water.

environment where evaporation of the closed-in Paradox waters left behind vast beds of salt. Evaporation occurred because the North American continent lay in a warm climatic zone, slightly north of the equator. Episodic flooding and evaporation of this sea produced a mile-thick layer of salt.

Salt has an unusual property: put enough weight on it, and it contorts like Silly Putty. Salt is also less dense than the surrounding sandstone, so it has a tendency to rise when it is forced to move. Under the intense pressure of

Eagle Point overlook on Grand Canyon West.

The latest evidence points to a combination of both.

Formation of a restricted basin in what is now southeastern Utah was the dominant event of the next geologic period, the Pennsylvanian (320–286 million years ago). Known as the Paradox Basin, this northwest-to-southeast trending trough allowed water from an ocean that lay to the west to flow into the area. This oval-shaped basin extended from northwest New Mexico through Moab up to Price, Utah, 120 miles (193km) south of Salt Lake City.

The Paradox Basin sea probably looked something like the modern Mediterranean Sea, with its narrow connection to the Atlantic Ocean. This thin neck created a restricted

☉ THE FINE STUFF OF SAND

Deserts are often associated with sand, and a visitor to the American Southwest will encounter countless varieties of the stuff, from the fine white gypsum of White Sands to the vibrantly burnt orange of Monument Valley. Sand, as intuition might suggest, is the result of weathering on rock. Wind, water, and abrasion grind down rocks into smaller particles that, when wind blown, must eventually gather in deposition, often as sand dunes, the most recognized symbol of the desert yet covering only 20 percent of the planet's deserts. Under the right conditions of time and geology, sand dunes may be subject to forces that turn them into sedimentary stone.

thousands of feet of rock, produced by sediments washing out of nearby mountains, the salt in the area around Moab and Arches National Park began to move and bow upward, creating mile-long ridges capped by a rock unit known as the Entrada Sandstone. Salt movement continued for about 100 million years.

Now jump forward to about 10 million years ago, when water began to percolate into and dissolve the beds of salt, which led to collapse of salt-created ridges. As the sandstone folded into the void, it stretched, cracked, and

town of Moab. This resulted in intermixed layers of sandstone, shale, and limestone. One of the most interesting limestone regions is southeastern New Mexico.

Two hundred and fifty million years ago, a constricted sea covered what is now the area of Carlsbad Caverns National Park and adjoining Guadalupe Mountains National Park. The warm waters were an ideal spot for the formation of a reef resembling Australia's Great Barrier Reef, except that algae and sponges built the 400-mile (640-km) -long by 4-mile (6.4-km)

Double O arch in Arches National Park.

produced a series of parallel cracks, which eroded into a system of parallel canyons and fins, or narrow ridges of rock. Good examples include the Devil's Garden and Fiery Furnace in Arches; fin and canyon formation created a perfect environment for the formation of arches in the park. Arches form when water mixes with atmospheric carbon dioxide to form a weak acid, which first weakens the fins and then erodes them. In addition, during winter, water may seep into fractures in the rock, freeze, expand, and crack the fins open, thus forming an arch.

Advancing and retreating seas were common across the Southwest during the period following the deposition of salt below what is now the

-wide complex, instead of corals, which make up modern reefs.

The caverns at Carlsbad began to form roughly 12 million years ago, during the uplift of the entire reef complex that formed the Guadalupe Mountains. Uplift allowed groundwater to percolate down into the limestone and dissolve it. Dissolution of the rock created passageways and caverns, while deposition of the dissolved elements formed stalactites, which hang down, and stalagmites, which rise upward from the cave's floor.

PETRIFIED TREES AND URANIUM

Throughout the time of advancing and retreating seas, the North American continent continued to move north. The climate was generally warm, with monsoon rains and intermittent dry seasons. During one of the periods when no sea covered the land, a purplish, yellow, and brown mottled rock, the Chinle Formation, was the most important unit deposited, at least from an economic viewpoint.

The Chinle contains huge reserves of uranium, produced from groundwater and most likely leached out of volcanic ash. As it moved through the rock, the uranium-rich water encountered plant remains and replaced the

One non-geologic feature at El Malpais National Monument is a 930-year-old Douglas fir, which must have started to grow within decades of the cooling of the site's lava.

organic material with uranium minerals, which settled out of the water. The Chinle is also the rock unit where one finds the petrified logs at Petrified Forest National Park. Petrified wood formed as a result of a similar process to the uranium but now the groundwater was silica-rich, so quartz precipitated out instead of uranium. The logs originally came from streams carrying material from nearby highlands.

DESERTS AND DINOSAURS DESCEND

By 200 million years ago, the southwestern portion of the continent had drifted into a climatic zone governed by dry, hot conditions. Deserts began their 40-million-year-long reign over the northern portions of the Southwest. The sand dunes of these early deserts have been preserved today as the 200–2,000-ft (60–600 meter) -high cliffs of red and tawny sandstone found in the national parks and surrounding lands of southern Utah.

Non-marine or continental conditions have mostly dominated the Southwest since the time of the deserts. Volcanoes at the edge of the region periodically spewed ash and lava into the lakes and streams. Alteration of these ashes created the green rocks found at Arches National Park. Other rock layers across the Southwest are tan, red, or grayish.

It was during this era that dinosaurs roamed the streams and lakes. When the dinosaurs died, some fell into the streams and washed down into the lowlands, where their bones collected. A good fossil locality is just outside Grand Junction in northwestern Colorado. Near here, paleontologists found the bones of Utahraptor, a 20-ft (6-meter) -long animal with a 12-in (30-cm) -long killing blade growing out of its foot. Utahraptors were a relative of the cinematic velociraptor.

When Steven Spielberg made his movie

Fossilized tree trunk in Petrified Forest NP.

Jurassic Park in 1993, he enlarged the velociraptors, which were actually about the size of a golden retriever, to create a more dramatic beast. Coincidentally, Utahraptor, which was indeed about the same size as Spielberg's velociraptors, but on steroids, was discovered the same summer the movie was released, thus adding a bit of credence to Spielberg's fantasy world.

Utahraptor was excavated from the Morrison Formation, the fossil-rich rock unit that makes up Dinosaur National Monument in northeastern Utah and northwestern Colorado. The extinction of the dinosaurs 66 million years ago occurred as the Rocky Mountains began to be uplifted.

RISE OF THE MOUNTAINS

Additional mountain-building events have occurred several times in the past 66 million years. Numerous small ranges, such as the La Sals, Henrys, Abajos, Sleeping Ute, and Navajo mountains, dot the Southwest and were all formed in this period. Geologists call these mountains laccoliths, while some less serious folk call them "hot humps between the sheets."

Laccoliths like these formed when molten rock or magma cooled within the earth. As the magma was rising it reached a zone of weakness

Valley of Fires Recreation Area, Carrizozo, New Mexico.

⊘ ALL ABOUT MINERALS

While "rock" and "stone" are often used interchange-ably, one can't use "mineral" in the same way: in fact, rocks and stones are usually made from minerals, which are inorganic substances with very specific chemical and crystalline structures. Most minerals are either pure deposits called ores or are blended with other minerals in rock. Many minerals are formed volcanically when magma surging up through the earth's crust forms deposits. The magma then cools, and the heavier basic minerals crystallize first and sink. Minerals may also form because of chemical action – heat causes reactions on surrounding rocks, resulting in mineral changes.

and began to spread laterally between sedimentary layers (the sheets). Continued pulses of magma bowed up the sheets and formed a mushroom-like structure (the hump). Over time, the softer sedimentary rocks eroded away, leaving behind rounded mountains that glaciers would eventually carve into jagged peaks.

In some places, though, the magma pierced the surface and erupted. One such volcanic event occurred in southeastern Arizona 27 million years ago, when six incandescent ash flows shot out of a crater near present-day Chiricahua National Monument. Eruption of the Turkey Creek caldera produced a 2,000-ft (609-meter) -thick layer of dark volcanic rock, known as rhyolite. Subsequent erosion by water, ice, and wind sculpted the rhyolite into columns, balanced rocks, and hoodoos.

Between 5 million and 13 million years later, lava and ash spewed out of a volcano at the southwestern corner of the state. The light and dark rocks make up the Ajo Range and Bates Mountains of Organ Pipe Cactus National Monument. At roughly the same time, another flow of lava spread across the Verde Valley in central Arizona. This was followed by eruptions 2 million years ago in New Mexico. Pumice (a rock that is light in weight and color and able to float in water), tuff (solidified ash flows), and obsidian (volcanic glass) from these explosions are found in Bandelier National Monument, in northwestern New Mexico.

The most recent eruptions of black lava (basalt) occurred within the past 1,000 years. Known in New Mexico as *malpais* – Spanish for "bad country" (anglicized to *mal-pie* in Arizona) – the jagged, fractured flows spread across the northwestern corner of the state. El Malpais National Monument is a good place to see these flows. The extensive Raton-Clayton Volcanic Field in northeastern New Mexico contains Capulin Volcano National Monument, the easternmost young volcano in the western United States. It was last active 40,000 years ago. Sunset Crater Volcano National Monument in northern Arizona, which first exploded in either 1064 or 1065, is the westernmost and youngest volcano in the United States. It is part of the large San Francisco Volcanic Field around Flagstaff.

The other mountainous terrain in the American Southwest, the Basin and Range province, can be found in southern Arizona and New Mexico and westward into California. It did not involve dramatic volcanoes. Instead, movement of the North American plate starting about 20 million years ago caused the crust to stretch and crack along a roughly north–south trend. When the land spread, some blocks of earth started to break and tilt like a stack of upright books tipping over. This forced some chunks of land to rise and others to drop. The ones that dropped formed the basins and began to fill with sediments washing out of the blocks that

In his classic tome on the region, *The Colorado*, writer Frank Waters sums up the place of geology in the life of the desert Southwest. "Geology here forever dominates life and gives it its ultimate meaning." This is a rather eloquent way of pointing out the interrelationships of plants, animals, humans, and geology. For example, soil types affect where plants grow, and elevation differences create climatic variation, with precipitation that varies across the region from less than 5ins (13cm) to over 30ins (76cm).

Big Bell Rock and Courthouse Rock, Sedona.

rose, which are now the mountain ranges. Some basins contain 15,000ft (4,600 meters) of fill. Crustal movement along these faults continues to the present day.

Erosion of the Grand Canyon occurred even more recently than the Basin and Range, beginning about 6 million years ago. Surprisingly, the significant downcutting by the Colorado River that created the canyon took place somewhere between 4.7 and 1.7 million years ago, which works out to a rate of about 1.2 to 3.2 feet (1 meter) per 1,000 years. All of that material was transported away from the canyon by the Colorado River and ended up in the Gulf of California. Downcutting still occurs in the Grand Canyon, but at a much reduced rate.

⊘ BIG ENCOUNTERS

The first Europeans to see the Grand Canyon were Spanish, in 1540, just a scant two generations after Christopher Columbus' voyage to the New World. These first Spaniards were treasure-seeking members of Coronado's futile expedition in search of the fabulous Seven Golden Cities of Cibola. One of Coronado's lieutenants, Garcia Lopez de Cardenas, was guided by local Indians to the South Rim of the Grand Canyon. The Spaniards were duly impressed by the size of the place, but they saw the canyon as an impediment to further exploration and left with no recorded regrets. It would be 300 years before the next European visit.

The Three Rivers Petroglyph Site,
New Mexico.

DECISIVE DATES

BEGINNINGS

c. 500 BC
The Hohokam develop an intricate system of irrigation canals in Arizona's Salt River Valley.

AD 700
Ancestral Puebloan, Sinagua, Hohokam, Salado, Fremont, and Mogollon people live in the Southwest.

1150–1299
The Great Drought causes ancestral Southwest people to abandon villages and move to protected cliffs and canyons with reliable water sources.

EUROPEAN ARRIVALS

1540–42
Conquistador Francisco Vasquez de Coronado heads an expedition from Mexico (New Spain) on a first Entrada into El Norte, the Southwest.

1598
Juan de Oñate and 149 colonists settle next to San Juan Pueblo in northern New Mexico.

1610
Santa Fe is founded as the administrative capital of New Mexico, the northernmost province of New Spain.

1680
Ancestral Puebloans kill 22 Franciscan priests and retake New Mexico in the Pueblo Revolt.

1692
Father Eusebio Francesco Kino establishes the first mission in Arizona; more soon followed.

Gadsden Purchase surveyors.

1705
Albuquerque is founded.

1775
Tucson is founded.

1776
Spanish missionaries arrive in the Utah region.

THE SETTLER YEARS

1822
Settlers begin arriving in New Mexico via the Santa Fe Trail; Mexican War of Independence.

1824
Founding of the Mexican Republic, including the Territory of Nuevo Mexico, a vast region that includes much of today's Southwest.

1846–48
The Mexican War.

1847
A group of rebels from Taos Pueblo kill the governor of New Mexico Territory and 20 Anglo settlers. Mormons, under the leadership of Brigham Young, begin to settle Utah and Nevada.

1848
Lands north of the Gila River are ceded to the US territory of New Mexico. Wagon trains on the Oregon Trail pass through.

1851
Fort Defiance is built to "control" the Navajo.

1853
The Gadsden Purchase secures lands between the Gila River and what is now Arizona's southern boundary; all of Arizona now under US control.

1857
Lt. Joseph Ives leads an expedition into the Grand Canyon and returns with the first geological descriptions and illustrations of the natural wonder.

1861
A Chiricahua Apache leader, Cochise, is wrongly accused of kidnapping a rancher's son, setting off a cycle of revenge.

1863
President Lincoln creates the Arizona Territory.

1863–5
Kit Carson is commissioned to move Navajos to a camp in eastern New Mexico; hundreds die along the 300-mile (480-km) journey known as the "Long Walk."

1868
Navajos are allowed to return to their homeland. Phoenix is founded.

1869
Major John Wesley Powell leads the first expedition down the Green and Colorado rivers and through the Grand Canyon. The transcontinental railroad is completed at Promontory Summit in Utah.

1881
The Gunfight at the OK Corral takes place in Tombstone, Arizona.

1886
Geronimo surrenders, ending 25 years of Apache wars. American settlement in the region gathers speed.

1887
Congress passes the General Allotment Act, dividing Indian tribal lands into parcels and deeding them directly to individual Indians, to encourage them to become involved in agriculture.

1888
Copper surpasses gold and silver as an Arizona export.

1896
After the Mormon Church repudiates polygamy, Utah is granted statehood.

Hoover Dam.

THE 20TH CENTURY

1910–23
The Mexican Revolution.

1910–15
Gold and silver mining peak in the Southwest.

1911
Roosevelt Dam is constructed in Arizona.

1912
The Arizona and New Mexico territories are granted statehood.

1916
Notorious Mexican revolutionary Pancho Villa raids Columbus, New Mexico.

1936
Hoover Dam is completed.

1945
The first atomic bomb is exploded at Trinity site near Alamogordo, New Mexico.

1960
The first planned retirement community, Sun City, west of Phoenix, is developed.

1963
Glen Canyon Dam completed.

1974–present
The Central Arizona Project diverts water from the Colorado River to irrigation canals across the Phoenix area.

1974
Huge deposits of shale are tapped on Colorado's Western Slope.

1980s
Celebrities discover Santa Fe Style and begin to move to New Mexico.

1990
The original London Bridge is rebuilt at Lake Havasu in western Arizona, becoming the top Arizona attraction after the Grand Canyon.

2000
Arizona's population reaches 5.1 million, an increase of 40 percent in 10 years.

2008
Senator John McCain (R-AZ) is defeated in the US presidential election by Senator Barack Obama (D-IL).

2014
Legalization of recreational marijuana turbo-charges Colorado's economy. Sales of related products reach $996 million in 2015.

2016
The Denver Broncos win the NFL Super Bowl for the third time; businessman Donald Trump (R-NY) beats former Senator and First Lady Hillary Clinton (D-NY) in the US presidential election.

2017
New Mexico's Organ Mountains–Desert Peaks and Rio Grande del Norte, Utah's Bear's Ears and Grand Staircase–Escalante, and other recent national monuments are reviewed by the new Republican administration with the intention of downsizing them and opening the way to more resource extraction. On October 1, Stephen Paddock commits the deadliest mass shooting in American history by an individual, killing 58 people and injuring 546 at a music festival on the Las Vegas strip.

White house ruins, Canyon de Chelly.

IN ANCIENT TIMES

After arriving across long-submerged land bridges, early migrants to the American Southwest evolved into six different but similar main cultural groups.

During the final stages of the Pleistocene epoch (1.8 million years ago–11,700 years ago), nearly one-sixth of the earth's surface was blanketed with ice, a period we know as the Ice Age, actually one of many. Massive glaciers formed from billions of tons of water, and the oceans receded. In some areas, the sea level dropped by as much as 300ft (90 meters) and long-submerged fragments of sea bottom were exposed.

One of these fragments of sea bottom – a 56-mile (90-km) strip of rocky earth between northeastern Siberia and northwestern Alaska, dubbed Beringia – became an early gateway for human migration to North America. It appeared approximately 12,600 years ago, according to a study using ancient DNA, pollen, and remains of humans, plants, and animals found in lake sediments.

Archeological evidence at the Monte Alto site in Guatemala indicates that aboriginal Asians were already in the Americas 20,000 years ago, and controversial DNA evidence at a mammoth kill site in California suggests an even earlier date: 130,000 years ago. So that begs the question: how did these pioneers arrive?

Recent studies suggest that they may have literally floated here, using hide-covered boats, or coracles – either down the West Coast of North America from Asia to sites like Monte Alto or by sea from southwest Europe, some 22,000 years ago, a theory popularized by archeologist Dennis Stanford, based on European flint-knapping techniques that predate the Clovis culture, first identified in northeastern New Mexico in the early 20th century.

However the earliest Americans got here, it would have been an arduous journey, made by just a few intrepid souls. It was only late in

Hohokam petroglyph in Saguaro National Park.

the Pleistocene, when interglacial sub-ages (warming trends) began to occur and sea-level ice began to melt, that large numbers of paleohunters made the trek. They were attracted by one major resource: mammoth, bison, and other Asian big game flocking to North America to graze on the grass, shrubs, and forage that flourished as the climate warmed.

THE FIRST SOUTHWESTERN SETTLERS

When did humans first reach the Southwest? Archeological evidence at the Clovis site in northeastern New Mexico – dateable artifacts found with bones of extinct animals – suggests that they were entrenched in relatively large numbers by 15,000 years ago. This same evidence has allowed scientists to reach some logical conclusions about early humans.

Paleo-Indians of the Clovis – later the Folsom – cultures were primarily meat-eaters, although they probably gathered wild plants for food as well. Using flint or bone-tipped weapons of their own creation and design, Paleo-Indians could kill animals 20 times their size. In part, early humans were social creatures; they hunted in organized groups in order to kill not just a single animal but an entire herd at one time for

Cliff House, Mesa Verde National Park.

the good of the community. Because constant expansion of hunting range was necessary, fixed habitations were seldom established.

For 7,000 years from about 7000 BC, human lifestyles in the American Southwest were changing significantly. This span of cultural amplification has been named the Desert Archaic period. Among the most important changes to occur during the Archaic period were: the acquisition of the fire-drill and the grinding stone; the utilization of foods other than meat – mainly seeds, wild grains, tubers, and berries; the construction of semi-permanent, seasonal dwelling places – primarily "pithouses," semicircular or rectangular holes in the earth that were covered with brush and mud; and the practice of spiritual ceremonies.

The development of the Paleo-Indian into the Archaic Indian was a sluggish process at best, dependent upon interactions among groups of people sometimes separated by hundreds of miles. This was not true, however, of the next

> *Of changes occurring during the 1,500-year-long Pithouse-Pueblo Period, nothing was more important that the development of discrete human societies over a wide area.*

period of cultural expansion – the Pithouse Pueblo Period – which began about 2,000 years ago and ended with the arrival of Europeans in the Southwest in the mid-16th century.

CULTURAL DIVISIONS

By AD 700, six distinct groups of people had evolved in the Southwest. In the north were the Ancestral Puebloans (formerly known as the Anasazi) – an intelligent, artistic society of farmers whose multistory adobe villages and later, seemingly defensive hidden cliff palaces and canyon cities were so well constructed that many have survived nearly intact for a thousand years. To the south, near the San Francisco Peaks area of northern Arizona, were the Sinagua, dry-land farmers (their name means "without water") whose culture became a melting pot of building techniques and increasingly complex social development. In the Gila and Salt River valleys near present-day Phoenix were the Hohokam, at their peak perhaps the greatest canal builders in North America. To the east, along the Salt River were Hohokam cousins, the Salado (their name means Salt People). In the rich mountain country of southwest New Mexico were the largely pithouse-dwelling farmers and ceramicists known as the Mogollon (Muggy-on). And along the Fremont River in south-central Utah around Capitol Reef were the enigmatic Fremont people – who, like the Mogollon, were largely pithouse dwellers, artisans, and farmers who lived a more modest lifestyle than their Ancestral Pueblo neighbors to the south.

We can only guess how and why these divisions of culture came about. One important factor may have been the introduction and development of agriculture – a concept introduced to the Southwest from Mexico, where teosinte, a hybridized grass, was developed into corn, later joined by beans and squash, the famed "three sisters" of Southwest cuisine.

Farming demanded huge changes in social structures. Because agricultural products could be stored for the winter, dependence upon hunting and gathering was drastically reduced. In turn, habitations became more permanent so that farmers could tend their fields. Permanency demanded security from enemies, and security required a large and stable population.

Whatever the reasons, there arose these six major cultures and many minor ones. Geographically separated by hundreds of miles, each bore striking similarities to the others. They were all agricultural societies, heavily dependent for survival upon crops of maize (corn), beans, squash, and melons. In their early stages of development, all lived in underground pithouses or caves, later moving to aboveground, apartment-style, multistoried homes called *pueblos* (villages) by the Spaniards. By AD 700, nearly all used pottery extensively and had acquired the bow and arrow. Three centuries later, cotton-weaving implements were widespread. More importantly, none developed the aristocracy (as far as can be determined) that marked the Aztec and Inca civilizations to the south; ritual leaders, who watched the skies and predicted when to plant and harvest crops, were apparently held in high esteem, however, and lived in special houses.

Similarities among the cultures occurred also in physical appearance, clothing, and daily activities. From burial evidence, scientists think that most prehistoric Indians were about the same size and build; men averaged 5ft 4ins (1.6 meters), women slightly less. They were muscular, stocky people with sparse body hair. Head hair was thick, however. Men wore it long; women preferred it bobbed or fashioned into elaborate coiffures.

THE GOLDEN AGE

Similarities amongst the differing groups were not coincidental. Throughout the 15-century span that encompassed the Pithouse and Pueblo periods, interaction undoubtedly took place among all prehistoric cultures in the Southwest,

as well as in northern Mexico, with each contributing something to cultural development.

So rapidly, in fact, did new ideas and methods spread among these Southwest cultures that by the mid-11th century a Golden Age occurred. Building techniques and irrigation systems had progressed to a sophisticated degree. Frivolities such as ball games and contests with dice were commonplace. In addition, increased rainfall had mellowed the often harsh environment; natural springs and streams ran full, and game and wild plants flourished. Because of

Hohokam red-on-buff pot and effigies.

the added moisture and new agricultural techniques, farming increased, and with surplus food available, populations grew. New farming projects were started in areas that could hardly have supported cacti a century before.

Existing towns grew more complex, and some became powerful pilgrimage centers known far and wide. Around 1000, in Chaco Canyon in northwest New Mexico, the hugely successful Chaco culture grew to prominence, influencing the whole Southwest region through trade and lifestyle, including as far away as Mesoamerica, California, and the Woodland and Mississippian cultures of the Midwest. Chaco's cultural influence was so widespread, it has been dubbed the Chaco Phenomenon.

DECLINE OF THE GOOD YEARS

This new life of relative comfort was only temporary, however, and although there are many plausible explanations as to why this prehistoric Southwest Golden Age was cut short, one of the most feasible is that by the middle of the 12th century, weather patterns had once again changed and the region saw the beginning of drought.

Where water was permanently available, farmers were little affected, but in areas where agriculture was dependent upon rainfall rather than irrigation, particularly the Chaco region,

10th-century painted pottery bowl.

⊘ ANCIENT FASHION

Clothing varied amongst the six main groups, but variations depended less upon tribal affiliation than upon time of the year. In hot weather, most people wore nothing but sandals woven from plant fiber or plaited from yucca leaves. As the seasons changed and the days cooled, skirts and aprons made from vegetable material or animal skins were added. In winter, hide cloaks, shirts and blankets – the latter made from rabbit skin, dog fur, or turkey feathers – were probably sufficient to keep out the chill. When cotton was introduced and people learned the art of weaving, more elaborate forms of winter clothing – mainly heavy cloaks – came into vogue.

life once again became difficult. Many towns and outlying family dwellings were abandoned, with the inhabitants migrating and petitioning to join other groups living in pueblos that had been constructed near natural groundwater sources, such as Aztec Ruins on the Animas River in northeastern New Mexico; Mesa Verde, Colorado; and the Pajarito Plateau above the Rio Grande in northern New Mexico. What possessions could be carried were taken along; all else was left behind. This sudden influx of refugees unsettled the communities they were joining, but, in most cases, room was found.

Around this time, a new threat appeared in the Southwest: nomadic foreign raiders intent on taking over resources. Dineh people from northwest Canada arrived in the Four Corners region from the 1100s. Once in the Southwest, they would split into the Navajo culture in the Four Corners farming areas and the Apache in the central and southern mountains along the Arizona/New Mexico border. And as with the Utes – a branch of the Shoshone culture of the Great Basin migrating into Utah and Colorado – and the Comanche, another branch of Shoshone that overflowed into southeastern Colorado, once the Navajo and Apache acquired the horse from arriving Spaniards in the 16th century, they would become a force to be reckoned with.

Although the Navajo and Pueblos would later live together harmoniously, in the early years, Ancestral Puebloans in the Four Corners found themselves the targets of continual harassment from the newcomers. Few in number, the Dineh dared not attack a fully protected village, but they easily raided fields, stole harvests, and picked off an occasional farmer or his family. In addition, towns and villages had, probably out of necessity, begun to prey on one another; there are strong indications of competition for resources, social unrest, and general stress among Pueblos at this time.

Sometime during the late 12th century, the combination of harassment, thievery, and steadily worsening drought conditions brought about a drastic change in lifestyle for Ancestral Pueblo and other traditional southwestern people. They abandoned valleys and mesa-top homes and took refuge in isolated caves and protected canyon amphitheaters. Whether the move ended the threat or only prolonged it, researchers don't know. They do know, however, that it did little to ease internal strife or alleviate the need for water.

Midway through the 13th century, as the great cliff houses of the Mesa Verde area of southwest Colorado and Betatakin and Keet Seel in northern Arizona were under construction, the drought was reaching its peak. Even permanent water sources began to run dry, and life became a matter of day-to-day survival. The soil was worn out and turned to dust; crops failed every year. Hunting and gathering had never been fully abandoned, but food supplies in the wild decreased in direct proportion to the decrease in moisture. There was simply not enough food and water for the population.

Although we have no idea of its exact nature, some type of social upheaval undoubtedly took place – perhaps a universal uprising against failing leaders, who, in this agricultural society, consisted of skywatching astronomer priests who likely failed in their central role: to predict accurately when to plant, hold ceremonies, and harvest crops.

By 1299, when the Great Drought finally ended, most villages and towns of the Ancestral Pueblo culture had been abandoned (including, by AD 1000, those of the Mogollon and Fremont, both of which appear to have been subsumed into Pueblo culture). Hohokam, Salado, and Sinagua communities near permanent streams survived longer but met the same fate within a century.

MIGRATING PEOPLES

It is here that the real mystery begins. The Hohokam and Salado would eventually become the Pima of southern Arizona and revert to a simple hunter-gatherer lifestyle, while the Sinagua of northern Arizona would move to the nearby Hopi mesas. But where did Ancestral Puebloan refugees from Mesa Verde and northern Arizona go?

According to traditional stories, some journeyed east to join or start pueblos along the Rio Grande in New Mexico, or stopped before getting there and formed the pueblos of Zuni and Acoma. Some may have gone south to Mexico or west to California, and a good many simply changed their lifestyles to meet current requirements for survival and remained nearby, the ancestors of today's Hopi.

The Hopi mesas in Arizona took in both the Sinagua and Ancestral Puebloans. Hopi people claim ancestral ownership of many of the great population centers, such as Mesa Verde, Betatakin, Keet Seel, and Wupatki. Prehistoric Hopi clan signs found in these ruins give validity to the claims, though many archeologists argue the point. Pictographs (prehistoric rock paintings) and petroglyphs (rock carvings) similar to those the Hopi claim as clan symbols were once freely used throughout both North and South America. This certainly suggests widespread interaction

Wupatki, New Mexico, home of the Sinagua people.

among early cultures but not necessarily the traditional ownership of the signs that Hopi legends proclaim. Hopi ancestors were probably an aggregation of several different cultures.

Wherever these early people went, they were gone, for the most part, by the early 1400s, shortly before the Spanish arrived, abandoning adobe homes they had so painstakingly constructed. Many of these prehistoric dwellings, preserved by dry desert air and remote locations that prevent desecration, and in some cases by the stabilization and restoration technology of modern science, still exist and may be easily visited. Remember, though: although they are old, these ancient dwellings remain fragile, so watch where you walk.

Painting of Father Juan de Padilla finding the cross set by Coronado.

SPANISH EXPLORATION

First seeking imaginary gold and then lost souls, the Spanish in the New World embedded their culture into Mexico and the American Southwest.

On an autumn day late in November of 1528, four half-drowned seamen – survivors of the ill-fated Spanish expedition of Panfilo de Narvaez – were washed ashore onto the beaches of Texas by the unfriendly sea. Naked, chilled, and starving, they were fortunate to be found alive by Indians, who fed and clothed them. These naked conquistadors were the first known Spaniards to set foot in the Southwest. So began one of the most remarkable journeys in American history. The shipwrecked, led by Alvar Nuñez Cabeza de Vaca, walked for thousands of miles through the desert until, eight years later, they reached Mexico City.

On the way, they learned to live and adapt to their environment like Indians. They adopted not only the clothes but the habits of the tribes they met along the way. The Indians most often feted the men as messengers of the gods, as the Aztecs had regarded Cortes farther to the south. Especially welcome in this group of four men was Esteban, a black Moor and Christianized slave of the Spaniards who was favored by the Indian women even more than the others. Although no records exist to document the theory, historians conjecture that the first *mestizos*, half Spanish and half Indian, were born of the lost conquistadors and Indian women. In his memoirs, Cabeza de Vaca mused wryly about "the possibility of life in which to be deprived of Europe was not to be deprived of too much."

SEEKING NEW CONQUESTS

On his arrival in Mexico City, Cabeza de Vaca told tales of walled cities with houses four and five stories tall and of Indians who were more civilized than the Spaniards. To Cortes's conquistadors, who had conquered most of Mexico and

Esteban the Moor exploring the American Southwest.

⊘ SEVEN GOLDEN CITIES

Las Siete Ciudades de Cibola, or the Seven Cities of Cibola, were the elusive goals of Spanish conquistadors in North America during the 16th century, following the failure to find similar cities in South America. These legendary centers of unbelievable wealth and splendor had first been suggested by the shipwrecked Alvar Nuñez Cabeza de Vaca, who was shipwrecked in 1528 and wandered through Texas and northern Mexico for eight years. Because of his reports, the viceroy of New Spain sent out an expedition under Esteban, a slave shipwrecked with Cabeza de Vaca, and Fray Marcos de Niza, who then claimed to have seen the golden cities from a great distance.

then fallen into fighting among themselves over the spoils, the reports meant new gold might be found in the desert to the north. The cry went up: *Otro Mexico! Otro Peru!* "Another Mexico! Another Peru!"

Enticed by Cabeza de Vaca's tale, the restless and bored conquistadors polished their rusting armor and prepared themselves for battle, and to conquer the entire continent. Under the orders of the Viceroy of New Spain, Antonio de Mendoza, an *entrada* – an expedition – set out for El Norte (the North) led by Fray Marcos de

> "To possess silver and gold, the greedy Spaniards would enter Hell itself," said the Franciscan Fray Zarate Salmeron of New Mexico, failing to dissuade them.

Deaths, hardships, and dangers challenged their sense of adventure and machismo, and, when that failed, the promise of great riches spurred them on.

Canyon de Chelly rock paintings depicting the arrival of the Spanish.

Niza and guided by Esteban, the black Moor. Its aim was to find the legendary Gran Quivira and the fabled Seven Cities of Cibola that Cabeza de Vaca had heard about – but never seen.

For months, Fray Marcos and his men wandered through the Sonoran Desert and into the Southwest, but, finding no cities of gold, they returned to Mexico City empty-handed. In the course of their ordeal, Esteban had been killed by the men of Zuni Pueblo, who said he had "assaulted their women." (For reasons no one understands, a statue of now Saint Esteban was raised in the nearby pueblo of Acoma, where it stands today.)

Despite the failure of Fray Marcos's expedition, the Spaniards were not discouraged.

Of all the conquistadors who set forth in search of the Seven Cities of Cibola and Gran Quivira, the one who would gain lasting fame was Francisco Vazquez de Coronado, the governor of the Kingdom of Nueva Galicia, the "Knight of El Dorado." With the blessing of the emperor and the viceroy, Coronado marshaled a small army in Mexico and crossed half a continent. He alone among the conquistadors created a romantic legend that would linger.

Coronado was the image of the poor *hidalgo* (gentleman): dignified, handsome, and so poor he had to borrow from his wife to fund the expedition. His pretension of courtly nobility in the inhospitable wilderness, epitomized by his wearing armor in the burning desert sun, made him the American Don Quixote; he was one of those rare men who perfectly fit his moment in history, for better or worse.

The men of Coronado's army, on the other hand, were the riffraff, cutthroats, and adventurers of Mexico City, It was an epic irony. The image of the conquistadors riding forth in resplendent armor of gold, with flags and plumes proudly flying as in a knightly pageant, is largely a myth, created in retrospect. The contemporary description of Coronado's men is not nearly so grand.

Most of Coronado's men wore "American" rather than European clothing, said one observer, and another noted that "many more [wore] buckskin coats than coats of armor." And while the majority were horsemen, few were high born. In Spain, only a gentleman was permitted – by royal decree – to ride a horse, and any knight found on a mule was subject to punishment. But in Mexico, anyone could ride. In 1554, the viceroy Velasco complained of these horsemen: "Very few are *caballeros* (knights) or *hijosdalgos* (sons of gentlemen).

A Spanish inscription at El Morro National Monument by Don Juan de Onate, from 1605.

⊘ CORONADO'S GOLDEN FAILURE

Francisco Vazquez de Coronado journeyed to the New World and New Spain (present-day Mexico) in 1535 with the new viceroy, Antonio de Mendoza. Coronado was quick to earn a reputation in the pacification of Indians, and he was soon appointed the governor of Nueva Galicia.

When the expedition ordered by Mendoza – to seek the legendary golden cities of Cibola led by Fray Marcos de Niza – returned to Mexico City confirming the richness of these cities, (which were, in fact, Zuni pueblo in present-day New Mexico), Mendoza organized yet another expedition. One part of this expedition, two ships commanded by Hernando de Alarcon, found no

cities but did discover the mouth of the Colorado River, in 1540. The main force, led by Coronado and consisting of 300 Spaniards, probably an equal number of Indians, and herds of livestock, moved overland northward. The pueblo of Zuni was captured but proved to be no city of gold; a secondary reconnaissance group sighted the Grand Canyon. Offshoot expeditions into Texas and Kansas proved futile, and two years later, in 1542, Coronado returned to Mexico.

Coronado was indicted for his failure by an official inquiry but found innocent. After another indictment in which he was fined, he stayed on the Council of Mexico until his death in 1554.

They are *gente comun* (common people). In these provinces, the *caballero* is a merchant." The nobleman Don Juan Garray added in total disgust, "Even beggars ride horses in Mexico."

For his entrada, Coronado mustered nearly 400 men, almost all of them volunteers. There were officially 235 mounted men and 62 on foot, but unofficially there were many more, ranging from teenagers to old men. It was rather a motley troop.

Not only were the soldiers not conquistadors, some of them weren't even Spaniards.

Francisco Coronado on his 1540 expedition.

The company bugler was German, and there were two Italians, five Portuguese, a Frenchman, and a Scotsman, Thomas Blake, who had changed his name to Tomas Blaque. And there were hundreds of Indians. No one knows how many Indians marched with Coronado, but it is known that they were not simply bearers and carriers. Most of them were hired to be scouts, guides, horse wranglers, herdsmen, *vaqueros* (cowboys), and bridge builders. All of them were well armed with lances, spears, and bows and arrows. Were it not for these Mexican Indians and the American Indians who later joined the expedition, it is doubtful that there could have been a successful expedition at all.

Coronado's army traveled north from Mexico for some 1,500 miles (2,400km) through the Apache lands of what is now Arizona into present-day New Mexico. On the Rio Grande, Coronado asked directions from a man he called The Turk (because he was dark-skinned), who explained that his people had no gold – it was all farther east in what is now Kansas, where the people were so rich that even their canoes were made of glittering gold.

Coronado headed for Kansas, with The Turk. He crossed the Pecos River into West Texas and went north through Oklahoma. He finally reached Kansas near the present-day town of Abilene, but found no gold canoes there. Frustrated, he turned back to Mexico after first ordering the execution of "The Turk."

Neither Coronado nor any of the other conquistadors found the gold and jewels they sought. Most of them returned to Mexico City in disappointment, and, after their discouraging reports, few followed them into the desert in search of fabulous treasure. The conquistadors themselves, weary and aging, had come to that time of life when even old soldiers have to settle down and retire. The conquest was over. Even the mighty Cortes lamented, "I am wasted, and exhausted, by all I have done..."

By themselves, the conquistadors could never have conquered the Southwest. In the rugged mountains and deserts, their medieval military tactics and armor were of little use, nor did they have the spirituality – despite the pervasiveness of the Catholic Church in the New World – needed to comprehend the deep religiousness of the Indians. So disillusioned were the latter-day conquistadors that they even forgot their discovery of California. Not until more than two centuries after the voyage of Juan Cabrillo did Juan Bautista de Anza set forth to settle California, in 1777. In the end, it was left to the Spanish missionaries to accomplish what the conquistadors could not: conquer the land.

MISSIONARIES SEEK SOULS, NOT GOLD

The missionaries came to conquer not by force of arms but by settlement and religious fervor. Of course, when the Indians rejected "peaceful" conquest, the religious conquistadors set down their plowshares, took up swords, and forced their rule on the native tribes.

The Franciscan *padres* in New Mexico and the Jesuits in Arizona and Texas did more than baptize and make Christians of these Indians. (From 1591 until 1631, the Jesuits alone baptized 151,240 Indians.) They tried to transform the Indians into Spanish peasants, to "attract the nomadic tribes to a peaceful, sedentary life." As the Jesuit father Juan Nentuig wrote in 1763, the Christian Indians were "more inclined to work... [and] ... to till their lands."

The missions of the Jesuits were more than churches. Into their hands was placed the responsibility for government and the economy. The missions became the centers of farming, commerce, and education. To the suspicious Spanish officials, the rather autonomous Jesuits seemed to be building an ecclesiastical empire within the Spanish provinces. What was worse, many of the Jesuits were not even Spaniards – not with names like Pfefferkom, Benz, Kino, Stiger, and Nentuig. Nevertheless, when Jesuits asked for permission to raise their own army,

Sandia pueblo's Indian church near Albuquerque, New Mexico.

⊘ LEGACY OF CONQUEST

From whence came the *conquistadores* (Spanish for "conquerors"), whose influence lingered in the American Southwest for centuries?

When Spain sought to colonize the Americas at the beginning of the 16th century, it was the military who led the way, first with the landing near Veracruz by Hernan Cortes in 1519, who then headed inland with 400 soldiers to begin the conquest of Aztec Mexico. He gained an ally with the independent city of Tlaxcala and conquered the Aztec capital at Tenochtitlan, now Mexico City. By 1524, most of present-day Mexico had been conquered by the conquistadores, with the help of the Tlaxcalans.

In South America, Inca Peru was subdued by two Spanish adventurers, Francisco Pizarro and Diego de Almagro, who had first settled on the Isthmus of Panama. In 1531, Pizarro left with 180 men and 37 horses to start his conquest of Peru, which was in civil war at the time. Pizarro captured the Inca ruler and, with the help of Almagro, took Cuzco, the capital, in 1533. Pizarro established a new capital at Lima. In 1538, Pizarro and Almagro were at each other's throats in their own war; Pizarro won but was murdered in 1541. From Peru, the conquistadores extended Spain's control over much of South America – soon replaced by Spanish administrators.

the Spaniards often agreed. (In one case, prisoners were released from the jails of Mexico City and sent out to protect the missions.)

In New Mexico, the mission churches of the Franciscans were more like fortresses than places of worship. The walls were sometimes 7ft (2 meters) thick. Following the Pueblo Revolt of 1680, when Pueblo Indians in New Mexico killed 22 Franciscans and fled over the border to Texas for a decade, returning missionaries in 1692 protected themselves with Indian slaves and mercenaries. aEven so, in 1792 Francis-

as brothers. One of the most courageous of the missionaries, he was said to have made 40 *entradas* to the Sonoran Desert and established many missions in the region, not to mention one of the first cattle ranches in present-day Arizona.

A true folk hero, Kino was known as the Padre on Horseback. He died at the age of 70 at the mission of Magdalena in Sonora, Mexico – his deathbed made up of two calfskins with a saddle for a pillow. His eulogist, Father Luis Velarde, said Kino died as he lived – as one with the Indi-

Spanish conquistadors using Native American captives to carry burdens in 16th-century New Mexico.

can priest Juan Domingo Arricivita called for the "protection of troops in order to propagate the faith." It was "impossible without them," he said. And from 1744 to 1745, when the *visitador* to Sonora, Juan Antonio Balthasar, traveled to the Tohono O'Odham mission of San Xavier del Bac just south of present-day Tucson, he requested "soldiers to force these Indians to live in the pueblo," as it was clear that "just a hint of soldiering is necessary" to make them go to church.

But not all of the missionaries were so eager to take up arms against their parishioners. Father Eusebio Francisco Kino, the Jesuit who founded San Xavier del Bac mission, objected to such a policy. He wanted the Indians treated

ans. Padre Kino's bones are displayed under glass in Magdalena and he is in the First Phase of canonization by the Catholic Church, where he is referred to as a "servant of God."

SETTLERS SETTLE DOWN

Shortly after the arrival of the missionaries came the settlers, mostly people escaping aspects of their past or lives in Mexico. They, more than the conquistadors, were the true explorers of the land. Once settled, they began detailed surveys of the countryside. As farmers, they had to know the flow and direction of every stream and river, the precise rise and fall of every canyon and valley, the grass and trees of every pasture and forest. The settlers explored the land the ways soldiers could not. Conquistadors rode swiftly for safety in hostile territory and mapped from horseback, but settlers walked the earth, foot by foot, and explored the territory intimately, surveying every inch of land. The historic Spanish land grants, extensive lands that were gifted to nobles by the Spanish Crown in return for services rendered during settlement, and passed down through generations in Arizona and New Mexico, were measured in such a way, as were village deeds.

a meager existence. "Not only have the settlers of New Mexico not enjoyed riches but the scourge of God has been upon them always, and they are the most oppressed and enslaved people in the world," the Franciscan father Zarate de Salmeron wrote of them in 1626. "As long as they have a good supply of tobacco to smoke, they are very contented and they do not want riches, for it seems as if they have made a vow of poverty."

In the palatial mansions in Mexico City, the American Southwest was known as the "Land

La Jornada statue at New Mexico Museum of Natural History and Science.

HARD TIMES

Many of the settlers in the Southwest were poor Spanish farmers and shepherds, Mexicans from the Sonora and Chihuahua desert areas of northern Mexico that border present-day Texas, Arizona, New Mexico, and California. Few wealthy noblemen or old conquistadors in Mexico or Spain had any desire or need to endure the desert's severe hardships to establish a new life. As always, the immigrants were poor men and women seeking new opportunities, hoping to escape a life of poverty.

But on the poor lands of the desert, the poor settlers became poorer. The dry farming and small mines they established offered

of the Barbarosos" – the barbarians – and that referred not only to the American Indians but to the "Spanish" settlers as well.

Few of the settlers who joined the 1598 *entrada* of Juan de Oñate into New Mexico were born in Spain. Most were Mexicans and *mestizos*, half-Indians, who, like de Oñate himself, were born in Sonora; he was married to an Indian woman said to be a granddaughter of Montezuma. Typical of the expeditions of the Southwest, Oñate's *entrada* included as many as 1,000 Mexican Indians, outnumbering the Spanish by 10 to one. Having lived on similar land in Mexico they understood the particulars of the terrain and survived more easily than the settlers.

ARRIVAL OF THE ANGLOS

Unlike the Spaniards, early Anglos to the Southwest sought only pelts and trade, but they were soon settling and bringing with them a less constrained lifestyle.

On the East Coast of the expanding United States, they were contemptuously known as "Squaw Men" and "White Indians." No one quite like them had ever lived on the American frontier before, and certainly no one ever will again. The mountain men who came to New Mexico and Arizona in the early 1800s were "a rare moment in history," wrote the American Indian author Vine Deloria. These men not only crossed the continent, they crossed from one culture to another.

Unlike the Spaniards, the first Anglos to settle in the Southwest came to hunt beaver and to trade, not to conquer. In the mountain wilderness where they made their homes, trappers most often lived in peace with the Mexicans and Indians already in residence.

Paradoxically, the mountain men who went West to escape the civilization of the East brought some of that civilization with them in their saddlebags and wagons. The trade goods they offered the native people forever changed the wilderness and paved the way for the storekeepers who replaced them. The mountain men made themselves obsolete.

One of the first mountain men in the Southwest, Baptiste le Land of the Missouri Fur Company, came to Santa Fe, New Mexico, in 1804, the same year as Lewis and Clark began their expedition of the land purchased from France. The first Anglo most Mexicans and Indians had ever seen, Le Land was, in fact, a French Creole who married an Indian woman. He was followed by James Pursell in 1805 and, in 1809, Zebulon Pike, a mapmaker and government agent who first arrived in Santa Fe as a prisoner on his way to trial in Mexico City. Pike built the first Anglo fort, of cottonwood trees, on the Conejos branch of the Rio del Norte, the Rio Grande.

Zebulon Pike on an expedition.

Spain ruled the land, but just barely. It was sparsely inhabited by Spaniards, and the royal authorities were nervous about the Anglo traders and wanderers who had entered their domain.

Between 1812 and 1821, several merchant adventurers were arrested by Spanish soldiers and locked up in Chihuahua's dungeons. Not until the Mexican War of Independence in 1822, and the founding of the Mexican Republic in 1824, did the atmosphere change. The Territory of Nuevo Mexico was established under Mexican ownership, a vast territory that included New Mexico and Arizona, and where the Anglo mountain men and merchants were welcomed in a friendlier manner.

In his "Report on Foreigners" in 1825, the governor of New Mexico, Antonio Narbona, wrote of 20 Anglos arriving in a single month, half of them merchants. By 1827, a similar monthly report listed 36 Anglos, of whom 31 were merchants who "to sell their goods remain for some time in the towns," but have "no intentions of settling themselves."

SANTA FE TRAIL

With the establishment of the Santa Fe Trail from Missouri, wagon trains and caravans

Wagons at the end of the Santa Fe Trail.

crowded the trails that led West. By 1821, the Missouri frontiersman William Becknell led his "company of men destined to the westward" to New Mexico. Of these traders, George Sibley wrote in 1825 that "the first adventurers were hardy, enterprising men who, being tired of the dull and profitless pursuits of husbandry, were determined to turn merchants and traders in the true spirit of Western enterprise," for these men believed the "many strange and marvelous stories of inexhaustible wealth" that were told about the West.

Becknell's expedition opened the way to the West. In Congress, Senator Thomas Benton introduced a bill to maintain a road to New Mexico. It made more sense. Since the distance was

> *From 1822 to 1844, the value of the merchandise carried on the Santa Fe Trail increased from an estimated $15,000 each year up to nearly $450,000.*

much shorter from Missouri than from Mexico City, goods could be sold more cheaply by the Anglo traders than by the Mexican entradas.

The merchant wagons brought with them a new way of life into the Southwest. Not only were luxury items such as champagne, beer, whiskey, and rum introduced, but also oranges, lemons, cherries, whale-oil candles, tobacco, Epsom salts, straw hats, silk handkerchiefs, dried fish, and hundreds of other products became available.

In their dusty wake, the merchant wagons also brought settlers. They homesteaded, planted crops, established ranches, and built towns – all on Mexican and Indian land grants to which they had no title. For generations afterward, the ownership of the land would be under dispute. It often still is.

AMERICAN SOLDIERS ARRIVE

The settlers were soon followed by soldiers. In 1846, President Polk sent General Stephen Watts Kearny to the West to conquer New Mexico, but the anticipated war with Mexico became more an occupation than a conquest. In a treaty signed with Mexico in 1848, the United States paid $15 million for New Mexico, Arizona, Utah, Nevada, California, and part of Colorado.

After the Mexican War, few federal troops besides General Kearny's small detachment were stationed in New Mexico and Arizona. With so few troops to defend them during the Civil War between the American North and South, the territories were nearly lost to the Confederacy, which had seen a vacuum in the Southwest and tried unsuccessfully to exploit it.

The supplying of merchandise and food to the troops became the region's largest and most profitable business. Many an old family fortune was built on government contracts, something of an irony for people who prided themselves on rugged individualism.

"Almost the only paying business the white inhabitants of the territory have is supplying the troops," General Edward Ord wrote to President Andrew Johnson after the Civil War. "Hostilities are therefore kept up [against the Apache] with a view of supporting the inhabitants..." Even that irony was compounded by the sending of the 10th Cavalry, composed largely of former slaves, to subdue and control Indians in the Southwest.

Settlement of Arizona's Sonoran Desert had long been a difficult proposition, due to fierce resistance from the Apache, who lived in mountain strongholds along the Arizona-New Mexico border and were skilled warriors whose prowess

Spaniards had to abandon nearly 50 settlements and 126 ranches throughout Arizona. By 1775, Padre Bartolomo Ximeno reported that there were only 10 horses and 56 cows left in the territory that the Apache had not stolen.

Those Anglos who did settle in Arizona were mostly Southerners. During the Civil War, Arizona, unlike New Mexico, sided with the slave states of the Confederate south. The citizens of Tucson voted to join the Confederacy, and in 1862, the Confederate Congress proclaimed Arizona a Confederate territory. There were few

Battle of San Gabriel in the US-Mexican War, 1847.

in warfare took on legendary status. By the American period, a small number of trading centers, farm towns, and ranches were established, primarily mining towns such as Tombstone and Bisbee in southern Arizona and Jerome and Prescott in north-central Arizona – which eventually produced billions of dollars in silver and copper ore.

The Apache were largely successful in keeping out Spanish settlers throughout the period of Spanish rule. In 1630, Padre Alonzo Benavides called them a "people fiery and bellicose and very crafty in war." In fact, the Apache were a nomadic people, less interested in conquering places and capturing people than in taking horses and cattle. By the 1760s, in spite of the efforts of the staunch Jesuit missionaries, the

⊘ GRIZZLED CHARACTERS

By necessity, mountain men were multicultural and multilingual, and by nature, they were invariably colorful figures. The flamboyant Pauline Weaver, a hunter and agent of the Hudson Bay Company, was a gun-toting adventurer who is sometimes called the Founder of Arizona. Christopher "Kit" Carson, one of the fathers of the Anglo New Mexico and known to most modern-day schoolchildren, began his career as a grizzled mountain man, then became a U.S. Army scout and officer, a respected citizen of Taos, and a civic leader. He himself was representative of the tricultural melting pot that constituted New Mexico by marrying, in turn, a Mexican, an Indian, and an Anglo wife.

slaves in Arizona, but settlers engaged in a lively slave trade in Apache children.

Despite their former rebel sympathies, Anglo settlers in Arizona were happy to welcome the U.S. Army after the Civil War ended. The Indian Wars, which were fought to open more territory for settlement, were largely conflicts between nomadic Indians and settlers, and when faced with modern American military campaigns, native people often surrendered.

In 1865, Mescalero Apache headman Victorio told Lieutenant Colonel N.H. Davis: "I and my people want peace. We are tired of war. We are poor and have little to eat and wear. We want to make peace."

Davis replied, "Death to the Apache, and peace and prosperity to this land, is my motto." General Edward Ord agreed. The Apache, he declared, were "vermin to be killed when met."

Not everyone among the conquering forces agreed. General George Crook, who led the capture of Geronimo, said of the Apache, "I wish to say most emphatically that [this] American Indian is the intellectual peer of most, if not all, the various nationalities who have assimilated to our laws..."

COWBOYS AND RANCHES

During the 1870s, ranching became a new way of life in the West. Huge cattle outfits spread out over the territory. The vast Matador, King, and Lumpkin ranches in Arizona ran tens of thousands of cattle on hundreds of thousands of open ranges. There were battles between sheepmen and cattlemen over grazing lands, and not long after the Civil War and the Indian Wars had ended, the so-called Range Wars began.

One of the most famous range wars was the Lincoln County War, in New Mexico, where Billy the Kid (who was actually born in Brooklyn) earned his reputation as a gunman. In reality, Billy the Kid worked as a busboy and waiter in a café in the town of Shakespeare (now a ghost town in the boot-heel of New Mexico). He was no more a cowboy than was Wyatt Earp, Bat Masterson, or Doc Holliday, the dentist. Few, if any, ranch-working cowboys ever fought in the Range Wars.

On the ranches of the Southwest, the cowboy of English-Irish-Scottish-German ancestry inherited the older Western traditions of the Mexican and Indian vaquero. Southerner and Easterner, Mexican and American Indian, Spaniard and Anglo – they all merged into a new and unique figure known as the Westerner.

Perhaps more than anything else, it was the earth and sky that shaped cowboy culture. There was nothing in their experience back East to prepare Anglos for such awesome vistas. In the beginning, the cattle ranches resembled those of Sonora and Chihuahua in northern Mexico, built in the adobe styles of the Southwest. And during the old days of Spanish rule, land grant ranches

Geronimo in the Sierra Madre Mountains.

⊘ THE LONG WALK

Like their Apache cousins – both tribes have common ancestry and cultures – the Navajo people had a fierce reputation. They were like "wolves that run through the mountains," said one U.S. Army general, and they needed removing by force. In 1863, Kit Carson was commissioned by the U.S. Army to round up the Navajos and ship them to a camp in eastern New Mexico. Rather then fighting the Navajo, Carson starved them out by destroying their livestock and crops. By 1865, more than 8,000 Navajo had been sent on the Long Walk of 300 miles (480km). Some 400 died on the walk, while thousands more died in the camp at Bosque Redondo.

> A cowboy ditty:
> "The cowboy's life is a dreadful life
> He's driven through heat and cold
> I'm almost froze with water on my clothes
> A-ridin' through heat and cold"

in southern Arizona were feudal fiefdoms with sprawling haciendas that contained entire towns. During the American period, however, ranches were composed of rough frugal buildings, reflecting the pioneer life of their owners.

THE BUCKAROO IS BORN

With the convergence of different cultures under the inhospitable desert sun, in time a new breed of cowboy – the buckaroo (an Americanization of the Spanish word vaquero) – emerged. As the old saying goes, buckaroos were "tough as a longhorn cow, and just as dumb." The cowboy "yell" was a way of proclaiming one's manhood, and one of the old cowboy yells of the Southwest says it all: "Whe-ee-o, I'm a bad man! Whoop-eee! Raised in the backwoods, suckled by a polar bear, nine rows of jaw teeth, a double coat of hair, steel ribs, wire intestines, and a barbed wire tail, and I don't give a dang where I drag it. Whoop-whee-ha!"

Ranch women of those days were not about to be outdone by their men, thinking themselves to be as tough as the men. One proper lady described herself in 1887: "My bonnet is a hornet's nest, garnished with wolves' tails and eagle feathers. I can wade the Mississippi without getting wet, outscream a catamount (mountain lion), jump over my own shadow... and cut through the bushes like a pint of whiskey among forty men."

The modest, laid-back, low-key, taciturn style of the 20th-century cowboy was nothing like that of the original buckaroos in the 19th century, who were lusty, ribald, raucous men who lived with a gusto that reflected the Victorian appetites of the era. With the passing of the open range and the fencing of the New Mexico and Arizona ranges, Anglo ranchers and cowboys were doomed. The turn of the century turned their memories into nostalgia. The last of the old-time cowboys, together with some of the old lawmen and outlaws, joined touring shows like Buffalo Bill's Wild West or Teddy Roosevelt's Rough Riders, and were largely recruited in New Mexico and Arizona.

When the cattle drives ended and the stage-coach trails faded, replaced by the railroad, the desert silence was shattered by the din of rail-roads and motorcars that brought thousands of newcomers. These were the new Anglos, the sick seeking the sun, the land developers seeking a tidy fortune, and the artists seeking a new light and new colors.

As the 19th century ended, East Coast artists

Billy the Kid.

discovered the Southwest. In 1898, Taos Society of Artists founders Ernest Blumenschein and Bert Phillips settled accidentally in Taos, New Mexico, when after riding the railroad to Denver from New York and taking a wagon down to New Mexico, they broke a wheel in Taos Canyon and fell in love with the area. They were not alone. In 1916, Mabel Dodge Luhan moved her New York salon to Taos. A few years later, novelist D.H. Lawrence, a temporary resident, was to proclaim, "There are all kinds of beauty in the world, but for a greatness of beauty I have never experienced anything like New Mexico."

The old-timers were to become a part of the artists' scenery and the writers' stories, and even a few legends.

Navajo Land

ARIZONA - NEW MEXICO

CONTEMPORARY TIMES

Air conditioning and the hot, dry weather gave the Southwest an appeal that lured people from colder climes to the area's warm embrace.

By World War II, the old frontier life was gone – but not quite. Gone were the longhorns and the great cattle drives on the Goodnight Trail. Gone were most of the gunslingers and bandidos, but by no means all. Even so, there was still plenty of the frontier atmosphere left. Many of the old gunfighters, those who had not died of "lead poisoning," were still alive. Pat Garrett, the sheriff who killed Billy the Kid, was himself dry-gulched in 1908 with a bullet in his head, at a time when such goings-on were presumably a thing of the past. The great gambling saloons of the Southwest closed their doors sometime between 1900 and 1911, outlawed due to an influx of "good women," but in the red-light districts the "soiled doves of the prairie" still did a land office business.

Mexican bandidos still strayed across the border to raise havoc on the wrong side of the Rio Grande. And trains were still robbed at gunpoint until the outbreak of World War I.

REVOLUTION TO THE SOUTH

The Mexican Revolution (1910–23) brought plenty of excitement, and it actually started on American soil in 1911, when Francisco Madero led a few hundred followers across the Rio Grande to start the civil war that would topple the Mexican dictator, the "Old Cacique" Porfirio Diaz. A decisive battle was fought at Juarez between the revolutionary army, led by Pancho Villa and Pascual Orozco, and the Porfiristas, led by Vasquez Gomez. The rebels won a brilliant victory, while Americans on the El Paso (Texas) side across the river had a grandstand view, watching the battle from their roofs and the tops of railroad cars.

In 1912, freshly escaped from jail and fleeing for his life, Villa holed up in a fleapit hotel in El

Government officials in Phoenix, 1907.

⊘ GERONIMO AND TECHNOLOGY

For American Indians, changes in the 20th century were bewildering. The Chiricahua Apache chief Geronimo, born in 1829, had grown up as a technologically stone-age man; his first weapons were stone-tipped arrows. Shortly before his death in 1909, as a member of the Dutch Reformed Church, he attended a convention of cattlemen in Tucson. In his hotel room, he was confronted by newfangled symbols of civilization – electric lights and the flush toilet, which he did not know how to use. As nobody had told him how to turn off the lamp at his bedside, he simply put his boot over it. Later, he was photographed at the wheel of an early Ford automobile.

Paso's Chamizal district. Soon he was back in Mexico to meet up with Zapata in Mexico City. Relations between the revolutionaries and the American Government fluctuated between good and bad. At a time when they were bad, in 1916, Villa made his famous raid on Columbus, a sleepy New Mexico frontier town where the only previous excitement in the town's history was a plague of rattlesnakes.

The battle in Columbus between the Villistas and Americans grew into one of the greatest shootouts the Southwest had ever experienced.

Francisco 'Pancho' Villa, 1908.

It resulted in the death of 16 Americans and a punitive U.S. Army chase under "Black Jack" Pershing in a fruitless pursuit of Villa.

The period around World War I has been described as a time of the *gringo*, a period of racial tension as Anglo newcomers engulfed the Spanish-speaking communities while looking down upon Hispanics. Statehood for both Arizona and New Mexico was held up as lawmakers and preachers alike opposed statehood. One congressman argued, "We don't want any more states until we civilize Kansas!" The Arizona legislature passed a law stipulating that 80 percent of workers in the state had to be American-born, a measure directed against immigrant Mexicans and Asians.

ECONOMIC UPSWINGS

Development proceeded slowly. After all, New Mexico's state motto is Crescit Eundo – "It grows as it goes." Frontier manners remained rough for many years. In Flagstaff, in northern Arizona, Sandy Donohue, barkeep at the Senate Saloon, greeted President Teddy Roosevelt by declaring, "By God, you are a better-looking man than your picture, you old son-of-a-bitch." Teddy, the one-time cowboy, took it as a compliment.

Modern amenities were slow to arrive in the Southwest. Flagstaff got its first telephone in

> *While considering statehood (granted in 1912) for New Mexico and Arizona, Congress considered making one state from both, to be called Montezuma.*

1900, with 85 subscribers throughout the county. The first steam-powered automobile arrived in 1902. Electricity came in 1904. Teachers were scarce, as their salaries were fixed at $75 a month while room and board cost $40.

Miners had infested the Southwest during the late 19th century, but gold's best year was 1915, when New Mexico produced $1,461,000 with what the ancient Indians had called the "Dung of the Gods."

Silver was found in some abundance throughout the region, though never rivaling the famed silver lodes of Nevada and Colorado. The most silver produced in New Mexico was $1,162,200, in 1910. By 1950 this had dwindled to about $100,000 per year.

Luckily, the Southwest had a wealth of other desirable minerals, and copper soon became king. When American industry began demanding copper, mines and mining towns once again mushroomed overnight. Coal also became important, particularly with the ever-expanding networks of railroads that needed the black stuff for their engines. After copper and coal came potash, and more exotic minerals, such as cobalt, antimony, and molybdenum. As one metal was replaced by another, new communities sprang up.

Early Anglo settlers had come to till the region's soil. In 1900, 5 million acres (2 million hectares) of land were under cultivation in New Mexico alone, and by 1910, the state had 35,000 farms. Lack of rain wiped out many of these farmers, and in 1911, the first of the big dams – Roosevelt Dam – was built in southern Arizona. Irrigation resuscitated much of the farming, and until the explosion of organic and local foods and the Slow Food movement in the early 21st century made such methods profitable, small farmers were replaced by large agribusiness.

Some 90 percent of Southwest land is unsuited to cultivation, yet is good cattle country. But although small ranches raising grass-fed cattle have become increasingly popular in the Southwest in recent years, mostly in local markets, cattle raised to satisfy the mainstream supermarket business don't grow fat on Southwest ranches and are sold and shipped to concentrated animal feed operations (CAFOs) in the Midwest and elsewhere. By 1910, there were 40,000 miles (64,000km) of barbed wire in Arizona alone, fencing off huge tracts of land.

The end of open ranges meant the end of old-fashioned cowboys. In 1892, a Western writer

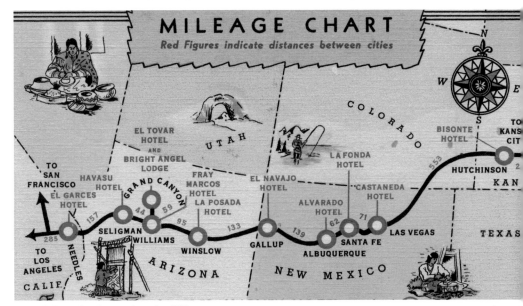

Santa Fe Route hotel poster from the 1930s.

⊘ BARBED-WIRE BLESSINGS

Ubiquitous not only in the American Southwest but throughout the country – anywhere land is plentiful but divided – is the barbed-wire fence, silvery threads of metal, strung from pole to pole, punctuated with sharp barbs.

There are actually several dozen types of barbed wire in use, though increasingly only one type is seen on America's open ranges: two longitudinal wires twisted together with wire barbs wrapped around the wires at regular spacings. There is a purpose to using two, inter-twined wires, as it not only makes the fence stronger but also allows the wire to contract and expand under the West's temperature and weather extremes.

Patents on barbed wire were first issued in the United States in 1867. But barbed wire wasn't widely used until 1874, when Joseph Glidden (after seeing a sample at a fair in 1873) devised a suitable machine for its manufacture. Within 15 years, barbed-wire fences, intended primarily to restrict movement of cattle, had enclosed most of the country's open range.

Although Glidden's patents on his manufacturing process were challenged, he eventually prospered by selling his business.

A modern variation is the electrified fence, which is typically a single strand of barbed wire, electrified.

lamented that "railroads and bobwire spell the demise of that colorful character."

SHIFTS IN AMERICAN INDIAN COMMUNITIES

Changes were coming to native communities, too. In 1919, American Indian men who had enlisted in the army to fight the country's enemies became eligible for U.S. citizenship. Oil was discovered on Navajo land, bringing income to the tribe that had wisely invested in education and other projects beneficial to all.

self-rule patterned after the system of government practiced by non-Indians.

Instead, they adhered to traditional dependence on elders or religious chiefs. This led, in some places, to a simmering conflict between the "Progressives" and the "Traditionals."

Meanwhile, lagging behind the Anglos in economic gains and the professions, Hispanic Americans in New Mexico concentrated on politics and wound up effectively running the state.

Gold and silver mining became mostly a distant memory, and many unproductive coal mines

Navajo people at a trading post, 1940s.

In 1922, Pueblos formed the All Pueblo Council in order to fight the so-called Bursum Bill, legislation that was designed to secure the right to Indian land for white squatters. In 1924, American citizenship was conferred upon all American Indians born within the borders of the United States.

In 1934, the Indian Reorganization Act gave the right of partial self-government to the tribes. As a result, tribal constitutions were framed and tribal presidents and councils democratically elected. It was a mixed blessing. The elected leaders often represented the more assimilated, educated, and English-speaking sector of the Indian population, while the traditional Indians saw no reason to adopt forms of

were shut down. (Still, potash mining started in a big way in 1931.) Natural gas became a source of income in the 1920s, and the Southwest enjoyed a number of moderate oil booms. Large copper mines opened in Arizona and New Mexico.

In 1936, Hoover Dam was completed. Water, or rather the lack of it, was becoming a problem. Many of the old-timers complained that modern industry, farming, ranching, tourists, and the increased population were "pumping the West dry." It was true.

SHADES OF SECRECY

In 1942, the US Army took over land belonging to a boys' school at Los Alamos, in northern New Mexico, northwest of Santa Fe. In the words of Erna Ferguson: "No secret was ever better kept than that of Los Alamos. The schoolboys had it that they were moving out for the Ethiopian Ski Corps or the Scandinavian Camel Artillery. Santa Feans saw lights against the Jemez peaks, but knew nothing." Meanwhile, a town of 8,000 people was springing up almost overnight in the vicinity of the state capital, without anyone being aware of it.

Landlocked and chronically thirsty, the Southwest at the end of World War II was remote but hardly unknown. Railroads, highways and scheduled flights made access easy. Inhabitants shipped out iron, T-bone steaks, and grapefruit and got back dude ranches and tourists doing the national park circuit. Yet each state seemed in a private trance.

Arizona, focus of frantic Air Force activity during World War II, returned to its three Cs: cotton, cattle, and copper. New Mexico, with its Pueblo and Hispanic agricultural traditions, changed primarily with the seasons. Southwest Nevada, in decline since the silver boom of the 1800s, was a polity of sand and collapsing buildings. Colorado rode a recreational boom as skiing in the Rockies became popular. And southern Utah deliberately stayed out of the postwar mainstream to preserve the isolation and purity of its Mormon culture.

The Southwest in 1945 resembled the Great Basin of Utah and Nevada, whose rivers deadend in separate valleys instead of reaching out to the sea. Like the Great Basin to its north, the Southwest was facing inward, fixed on its several selves.

GREAT AND MIGHTY DAMS

A federal role was crucial in developing what all Southwesterners demanded: more water. Reclamation was hardly a new idea. The Southwest had received the Reclamation Act in 1902, the Hoover Dam on the Colorado River in 1935, and countless dams built by federal, state, and private concerns. But with the war effort over, the Bureau of Reclamation could direct its attention westward in a major way, and it made proposals for every watercourse. Its grandest single monument was Glen Canyon Dam, completed in 1963 near Page, Arizona, and backing water 180 river miles (290km) into some of the Colorado River's least-known and most spectacular canyons. Its

most ambitious scheme is the ongoing Central Arizona Project, to channel water from the Colorado River to Phoenix and Tucson at a cost of more than four times the original estimate of a billion dollars.

Federal stimulation of the Southwestern economy developed a wide spectrum of activities and shifted the balance of power in the Southwest. Much of the driest and least productive land had been allotted to the military during World War II, and the military kept it. During the 1950s, the salt and alkali basins of Nevada became the site

Glen Canyon Dam.

⊘ TIMELESS SOUTHWEST ART

The Southwest has lured artists and writers to its embrace in the past century, among them, one of America's important women artists, Georgia O'Keeffe, who arrived in Taos for the first time in 1917 and immediately fell in love with the place. In a letter back east to her photographer husband Alfred Stieglitz, she described the New Mexican landscape as "a perfectly mad-looking country – hills and cliffs and washes too crazy to imagine all thrown up into the air by God and let tumble where they would." By the time she died in 1986, O'Keefe had painted not the Old Southwest or the New Southwest, but a timeless Southwest of light and color, of geology and life.

of hundreds of underground nuclear tests, and Hill Air Force Base in Utah became the West's leading missile center. Towns like Yuma and Sierra Vista, in Arizona, are virtual adjuncts to the military, and many of the emptiest reaches of the Southwest are off-limits to civilians.

Ironically, much of the land in the hands of the military – scarred by tanks, pounded by artillery, glittering with shrapnel – has remained relatively intact, while the drive for minerals, lumber, and cheap energy has caused more lasting devastation. Mining on federal land was

Copper mine at Silver City, New Mexico.

⊘ AN EXPLOSIVE START

The atomic bomb was designed and built on a plateau in the Jemez Mountains, northwest of Santa Fe, home to hundreds of cave dwellings carved from the soft tuff rock by prehistoric Pueblo Indians. It was first exploded at the Trinity site, near Alamogordo in southern New Mexico, in 1945. "A blind girl saw the flash of light, a rancher thought the end of the world had come," but the country at large knew nothing. It was a New Mexican officer who "armed" the bomb before it was flown to Japan and dropped on Hiroshima, and it was Paddy Martinez, a Navajo man, who, in 1950, found the first lump of uranium in the Arizona desert. Thus did the Nuclear Age take root in the American Southwest.

encouraged by minimal fees and scant regulation, while lumber contracts didn't – and still don't – make that most basic requirement that a new tree be planted for each cut down.

In the early 1950s, uranium prospectors gouged roads at random across southern Utah, leaving permanent scars. Uranium was developed more systematically in northwestern Colorado, around Grand Junction, and in northwestern New Mexico in the 1970s, leaving behind carcinogenic mill tailings for the Indian inhabitants. But it was coal, abundant and often lying near the surface, that became the most coveted resource.

In 1957, a Utah coal company made the first contract with the Navajo Tribal Council to extract coal beneath Navajo land. The major oil companies, sensing that the coal beds of the Colorado Plateau were a vital energy source, began acquiring coal companies and turning them into subsidiaries. Cities like Los Angeles and Phoenix badly needed new energy but had to generate it elsewhere. Ample coal in southern Utah and northern Arizona could be burned on the spot. Power would surge through transmission lines to immense cities hundreds of miles away.

In 1974 a consortium of 21 utilities, representing seven states, banded together and proposed a mesh of strip mines, power plants, and transmission lines of unprecedented complexity. Not all of the proposed grid came into being, but major coal-fired power plants went up in Farmington, New Mexico, and Page, Arizona. The Page plant, near Glen Canyon Dam, was linked by a company railroad to a strip mine run by Peabody Coal, 70 miles (113 km) east, on Black Mesa, a formation sacred to the Hopi.

RETIREES AND REAL ESTATE

While energy battles were being fought on the Colorado Plateau, the warmer lands to the south were filling up with humanity. With the introduction of air conditioning during World War II, suddenly no desert was too hot for colonization. Snowbelt retirees settled in vast planned retirement communities such as Sun City; in tracts and trailer parks along the Colorado River from Boulder City, Nevada, to Yuma, Arizona; and even in the small towns of southern New Mexico, in places like Truth or Consequences.

While traditional industries like copper mining and small-scale ranching fell into decline, high-technology industries in Albuquerque, Phoenix, and Tucson drew ambitious young people from elsewhere to the area, balancing the demographics and at the same time inflating the population. Mesquite gave way to mobile home communities, to pseudo-adobe duplex compounds, and to townhouse labyrinths around artificial lakes that obliterated the desert. One developer brought the original London Bridge to the Colorado River in the 1970s and ran the world's tallest fountain on subsiding groundwater merely to promote his ventures. Easier on the terrain was outright land fraud, wherein development took place on paper, and the land, if any, was spared.

21ST CENTURY CHANGES

As the 21st century dawned, the runaway growth in residents and tourists throughout the Southwest forced planners to confront the need for better roads, better housing developments, better airports, better public transportation, and better management of scarce and fragile resources. Once a land of boom and bust and endless frontiers, the Southwest took a long look at itself and a future of declining resources and decided to make lasting changes. There have been many surprising developments.

Light rail, shuttle buses, and streetcars have been successfully introduced in recent years to even the most sprawling of cities, such as Tucson and Phoenix, as well as national parks like Zion, Bryce Canyon, and Grand Canyon. Historic downtowns and some industrial zones have been redeveloped into more pedestrian-friendly, multi-use places, with coordinated public transit, wider boulevards, attractive xeriscape desert landscaping, and popular green spaces and community gardens. They have attracted local businesses, farmers' markets selling locally grown food, and farm-to-table restaurants headed up by chef-owners with national credentials and a penchant for grow-your-own. Many cities have built or expanded cultural museums, including Scottsdale's Museum of the West, which opened in 2016 under the leadership of the former director of Phoenix's Heard Museum.

Water recycling, conservation, and other environmental programs have been surprisingly successful, considering the region's profligate use of resources in the past. They have become models of what can be achieved, both in national parks like the Grand Canyon, a leader in recycling in the parks, and metro areas like Phoenix, which began recycling graywater from its numerous golfcourses and reducing its environmental footprint through a number of public-private partnerships.

Colorado has led the way on a variety of fronts, symptomatic of its influx of new Front Range residents, many Latino, who hail from progressive California. Medicinal marijuana was legalized in the state in 2014, immediately attracting new

Urban sprawl near Phoenix.

small growers and stores selling marijuana to health tourists. Massive sales have jumpstarted its economy following the devastating international Great Recession that began in 2008. Marijuana is now a major contributor to state coffers, to the tune of $996 million in sales in 2015.

More soberingly, Colorado has been the site of several mass shootings by disaffected males, including at Columbine High School, an Aurora movie theater, and more recently, a Planned Parenthood clinic. The shootings led to the passing of important gun control legislation by Democratic governor John Hickenlooper in March 2013, a move widely applauded. Later that year, however, two lawmakers who had sponsored the bills were recalled, a first in

Colorado, demonstrating the lasting influence of the gun lobby and gun culture in this state, and many others. This has continued in Congress, despite the near-fatal shooting of popular Tucson congresswoman Gabby Giffords and several members of her staff at a meet-and-greet with the public in 2011. In 2016, however, Colorado's gun control laws were upheld by its legislature and remain in force.

Climate change is severely impacting the Southwest, with temperatures continuing to rise, ongoing severe drought conditions, mas-

Children holding signs in support of Bears Ears NM.

sive flooding, and extensive wildfires along the wildland-urban interface surrounding cities like Denver, which come earlier and grow worse each year, and cause millions of dollars worth of damage.

Same-sex marriage, federally recognized since 2014, is now recognized in all Southwest states, and LGBTQ tourism has grown significantly. Meanwhile, as more people move to Southwest cities like Tucson, Phoenix, and Denver, particularly from the West Coast, these traditionally red states have become increasingly blue, particularly Colorado, which hosted the Democratic Convention where Senator Barack Obama was nominated as the presidential candidate and went on to win two terms,

beating Arizona senator John McCain. For the first time, Southwest states like Colorado are on the national radar during presidential elections, as a result of changing demographics, and have moved beyond being "flyover country" for Washington. Reliably red states like Arizona and Utah have held on, though, with Arizona's desert border with Mexico the subject of continued measures to quell illegal immigration, supported by its ambitious Republican senators, state legislators, and at least one controversial local sheriff.

Barack Obama's historic presidency, as the country's first black president, brought significant changes in civil rights but went hand in hand with an increasing divide between thriving blue cities and surrounding red rural areas whose citizens struggle to make ends meet. Discontent and disaffection bubbled below the surface, popping into view from time to time through the actions of the Tea Party, an activist right wing of the Republican party, which used Barack Obama's half-Kenyan parentage and birthplace in Hawaii, to try to introduce a "birther law," requiring proof of US citizenship for presidential candidates.

This discontent erupted countrywide in the 2016 presidential election, when businessman Donald Trump, who had never worked in public office, unexpectedly won the presidency, beating former First Lady and New York senator Hillary Clinton. From inauguration day 2017, the Trump administration unleashed an onslaught of rushed congressional actions designed to undo landmark laws protecting the environment, public lands, abortion access, and civil rights, some of which go back decades.

At the time of writing, several recent Southwest national monuments, set aside for protection of scientific and cultural resources by President Obama under the Antiquities Act of 1906, are being recommended for downsizing. This includes Bears Ears National Monument in southeastern Utah, newly declared in December 2016, and Grand Staircase-Escalante National Monument in southwestern Utah, declared by President Clinton, which have been the focus of persistent recall efforts by powerful Republican congressional leaders like Senator Orrin Hatch. The intention is to redraw the map at both the federal and local level and reframe US policy.

DEVELOPMENT IN THE GRAND CANYON

Throughout its history, the park has faced environmental challenges – never more so than now.

In March 2016, the US Forest Service rejected a plan from an Italian developer to build a luxury resort in the small gateway town of Tusayan, just outside Grand Canyon National Park's South Rim. Despite the developer's influence – they already had bought up much of Tusayan and funded the town's successful but controversial 2010 incorporation effort – the development was voted down. However, with over 5 million visitors a year, parking at a premium, hotels within the park's Grand Canyon Village booked a year ahead, long waits at restaurants, and amenities in little Tusayan maxed out, addressing visitor needs (and employee housing) at the Grand Canyon remains a work in progress.

The federal government first proposed developing Tusayan (pop. 558) in the late 1980s. One promising plan was put forward in 1999 by a local developer and was applauded as a model for the future by developers, government, and environmentalists. Canyon Forest Village, planned to truck in water rather than pump it out of the Canyon.

Most importantly for drivers frustrated by the traffic jams at the Canyon, the plan included a light-rail system from Tusayan to the South Rim, which it was estimated would cut traffic in the park by 80 percent. (Ironically, it was a train that first brought tourists to the canyon; Williams, another major visitor gateway, off I-40 southwest of the park, still runs its historic steam train daily.)

Development was to have been made possible by land swaps of national forest land around Tusayan and private parcels. The Forest Service was to exchange land at Tusayan for 2,200 acres (890 hectares) scattered elsewhere in Kaibab National Forest, land that could have been developed with no environmental safeguards. In this case, everyone involved – the US government, private landowners, developers, environmentalists, tribes – was happy with the exchange of land, but the development itself foundered and was abandoned. At which point, the Italian developer stepped in.

The sections of the East and West Rims of the Grand Canyon on tribal lands outside the park are experiencing development pressures as tourism continues to boom. Grand Canyon West on Hualapai Indian land, north of Kingman, built a popular see-

Helicopter flying over the Grand Canyon.

through high viewing platform above the West Rim called Skywalk, attracting visitors from Las Vegas; while on the East Rim, the $1 billion Grand Canyon Escalade proposal from a private company to develop hotels, restaurants, stores, and a gondola on Navajo Nation land has been voted down by the Navajo Tribal Council but not yet finally declined.

In the last few years, Grand Canyon National Park has worked to improve the visitor experience at the South Rim by creating a new visitor center, park-and-shuttle operation, bicycle rentals, and trails just within park boundaries. Popular scenic drives are closed to private vehicles in busy summer periods now (as is true at Zion National Park), getting visitors out of their cars and onto buses and hiking trails.

But in 2017, with a new pro-big-business federal government moving fast to open up national parks to development and resource extraction, Grand Canyon's challenges have only grown. Uranium mining, which had been allowed in the past but was responsible for polluting the Navajo water supply, may once again be permitted. The park also continues to contend with noise from helicopter flights, encroaching non-native species, and air pollution from nearby power plants.

📷 THE MILITARY'S PLACE IN THE SUN

The Southwest's important military bases are used for the development of stealth technology, atomic weapons, missiles, aircraft, and training.

The sparsely populated Southwest houses a number of military installations – depots, attack aircraft training centers, fighter weapons centers, research and development weapons test centers, and fighter wings. Spacious, cloudless skies ensure ideal flying conditions. As pilots know, huge restricted air zones must not be entered by unauthorized aircraft to avoid being blown to smithereens in a missile test. The secrecy and human love of intrigue spark curiosity about these remote, fenced, and heavily guarded sites.

Take Site 51, a restricted air force base in the Nevada desert. The government first denied its existence then issued this statement: "We do have facilities within [Site 51]. The facilities of the Nellis Range Complex are used for testing and training technologies, operations, and systems critical to the effectiveness of V.S. military forces. Specific activities conducted at Nellis cannot be discussed any further than that." The site was selected in the mid-1950s for testing of the V-2 spy plane, due to its remoteness, proximity to existing facilities, and presence of a dry lakebed for landings.

ATOMIC SECRETS

In 1942, the secluded Pajarito Plateau in northern New Mexico was perfect cover for Los Alamos physicists developing the first atomic bomb, code name "Manhattan." It was tested in July 1945 at the Trinity site in the Jornada del Muerto, near Las Cruces. A second bomb was dropped on Hiroshima on August 6; a third on Nagasaki on August 9. Nearly 100,000 people died.

An MQM-107D Streaker drone, used for training with every surface-to-air and air-to-air weapon in the Air Force and Army inventory. The White Sands Missile Range Museum is the largest military installation in the US and was the site of the first atomic bomb test on July 16, 1945.

These soldiers at Lackland Air Force Base in Texas find that basic training has not changed with advances in military technology.

The first Atomic bomb experimental explosion, code named Trinity.

United States Air Force Rockwell B1-B bomber landing at Nellis AFB.

The 1947 Roswell incident

On June 14, 1947, a rancher in Lincoln County, New Mexico, found unusual debris on his property. He had found weather balloons twice before, but not like this one. On July 7, having heard reports of crashed "flying discs," he reported his find. The military examined the wreckage – a bundle of tinfoil, paper, tape, sticks, and rubber weighing about 5 pounds (2kg) – and determined it was the remains of a weather balloon. All was quiet until 1978, when the drama resumed in books, tabloids, and TV, all crying cover-up. A conspiracy theory posited that the debris was the result of an alien spacecraft that had crashed at Roswell, which was then recovered and covered up by the U.S. government. In the years subsequent, the claim became possibly the most debated and investigated rumor of its type. The furor grew until the 1990s, when the government published two reports disclosing the true nature of the crashed object: a nuclear test surveillance balloon from Project Mogul. Just enough discrepancy remained, however, to keep the conspiracy theory alive.

Edwards Air Force Base has seen more major milestones in flight than any other place on Earth.

A Textron Scorpion experimental aircraft conducting handling and flying quality maneuvers above White Sands Missile Range near Alamagordo, New Mexico.

Major Jesse Marcel, intelligence officer at Roswell Army Air Field, in July 1947, displaying the mysterious wreckage that many people believe was an alien spaceship.

Native American Hopi dancers perform ritual chants, Arizona, 1902.

53813 ANTELOPE PRIESTS CHANTING AT KISI, MO—

A mural of a Navajo girl on Route 66, Albuquerque.

A Navajo man wearing ceremonial clothes at a Festival Navajo Nation Fair.

THE NATIVE AMERICANS

Living in this part of the world for more than 100 centuries before the Spanish discoverers arrived, these proud and varied people are the "original Americans."

Whether they are called "American Indian," "Native American," or simply "Native" seems to matter less to individuals than their tribal identity. American Indian people think of themselves first as members of a particular tribe, and many tribes further differentiate according to specific locales. Even tribal names such as Navajo, Ute, or Pueblo are mere labels attached to the tribes by Europeans who were unable to pronounce – or did not bother to discover – the name each tribe has to identify itself.

The myth that all American Indians are alike still persists, but nowhere is this falsehood easier to disprove than in the Southwest. For here, often within a few miles, are Native communities whose cultural and linguistic differences are as pronounced as those between England and Turkey.

CREATION OR MIGRATION?

All tribes in the Southwest have religious beliefs connecting their creation and the creation of the Universe with a higher force or being. Each tribe has its own particular story of Creation, and anthropological theories about origins in Asia or the South Seas are firmly rejected by many American Indian people.

Regardless of how they came to the Southwest, when the Spanish arrived in 1540, Native people had already been living there for some 10,000 years. It is within this immense span of time that the tribes of the Southwest have come to understand their intimate relationship with Earth, the Mother Creator for many Pueblo tribes. Mountains, hills, streams, and springs are sacred; they can point to them and say, "This is where our people come from." They can point to the ruins of ancient villages

A Native American woman working at La Posada Hotel.

⊘ SPIRITUALITY

Religion is the cornerstone of American Indian identity, with many people combining ancient religious traditions with the practice of Christianity. Perhaps the most visible form of contemporary Native religion, however, is a loosely defined movement that can be termed "American Indian Spirituality," which draws on some general religious themes in order to forge a common intertribal spiritual identity. It exemplifies harmonious living and spiritual interconnections with the natural world; politically, it is firmly opposed to environmental exploitation and Western materialism. Also appealing to non-Indians, it is a mainstay of the New Age movement.

and say, "These are the footprints of our ancestors." Even today, there are American Indians who can trace the migration of their ancestors for thousands of years. It is no wonder, therefore, that they feel spiritually rooted to the land.

It is difficult to gauge the impact of the arrival of the Spaniards and later European settlers upon the tribal cultures of the Southwest. The difficulty lies in the fact that any attempt to evaluate or compare the "before" of American Indian cultures with the "after" is

Southwest have continually demonstrated their belief in and respect for many alternative ways and beliefs. This adaptability and intellectual breadth enabled these cultures to survive and even thrive in the harsh Southwestern climate. Within the world view of these Southwestern Indian cultures, the fact that a medicine man has a television in his house does not necessarily mean that he has rejected ancient beliefs and traditions; what it means is that his curiosity and belief in knowledge about all humanity have prompted

Taking the Pledge of Allegiance at the Crystal Boarding School in the Navajo Nation.

impossible. Furthermore, implicit in such an assessment are Western assumptions about "change" or "loss of cultural purity," which are appropriate only when applied to Western cultures. Western views of life and culture tend to place an inordinate emphasis on material evidence, while the Native cultures of the Southwest tend to assert the spiritual dimension. No outsider, no matter how "expert," can truly comprehend what lies at the heart of the Navajo or Pueblo or Apache cultures.

What is visible is evidence that deep within these cultures is the profound philosophical belief in coexistence with all living things, including human beings of other races and cultures. The American Indian cultures of the

him to include within his world this artifact of high-tech culture. His view is that what he might see, or learn by seeing, can strengthen his traditional healing powers.

While some of the sacred dances and ceremonies are closed to outside visitors (as a result of several centuries of onlookers displaying boorish behavior), a great many are performed for the renewal of all human beings, and these ceremonies do welcome outside visitors.

NO-NONSENSE PATRIOTISM

At the same time, it is important to remember that nearly all Native people, no matter which tribe they come from, are intensely conscious of being Americans; of being not only the original, or First, Americans, but fiercely proud Americans who have fought and died for this land in every major war. The overwhelming richness and intensity of tribal identity may occasionally obscure this plain patriotism, also a key ingredient in the identity of a White Mountain Apache or an Isleta Pueblo. The "trusteeship" of the US Government over tribal lands is not an American Indian scheme. The Founding Fathers conferred this unique (and, as some Indians see it, paternalistic) legal

deer as they see fit, without state intervention. The result is a paradise for big-game hunters and for trout fishermen at the Jicarilla's Stone House Lodge Resort on Stone Lake.

On the negative side, many Indian communities do not have direct control over the leasing or development of their tribal lands. Before these tribes can do anything on their land, they must secure the approval of the Secretary of the Interior and the Commissioner of the Bureau of Indian Affairs. The results of this 200-year-old policy toward Indian tribes

Navajo Code Talkers.

status upon Indian Tribes in the Commerce Clause of the US Constitution.

The unusual legal status of communities located on federal Indian reservations often brings strange or interesting results. For example, in Arizona, the New Pascua Tribe of Yaqui Indians can conduct million-dollar bingo games 10 miles (16km) west of Tucson because Arizona state laws limiting the size of bingo jackpots do not apply to the Pascua Yaqui Reservation, which lies under the federal jurisdiction of the United States Department of the Interior.

The special legal status also means that the Jicarilla Apache Tribe in northern New Mexico may manage their trophy-size elk and mule

⊘ FIGHTING FOR THEIR COUNTRY

American Indians have the highest record of US military service per capita of any ethnic group. It is thought that their distinctive cultural values – particularly a proud warrior tradition – drives them to serve their country. The courage, determination, and fighting spirit of American Indians were recognized by American military leaders as early as the 18th century, and from the War of 1812 right through the Iraq and Afghanistan campaigns, their numbers have been strong: One veteran says they go to war because they are "super-patriots.... Any pow-wow you go to – after all the American government has done to Indian people – the American flag is still there. Always."

is readily apparent: Native American communities are notoriously lacking in many of the modern amenities other American communities take for granted. Because neither individual tribal members nor the tribe itself has "ownership" of the land, financing for housing, sewage treatment, and solid-waste disposal were in past years impossible for Indian communities to obtain.

Very few of the businesses located on reservations are controlled by the tribe. Again, until recently, it has been extremely difficult for enterprising American Indian businesspeople to obtain bank financing since reservation lands cannot be used as collateral. Because of these complexities, in past years tribes in the Southwest had little control over land use and development of natural resources on tribal lands. Large mining corporations, aided by apathetic bureaucrats in the Department of the Interior, obtained vast mineral and petroleum leases on tribal lands without paying more than token sums for these lease privileges. Although these unfortunate leases were

Navajo children on their family ranch in Sweetwater, Arizona.

⊘ RESERVATIONS

There are more than 50 Indian reservations in the Southwest. They encompass the modern tribal lands of more or less separate groups. The largest and most culturally intact of these groups are the Pueblo, Navajo, Hopi, Apache, Tohono O'odham, and Pima. Smaller tribes include the Havasupai of the Grand Canyon, the Ute of southern Utah, and the Paiute of northern Arizona. The Walapai, Hualapai, Mojave, Yavapai, Chemehuevi, Yuma, Cocopa, Maricopa, and Yaqui live in western Arizona, but many have friends or family in Mexico.

The 27,000-square-mile (69,333 sq.km) Navajo Nation, which dominates the northeast corner of Arizona and spills over into New Mexico and Utah, is the largest Indian reservation in the country and is arguably the most dramatic and beautiful scenically.

When traveling on Indian reservations, it is important to remember that you must obey all tribal laws and regulations. It is advisable to contact tribal councils before your arrival and ask about any rules or prohibitions of which you need to be aware. These may include restrictions on photography, travel, fishing, hunting, hiking, and carrying or consuming alcohol. If there is one golden rule it is "Be respectful": reservations are living, working communities, not elaborate tourist displays.

made in the mid-1950s, many had a duration of 40 or 50 years, so it is only now, in the 21st century, that Indian tribes are taking charge of their own destiny.

Equally unfortunate was the policy of the Department of the Interior allowing mining operations to strip-mine coal and uranium without requiring reclamation of the land. Evidence of these past abuses is visible on many reservations.

For people who trace their origins to Mother Earth, the natural-resource policies of the

technological age is quite a shock to the eye. High-tech sewage plants are juxtaposed with sandstone walls built in AD 1000. Casino-resorts and golf courses sit across from sacred landmarks on tribal lands.

This juxtaposition of ancient non-European culture with a high-tech world disturbs many people, because it raises many questions and provides no answers about the multiplicity of cultural identities. Clearly, tribal people living in the Southwest are very much part of the present and its attendant material culture.

San Juan Indian Pueblo Eagle Dance.

Department of the Interior have been particularly painful. But in recent years, a gradual shift has been taking place, in which young Indian lawyers and PhDs have helped their tribes assert more control over their lands and natural resources. But always there remains a deep conflict between the traditional reverence for Mother Earth and the critical need for jobs, money, and housing in communities where unemployment may run as high as 75 percent, and woefully scarce housing is often without electricity or indoor plumbing.

Because the tribes of the Southwest remained relatively untouched by Western influences for so long after the arrival of the first Spaniards, the appearance of the modern

⊙ MINERAL WEALTH – OR WOES?

When American Indians in the Southwest were assigned reservations in the late 19th century, many were sent to land thought nearly worthless for mining or agriculture. That was before uranium became the driving force of the nuclear age. About half the recoverable uranium within the United States lies within New Mexico – and about half of that is beneath the Navajo Nation. Many Navajos, however, have come to oppose mining, particularly after one morning in July 1979, when tons of radioactive uranium waste spilled into the Rio Puerco, a major source of water on the reservation in west of Albuquerque. The detrimental repercussions of that event are still being felt.

Outsiders have often seriously misjudged the visible and superficial evidence. In 1900, Franz Boas, a towering figure in cultural anthropology, announced that the Pueblo tribes faced cultural extinction within a decade. More than a century later, cultural anthropologists are just beginning to realize that, as "outsiders," they are unable to understand that ineffable core of tribal identity that lies intact beneath layers of external debris left behind by successive waves of explorers and invaders.

are still here. Now the Americans come with electricity, automobiles, and television. And perhaps, one day, they too will go away. And the Hopis will still be here."

There's no question that American Indians will still be here. But the conundrum disturbing middle-aged Indians today is "In what form will we exist?"

Many Indian people of this generation have become "modernized" for various reasons, largely economic. As in most parts of the world where there is movement by a younger

The Navajo Flag, painted on a wall.

But as one old Pueblo woman said in the late 20th century, "How much could you expect Franz Boas to know? The United States of America hasn't even existed 250 years yet. But we have been around 9 or 10 thousand years at least."

In fact, there is a story that people in the Southwest tell about a Hopi elder who was asked if it was possible for traditional Hopi ways to survive the influences of modern American life. "The Navajos came a long time ago and raided Hopi villages," the old man is supposed to have said. "But the Navajos went away, and the Hopis are still here. Then the Spanish came with their horses, guns, and Bible. The Spanish disappeared, and the Hopis

generation from the lifestyle of their parents, this creates a difficulty with upholding the responsibilities and practices of old, while living a modern life, with all its attendant demands. For many younger Indians, this can result in a feeling of leading two entirely separate lives. They are caught between two worlds: Navajo and Anglo, switching back and forth, never able to bring them together. Modern and traditional worlds overlap, and people are forced to accommodate both as best they can.

Time and again, through centuries of war, epidemics and hunger, Native Americans have proven their resiliency, their ability to adapt. In the end, they will endure.

LAND AND CULTURE

Whatever the tribe, the determining factors in the life patterns that were (and still are) followed have always been the weather and the terrain.

The American Indian people of the Southwest, no matter what their linguistic or philosophical difference, have always seen themselves in relation to the landscape around them: they regard the earth as their mother and the sky as their father. Survival until very recently has depended upon powers of adaptation, not change, and upon intimate knowledge of weather patterns, clouds, animals, and plants.

SETTLEMENTS

In places where annual rainfall and drainage patterns allowed farming, and where nearby hills and mountains offered small game or deer, groups like the Pueblo people of New Mexico and the Hopi of northern Arizona established permanent villages with massive stone-and-mortar walls to ward off the rigors of winter. The Pima and Tohono O'odham of southern Arizona settled in villages near desert springs since water was of primary concern in their location. Their villages, while permanent, did not require elaborate masonry walls but rather cool, airy thatching woven from local cane to provide protection from the sun and to allow the wind to circulate throughout.

Although, vast cultural and linguistic differences existed among them, these communities, which farmed and supplemented crops with hunting and gathering, shared similar concerns with regard to clouds and rainfall. In religious ceremonies, the focus was always, and continues to be, on adequate rain throughout the year. Prayers for rain and careful surveillance of the sky are activities understood by all cultures engaged in farming without benefit of modern technology.

KACHINAS

In Pueblo culture, kachinas are spiritual beings that serve as intermediaries between people and the Great Spirit – and also act as messengers between the Pueblos and the domain of the Rain People. They manifest themselves as clouds and bring life-giving rain to the arid fields. With only 10ins (25cm) of rain falling each year on Pueblo land, the main concern of their religion is rain and the growth of corn, their most important crop.

Figure of a Hopi kachina.

Because the terrain and climate of the Southwest are so unpredictable and the consequences of long droughts irreparable, tribes in the Southwest have survived here, as one Hopi elder put it, "By prayer... we live by our prayers." Thus, the figure of the Rainbow Woman arching over the Great Seal of the Navajo tribe (displayed prominently on tribal motor-pool vehicles) symbolizes, literally, the sustenance that the Rainbow Woman is believed to provide the Navajo people.

A Native American guide leads a tour group through Taos Pueblo.

THE PUEBLO PEOPLE

Sought long ago by the Spanish as legendary cities of gold along the Rio Grande, the villages of the Pueblo are functional and communal towns of the desert.

Detail may vary from village to village, but the Pueblo people's story of the Creation begins with a single Mind that "thought" the entire Universe into existence. Once the Creation had been completed, the people and animals found themselves in a dimness full of running water, which was the First World, or the Blue World. They journeyed upward into the Red World, then into the Yellow World or Third World, where they rested before climbing upward into the White World, which was full of flowers and grass and beautiful running water. Many wanted to remain because it was a paradise, but they had been told that theirs must be the Fifth World, and a certain way of life that could be accomplished only by traveling there.

The animals, insects, and plants decided they must accompany their brethren, the human beings, into the Fifth World. But when the people and creatures arrived at the opening into the Fifth World, they found the hole was blocked by a large stone.

The people tried but were unable to move the stone. The Badger People began digging with their long claws and managed to loosen the stone. But it was one of the Antelope People who decided to butt the stone. The fourth time he struck it with his head, the stone flew out of the hole and Antelope led all the people and the creatures into the Present World.

From the beginning, the Present World was filled with a great many challenges and difficulties for the people. But it is by these struggles that the people realize their spirituality and humanity and, most important, their place with all other living beings in the Universe. Thus, the Pueblo view of the world emphasizes the interdependence of human beings and animals,

At the Indian Pueblo Culture Center, Albuquerque.

the lowliest insects, and the plants and trees. Pueblo clans further recognize this familial relationship by calling themselves, say, the Badger Clan or the Corn Clan. Each animal, plant, and tree that the people use to satisfy human needs has always been prayed to and asked to give itself to the people.

Among the Keresan-speaking Pueblo, for instance, a deer brought home by the hunter is placed in the center of the home and treated as a guest of honor. Turquoise is draped on the dead animal's neck and antlers, and family and guests approach the deer to "feed" it ceremonially by placing pinches of blessed corn meal on its nose. No part of the deer's body is wasted or in any way dishonored. The hunter must participate in the Deer Dance rituals and "dance" the soul of the deer back to the mountains, where the people believe the soul will be reborn into another deer, which will remember the love and respect of the humans and thus choose to once again give its life.

The land the Pueblo people call Mother is beautiful but unpredictable, and extremes of drought or winter cold have made human survival a great challenge. For thousands of years the Pueblo people have met this challenge, but only with the grace of the spirits of all living beings and the love of Mother Earth. The Pueblo people are by necessity among the greatest skywatchers. In ancient Pueblo observatories, winter sun symbols were inscribed on sandstone, and special windows allowed the sun to illuminate the petroglyphs only on the winter solstice. In a land where the sky determines the fortunes of farming, religious devotion to cloud formations, winds, the positions of the sun and the moon, and the tracking of the planets gave the Pueblo people the information necessary for successful agriculture.

DANCES OF CELEBRATION

The Present World of the Pueblo people is comprised of around 20 separate Pueblo tribes in New Mexico and the Hopi tribe in northeastern Arizona. Although the Pueblo people share similar religious beliefs that reveal a common worldview, linguistic differences distinguish each group from the other.

What a visitor may see at a *pueblo* (Pueblo village) today is not nearly so important as what will never be seen. Outsiders may attend a Pueblo dance, but it is only part of a longer religious ritual, and certain ritual dances are now off limits to visitors after years of bad manners by those visitors. Dances that are still accessible to visitors are important religious acts, regardless of the apparent informality of the Pueblo crowd around them. Smartphones, cameras, and filming are usually prohibited.

Jeweler of Navajo and Isleta Pueblo descent.

⊘ THE PUEBLO REVOLT

When the Spanish *conquistadores* arrived at Zuni Pueblo, in 1540, they found prosperous fields of corn, beans, squash, melons, and cotton. Under Spanish control, *encomienda*, or "tribute," a tithe of corn, woven cotton, and other valuable products payable to the local authorities, was instituted at the pueblos. Struggling with drought conditions and more mouths to feed, agricultural output was barely enough to feed the people of each pueblo, let alone their new masters, and the people began to starve and revolt against the impossible burden.

In 1680, the people of several pueblos organized a military maneuver still marveled at because of the great distances between the pueblos. Under the clandestine leadership of a San Juan Pueblo medicine man named Po Pay, the pueblo staged a great revolt on August 10 in which Spanish priests, soldiers, and settlers were slaughtered and the survivors driven out of pueblo country, to El Paso.

However, 12 years later, in 1692, the Spanish returned under the leadership of Diego de Vargas, who managed a Reconquest. This time the Spaniards were more cautious in their dealings with Pueblo people and softened their insistence on religious conversion. Spain acknowledged Pueblo governmental entities and granted each pueblo limited powers of self-government and modest or land grants. The Spanish retained power over the pueblo people until 1821, when Mexico gained its independence.

Among the ceremonies open to the public is Taos Pueblo's San Geronimo Festival in September. For centuries, this event has included an intertribal trade fair. On display are cottonwood drums, undecorated micaceous pottery (a gleaming pinkish ware with occasional smoke spots), and beadwork on moccasins.

In Santa Clara Canyon every November 1, the Puye Cliff Ceremonial takes place high atop the mesa opposite the pueblo, featuring traditional dances performed against a backdrop of stone and adobe ruins. Puye Cliff Dwellings, a national historic landmark, is the ancestral home of Santa Clara Pueblo, and part of the Pajarito Plateau. The ceremony is closed to outsiders.

Indian dances are requests to the spirit world for blessings, and they are often combined with Christian feast days. On Christmas Eve in the Catholic church of San Felipe Pueblo, for example, the spirits of the animal kingdom – as dancers representing deer or buffalo – pay homage to the Christ Child; elaborately dressed women dancers enter the church after midnight Mass. In hushed closeness, onlookers await the arrival of the procession. No one is supposed to see the dancers emerge from their kiva. Buffalo dancers, wearing the dark fur and horned headdress of the buffalo, with their exposed skin darkened, stomp on the floor. Deer dancers, who are bent over their sticks and whose headdresses are decked with antlers, move more lightly.

The Corn Dance is held at various times at different pueblos. Santo Domingo holds it in August on the feast of St Dominic. It's an open-air extravaganza that involves 500 dancers aged from two to 80. Barefoot women have blue-stepped *tableta* headdresses atop their glossy black hair to symbolize a mountain with an indication of rain. They each wear a one-shouldered *manta* (woven sash), adorn themselves with the best family jewelry, and hold a pine bough in each hand. The men wear short white embroidered kilts, long bold sashes, armbands, and moccasins. Like the women, they carry pine boughs.

In late November or early December, Zuni Pueblo holds the Shalako Ceremonial, among the most spectacular Indian celebrations (but now, sadly, closed to visitors). The all-night event centers on the coming of 12-ft (3.5-meter) Shalako and their retinues, who bless new or renovated homes. Pits are dug in the floor to enable the tall Shalako to enter and dance. The costly costumes are draped over a wooden framework, which includes pulleys to move parts like a puppet.

Complex social relationships grow out of the Pueblo worldview, in which the well-being of all creatures is tied to the well-being of every individual, and thus the community.

Performing the colorful Commanche Dance.

⊘ PUEBLO PRIVACY

The best time to visit a pueblo is usually to observe ceremonial dances on feast days. Indian dances are ceremonial events – prayers for rain, ample crops, a good hunt, or thanksgiving – and should be observed quietly and with respect. Cover up (do not wear shorts or have bare arms); refrain from clapping or talking to dancers about the meaning of ceremonials. Not all dances are open to the public. Most Pueblo people share an ambivalence toward tourism; there are factions within most pueblos that consider it a threat to traditional culture. Privacy is highly valued. Pueblo people may not always be warm, a response to being treated as objects of curiosity or camera fodder.

A Navajo man at John Ford's Point in Monument Valley Navajo Tribal Park.

THE NAVAJO

Inhabitants of the Southwest for nearly a thousand years, the vigorous and independent Navajo are known for their exquisite jewelry and rugs.

White men called them Navajo but they call themselves Diné – the People – and they came a long way to settle in the American Southwest. Of Athabascan stock, their ancestors came from the forests of northwest Canada, drifting into the Four Corners area – where Colorado, Utah, Arizona, and New Mexico meet – as small groups of skin-clad hunters during late Ancestral Pueblo times. By 1400, they were well established in their new homeland, a land of ever-changing colors, yellow deserts, blood-red mesas and canyons, green fir- and aspen-covered highlands, and silvery expanses of sage overspread by a turquoise sky. This beautiful land was sacred to them because it had been created by the Holy Ones for the People to live in.

They came as hunters, bringing lances, sinew-backed bows, and hide shields. Nomadic and war-like, they raided the villages of the Pueblo people, who had lived on the land long before them. They took from the peaceful Pueblo many useful things, including women, who taught them how to plant corn and squash, weave, and make pottery.

The Navajo were quick learners. In time, their weavers even outstripped their Pueblo teachers. Much later, they learned from the Spaniards how to ride horses and raise sheep, introduced by the Spaniards, and, still later, to be superb silversmiths.

THE "LONG WALK"

Planting and shepherding turned the roving nomads into sedentary herdsmen with a settled home region whose ancient center was beautiful Canyon de Chelly in northern Arizona. Then, in 1851, the U.S. Army built Fort Defiance in order to "defy" and control the Navajo, and in 1863, Kit Carson was sent to subdue and remove them.

Traditional Navajo dress.

⊘ THE NAVAJO AND THE SPANISH

The Navajos did not always enjoy peaceful relations with the incoming Spanish. In, the 1770s, the Spanish made brutal forays into Navajo country, beginning a long and bitter period of slave-raiding and land encroachment; at the same time, Catholic missionaries sought to convert souls and diminish local traditions and beliefs. In 1804, the Navajos made war on the Spanish but suffered a bloody defeat at Canyon de Chelly, in the eastern part of present-day Arizona (Kit Carson would later rampage through Canyon de Chelly, rounding up Navajos for the Long Walk). In 1821, at a truce conference with the Spanish, 24 Navajos were stabbed in the heart.

Carson waged a cruel war. He did not hunt down the small groups of Navajo hidden in the depths of their canyons; instead, he practiced a "scorched-earth policy," making war upon their crops and sheep. Livestock was killed and corn supplies burned. Winter came and many Indians, isolated in their canyons, starved or froze to death. At last, they surrendered to the army.

They were forced to make the "Long Walk" to Bosque Redondo, over 300 miles (500km) away to the east, in New Mexico. Their destination was

A traditional Navajo hogan in Monument Valley.

worse than the march itself – a flat, inhospitable land with alkaline water that made them sick. They had no materials to build shelters and lived in earthen holes. They never had enough to eat, as their crops withered in the hostile soil. Of 8,000 Navajo moved to Bosque Redondo (along with many Apaches), several hundred died during the march, and over 1,500 died after settling in the internment camp. After four years, the government relented and let the survivors go back to their homeland. And so the Navajo set out once again on the punishing five-week trek homeward, to the west.

Today, the Navajo tribe is among the largest in the United States, but this speaks only of the tribe's hardiness and resilience. More than

150 years after it took place, the Long Walk still haunts memories.

THE *HOGAN*

Navajo home life revolved around the *hogan*, or dwelling. The earliest type was the "forked stick" hogan made of three crotched poles interlaced at the top, covered with sticks and plastered over with mud, known now as male hogans and still used for rituals. In the center of the sunken floor was a firepit below a smoke hole. The hogan was well suited to the country – cool in summer

> *Canyon de Chelly in northern Arizona is the very heart of Navajo country. First occupied by the Kayenta branch of Ancestral Puebloans, this canyon has been inhabited for over 1,000 years.*

and snug in winter. People slept with their feet toward the fire, like spokes in a wheel. Modern hogans are cribbed-log octagonal cabins with a domed roof through which the stovepipe rises, known as female hogans. Many have electric lights and appliances. They are roomier than the old-style hogan but preserve its original design.

In the oldest of traditions, if a Navajo dies in the hogan, an opening is made in the back of the dwelling; the body is removed through this hole. The hogan and its contents are then burned, and the place is considered the haunt of *chindi*, the ghosts of the dead.

Although taboos are sometimes broken, Navajo tend to honor strictly the most serious taboos and, in time of misfortune, try to determine how they have erred and seek to propitiate the spirits.

Communicating with the spirits needs song and a medicine man, the *hatathli* or chanter, who can bring evil under ritual control. His knowledge is not gained easily. Before a "sing," he fasts for days, taking sweat baths and communing with the powers. He searches for the cause of evil through listening or trembling. His whole body shakes, and his trembling hands hover over a patch of corn meal. Finally, the finger traces an ancient design that indicates the cause of the disease and the appropriate ritual to exorcise it.

This tracing, called sand painting, can last several days. If the "sing" is performed correctly, the song chanted beautifully, and the sand painting properly completed, then all will be well. Some sand paintings are small and can be finished by one man in an hour or two. Others may be 20ft (6 meters) long, requiring several assistants. The patient who is sung over sits in the center of the painting and their living body is part of the sacred altar. When the ritual is over, patient and painting are symbolically united when the medicine man dips his wet fingers into the sand painting and transfers some of it (and its power) to the patient. Finally, the painting is destroyed and the sand scattered in the six sacred directions. The "sand paintings" on plywood or certain rugs sold to tourists as curios have their roots in this Navajo religious symbolism.

THE HOLY PEOPLE'S FAMILY TREE

Navajo religion is complex, and its teachings, legends, songs, and rituals are beautifully haunting and poetic. The Navajo believe

In the Navajo Nation, the medecine man Eugene Baatsoslani Joe is also a sand painter.

Ø SAND PAINTING

The exact origin of sand painting (once known as dry painting) is lost in the mists of Navajo mythology and legend, although it seems possible that the practice was borrowed from the Pueblo people to the east after the Navajos' ancestors migrated into the Southwest nearly 1,000 years ago. (Today, designs have been adapted to weaving.)

Traditionally, sand paintings are made during night-long healing rituals known as "sings." They are created on the floor of a ceremonial hogan by medicine men, who often spend years learning the elaborate prayers, chants, and designs. The most common designs of the sand painting feature the Navajo gods, or yei, who are invoked through chants during the ceremony to help cure an ill person. At the end of the ceremony, just before dawn, the sacred images are destroyed. The sand is then collected and buried north of the hogan.

Little was known of sand painting until the 1880s, when Washington Matthews, a military doctor stationed on the Navajo reservation, became the first white person to observe and study the ceremony. Some 30 years later, a scholar, Gladys Reichard, committed herself to learning the ceremonies, first by mastering the complicated Navajo language and then learning the chants herself.

in the Holy People, powerful and mysterious, who travel on the wind, a sunbeam, or a thunderbolt. At the head of these supernaturals stands Changing Woman, the Earth Mother, beautiful, gift-giving, and watching over the People's well-being. Changing Woman was found by First Man and First Woman as a baby, lying in a supernaturally created cradleboard on top of the sacred mountain of Dzilth-Na-O-Dith-Hle in the original Navajo homeland, or *Dinetah*, of northeastern New Mexico. Within four days, Changing Woman grew to maturity.

It was She who taught humans how to live in harmony with the forces of nature. She built the first hogan out of turquoise and shell.

The Navajo's chief ritual, the Blessing Way, came to them from Changing Woman and other Holy People. Changing Woman was impregnated by the rays of the sun and gave birth to the Hero Twins, who killed many evil monsters and enemies of humankind, many of whom were then petrified into the oddly shaped landmarks around the Dinetah that remind the People to live harmoniously with

Miss Native American USA pageant at the Festival Navajo Nation Fair in Window Rock.

⊙ FROM GIRL TO WOMAN

Coming of age is the occasion for many rituals, typical in most cultures that have retained traditional ties and attitudes to the natural and spiritual worlds. In the case of Navajo girls, traditional coming-of-age rituals and celebrations are very elaborate. The time of a girl's "first bleed" is a proud moment for her, and she hurries to tell her parents, who joyfully spread the news. The event is celebrated by a ceremony called a *kinaalda*.

The girl has her hair washed in a shampoo made from yucca roots. Then, for three days, wearing her best jewelry, she grinds corn on the old family *metate*. During each of the three days, she undergoes a "molding" rite. Lying on a blanket; she is kneaded and "shaped" by a favorite female friend or relative to make her as beautiful as Changing Woman.

Each dawn, the girl races toward the east, each time a little faster. Others are allowed to run with her but are careful not to pass her, so that they do not grow old before she does. On the fourth day, older women make a big cake from the corn that the girl has ground, sometimes as big as 6ft (2 meters) across.

When the cake is ready, after racing for the last time, the girl distributes it to all of the guests. After that, she is considered a woman, ready to marry and start a family of her own.

the land. Changing Woman allowed old age and death to exist, however. They have their part in the human scheme, She said.

THE TOUCHSTONE OF RELIGION

Religion remains an integral part of daily life for many traditional Navajo. Men go into the fields singing corn-growing songs, weavers make a "spirit path" thread in their rugs, and hide curers put a turquoise bead on their tanning poles to keep their joints limber. When a woman has a difficult birth, her female relatives and friends

Not observing taboos can arouse the anger of powerful spirits, but traditional Navajo life was highly regulated and people inevitably did break a few rules.

blankets were woven; the famous Navajo rug was an invention of Lorenzo Hubbell at Hubbell Trading Post in Ganado, Arizona, a white trader and friend to the Navajo who arrived on the res-

A Navajo woman works on a wool rug while sitting in her booth at the Santa Fe Indian Market.

loosen their hair to "untie" the baby. A chanter might be summoned to coax the baby along with an eagle-feather fan. Twins are a cause for great joy because they are a sign of the Holy People's blessing. The father makes the cradleboard. When the baby is placed in it, a special song is chanted:

I have made a baby board for you, my child.
May you grow to a great old age.
Of the sun's rays have I made the back.
Of clouds have I made the blanket.
Of the rainbow have I made the head bow.

Religious symbolism has influenced Navajo art, which is rich, beautiful, and economically important to individual families who typically pass skills between generations. Navajo weaving, is particularly impressive. Originally only

ervation soon after the coming of the railroads and tourists. Traders like Hubbell didn't take long to find out that travelers from the East had little use for blankets worn like ponchos and some of the color schemes and patterns. Instead, they renamed them rugs, brought in new dyes from the East, developed new patterns with Navajo weavers, and purchased the rugs to sell on, giving birth to a new industry.

Different regions of the Navajo reservation developed their own characteristic styles – Ganado Reds, geometric Two Gray Hills, figural Shiprock, and a great many others, and nowadays, Navajo men weave as well as women. Women also weave fine baskets, of which complex Wedding Baskets are prized gifts to mark marriages; while men excel in creating some of the best silver and turquoise work to be found in the Southwest. (At the tribal capital of Window Rock, one may visit the Navajo Arts and Crafts Center. Rugs, baskets and jewelry are also sold in stores throughout the area.)

The modern Navajo who does not choose to live the traditional life in the hogan might be a lawyer, electrician, law enforcement officer, or telephone operator. He might operate one of the giant cranes at the nearby strip mine or operate one of the complicated Japanese-built machines at the huge tribal sawmill. He might be a newspaper editor on the *Navajo Times* or a professor at Navajo Community College – all glass and steel but built in the shape of a traditional hogan. The modern Navajo man or woman shares some of the advantages and all of the frustrations, problems, and anxieties of fellow Americans.

With a population of more than 300,000 enrolled tribal members, the Navajo comprise one of the largest tribes in the United States. In fact, the Navajo Nation, as the reservation is

The Red Mesa Redskins are the football team of a small Navajo school in northeast Arizona.

⊘ NAVAJO AND HOPI DISPUTES

The Navajo and Hopi tribes have had their differences. The Hopi, whose mesa-top homes are completely surrounded by the larger Navajo reservation, had long claimed that the Navajo were robbing their fields and stealing cattle. Tensions escalated to a peak in 1974, when Congress passed the Navajo-Hopi Relocation Act. The law, which divided nearly 2 million acres (800,000 hectares) between the tribes, was supposed to partition the Joint Use Area in northern Arizona and compel 11,000 Navajo and about 100 Hopi to leave their homes. Many of the Navajo moved to new government housing; some traditional Navajos around Big Mountain protest the law and still resist relocation.

called, is bigger than New Hampshire, Connecticut, Vermont, and Rhode Island combined. It has oil, coal, uranium, and lumber. These resources bring in money but also wrenching changes: pollution, dependency on outside forces, industrialization, and the relocation of people.

Despite natural resources, poverty persists and housing and health care are sub-standard. Schools often don't prepare students for the problems they will face in an Anglo-dominated world. Religion and language fight against the inroads of a powerful, alien culture. Offered one Navajo: "We have survived the Spaniards, the missionaries and the Long Walk. We still walk in beauty. We will still be here, still be Navajo, a hundred years from now."

Pointing out detail in a hand-woven rug at the annual Santa Fe Indian Market.

THE HOPI

Comprising 11 mesa-top pueblos surrounded by the Navajo Nation, the Hopi reservation in northern Arizona appears desolate to outsiders, but to the Hopi, it is a spiritual home.

Approaching Hopi country from any direction may be a bleak or nondescript experience for some travelers, but once they meet and mingle with its inhabitants, a visitor generally comes away from the experience with anything but bleak or nondescript impressions. If Hopi people were inclined to describe themselves, which they are not, they would say they aspire to be industrious, hospitable, and helpful. Pueblo tradition and custom mandate such attitudes and behavior. Hopi country can be loosely described as high desert supporting little else beside the tenacious Hopi. They manage to coax the most wondrous yield of cultivated farm products out of it, notably an infinite variety of com.

Hopi country is comprised of 11 distinct villages located along the 35-mile (55-km) perimeter of Black Mesa, in northeastern Arizona. These villages – some settled for centuries, others founded as recently as 1910 – are home to 10,000 people closely knit by tradition, blood, and custom, but often separated linguistically and politically.

Speech patterns and vocabulary differ from village to village within the same general language structure, providing natural boundaries. These differences also provide a great deal of chauvinistic interplay with words among residents of each village. The traditional governing system also encourages a political distance between villages. However, the differences are not easily discernible to those unfamiliar with Hopi society.

KINSHIP AND FAMILY

The kinship system, which is still intact, provides the unity that allows free intercourse

Hopi tribes perform in the Hoop Dance Contest.

⊘ HOPI STEWARDSHIP

The Hopi are, above all, a deeply religious people. Religion is so completely intertwined with the rest of life that isolating it is like unraveling the entire Hopi universe. For the Hopi, spirituality is a universal concern. Hopi elders believe that they have inherited stewardship over Mother Earth, and are obliged to protect her and maintain the religion on behalf of humanity. This stewardship is carried out through priesthood societies called wuutsim, which conduct ceremonies to ensure the temporal and spiritual well-being of all people. There are also priestess societies and other religious groups, such as the *kachina* societies, that form the spiritual foundation of Hopi society.

between villages in all the important functions of communal living: family relationships, rites, and ceremonies. It is not overstressing the point to say that most Hopi growing up and living on the reservation know who they are and from whence they came.

The matriarchal kinship system, in which lineage passes through the female line, is crucial in maintaining familial and spiritual unity. All children of maternal sisters and paternal brothers, for instance, become brothers and sisters and share common parent figures,

Mexico. The storytellers are able to identify landmarks as far away as central New Mexico, southern Colorado, and Utah. Mythic tales of creation provide the basis for a system of beliefs

> When a Hopi meets someone, they will first give the name of their village, and if prodded further, will most likely tell you their clan affiliation followed by their Hopi name.

Hopi girls in 1906.

although in lesser degrees of intimacy beyond the immediate family. Paternal sisters and maternal brothers are aunts and uncles, but within the second generation, only the uncle's children are named nephews and nieces. The aunt's children fall into relationships dictated by clan formulas.

Superimposed on biological kinship is the clan system, which sees people within a single relational universe, that of brother and sister. The clan line is also matrilineal.

Legendary tales, guarded by hereditary caretakers within each clan unit, recount the extensive prehistoric migrations of one ancestral group after another over a vast area of the American Southwest, southern California, and

and practices so complex as to mesmerize generations of scholars throughout the world.

RITUAL AND CEREMONY

Visitors will find Hopi people naturally open and friendly in the privacy of their homes, though somewhat distant at public, social, and ceremonial gatherings – unless, of course, you have "Hopi friends." It is not uncommon to find at least one *pahaana* (white son) among the participants at wedding, natal, and *kachina* ceremonial preparation parties.

Hopi are particularly sensitive to the aesthetic tastes of the traveling public, whether these tastes be for art, services, or showmanship, such as the dancing kachinas, which have become such a magnetic attraction for countless outsiders. In fact, ritual and ceremony may be the most distinctive aspects of Hopi culture today. A serious issue among them today is how best to preserve Hopi ways that are rapidly changing because of pressures, both within and without, created by modern living and technology. There is no doubt that Hopi do not want to let go of all the "old" ways of doing things. The specter of losing tradition and custom to modem technology and lifestyles hovers constantly.

The modern Hopi wedding was being discussed around the breakfast table in a Hopi home. One man remarked at the marshaling of a caravan of automobiles to escort the new bride home at the culmination of wedding festivities. He counted around 20 trucks, each loaded down with gifts to be distributed among the bride's relatives. He was obviously saddened at the blatant ignorance displayed by the relatives about the original significance of the bridal homecoming.

"The bride goes back to her mother's house alone to await her new husband's pleasure.

The Hopi High School boys cross-country team head down a trail near Polacca, Arizona.

☉ KACHINAS: HOPI SPIRIT BEINGS

Since time immemorial, Hopi men have carved wooden replicas of the Hopi spirit-beings known as *katsinam*, or kachinas to non-Hopi. Called *tihu* in Hopi, these effigies are given to Hopi children to teach them about religion.

Kachina carving is deeply rooted in Hopi religion, and the kachina spirits are as innumerable as the laws of nature, for that is what they are. Some are the spirits of ancestors hidden by clouds, others make the rain fall and the corn grow. For half the year, from the winter solstice in December until the Niman Kachina ceremony in July, these spirits live among the Hopi in the mesa villages. During these months, they are represented by ornately costumed men – kachina dancers

– who perform dances. The rest of the year, the kachina reside in the high San Francisco Peaks, just north of Flagstaff.

It is thought that there are around 350 kachinas depicted in carvings, but no two are exactly alike. Although dolls, kachinas are not toys and are, in fact, considered sacred. There are two types: traditional and sculptural. Traditional kachinas are crafted from the soft root of the cottonwood tree and are typically carved in rigid poses with legs together and arms to the side. Sculptural kachinas are more interpretive and feature the virtuosity of the artist as much as traditional religious symbolism.

When he decides to accept her as a bride he will follow her, bearing appropriate gifts," he said. (Even second-generation Hopi born this century might be hard put to know that the right gift for him to bring is a load of wood, symbol of hearth and home.)

Young people sitting around the table in that modern house were quite surprised and fascinated to hear this; no one had really explained these things to them. Their only experience with weddings consisted of the mixture of Western and Hopi ceremonial activities that has become the modern Hopi wedding: at most, a two-day affair, replete with an abundance of foods from the traditional pantry as well as the supermarket, wrapped gifts mingling with the native foodstuffs customarily given to the bride and groom's families, table decor contrasting with makeshift outdoor open fires for cooking.

So it goes. And so it goes in other rites that are still vital, such as natal rites and initiation into ceremonial societies. It is this innovative mixing of the old and new that separates one generation from the other, because, if the truth be told, these hybrids have an ambience of their own, and an appealing vitality.

KACHINA DANCES

This attractive mixture of the old and new can also be seen during one of the many summer weekends on which kachina or other dances are sponsored. Less than a generation ago, kachinas were first introduced to the Hopi child as spiritual beings who come to this world from the Spirit Home, which may refer to either an opening, or *sipapu*, in the floor of a ceremonial room, or *kiva*, or to a shrine on the San Francisco Peaks near Flagstaff, a "secret opening."

Kachinas are commonly present in the dances held indoors in kivas and outdoors in village plazas, depending upon the time of year. These colorful, masked beings represent elements, qualities, and inhabitants of the universe; they may be cast, in their spiritual state, in roles for various purposes, some didactic (bearing lessons) and others more inspirational.

Kachina dances are an accepted way of life for the Hopi; there is at least one dance per village each year. Attending kachina dances has become important to a new generation of Hopi who now live in cities far from the reservation but return as spectators and participants.

An upcoming dance mobilizes, as nothing else can, all the combined resources of a village. It is not unusual for Hopi to travel from Los Angeles, San Francisco, Denver, or Oklahoma City for these events; coming in from Tucson, Phoenix, and even Salt Lake City can be a weekly or monthly habit with some families. When all the relatives have gathered, there may be a fleet of five to 10 vehicles, mostly trucks, in

Buffalo hide kachina mask representing the sun.

front of each house in that village. Even though these autos may have come loaded with provisions from the supermarkets of the urban centers, the preparation of traditional feast foods is not abandoned.

Corn, the symbolic Mother to the Hopi, is the most visible traditional food, secular and sacred, for this occasion as it is for most rituals and religious ceremonies.

The ceremony consists of a series of dances, usually seven or eight, performed every two hours with 30-minute breaks, beginning about midmorning and ending at sundown. The staging of a kachina dance is an example of the refined sense of the dramatic, a trademark of the Hopi and the other Pueblo peoples.

THE APACHE

Typically depicted in the media as the most ferocious and warlike of the Southwest tribes, the Apache were traditionally peaceful nomadic hunters.

Like most other Southwest tribes, the Apache dispute the anthropological theory that they migrated to North America across the Bering Strait. An elderly San Carlos Apache tells the story handed down for centuries:

"Our ancestors tell us that we were created in the area where we now live. In the beginning, there was no living person upon Mother Earth, only supernatural beings. When our people were created, there were wicked creatures who killed them. During this time, the White Painted Lady gave birth to twin sons. One of these sons went to his father, Sun, and returned to Mother Earth dressed in proper Apache clothing, carrying a bow and arrows and leading several horses. After he taught our people how to use these things, he helped kill the evil creatures. Mother Earth then became a good place to live for our people."

All Apache have a creation story with ideas similar to this one.

Before contact with the Spaniards in the middle to late 1500s, Apache bands mingled freely with each other and with their close kin, the Navajo. The Apache, like the Navajo, are of the Athabascan-speaking family originally from northwestern Canada and have no written history or language.

The Apache called themselves the People, but to others they were the "Enemy." The land the Apache roamed traditionally encompassed present-day Arizona, New Mexico, and northern Mexico. While they were, in essence, one family, each group had its own hunting territory and did not encroach on that of its neighbors. The relatively peaceful, nomadic life of the Apache was drastically altered by the appearance of outsiders into the Apache domain: Spaniards, Mexicans, and finally Anglos.

Apache Mountain Spirit Dancer.

ANGLO AND SPANISH COLONIZATION

When Coronado made his expedition into the Southwest in the 16th century, he unwittingly introduced a new mode of travel to the Apache, which they would adopt and use more skillfully than any other Southwestern tribe. The horse became a beast of burden, a source of food, and a reliable form of transportation that enabled the Apache to expand their geographical range far beyond their original territories.

Apache reaction to Spanish and Anglo colonization was raiding and warfare, which was so effective that twice the intruders were driven out for as long as a decade. Indeed, southern Arizona was one of the last areas of the Southwest to be settled by the Spanish and Americans.

> *The sunrise ceremony is the most important ritual for the Apache: girls are believed to possess curative powers at puberty and treat the ill by touching them.*

Contrary to popular belief, Apache raiding did not include wanton destruction; its aim was generally to steal livestock.

When the Gadsden Purchase was made in 1853, all of Arizona came under the control of the United States. This, and the discovery of gold in western Apache territory 10 years later, brought an influx of Anglo settlers and prospectors. The Arizona Territory legislature officially decided that the only way to control the Apache was to exterminate them. The Department of War in Washington disagreed with this policy, and the Territory lacked the means to carry out the extermination. This fact, together with the slaughter of 75 unarmed Apache women and children near Tucson by a mob of outraged citizens and a group of Tohono O'odham Indians, led to the implementation of the so-called Peace Policy.

This policy called for rounding up Apache and confining them to reservations, where they would have to make a living by growing crops and raising livestock. This plan required the removal of some tribes from their homelands. The removals were met with ambivalence by the Apache. Some had become weary of the hardships of war and preferred to settle down in peace. Others, however, waited for a chance to escape. Two of those who bolted were Geronimo and Victorio. But by 1890, the Apache wars were finally over.

Today, the Jicarilla and Chihuahua Apache tribes in New Mexico and the San Carlos, White Mountain, and Mescalero Apache in Arizona have become economically self-sufficient through ranching – the Apache are excellent cowboys, and rodeo is very popular – and welcoming visitors for numerous outdoor pursuits on their spectacular mountainous lands, including hunting, camping, fishing, and skiing. The tribes also produce basketry and other arts and crafts, offer cultural tours, and run several successful casino-hotels.

CEREMONY AND CELEBRATION

The Apache sunrise ceremony – a girl's puberty rite – can be seen several times a year on the San Carlos and White Mountain reservations in Arizona and the Jicarilla reservation in New Mexico. The Mescalero Apache ceremonies in southern Arizona are all performed in summer.

The awesome and colorful masked mountain spirit dancers – *gans* – still perform at the puberty rites of the San Carlos, White Mountain, and Mescalero tribes. (The Jicarilla Apache have

Rodeo at the Mescalero Apache Rodeo grounds.

not used the dancers as part of their ceremonies since the introduction of the vaccination program on their reservation. The Jicarilla leaders decreed that anyone who had been vaccinated could not participate as a mountain spirit dancer, and the result was the disqualification of nearly all Jicarilla youth.)

The sunrise ceremony is held after a girl has first menstruated and enters womanhood, assuming her family can afford the costly preparations. The ceremony recognizes that the girl will need strength, patience, good luck, and wisdom in life. These qualities are possessed by the White Painted Lady and are acquired by the girl during the four-day ceremony when the White Painted Lady resides in her body.

Fancy Dance contest at the Red Mountain Eagle pow wow, held at Salt River Pima-Maricopa Indian Community.

TOHONO O'ODHAM AND PIMA

Little known outside southern Arizona, the Tohono O'odham and Akimel O'odham (Pima) live in the Sonoran Desert and are the most assimilated tribes in the area.

The Tohono O'odham ("People of the Desert"), formerly known as the Papago, live on a sprawling 2.8-million-acre (1.1 million hectare) reservation in the Sonoran Desert, southwest of Tucson. Their tribal headquarters is in Sells, nestled beneath the sacred mountain of Baboquivari, protector of the Tohono O'odham people.

The Pima, or Akimel O'odham ("People of the Water"), live on the Gila Indian Reservation with the Maricopa, just south of Phoenix. As their name suggests, they were once highly successful irrigation farmers along the Santa Cruz and Gila rivers until whites arrived and usurped their resources.

A SENSE OF PLACE

Archeological and anthropological evidence indicates that the Akimel O'odham and Tohono O'odham were once culturally the same. They are said to be descendants of the now-vanished Hohokam, or, as they are called by the people, Hukukam, "the ones that have gone now." Linguistically, the two groups are closely related and their languages mutually intelligible. Many of their rituals, stories, and songs are similar. The only distinction is place – the area of the Sonoran Desert where they are from.

The Pima, and to a lesser extent the Tohono O'odham, are the most acculturated Indian tribes in the Southwest. Since their earliest recorded contacts with whites, the Pima especially have been looked upon as friendly. During the California Gold Rush of the mid-19th century, Pima agricultural entrepreneurs sold their own homegrown flour and other provisions to white prospectors and escorted them through Apache territory. At the time of the Apache wars in the 1860s, a large number of the Pima served as scouts for the U.S. Army.

Maricopa women gathering Saguaro fruit, 1907.

White settlers took over water sources used by the Pima, destroying their culture for over a century. Lawsuits in the 1980s returned water rights to the tribe, however. This has enabled them to farm once again, and build a multimillion dollar casino-resort on a lake near Chandler, well known for its views of the Estrella Mountains and onsite fine dining restaurant serving locally-sourced native cuisine. The Maricopa are renowned for their reddish pottery, on display at the resort.

The Tohono O'odham run an attractive cultural center and museum in Topawa, which houses a library, an archive, classrooms, and exhibits about Tohono O'odham culture, as well as a restaurant showcasing native cuisine. The Tohono O'odham are famed for their finely woven baskets.

📷 AMERICAN INDIAN ART

American Indians of the Southwest have a legacy rich in symbolism, found in kachina figures, sand paintings, and other creative forms.

American Indian spirituality can be viewed more as a way of life than a religion. Traditionally, daily life among Native people has not been compartmentalized; instead, work, play, and worship are all intertwined in experience and belief. Symbols come from all that the People see and imagine in the world around them. Rain clouds, corn, rainbows, animals, spirits, shapes, and colors all have symbolic meaning relating to the six directions: above, below, north, south, east, and west.

Indian people do not readily share the meanings of their symbols. As a result, Navajo sand paintings made for sale to the public always contain one mistake, insignificant to the non-Navajo eye but obvious to a *hatahli*, or medicine man. It may be an altered color sequence or a change of a small detail, but it is enough to avoid trespassing into sacred – and secret – traditions.

Though widely known, carved and painted rock inscriptions, or petroglyphs and pictographs, some of them hundreds of years old, are poorly understood. They do not represent language, but may mark special occasions, visions, boundaries, prayers, hunts, deities, or other concepts.

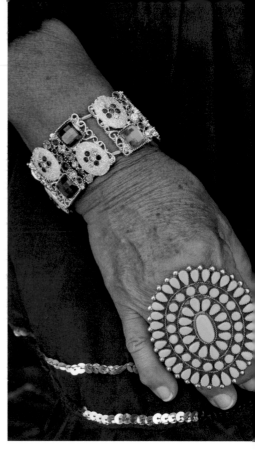

Traditional jewels displayed at Festival Navajo Nation Fair in Window Rock, Arizona.

When American Indians gather for an inter-tribal pow wow, the scene is lavish with costume and color. Warrior regalia adorns this Navajo man.

A traditional Hopi kachina doll, carved from cottonwood and representing a dancer with gourd rattle, dance staff and bull headdress mask.

A Navajo Yei Bichei figure, or Rainbow God, engraved on a man's bolo tie.

Creativity in silver and stone

Of all American Indian arts and crafts, jewelry must rank highest in demand on the tourist market. It comes at all prices and is widely available, whether you buy old pawn from a trading post, stop at a roadside stand, or visit artisans in their homes. While no group makes only one style, they do have specialties. Navajo silverwork, first taught to the tribe by Spanish craftsmen in the 1800s, usually incorporates locally mined turquoise, a stone sacred to Southwest Indian people from ancient times. Silver overlay is distinctively Hopi and was popularized by contemporary Hopi jeweler Charles Loloma. The Zuni are known for channeled inlay designs using small stones, each set in its own bezel. Santo Domingo Pueblo artisans make mosaic jewelry, liquid silver necklaces, and *heishi*. Aside from the customary rings, earrings, necklaces, and bracelets, you will find concho belts, hat bands, watch bands, bolo ties, and belt buckles in every style. Modern Pueblo Indian jewelry usually shows the influence of Ancestral Pueblo people, but artisans continually have new visions for their work, and it takes delightful turns.

Some images on this Utah panel may be 2,000 years old. The horse-mounted hunter was etched after 1540, when horses were brought to North America.

American Indians see habitation sites as stopping places on their journey to the center of their spiritual world, rather than abandoned homes.

If this Navajo rug features a border, an "escape" thread, or a spirit line, would probably be woven across it so that spirits would not be trapped therein.

Annual Mariachi Festival
performance in Tucson.

THE HISPANICS

The influence of the energetic Hispanic culture not only lingers on but also permeates nearly every facet of the Southwest, from place names to architecture.

In 1598, Governor Don Juan de Oñate led 130 families and 270 single men from Mexico to an area just north of present-day Santa Fe. They were the first European settlers in the Southwest, and the Pueblo Indians who lived along the nearby Rio Grande were linked forever after to the destiny of the new colonists.

For over a century, the Hispanic villages, surrounded by towering mountains, clung to the Rio Grande. Villagers made a living from fields and flocks. The settlers were *Hispanos* and *Mexicanos* who had come in search of a new life, while the Catholic friars had come, not surprisingly, for Indian souls to convert. El Paso in modern-day Texas was the resting point and link between Old Mexico and New Mexico, just as it and adjoining Juarez, on either side of the Rio Grande, are today.

Heading north from El Paso through an expanse of desert called La Jornada del Muerto, or The Journey of Death, the colonists were rewarded with the high plateaus and mountains of the Sangre de Cristo (Blood of Christ) range in the Southern Rockies, a topography that reminded some of southern Spain and others of Mexico.

A STYLE IN THE LAND

From these first villages, the settlers began to extend their influence. Groups of families petitioned the Spanish authorities in Mexico for land grants, and communities spread along the river and into the mountains. When Mexico broke from Spain in 1821, the land-grant system continued, and when Anglo-Americans arrived in the Southwest, they found a communal land system they did not understand.

The land-grant system played a crucial part in the formation of the Hispanic culture and the

Roasted corn at the annual Spanish Market in Santa Fe.

⊘ HISPANIC DOMINANCE'S END

When Mexico won independence from Spain in 1821, American traders began to trickle in, followed later by settlers. In 1845, the United States annexed Texas, setting off the Mexican War. The U.S. Army captured Mexico City two years later and, under the terms of the Treaty of Guadalupe Hidalgo, the United States took possession of New Mexico including present-day Arizona and California, and also solidified its hold on Texas. After more than three centuries of overbearing influence, Spanish and, briefly, Mexican, dominance over the region diminished, and Hispanics in the Southwest suddenly found themselves second-class citizens.

character of the Hispanos. The original grants provided space for homes, fields, irrigation water, firewood, and the grazing of animals. But in 1846, the Anglo-Americans brought a new system of land ownership, and many land grants were lost or greatly diminished. Those that still remain struggle for survival, and as the Hispanic people move away from their villages into larger urban centers, a cultural transformation is underway. Hispanic culture in the Southwest today is one of rapid assimilation into the mainstream Anglo culture.

Our Lady of Perpetual Help Mission, Scottsdale.

PUEBLO NEIGHBORS

The Hispanos were the neighbors of the Pueblo Indians. A sharing of cultures continued until 1680, when the Pueblo Indians of New Mexico, enraged because Hispanic colonists got preferential treatment and Catholic friars insisted that the Indians give up their traditional religion, took up arms and drove the Hispanos out of New Mexico into El Paso in the bloody Pueblo Revolt. But in 1692, the Spanish returned, led by Don Diego Vargas. During the Reconquest, they once again took over Santa Fe and reestablished Spanish rule.

A SENSE OF EARTH AND VILLAGE

Three elements seem to characterize individuals and communities in the Southwest: earth,

> *During Spanish colonial times, the towns of Spanish California developed slowly compared with those of New Mexico. Life was austere, but they prospered.*

water, and air (sky). The Hispanos discovered that Pueblo Indians had a sacred partnership with the earth. They understood the earth and its creatures and knew they needed tending. In Spanish the earth is *la tierra*, and the land that belongs to the community of the land grant or village is to be guarded for the well-being of all.

Hispanics love their village; their sense of place is strong. They are honor-bound and loyal to family and community, and this long history of attachment to the land of the village evolved into a close relationship with *la tierra sagrada*, the sacred earth. Like the Pueblo Indians before them, the Hispanos learned to live in close harmony with their native land.

Two rivers dominate the Hispanic Southwest. The Colorado River rises in the Rockies in Colorado and flows southwest across the Colorado Plateau, through southeastern Utah and the Grand Canyon in Arizona to the Gulf of California. The Rio Grande originates in southwestern Colorado and flows through New Mexico and along the U.S.–Mexico border on its way to the Gulf of Mexico near Brownsville, Texas. Historically, the Hispanic population clung to the life-giving Rio Grande. The river is not only an important source of water; it is a corridor of Hispanic culture that straddles the border between Mexico and the United States. The Rio Grande is to Southwestern Hispanics what the Mississippi River is to the Midwesterner.

Another element in the fragile desert completes the picture: the sky (air element) that delivers the light and determines the tone, color, and mood. The sky is clear, the air is crisp and the colors sharp. Sunrise and sunset are definite times, and summer's clouds are unrivaled in beauty.

FAMILY AND HOME

Hispanics have lent their unique character and industry to the land. They gave rise to the first mining industry in the Southwest, and they were the original horsemen (the Spanish *caballeros* from which the Mexican word *vaqueros* derived) who introduced the lore and trappings of the cowboy. They learned from the Pueblo Indians how to build humble mansions of sundried adobe mud bricks, and like Pueblo people, used a system of *acequias*, or irrigation canals, to water their fields – in their case, learned from the Moors in Spain.

Spanish is spoken all over the Southwest, and the place names attest to centuries of Hispanic influence. From San Francisco to San Antonio, the corridor of the border region bears a strong Hispanic stamp. Santa Fe, Española, Albuquerque, Belén, Socorro, Las Cruces, El Paso – they

– godfathers and godmothers – extend the family ties. Godparents are selected for baptisms, confirmation in the Catholic Church, and weddings. This cultural tradition helps to extend the nuclear family into the larger community. A New Mexican family may have compadres as far away as California, Texas, or the Midwest, and they are all included in the family.

This vast network of communication also helps keep cultural traditions alive.

Likewise, the migration of Mexicans northward into the United States – legally and illegally

Christmas Eve luminarias in Albuquerque's Old Town.

all sit along the Rio Grande, and all were Hispanic settlements.

Hispanic culture was nurtured by Catholic faith, family, and community ceremonies, oral storytelling, and other folk arts. The Spanish language is still at the core of the culture, but as more activities take place in an English-speaking world, the dilution of the language is inevitable. It is common to find people speaking a combination of both languages, or Spanglish, in northern New Mexico. Even so, Spanish is typically the primary language of most Hispanics in the Southwest.

Family and home are at the center of the value system, as is strong identification with family name. Family relationships are extended by the *compadrazco* network. *Compadres* and *comadres*

⊘ LASTING IMPRESSIONS

The influence of Hispanic culture in the American Southwest remains profound. Much of cowboy culture for example, has Spanish origins, from the names of clothing – *chaparrejos*, or chaps, and *la reata*, or lariat to old-time cowboy traditions like the roundup and rodeo. Spanish place names, extending geographically from Texas to California, testify to Spanish exploration: El Paso, Santa Fe, La Cruces, Los Angeles, San Francisco. In Arizona and especially New Mexico, Spanish folk art is still created, and Spanish colonial architecture, with its graceful Moorish and Indian touches, has been emulated by designers around the world.

– reinforces the culture. As workers move north, to El Norte, so do their music, lifestyle, social needs, and language. There are millions of Hispanics in the United States, with a considerable proportion – and often a majority – living in the Southwest.

CHICANO PRIDE

Of all the border societies, Hispanic society has been most actively involved in the development of the Southwest. The contemporary social and political movement began in the late 1960s with the so-called Chicano movement. Like the parallel black civil-rights movement, Chicanos demanded equality in schooling and health care, along with acceptable working and living conditions for all Mexican-Americans. The movement led to a resurgence of ethnic pride, and the word Chicano reflected that pride.

To find their roots, Chicano leaders and artists returned to the mother country, Mexico. By asserting their heritage, they reinforced their pride. Political leaders, folk heroes, and the role of Chicanos in mining, ranching, farming, and the railroad industry revealed an active commu-

Cinco de Mayo celebration in Scottsdale.

⊘ WHAT'S IN A NAME?

There are nuances, often politically loaded, to the words used to describe people of Hispanic descent in the United States, and it may be helpful for travelers to understand the distinctions:

The word Chicano is typically used to describe Mexican immigrants to the US.

Latino is used to describe immigrants with roots in Latin America.

Hispanic (which is more commonly used) and Hispano refer to someone who can trace their lineage to Spain; these latter terms are most often used in the Southwest and are a source of pride for the long history in the region that they infer.

nity. Folk arts, oral storytelling, religious music, and the presentation of morality plays during the Christmas season all display a creative imagination kept alive and well by the elders.

The Chicano movement inspired a renaissance of artistic expression. Art groups sprang up in every community. A resurgence of ethnic pride and creativity carried the Chicano into new fields: cinema, mural artworks, and innovations in music.

The Southwest today is not so much a melting pot as a sharing pot. The various cultural groups try to give and take, share and learn to grow with each other, but Hispanic culture takes the lead.

For Christmas, locals and travelers in the Southwest enjoy the festive lighting of the *luminarias*, the candles in brown paper bags that illuminate churches and homes. (In northern New Mexico, these are called *farolitos*, little lanterns; *luminarias* are bonfires lit to show the way to the Christ child on Christmas Eve.) *Luminarias* or *farolitos* are a staple item at Christmas – often the electric version these days, for ease of use; even more so, traditional foods such as *tamales, posole, chile* (the Spanish spelling is used to denote both the green and red chile vegetable and the sauce, with or without meat, made with it), *carne adovada, natillas, biscochitos,* and *enpanaditas.* The rest of

> *By 1545, a quarter of Mexico City residents were Jews, and more Jews than Catholics lived in New Spain. In New Mexico, crypto-Jews escaping the Spanish Inquisition hid their identities for generations by becoming Catholic.*

Isidro, patron saint of all who till the soil, with his yoke and oxen, his plow and his helper, a diminutive angel – a fine example of traditional wood

Old Spanish hand-made chests at El Camino Real International Heritage Center, Soccorro, New Mexico.

the year, beans, red or green chile, enchiladas, burritos, and tacos are the usual fare. For Hispanics, the kitchen is still the heart of the house.

AN EXPRESSION OF TRADITION

Traditional art and ritual are at the root of this renaissance. Picture, for instance, a solemn procession winding its way down the wash (*arroyo*), meandering like a long, colorful ribbon through fields and chaparral, finally coming to a halt on top of a hill crowned by an ancient adobe chapel. There is a ringing of bells, the sound of fiddles and voices singing. At the head of the procession stands a man holding aloft a gilded cross; by his side, the village priest. Behind them four men carry a wooden image, or *santo*, representing San

carving. Behind them follow the worshippers – men in old costumes, devout women in black shawls beneath black umbrellas shading them from the sun, children, and tourists.

The procession blesses the fields in spring and gives thanks for a plentiful harvest in the fall. It takes place at El Rancho de las Golondrinas, a working 18th-century Spanish ranch and living museum just south of Santa Fe on the historic Camino Real, linking Mexico and El Norte. The procession heralds a two-day fiesta of music and dance and a gathering of Hispanic craftsmen – *santeros* (carvers of holy images), painters of religious *retablos*, smiths handcrafting objects, women weaving colorful Chimayó blankets, basketmakers, and women ladling out devilishly hot chile. All this activity is set against the backdrop of ancient chapels and buildings that underscore the historical roots of today's traditional artists and *artesanos*.

Hispanic artists relied upon their own resources, using materials their environment offered. Even the homes of the *ricos*, the *gente fina* (fine folks, or well-to-do), were simple, with only essential furnishings. Finery belonged to the rich.

The main piece of furniture in the Hispanic house was the *trastero*, or cupboard, often richly carved and painted. Chests, in which a family's

Playing the guitarron, an acoustic bass instrument.

⊘ ART IN ISOLATION

Traditional Hispanic art was, and is, homemade – rustic and original, often fashioned by simple farmers who became artists. This art was created with little outside influence, as for centuries the Southwest was all but cut off from the rest of the world. The populous cities of Mexico were more than 1,000 inhospitable desert miles (1,600km) away. Maybe two, or three times a year, a mule train or maybea caravan of *carretas* – lumbering oxcarts prone to breakdowns and agonizingly slow – made their way to Santa Fe. Yankee goods arrived via the long Santa Fe Trail, but until the arrival of the railroad, the region remained relatively isolated.

possessions were kept, also served as tables or benches. Fancy chests and boxes had elaborate hand-forged locks and were richly decorated with carved lions and scalloped wheels, less often with designs of Moorish origin. Chairs were sturdy, rough-hewn and thick legged. Built into the rooms were *nichos*, or niches, to hold the images of saints and other religious objects, and molded whitewashed adobe seats, or *bancos*. Lithographs of saints or biblical figures were displayed in punched tin frames. There were also usually a number of *retablos*, or pictures of saints painted on wooden boards.

Many churches held naive paintings on tin, showing the person who ordered them on his or her knees, giving thanks to some saint for having cured them of an illness. Other such *retablos* might show a fire, or a fall from a horse that someone had survived, thanks to the intercession of a patron saint.

THE RELIGIOUS ART OF SANTOS

Santeros were the men who carved *santos* – figures of the Savior, the Virgin, saints, and angels. The images were not anatomically correct but were rather works of faith instead of art. Angels were short-legged; saints were elongated, narrow-waisted, and big-footed. Anglos, used to the realistic, formal art of white America, first said *santos* were "fearful artistic abominations." Today, these "abominations" are highly prized works of art eagerly sought by museums and serious collectors, who value them for their peculiar charm. One also often encounters tragic figures of the suffering Christ, hollow-cheeked and emaciated, the body chalk-white, hair and beard coal-black, with bright blood trickling from many wounds.

Death and suffering have traditionally played a large part in Hispanic art, possibly as a reminder of centuries of oppression of Spanish Christians by the Moors of northern Africa. They are uppermost in the mind of the mysterious sect called Penitentes, who will scourge themselves until the blood flows and whose prayer is, "Lord, give us a good death." This preoccupation with the inevitability of dying, and with damnation and salvation, shows itself in the most impressive of Southwestern sculpture, the large death cart with its skeleton of Doña Sebastiana, who admonishes the viewer, "As I am now, so you will be. Repent!" Typical also are statues of La Conquistadora, patroness of Santa Fe, who accompanied De Vargas and his men during the 1692 Reconquest of New Mexico and is still annually paraded on the streets; of Nuestra Senora de Guadalupe, the Indian Virgin sacred to Mexico, with her own shrine in Santa Fe; and of the Holy Trinity. More ambitious sculptures are known as *bultos*.

Material used for *santos* is usually cottonwood and plaster made from locally found gypsum. Colors came out of the native earth – the red and orange from pulverized iron ocher; white and yellow from the abundant clay; black from finely ground charcoal; and green from boiled herbs. Blue had to be imported and was not much used before the 1850s. *Santos* are an integral part of every household, particularly patron saints after whom family members have been named.

Women excel in needlework, embroidering coverlets – *colchas* – using designs of humans, birds, and flowers, usually on a white background. Churro sheep, brought to New Mexico by the earliest Spanish settlers, survived well in the high desert on little browse and provided cheap, abundant wool.

San Jose Mission church's interior, Laguna Pueblo, New Mexico.

☉ TRADITIONAL CRAFTING

The arts and crafts of Hispanic society were both necessarily functional – whether for food or for worship – and highly aesthetic and personal.

Silversmithing is done by a *platero*, who sometimes still fashions his wares with the help of a homemade mud oven (*horno*), charcoal, bellows of goatskin, and a blow pipe. Often also doubling as blacksmith, traditionally the *platero* melted down silver peso coins to make crosses, necklaces of hollow beads, rosaries, bracelets, earrings, tobacco and powder flasks, silver buttons, headstalls for horses and spurs for the rider. It was Spanish *plateros* who taught the craft to Navajo Indians in the 1850s.

Pottery was simple and made for everyday domestic use, although nowadays some ceramicists also make a range of charmingly painted and fired clay figures of Mary, Joseph, and the Holy Child in his manger, the three wise kings and praying shepherds – all of them typical Hispanic farmers surrounded by burros and lambs, oxen and goats. These may be admired and bought in museums and antiques shops throughout the Southwest, particularly in Taos and Santa Fe.

Much of what is now sold to tourists as art does in fact have its origins in the traditional crafts of yesteryear.

Trail riding at White Stallion
Dude Ranch, Arizona.

THE ANGLOS

Originally lured by furs and trade, the Anglo population is now drawn to the Southwest by warm weather, outdoor pursuits, arts and culture, and high-tech jobs.

So diffuse is the Southwest's Anglo population, it is difficult to say who is included, except that few Anglos actually descend from the Angles, a small German tribe that invaded England in the 5th century. The label was given currency by Hispanic Southwesterners and generally refers to anyone without a Spanish surname, no matter their ethnicity.

The first Anglos to reach the Southwest were explorers, fur trappers, and traders who brought long-coveted goods along the Santa Fe Trail and introduced a dominant Anglo cultural trait: free trade and commerce. That small breach through the formerly self-enclosed New Spain soon became a flood. The American military presence began with forts and garrisons to protect trade routes from outlaws and raiding Apaches, but it was soon engaged in the largely trumped-up American war with Mexico that resulted in Arizona and New Mexico being ceded to the United States by treaty in 1848. Before long, the Southern Pacific and Santa Fe railroads had opened the Southwest to the American public.

THE GREAT MOVE

The enterprising Yankees who built the railroads also built the first grand hotels, and the pleasure-seeking, self-indulgent Southwesterner of the future was imported, along with numerous academics, artists, and others interested in native cultures. Within decades, paved highways, air services, national promotion, and importantly, air conditioning, opened the Southwest to tourism. Patients suffering with tuberculosis in overcrowded cities back east were largely responsible for the influx of artists, writers, and other creatives who settled in Santa Fe for their health. They found clean, dry air and an

Cowboy at Rancho de los Caballeros dude ranch.

ideal – and warm – place to resettle.

By the 1960s, a national migration had been launched that organized Southwestern retirement into vast planned communities in sunbelt cities like Phoenix and Tucson. By the 1970s, resorts had passed through the grand-hotel and dude-ranch phases to emerge as lavish resort complexes with restaurants, nightclubs, and golf, tennis, and national convention facilities. Trailer parks staked out mile after mile, motorcycles and dune buggies roared across the open desert, post-World War II surplus rafts were used to run the Colorado and other rivers by enterprising locals, and motorboats and houseboats plied the reservoirs. Organized leisure became the Southwest's most visible industry.

Traditional agriculture and manufacturing, meanwhile, went into relative decline. Mining – subject to falling demand, foreign competition, shrinking deposits, and labor disputes – suffered the most, and many smelters and open pit mines closed (only to reopen later, when the price of uranium and precious metals rose). Ranches, faced with expensive mechanization, have further consolidated into large spreads. Cattle are fattened more in concentrated animal feed operations (CAFOs) than on the open range – although the increasing demand for grass-fed cattle has

still control the availability of alcohol. Like Indian tribes, who have had embraced casino-resorts and gambling over the opposition of traditional elders, Mormons have had to strike compromises that allow them to operate casinos and tourist facilities.

Environmentalism and a desire to save the last untouched wild places in the western United States grow increasingly passionate as the landscape disappears. The matter has taken on even more urgency in the 21st century, as climate change brings extreme drought and weather changes globally, and resistance to conservation at

Medidating at a vortex site in Sedona.

sparked a renaissance of small family ranches in the Southwest. For the most part, though, cowboys work on dirt bikes or out of trucks, not on horseback, or don't work at all.

Water-intensive surplus crops like cotton no longer make economic sense, and municipalities are clamoring for water, a rare and contentious commodity in this arid land. Ranches, citrus groves, and cotton fields increasingly have been bought out by agribusiness or have given way to the walled-in multiplex developments.

The trend toward consumerism and resource exploitation finds its strongest opposition within the Anglo community itself. Mormons, powerful in Arizona as well as Utah, have held out for conservative, family-oriented values, and in Utah

the federal level, not just the local level, threatens to undo many of the gains and legal protections of the second half of the 20th century. Environmentalists look to traditional Indians, particularly Hopi and Navajo elders, as allies and often join tribal councils in suing outside corporations.

SOUTHWESTERN RETIREES

The phrase "retired to the Southwest" invariably conjures up images of the swimming pool and deck chairs, the golf, and hot sun of a Snow Belter's afterlife. The reality, while including those items, is fortunately far livelier and far more reflective of the American spectrum.

The terrain itself does not permit uniformity. Much of the Southwest is higher in elevation than outsiders realize and suffers classic northern winters, particularly places like Santa Fe in the high desert, at an elevation of 7,000ft (2,100 meters). A few individuals settle in mountainous small towns like St George in southwestern Utah and Flagstaff in northern Arizona, knowing that they will enjoy temperate summers while their contemporaries are holed up with their air conditioning. A few more will strike some compromise in Santa Fe and Taos in northern New Mexico, or Sedona and Prescott in northern Arizona, where the summers are slightly too warm and the winters just overch-

1960 and the granddaddy of American planned-retirement communities. Around 38,000 people now inhabit this walled-in labyrinth of curving streets, golf courses, single-story dwellings, artificial lakes, recreational centers, churches, medical centers, and subdued commercial areas. To own a home, one must be at least 50 years old. Residents gather in travel clubs, bicycle clubs, alumni clubs, even a club for retired union members, and a giant Sundome hosts a symphony made up of Sun City residents and visiting celebrities. So calm and safe is the environment that circulation is largely

Teeing off on the golf course at Nautical Inn and Resort, Lake Havasu City, Arizona.

illed. But most of the incoming retirees have spent previous Januaries numb to their very bones, so they go to the opposite extreme, demanding perfect winters, summer discomfort be damned.

The Southwest has a sunbelt tilt – high in the north, in the elevated high desert region known as the Colorado Plateau, and falling as the Rio Grande and Colorado river basins drain southward into the deserts and eventually, the Gulf of Mexico. This means that retirement country thickens in southern New Mexico and reaches peak density in the Sonoran Desert of central and southern Arizona, where the winters are mostly celestial.

Most responsible for the popular image of Southwestern retirement is Sun City, west of Phoenix, invented by the Del Webb Corporation in

by bicycle and golf cart. With a long waiting list for potential residents, Sun City has spawned such kinsmen as Sun City West, Green Valley, and the euphemistically named Youngtown.

Arizona's over-planned communities offer a bewildering range of activities, yet on streets where nearly identical houses are tinted complementary pastels, and graveled yards are sprayed minutely divergent shades of green, one can't help feeling that individuality is being held onto only lightly.

Far more numerous are the mobile-home communities found outside El Paso and Albuquerque, and along the Colorado River from Boulder City, Nevada, to Yuma, Arizona, and in diminishing perspectives from Tempe through Mesa to Apache

Junction, east of Phoenix. Owing to population density, social life is intense, with evenings of bingo and cards, community meals and dances, and the floating coffee klatsch that slides into a cocktail party.

Forays outside the community are often by recreational vehicle: dune buggies for the hills, motorboats on the reservoir. To give each residence a personal stamp, care is lavished on gardening and decor, but the turnover is far greater than in communities like Sun City in west Phoenix or Carefree, adjoining Scottsdale. Strangers overcome the sense of impermanence with immediate exchanges of life stories and watch over each others' comings and goings.

Most evanescent and fascinating of all retirement groups are the snowbirds – people who converge on the Southwest each winter in campers, trailers, and even trucks with homemade cabins to improvise life wherever they pull up. Some retain roots where they spend the summer, but many are too nomadic even for the tax collector.

They range throughout southern New Mexico and the Sonoran Desert but can be found in great-

A local business in Flagstaff, Arizona.

⊘ HIGH-TECH LIFESTYLES

Two industries important in bringing white migrants to the Southwest are the high-tech and military research industries. Arizona and New Mexico have a major stake in high-tech industries. Defense-oriented research into microbiology and particle physics are major employers at research centers such as Los Alamos and Sandia Laboratories, while a new Facebook data center was just built in Las Lunas, south of Albuquerque. The Silicon Desert has brought with it an upwardly mobile, career-oriented subculture represented by singles bars and club-like apartment complexes, all aesthetically dissected by regional lifestyle magazines.

est concentration at Quartzsite, a two-café desert crossroads in western Arizona, near the California border. During the winter, Quartzsite swells from a few hundred residents to tens of thousands of Snow Belt refugees. A few hook up to utilities in compounds, but most just stake out a spot in the surrounding hard sand. The town's one thoroughfare, lined with acres of open space, awaits the winter-long flea market. Up go the tables of glassware, antiques, tools, old bottles, and campaign buttons collected the previous summer, along with jewelry, ceramics, wood carvings, and clothing that the retirees have made. The season climaxes with February's white-man powwow, an annual "rock festival" of minerals and gems that draws more than a million visitors to the town.

ART IN THE SOUTHWEST

An eclectic range of art and artists, from Pueblo Indian to Europeans, give the Southwest an especially rich and satisfying aesthetic.

In one of the most ambitious art projects the Southwest has ever seen, a long-dead volcanic cinder cone in northern Arizona becomes one of the world's largest works of art. Visitors descend to the bottom of the crater bowl and look up to experience the illusion of the sky as a tangible object stretched over the crater, like plastic wrap (cling film) spattered with stars. Artist James Turrell's Roden Crater project is unprecedented in its scale and ambition, yet it still follows the lead of centuries of art in the American Southwest, because it is inspired by light and landscape. No other region of North America is blessed with such extravagant, penetrating, radically changeable light; no other place on our planet has such an astonishing repertoire of landforms and biological zones. No wonder artists never cease to draw inspiration from it.

"Races" (David Tineo) on Museum of Art Tucson's exterior.

AWESOME IMAGES

The artists who first dribbled westward in the mid-19th century were romantics, and the land they encountered sent their imaginations spinning. Exotic Indian cultures and monumental mountains and canyons became epics on their canvases. Paintings such as Albert Bierstadt's *The Rocky Mountains* and Thomas Moran's *The Chasm of the Colorado* took grandeur and raised it to the second power, calling in otherworldly light, Wagnerian storms, and impossible peaks and abysses. The Southwest's natural landscapes hardly needed exaggerating, but such paintings were the products of their time.

The whole country imagined the West as something even more awesome than the reality, and the artists gave us what we craved.

☉ NAVAJO SAND PAINTINGS

Sand paintings were, traditionally, made during night-long Navajo healing rituals. (Nowadays, of course, permanent sand paintings are made specifically for the non-Indian buyer.) Softly singing the various chants of the rite, and depending upon the cure required, the medicine man sifts the colorful crushed stone, corn pollen, and other sacred materials through his thumb and index finger, slowly creating the appropriate design – Navajo gods, rainbows, feathers, or representations of animals. Most sand paintings are about 3ft (1 meter) across, although some reach as much as 20ft (6 meters) and require helpers to complete.

Commercial interests encouraged them. By the 1880s, the Santa Fe Railway was hiring artists like Moran to paint the pristine wonders of New Mexico and Arizona, luring tourists and settlers from the over-industrialized East.

Art didn't actually need the patronage of the railroad industry; the land itself was attraction enough. "Any man who is really an artist," wrote journalist Charles Lummis in 1892, "will find the Southwest... a region where the ingenuity, the imagination, and the love of God are... visible at every turn."

Two academically trained New York artists, Ernest Blumenschein and Bert Phillips, came under its spell in 1898. The two were on a sketching pilgrimage through the Rockies from Denver to Mexico when one of their wagon's wheels collapsed near Taos, in northern New Mexico. Blumenschein later wrote, "No artist had ever recorded the New Mexico I was now seeing.... My destiny was being decided." They stayed, and in 1915, along with four colleagues, founded the Taos Society of Artists. The Society won national recognition for its

Georgia O'Keeffe beside an easel with a canvas from her series, "Pelvis Series Red With Yellow," Albuquerque, 1960.

⊘ GEORGIA O'KEEFFE

Born in Wisconsin and trained primarily in Chicago and New York, Georgia O'Keeffe is the artist most closely associated with the American Southwest. She first came to public notice in 1916 when Alfred Stieglitz, an influential photographer and art collector, exhibited her drawings at his New York gallery. "The purest, finest, sincerest things to have entered (the gallery) in a long while," he said.

Stieglitz and O'Keeffe were married in 1924 as part of an often tumultuous relationship. An independent woman, she retained her name. "I've had a hard time hanging onto my name, but I hang onto it with my teeth. I like getting what I've got on my own."

At times, O'Keeffe felt frustrated by the unwillingness of the male-dominated art world to take her or her work seriously. "Women can only create babies, say the scientists, but I say they can produce art – and Georgia O'Keeffe is the proof of it," wrote Stieglitz.

She wasn't especially comfortable with the elaborate interpretations critics made of her work, once scolding a writer who asked about the meaning of a painting. "The meaning is there on the canvas. If you don't get it, that's too bad. I have nothing more to say than what I painted."

O'Keeffe died in Santa Fe in 1986, aged 92, one of America's finest 20th-century artists.

work, and Taos became a mecca for artists.

Taos today claims some 250 serious resident artists (out of a 2016 estimated population of 5,763) and a century-long heritage of interpreting the landscapes and cultural stew of its immediate neighborhood. Even the seemingly hackneyed subjects – Taos Pueblo, Taos Mountain, the famous Rancho de Taos church – keep hurling fresh challenges and insights at any artist open to interpretation. A rusty twilight, a dusting of snow, even the sunburn of a bone-dry afternoon in June changes not only their

An excellent place to see some of the best pueblo pottery and ceramics, including those of Maria Martinez, is the Millicent Rogers Museum, near Taos.

interpretations of what she saw and felt. She explained near-obsessive paintings of bleached bones: "The bones seem to cut sharply to the center of something that is keenly alive on

Artist at work under an umbrella in Sedona.

color but also their spirit. In the Southwest, landscapes and architecture have long been acknowledged as living things.

No one understood this better, or made more of it, than Georgia O'Keeffe, who adopted New Mexico as her summer residence in 1929, and moved permanently to the sheepherding village of Abiquiu in 1946. Her art, now properly celebrated in the Georgia O'Keeffe Museum in Santa Fe, is recognizable and yet impossible to categorize. On her canvases, bare hills become voluptuous swirls, flowers bloom with erotic energy, slumping adobe walls exude timeless nobility. The paintings are not quite realistic, not exactly expressionistic, and seldom entirely abstract; they are pure, emotional

the desert even tho' it is vast and empty and untouchable... and knows no kindness with all its beauty."

IT'S IN THE LIGHT

Light teases, probes, and reveals O'Keeffe's landscapes. David Muench, the prolific landscape photographer, says that light is "what gives meaning to form," demonstrating with a portrait of white sycamore bark in Arizona's remote Aravaipa Canyon. Muench chose to ignore the sunny side of the trees and photographed the trunks veiled in shadow instead, because "It wasn't a mute black shadow. It incorporated the light reflected from a creek, a riparian forest, and a desert canyon wall. The whole life of the canyon was wrapped up in the soft shadow on this sycamore trunk."

Since moving to Arizona from Chicago decades ago, painter Lynn Taber-Borcherdt, who was born in Bakersfield, California, in the Mojave Desert, has painted landscapes that have evolved from a fascination with deep, jagged shadows, then iridescence and luminosity, and more recently, the pure drama of sky. "If I hadn't come to Tucson, none of this would have found its way into my work," she has said. "My paintings in Chicago were dark, dark, dark."

The Southwest's swirl of cultures has also motivated and inspired artists, not always to the good. Western art, while still prized by its devotees, seems, after a 170-year-long run, rather stale and repetitive. But it did (and perhaps still does) play a role in perpetuating the mythology of the noble cowboy, which in turn made the West appear to be a fabled land of adventure, heroism, and virtue – and therefore a place that has acted as a repository of dreams for many successive generations of Americans.

Old West-themed sculpture for sale at an art gallery.

⊙ OF NOBLE COWBOYS AND GLORIFIED LANDSCAPES

The genre of Western art may have become irreversibly stale and tired, but it is almost inescapable for most of us, and that includes the good, the bad, and the schlock.

As for good Western art, not only was the notion of the noble cowboy explored and perpetuated but often the West's natural splendors were also embellished.

Thomas Moran, for example, was the first artist to celebrate the grandeur of Yellowstone – his work helped to persuade Congress to designate Yellowstone a national park – and later the Grand Canyon, with a romantic and glorified atmosphere. Moran didn't intend to make an exact rendering but, rather, tried to imbue

his work with the emotional power of the landscape. To those critics demanding accuracy, Moran was quick to respond: "I did not wish to realize the scene literally... (but) to preserve and convey its true impression."

For artists of the late 19th century like Frederic Remington, the Western story was not about the landscape but about the cowboy and his response to his environment. But as the 19th century drew to a close, the West of Remington's youth was quickly fading. In 1900, he visited Colorado and New Mexico, only to find that the rugged frontier had given way to "brick buildings and derby hats... It spoils all my early illusions, and they are my capital."

NATIVE ART AND CERAMICS

Southwestern pottery has produced and fulfilled a different form of dream for the Southwest's Indian tribes, especially the Pueblo people around the Four Corners region. Their artistic traditions date back more than a millennium, but their art suffered hard times, as the people themselves did, beginning with the Spanish *entrada* in 1540. But late in the 19th century, pottery began a spectacular and lucrative revival as the tribes discovered a market for their wares in the enchanted Anglos. Two women, Maria Martinez of San Ildefonso

abstracted feathers, butterflies, and shapes that originate from worlds that Anglo collectors will never understand. As one Hopi potter told writer Stephen Trimble, "Most of my designs are from the dreams that I had, from looking at the earth, everything in the universe." Other Indian artists have invented their own traditions, although nearly all have been influenced in some way by the land itself.

The late R.C. Gorman, the celebrated (and widely imitated) Navajo painter who maintained a studio in Taos, recalled his first experience in

Native American art for sale.

Pueblo, in New Mexico, and Nampeyo, a Hopi from Hano, Arizona, led the way. Encouraged by archeologists excavating ancestral tribal lands, they studied the pottery of their ancestors, then layered their own creative force over the traditions.

Today, thousands of skilled Indian potters produce exquisite, immaculately detailed handmade pots, sometimes selling them for thousands of dollars. Each tribe or pueblo maintains a distinctive aesthetic signature. Navajo pottery is generally undecorated, letting the architecture of the vessel form the artistic statement. Acoma jars feature black-and-white interlocking geometric patterns of dazzling complexity. Hopi potters are still inspired by their ancestors' red-and-black-on-yellow designs featuring

art as drawing in the ruddy mud of Chinle Wash in Canyon de Chelly. The economical lines of his swirling human figures sprang from that source.

Contemporary Indian jewelry frequently borrows the symbolic designs of nature – mountains, lightning, rainbows, clouds, snakes, and birds. Whatever the tribe or artistic endeavor, few American Indian artists ever stray far from the inspiration of nature itself. It is an integral part of their tradition, religion, and what outsiders might call soul.

OTHER LOCAL ART FORMS

Hispanic art also thrives in the Southwest, from the naive folk-art *santos* – carved statues of Catholic saints – to politically charged murals in urban *barrios*. One of the most notable Hispanic artists in the Southwest was the late Mexican-American Luis Jimenez, whose monumental fiberglass sculptures celebrated people who have been overlooked or downtrodden. His *Border Crossing*, planted outside the New Mexico Museum of Art in Santa Fe, depicts a larger-than-life barefoot man carrying his wife across the Rio Grande. This is illegal, according to American law. Jimenez thinks it is full of courage and nobility. Looking up at the sculpture, we are left to ponder the truth.

from Kansas to Los Angeles. Even regional architecture was affected by entanglement with the railroad. Mary Jane Colter, the first female architect in the United States, became architect and decorator for the railroad in 1902, and eventually designed and decorated 22 buildings for entrepreneur Fred Harvey. Her perfectionism and cantankerous manner caused workmen to dread her arrival at a building site, and she showed up often, even to supervise the laying of individual stones.

The Desert Watchtower on the East Rim of

"Verde Mural Connection" in Cottonwood, Arizona.

One important genre of southwestern art is often overlooked or scorned by the serious art establishment – Southwestern kitsch. We all know it: the saguaro-in-the-sunset, the mauve coyote launching his arias toward the moon, the prehistoric flute-player Kokopelli gracing earrings, light sconces, or toilet-paper holders. Purists will cringe, but the Southwest has always needed simplified symbols. This is an awesome land, where reality and mythology are entangled in a complex weave, where nature is often too overwhelming to comprehend, and where many cultures are thrown together in a tense and intricate dance.

The Santa Fe Railroad triggered a cultural exchange when, in 1883, it began to lay tracks

the Grand Canyon is a masterpiece of Colter's "indigenous" style and use of local materials. She hired the young Hopi artist Fred Kabotie, who later gained worldwide acclaim, to paint its Hopi Room.

Kabotie later related: "She could be difficult, especially when it came to matching colors... One day she kept sending me up in the tower with little dabs of oil colors, too small to match... I finally lost my patience. 'Let me have the tube,' I said [and] squeezed everything out and stirred in the color I felt was right. 'You've ruined everything and you've used up all the paint,' she cried. I took a little dab and ran back up in the tower. Fortunately it matched... saving my life and hers."

PREHISTORIC INDIAN ART

Pottery, rock art, and jewelry made by the ancestors of today's native people of the Southwest is culturally diverse, enigmatic, and a clue to their worldview.

A painted track resembling a roller coaster loops around a clay pot, encircling a flock of lizards. Two clowns, part human and part turtle, cavort like circus acrobats in the interior of a bowl. In what we now know as Utah's Canyonlands National Park, bizarre and chilling mummy figures drift like dark, two-dimensional ghosts across a canyon wall. These art works are as enigmatic as anything hung today at the Museum of Modern Art, but they were created by anonymous artists nearly a millennium ago.

At the peak of prehistoric civilization in the Southwest, from around AD 1100 to 1300, art flowered in dizzying profusion – a sign of people enjoying enough affluence to spend considerable time in creative pursuits. Unfortunately, when these cultures – those of the Ancestral Puebloans, Hohokam, Mogollon, and others – collapsed and dispersed, most of the stories underlying their paintings and pottery evaporated. Modern Puebloans, descendants of Ancestral Pueblo people, can sometimes "read" ancient petroglyphs. But they don't agree on the meanings.

Prehistoric Southwestern art mostly falls into three categories: ceramics, body ornaments, and rock art. Pottery begins to appear in the archeological record almost as early as agriculture, around AD 300, but it was several more centuries before it occurred to anyone to paint it. After AD 700, ceramic art blossomed with fantastic geometric and zoologic art. The different branches of the Ancestral Puebloan culture, clustered around the Four Corners canyons and plateaus of the Colorado Plateau, usually decorated their pots with tense geometric abstractions of checkerboards, triangles, diamonds, zigzags, spirals, and mazes.

The most sophisticated and most startling ceramic designs came from the Mimbres people, a branch of the Mogollon of southwestern New Mexico who were the first to learn pottery, probably from travelers from Mesoamerica. Mimbres bowls serve up an astounding

mixture of dramatic geometry, phantasmagorical beasts, and pictorial scenes of hunting, fishing, or dancing. Pioneer archeologist Jesse Fewkes believed the pottery depicted the Mimbres' mythological world, a theory that still seems plausible today. The Mogollon eventually merged with the Ancestral Pueblo, and it is easy to see their influence in ceramics.

Petroglyphs in the Bears Ears National Monument, Utah.

Prehistoric art often was designed to be worn as necklaces, pendants, earrings, bracelets, or rings. Many pieces were effigies of birds, antelope, or mountain lions carved from stone or bone. They likely had religious significance, counterparts to modern Christian cross necklaces or good-luck charms. Other pieces appear (to us) to be purely ornamental

The rock peckings (petroglyphs) and paintings (pictographs) scattered throughout the Southwest's hillsides, mountains, and canyons are the most prevalent remnant of prehistoric art, and also the most bewildering. But the most fundamental question remains to be answered: what were these illustrations intended to do? Depict history, mark territory? Record a census? Offer prayers for rain, fertility, or successful hunting?

One thing seems certain: rock art was designed to communicate across centuries and cultural lines. Wherever possible, rock artists created their works under erosion-protected natural stone eaves. And many symbols appear throughout the region, forming a *lingua franca* that would have been understood by a speaker of Hohokam, Kayenta Anasazi, or Mogollon.

Edward Abbey in Moab in 1969.

LITERATURE

Writers and travelers have written wondrous things about the Southwest, grappling with social upheaval, murder mysteries, and philosophical musings.

The author of this book," a reviewer once wrote of *The Monkey Wrench Gang*, "should be neutered and locked away forever." The author of the book, Edward Abbey, liked that critical snarl so much that he quoted it in an essay about his own work nine years later. You can almost hear Abbey chuckling even now. It was a validation, an assurance that his writing had hit the mark he intended. It had provoked and inflamed – which is what much of the best Southwestern writing has been doing for the last couple of centuries.

The Southwest is a fierce, prickly, obstinate, unforgiving land, replete with natural peril and human conflict. It is only right that its literature reflects this. It is also a place of exotic and delicate beauty, and writers have heaped up mountains of words, often great words, trying to understand and defend it.

"We are learning finally that the forests and mountains and desert canyons are holier than our churches," Abbey wrote in *Desert Solitaire*, probably his masterpiece. "Therefore, let us behave accordingly."

The earliest Southwestern writers were the soldiers and missionaries who came under the Spanish flag, and they kept exhaustive diaries to satisfy the Spanish mania for bureaucratic documentation. A few managed to create literature in the process. The best was Fr Ignaz Pfefferkom, an 18th-century Jesuit priest who described in meticulous detail and frequent delight such things as the comings and goings of scorpions, the effects of eating chiles, and the native customs regarding adultery. "Most of them are satisfied with one wife," he deadpanned in *Sonora: A Description of the Province*, "a fact which makes their conversion [to Christianity] easier."

The late Tony Hillerman at the foot of Sandia Mountain.

LANDMARKS IN LITERATURE

The Anglos who followed in the next century were a motley bunch, mostly amateurs when it came to journalism or writing poetry or fiction, but their work nevertheless forms a fascinating, mosaic-like picture of frontier life. One of the accidental masterpieces of 19th-century Southwest literature is John G. Bourke's *On the Border With Crook*, a painfully vivid account of US Army General George Crook's war against the Apaches. Bourke was an army general but no knee-jerk defender of his side's campaign. His visionary observations crackle across a century: "Promises on each side have been made only to deceive and to be broken; [and] the red hand of war has rested most heavily upon shrieking mother and wailing babe."

Perhaps the greatest early landmark in Southwestern literature was produced by an even less likely character, an asthmatic New Jersey art professor named John C. Van Dyke, who wandered the Southwestern deserts alone from 1898 to 1901. Van Dyke chronicled their unfamiliar beauty in rhapsodic but accurate detail: "Somehow (the desert mountains) remind you of a clinched hand with the knuckles turned skyward... Barren rock and nothing more; but what could better epitomize power!"

After *The Desert* appeared in 1901, its sub-

Christopher Walken in "The Milagro Beanfield War" movie.

ject was no longer a wasteland in the American imagination, and this slim book formed a foundation for what would become a flood of interpretive nature writing about the American deserts.

CLASSIC SOUTHWESTERN FICTION

Southwestern fiction of the 20th century also breathed deeply of the land, as well as from the many human cultures that inhabit it. "I don't believe a person can be born and raised in the Southwest and not be affected by the land," wrote the celebrated New Mexico novelist Rodolfo Anaya. His most celebrated novel, *Bless Me, Ultima*, published in 1972, is a fantastic swirl of violence, familial love, sorcery, and faith, and both good and evil are personified in the elements of nature itself. The

whirlwinds of summer "carry with them the evil spirit of a devil." The wild herbs have spirits, "and before I dug she [Ultima, the *curandera*] made me speak to the plant and tell it why we pulled it from its home in the earth." Few Anglos have any understanding of the Hispanic world of Anaya's novels, but *Bless Me, Ultima* provides an intimately scaled introduction.

American Indian writers have done much the same for their cultures. Leslie Marmon Silko's classic 1977 novel *Ceremony* tells the story of Tayo, a returning World War II prisoner of war, who struggles to purge his nightmares through the mystical ceremonies of his people. Former Albuquerque journalist Tony Hillerman, although no Indian himself (and Navajos have been surprised to learn that he isn't), penetrated Indian society in the Southwest to a remarkable depth within the framework of his page-turner mysteries set on the Navajo Nation and featuring Sgt Joe Leaphorn and his deputy, Jim Chee, of the Navajo tribal police.

The thorniest cultural novel of the Southwest is John Nichols' *The Milagro Beanfield War*, set in rural northern New Mexico where working Hispanic families struggle to hold off wealthy Anglo developers. It is hilarious, outrageous, profane – and profound, because it illuminates the real-life epic battle for the little towns and ancient family farms in the orbits of Taos and Santa Fe. When lawyer Nichols first arrived in Taos in 1969, land in Taos valley sold for about $500 an acre; by 2000, an acre was worth $50,000 and up. An entire culture has been challenged by changing demographics; novels like *Milagro* may soon be the most insightful record of it we have.

The classic novel about Southwestern development – the central story of the land right up to the present moment when it is under attack from within the federal government, supposedly its defenders – is, of course, the one for which it was proposed that Edward Abbey be neutered. *The Monkey Wrench Gang* is a badly flawed polemic. But its theme of eco-hooliganism seemed to collect and catalyze the outrage and frustration many Southwesterners feel about the exploitation and abuse of the land. Abbey always claimed that he wrote it mainly as entertainment, and with an "indulgence of spleen and anger from a position of safety behind my typewriter."

But one of Abbey's biographers, James Bishop Jr, wrote that *The Monkey Wrench Gang* "comes the closest to reaching that place of Abbey's most steadfast convictions: a romantically ideal-ized world in which the Industrial Revolution has been aborted and society has reached a steady-state equilibrium where man and the land can exist in harmony."

NON-FICTION

With his earlier *Desert Solitaire*, a collection of essays loosely based on Abbey's abortive career as a national park ranger in southeastern Utah, Abbey opened a vein of Southwestern literature that continues to be mined by many superb writ-ers, from the Mormon naturalist Terry Tempest Williams to adventurer Craig Childs. This genre may resemble nature writing, but at a deeper level it is really about the relationships between humans and the land. And it is far more emotion-ally charged than the work of pioneer naturalists like John Muir, Aldo Leopold, and Van Dyke.

The late Charles Bowden summarized it perfectly in the opening lines of his 1986 book *Blue Desert*, which picked up where *Desert Solitaire* trailed off. "This is the place where they hope to escape their pasts – the unemployment, the smoggy skies, dirty cities, crush of human numbers. This they cannot do. Instead, they reproduce the world they have fled. I am drawn to the frenzy of this act." Bowden's essays were themselves frenzied – overheated, dis-tinctively styled, often angry, but finally profound.

One of the finest recent books in this vein is the curiously titled *America, New Mexico* by Robert Leonard Reid. In its 10 essays, Reid masterfully paints the natural environment of New Mexico as a stage set – "a time-scented garden where nature is foremost and rocks are truth, and where dawn is a paean to fresh starts and reckless plans" – and then fills in real-life characters who are struggling with issues such as poverty, racism, and the weight of the Southwest's tumultuous history.

Reid willingly plunged headfirst into raw adver-sity and sinister forces – gang violence in Albuquer-que; the remnants of the Trinity Site, where the first atomic bomb was exploded – and found, "standing staunchly against them a quiet and unshakable confidence rooted in the natural world."

The sweeping grandeur and miniature mira-cles of the land itself seemed to offer, somehow, a redemptive counterpoint to the human frenzy that both Reid and Bowden described. And more than anything else, this is the long, tough thread coursing through more than two centuries of writ-ing about this region. Yes, the land is achingly beautiful and so, consequently, it is hopelessly fragile. But the land will abide. "When I touch the earth, I feel the rock hard face of eternity," wrote Bowden in *Blue Desert*.

Any bookshelf packed with the best reading on the American Southwest will be hot to the touch, sizzling with pain, passion, fury, violence, and moody volatility – all classic characteristics of the Southwest and its people. But under all of these qualities will lie a foundation of deep faith.

Charles Bowden in Tucson, Arizona, in 1998.

⊘ BEANFIELD HINDSIGHT

"I don't know if *The Milagro Beanfield War* is a good book, or just one with a lot of upbeat energy that has captured a certain fancy. To be truthful, though, I do have a few minor regrets. For exam-ple, given the opportunity to rewrite the novel, for sure I would cut out two-thirds of the cussing, which often seems gratuitous. And believe me, only one character, and just *once*, during the entire novel, would dare exclaim, *"Aiee, Chihuahua!"* Other than that, I still haven't reread the book in its entirety since the galleys were returned... so long ago. "
John Nichols, 1993

THE SOUTHWEST ON SCREEN

For decades, film makers have struggled to recreate the old West "as it really was." The results range from kitsch to memorable Oscar winners.

In John Ford's *The Man Who Shot Liberty Valance*, a senator played by James Stewart confesses to a newspaper editor that for decades he has lived a lie. The senator admits that 30 years earlier he did not actually gun down a sadistic outlaw, an act that launched his political career. Having heard the whole story, the editor tosses away his notes and declares, "This is the West, sir. When the legend becomes fact, print the legend."

DUELS IN THE SUN

By the time *Liberty Valance* came out in 1962, the makers of Westerns had instinctively followed that creed for nearly 70 years. They portrayed a West of duels in the sun, cavalry charges across desert dreamscapes, and savage Indians lined up on ruddy buttes.

These films offer little sense of everyday life, just an idealized world where things usually go according to plan: the bad guy embodies evil, while the hero upholds all that is good, reluctantly resorting to violence to right a world gone wrong. It's a simple scheme, and one that prevailed in countless "B Westerns," those second-billed features at old-time movie houses. Wildly popular, B movies both influenced the public's image of the West and cemented a perception of the Western as simple, light entertainment.

That perspective disregards the artistry of leading filmmakers, from silent-movie star William S. Hart to John Ford and Clint Eastwood. Traditional elements run through their work, but all three take the Western beyond simple formula, an achievement long ignored: Ford won six Academy Awards, but none for his Westerns. Only in latter decades, during a minor revival, did the genre earn greater respect, from Kevin Costner's *Dances with Wolves* to Clint Eastwood's

Henry Fonda in "My Darling Clementine" (1946).

Unforgiven. Both won Academy Awards for Best Film – the first Western winners since *Cimarron*, 60 years earlier. In more recent years, critically-acclaimed Westerns have included the Coen brothers' remake of *True Grit* (2010) and *Slow West* (2015), while many other filmmakers have worked in the genre, including Quentin Tarantino in *The Hateful Eight* (2015) and Seth MacFarlane's comedy *A Million Ways to Die in the West* (2014).

HISTORY OF WESTERNS

Western mythologizing was well underway by the time movies flickered into the public consciousness. Even before the Old West rode off into the sunset for good, 19th-century novels, stage plays, and Wild West shows had reshaped it. Film just offered a new medium for an already popular genre.

One of the first movies filmed in Hollywood was also a Western, Cecil B. DeMille's *The Squaw Man* (1913). Originally produced for stage, *The Squaw Man* played another pivotal role in film history. It launched the film career of actor-director William S. Hart, who won Broadway acclaim in the play as a cowboy named Cash Hawkins.

Hart knew and loved the West. Born in New York State in 1865, his family took him to the Midwest, where he grew up playing with Sioux children in the frontier towns where his father set up gristmills. He traveled with his father deep into Sioux Country before the family returned east. After *The Squaw Man*, Hart began getting more Western roles, such as the lead in *The Virginian*, enhancing his cowboy reputation. None other than Bat Masterson touted Hart's portrayal as "a true type of that reckless nomad who flourished on the border when the six-shooter was the final arbiter of all disputes between man and man."

Committed to an honest depiction (and chronically in need of money), Hart had a revelation while watching a Western movie in 1913. Horrified at its inaccuracies, he likened the film to burlesque. But he also recognized that if this movie succeeded, then his truer vision of the West should be able to capture movie audiences.

A WESTERN REVIVAL

By the time Hart arrived in Hollywood, producers were sounding a death knell for Westerns, one of several times the genre seemed to be on its way to the last roundup. Under film pioneer Thomas Ince's guidance, he began his career, and many credit Hart with reviving the Western. His sober face and hunched, two-gun stance became as famous as Charlie Chaplin's Little Tramp.

Unlike the glossy, stunt-filled Tom Mix movies, Hart didn't depict a rhinestone West. His had dust and grit; the plots generally strong and adult. Wild West shows had popularized flashy western duds, more Liberace than Laramie. Hart righted that image with a plaid shirt, simple kerchief, and a vest. He prided himself on his vision and in his autobiography wrote, "My pictures of the West in the early days will make that colorful period of American life live forever."

Western expert William K. Everson agreed with Hart and wrote, "His films were raw, unglamorous, and gutsy... the ramshackle Western towns and their inhabitants like unretouched Matthew Brady photographs, the sense of dry heat ever present (panchromatic film stock, developed in the 1920s, softened and glamorized the landscapes in later Westerns), and the clouds of dust everywhere."

Other directors had wetted the ground for a cleaner look. Considered Hart's masterpiece, *Tumbleweeds* (1925) has a documentary feel, especially the scenes of Oklahoma's Cherokee

Silent-film star Tom Mix.

⊘ PAVING THE WAY

It may be hard to imagine a Western without the sound of gunfire or the thundering of horses' hooves, but some real gems of the genre are the early silent films. Although *Cripple Creek Bar Room* (1898) is considered the "first cowboy film," it was 1903's *The Great Train Robbery* that gave birth to the Western genre. The 10-minute-long film was actually shot on the East Coast, rather than the Wyoming locale that it portrayed, but all the essential elements of a Western were there: good guys, bad guys, a robbery, a chase, and a final showdown. And it all wrapped up with the first-ever closeup of a gunman firing directly into the camera (and delighted audience).

Strip Land Rush. The film is considered by many to be an honest and accurate – even poetic – depiction of an important historical event. Pioneers race across the screen with a sense of urgency and danger, on horseback, in wagons, even on bicycles. Filmed by a semiburied camera, ground-level shots of thundering hooves and wagon wheels mesmerized audiences and became Western classics.

Hart's character declares, "Boys, it's the last of the West," and indeed *Tumbleweeds* proved to be Hart's final film. Hart pioneered the Western

Marion Michael Morrison, better known as John Wayne, was discovered by director Raoul Walsh. His first starring role was in The Big Trail (1930).

hero as a loner, the austere good-bad man who finds purpose and redemption in riding to the rescue. There was plenty of good old-fashioned chivalry, and many a rough outlaw became reformed by the love of a good woman. Hart's films often ended by linking the villains with the saloon and the "good guys" with the church. That strict, moralistic quality appealed to World War I audiences, but seemed heavyhanded by the Roaring Twenties.

Clashing with the studios, Hart retired to his ranch north of Los Angeles. Over the years, a steady stream of notables, including Charles Russell and Will Rogers, visited him at his Spanish-style home. Hart died in 1946 and gave the Newhall estate to Los Angeles County to be used as a museum. In typical Two-Gun Bill fashion, he explained, "While I was making pictures, the people gave me their nickels, dimes, and quarters. When I am gone, I want them to have my home."

JOHN FORD COUNTRY

There are statues of John Wayne in California; they even named an airport after him. To the public, John Wayne is the Western. But no man dominated the genre like director John Ford. Within the film community, Ford's legend is as big as Wayne's. Ingmar Bergman called him the world's greatest film maker. Orson Welles watched Ford's 1939 movie *Stagecoach* 40 times

and declared his three great influences "John Ford, John Ford, and John Ford."

Born in Maine to Irish immigrants, Seamus Ford (he later changed his name to John) headed west following the Hollywood acting success of his brother Francis. As he explained in an interview with Peter Bogdanovich, he got his chance when a director failed to show for a big scene the same morning that Universal Studios chief Carl Laemmle visited the lot. Someone needed to look in charge, so Ford took control of the action, ultimately burning down the street

Will Rogers.

in a scene he described as "more pogrom than Western." Later, when a new film needed a director, Laemmle said, "Give Jack Ford the job. He yells good."

Yelling good and using his sharp eye for composition, Ford first directed silent two-reelers, then moved on to some of the earliest Western epics, most notably *The Iron Horse* (1924). Like Hart, Ford sought authenticity. He often consulted old-timers and eschewed quick-draw duels and showy costumes. Ford met Wyatt Earp on the back lot a few times and based his 1946 O.K. Corral tale *My Darling Clementine* on Earp's accounts, although by that time the old gunfighter was printing the legend, rather than the facts.

Ford rode out to locations and slept under the stars during shooting. In 1938, he headed out to a more distant location than usual – Monument Valley – to film his first sound Western, *Stagecoach*, starring John Wayne. Dubbed "Ford Country," the valley and its towering red rock formations evolved into a famous trade mark. Ford, Wayne, and Monument Valley have grown into a kind of holy trinity of the classic Western. But the West they portrayed was one of considerable complexity. The early Wayne is as different from the icon Duke of later years as Hound Dog Elvis is from Vegas Elvis. Jane Tompkins, in *West of Everything*, writes, "The expression of the young John Wayne is tender... pure and sweet."

Ford cast Wayne in the roles of men with clashing emotions and loyalties, such as the cavalry officer who is torn between obedience to his commanding officer and his better judgment in *Fort Apache*. And the classic Monument Valley films often ended ambiguously, allowing audiences to reach conflicting conclusions, something that never happened in good-guy bad-guy

John Ford and a cast of Indian actors.

⊘ ON LOCATION IN THE SOUTHWEST

The Southwest has long provided filmmakers with varied and picturesque settings for their epics. Utah's Monument Valley is probably the most recognizable Western film locale, a favorite of director John Ford. The red rocks of Arizona's Sedona and Utah's Moab and the canyons around Kanab also have their share of film credits. But probably the most prolific Southwestern "movie studio" was – and still is – Old Tucson. Located about 15 miles (24km) from Tucson itself, the old walled city of Tucson was actually built in painstaking detail for the 1940 motion picture *Arizona*. More than 20 additional films were shot there in the 1940s and 1950s, but the site was continually deteriorating until

the Old Tucson Development Company leased the locale from Pima County and began restoration. In January 1960, Old Tucson opened with a "new look" and dual purpose: as both a movie location and family-oriented "entertainment park." John Wayne is particularly associated with Old Tucson; he made four films there, including the acclaimed *Rio Bravo*. The locale also moved smoothly into television, with the series *High Chaparral* shot there from 1966 to 1971.

A fire destroyed a huge portion of the studio in 1995, but the facility was quickly rebuilt, and continues to be both a working film location and popular family destination.

Westerns. In *Fort Apache,* Henry Fonda plays the commanding officer, a martinet who leads his troops on a suicidal charge against Apaches. Based on Custer's last stand, the film feels almost like a Vietnam-vintage attack on military incompetence. But as the movie closes, Wayne, whose advice Fonda disastrously ignored, tells myth-seeking reporters of the officer's heroism and eulogizes, "No man died more gallantly."

Critics chastise Ford for his depictions of Indians as bloodthirsty marauders. Certainly, in *Stagecoach* they appear as anonymous killers, while in *The Searchers* (1956), the white women captured by Indians have gone insane. Wayne's character is even ready to shoot his captive niece, the one he spent seven years searching for, declaring, "Living with Comanches ain't being alive." Yet in *Fort Apache*, Cochise appears as the man of reason, and it is Fonda who displays the bloodlust and bigotry that draw the Indians into reluctant battle.

Yet another picture depicting American Indians negatively was *Northwest Passage*, a great adventure saga starring Spencer Tracy as the leader of Roger's Rangers, battling Indians for territory.

"Let's face it," Ford told Bogdanovich, "we've treated them very badly. It's a blot on our shield. We've cheated and robbed, killed, murdered, massacred, and everything else, but they kill one white man and, God, out come the troops."

Certainly, if you've seen one Ford film, you haven't seen them all. Ford's West was one of shadings, not unlike the changing play of natural light and shadow found in his movies. It reflects the man himself, who could charm his actors or, as he did to Wayne, reduce them to tears. As James Stewart said of the director, "Take everything you've heard, everything you've ever heard, and multiply it about a hundred times – and you still won't have a picture of John Ford."

MAN WITH NO NAME

Ford filmed his final Western in 1964, while John Wayne continued until 1976 and won an Oscar for his portrayal of Marshal Rooster Cogburn in *True Grit* (1969). But reflecting the social pressures of the 1960s, Westerns underwent major changes. The cavalry song that accompanied an Indian surrender in *The Searchers* was used to ironic effect behind a scene of slaughter

in *Little Big Man* (1969). And the new Western man had as much Liberty Valance in him as he did John Wayne.

He smoked a foul little Italian cigar, wore a poncho, and sported stubble and a scowl. He was Clint Eastwood as the Man With No Name in a trilogy of mid-1960s Westerns shot in Spain by Italian director Sergio Leone.

The low-budget Spaghetti Westerns helped revive the genre at a time when big-money American epics had bombed. Eastwood told Kenneth Turan of the Los Angeles Times, "When

Clint Eastwood in "The Good, The Bad and The Ugly."

⊘ WOMEN IN WESTERNS

Although women were strong heroines (*The Perils of Pauline* types) in the silent era's Western serial melodramas, females in later Western films were either portrayed as good-natured dance hall entertainers or "virginal guiding lights." In many cases, women filled a domestic role; possibly a love interest to be fought over and possessed by the "hero." They were often the motive for male activity. But perhaps the notion of woman as less-than-privileged characters stems from the fact that white women were not among the first trappers or hunters to explore the region; they came instead with the establishment of farms, settlements, and towns.

I first went and did *A Fistful of Dollars*, there were a lot of predictions in the trade papers that Westerns were through. And I said, 'Swell. Now that I'm doing one, they're through,' but that film turned out to have its place in the world."

With a long and varied credits list that extends to the present day, Eastwood is not exclusively a Western actor and director, but his career follows some of the genre's trends. His break came in the television show *Rawhide*, where he played the amicable Rowdy Yates. His appearance in the musical *Paint Your Wagon*

Graham Greene in "Dances With Wolves."

> Kevin Costner's 1990 success, Dances with Wolves, was one of the few Westerns to cast Indians in acting roles, use Lakota Sioux subtitles, and view American Indians in a sympathetic way, not as bloodthirsty savages.

evoked the heyday of Roy Rogers and the singing cowboys.

But the Man With No Name had no Hollywood precedent. He subscribed to no moral code like William S. Hart's characters. He and his cohorts did what they had to do in order to survive in a moral and physical desert. In *The Good, The Bad,*

and *The Ugly*, the Eastwood character kills three men before the audience even sees his face, then takes the man he saved captive so he can collect the bounty.

A CYNICAL LONER

In an essay on Eastwood, writer Jim Miller describes the character as "a cynical loner at a time when the mood of the country was shaped in much the same line of thought... he brought a whole new look at the Western hero as a lone wolf, anti-hero that was totally different than characters John Wayne played."

Westerns declined steadily during the 1970s and 1980s; Eastwood went nearly 10 years without making a Western after he directed and starred in the modern classic *The Outlaw Josey Wales* (1976). Then, in 1980, one of the biggest movie bombs of all time, *Heaven's Gate*, convinced Hollywood that, finally, Westerns were well and truly dead.

WESTERNS REVIVED

In 1990, Kevin Costner's *Dances with Wolves*, a kind of New Age eco-Western, stunned Hollywood with its success and launched a revival that had everyone back in the saddle again. And after years of waiting, Eastwood decided that he had aged enough to portray reformed killer William Munny in *Unforgiven* in 1992, which he also directed.

Now a widower and hog farmer, Munny tries to convince himself that he is truly a changed man, even as he heads out again as a bounty hunter. He struggles with almost everything – his past, his horse, and his shooting – and looks as weary as the Man With No Name looked invincible. When his young partner asks him about what the Old West days were like, Munny replies, "I can't remember. I was drunk most of the time."

Every murder has its consequences, and Eastwood demythologizes killers and sheriffs alike by exposing the fictions of a reporter who would twist their exploits into the kind of dime novels that inspired Westerns in the first place. As in *Liberty Valance*, the genre turned in on itself, exposing its own false origins. Eastwood told the *Los Angeles Times* that *Unforgiven* would be his final Western. "Maybe that's why I didn't do it right away. I was kind of savoring it as the last of that genre, maybe the last film of that type for me."

THE GREAT EQUALIZER

A Western without a gunfight and lots of shooting would not be worthy of the name and is largely responsible for America's love affair with gun culture.

"God made some men big and some small, but Colonel Sam Colt made them equal all." So went a popular saying in Texas, where the Colt revolver made its mark early on. Firearms went by many names: six-shooters, hog legs, peacemakers, belly guns, lead chuckers, and equalizers. Whatever the name, they were an essential piece of equipment in the shoot-'em-up West.

ARRIVAL OF THE REVOLVER

In the early days, guns weren't terribly effective for either hunting or protection. An Indian could unleash several arrows in the time it took to reload a single-shot firearm. And then came Sam Colt in the 1830s with revolving pistols and rifles capable of firing several shots without reloading. Their impact was almost immediate. At Plum Creek, in 1841, Texas Rangers armed with five-shot Paterson Colts overcame four-to-one odds against 100 Comanche warriors. By the 1850s, the Colt revolver was the gun-of-choice, although the most popular Colt of the frontier era, the .45-caliber Peacemaker, didn't appear for another two decades.

But not every gunman preferred a Colt. After surrendering in 1882, the notorious outlaw Frank James called his Remington "the hardest and surest shooting pistol made." Lt Col George Armstrong Custer was said to be carrying a pair of Webley "British Bulldog" revolvers when he fell at Little Bighorn. Wyatt Earp probably drew a Smith & Wesson at the OK Corral. And Mark Twain packed a .22-caliber pistol known as a "suicide special," which he claimed had just one fault: "You could not hit anything with it."

Because low-caliber guns were used in much of the Wild West's "gun play," it usually took more than one shot to disable an opponent. That's why

shootists came to prefer a revolver of at least .44 caliber, which was often enough to drop a man with one hit. Most Westerners also owned a rifle or carbine, because they were far more accurate at long range than handguns. The Winchester rifle was called the "gun that won the West," and was standard issue among Texas Rangers, who put it

Wyatt Earp actor in the town of Tombstone.

to use against outlaws and Indians. As the manufacturer, Oliver F. Winchester, liked to say, "It has become a household word and a household necessity on our western plains and mountains. The pioneer, the hunter and trapper, believe in the Winchester, and its possession is a passion with every Indian."

Lever-action repeating rifles were just the thing to give a man confidence even if he was only a fair shot. More than 300,000 Spencer rifles, personally tested by Abraham Lincoln, were issued to Union soldiers during the Civil War.

Carne seca at El Charro Cafe,
Tucson.

SOUTHWEST CUISINE

Take the traditional foods of American Indians, Spanish settlers, and cowboys; add fresh ingredients, spices, and worldly techniques; et voila! Modern Southwest cuisine.

At its heart, Southwest cuisine is comfort food – home-style bean and meat stews and chile sauces you'll find bubbling on the stove in any traditional Hispanic kitchen in New Mexico and Arizona, southern Colorado, and Texas. Centered on corn, beans, and squash, the "three sisters" of Southwest ingredients grown here since prehistoric times, numerous variations-on-a-theme classic dishes have been handed down through families featuring marinated beef, pork, and chicken and sparked with fiery red and green chiles. From chile rellenos, burritos, tacos, and tamales to *huevos rancheros*, *carne adovada*, *posole*, and green chile stew – no true Southwesterner can leave the region for long without experiencing chile withdrawal.

From these humble origins, Southwest cuisine took a leap into the big time in the 1980s, when Santa Fe became a major travel mecca for the well heeled. For the second time in a century – the first being with the advent of tourism, the railroad, and Fred Harvey hotels – all things "Santa Fe style" became a major craze. Soon, an increasing number of well-traveled visitors were beating a path to Santa Fe, bringing with them sophisticated tastes in art, food, clothing, and architecture that brought the world to the remote high desert of New Mexico.

SOUTHWESTERN FOOD MOVEMENTS

First to popularize the idea of Southwest cuisine was a group of Texas chefs dubbed The Big Five. Tex-Mex cuisine combines Western and Mexican ingredients in a particularly American way and is heavy on the meat, cheese, and chile. The lighter New Southwest cuisine we know today was born in California, home of fresh, local, fusion cuisine, and arrived in Santa Fe when several chef alumni

Chile wreath with dried flowers at a market, Santa Fe.

of Alice Waters' revered Café Panisse in Berkeley – temple of everything fresh, local, and organic – moved to Santa Fe and opened restaurants. Prominent among them were Mark Miller, often dubbed the father of Southwest cuisine and an anthropologist by training, who opened the perennially popular Coyote Café, and Katherine Kagel, whose charming Café Pasqual's – housed in a tiny former corner drugstore – feels like a Mexican fiesta.

Both restaurants developed a lighter, Asian-influenced take on traditional Southwest fare that has stood the test of time. At the same time, classically-trained chef John Rivera Sedlar, a native of Santa Fe, opened Abiquiu, a popular restaurant in Los Angeles inspired by the dishes he grew up with, and more recently returned to

Santa Fe, opening the acclaimed Eloisa in the historic Drury Hotel downtown.

All three chefs are creative and fearless innovators, cultural historians, teachers, and most importantly, wrote books popularizing Southwest cuisine. Sedlar's ground-breaking cookbook, *Modern Southwest Cuisine*, remains a classic.

Today, a host of talented chefs have expanded Southwest cuisine beyond Santa Fe. Among the luminaries are Robert Del Grande, owner of Café Annie in Houston, Texas, a James Beard award winner for Best Southwest Chef; Vincent Guerithault, owner of Vincent on Camelback in Phoenix, Arizona, known for his classic French treatment of New World recipes; and James Beard award winner Jennifer Jaskinski of Rioja in Denver, one of several Front Range chefs whose stars are on the rise.

ANCIENT TRADITIONS

The basic Southwest cooking style is rooted in the ancient staples of its indigenous population, whose diet consisted of wild game, including deer, elk, buffalo, and wildfowl, as well as wild

Close-up view of dried flint corn, Santa Fe.

⊘ EDIBLE CACTI

As forbidding as they may look, some cacti provide delicious delicacies to eat. The best known is the fruit of the prickly pear, but also edible is the "vegetable" part of the plant: its "pads", known as *nopales*. Both the fruit and *nopales* are often found in Southwestern grocery stores. As a vegetable, the somewhat tart *nopal* – carefully prepared – can be used in many ways, including in salads, casseroles, and soups. Its taste has been compared to green beans or asparagus. The saguaro, too, produces a fruit that is particularly valued by the Tohono O'odham people of southern Arizona, who labor long hours to process the fruit into syrup and jam.

berries, acorns, pinon and other nuts, herbs such as sage, prickly pear cactus and fruits, and of course, the ancient, cultivated foundations of life: corn, beans, and squash.

The introduction of blue corn in the 1980s brought an added dimension to what was once a ubiquitous food: the tortilla. Blue corn, grown for centuries by the Navajo and Hopi in Arizona and the Pueblo peoples in New Mexico (along with other little-known varieties), is healthier and more easily digested, and a large segment of the health-minded public has embraced it. It's a rare instance of people developing a taste for blue food, bringing what was once a uniquely indigenous food into the mainstream and in the process, expanding the market for traditional indigenous foods and growing tribal economies.

The fiery catalyst in Southwest cuisine – chile – arrived in the Southwest via Europe in the 1500s. Chile is from South America, but it was unknown both in North America and Europe before Columbus arrived in the Americas in 1492. He was searching for black pepper and came upon the chile pepper (he erroneously thought he was in India, which is why he called the locals "Indians").

Chile has been eaten since about 7000 BC in Mexico and grown in South America since about 5200 BC. According to Carmela Padilla, author

By the time Don Juan de Oñate established the first Spanish settlement in New Mexico, near San Juan Pueblo in 1598, chile had already become established in northern New Mexico, grown with water from the nearby Rio Chama channeled to the fields by a traditional system of *acequias*, or ditches, still in use today. It has been a cultural and agricultural staple ever since. In fact, New Mexico (which is sparsely settled and considered economically poor) produces some 60 percent of the country's chile, which has gained even more importance since salsa usurped ketchup as the

Making fry bread, Coyote Canyon, Navajo Nation.

of *The Chile Chronicles*:

"By the time Spanish explorers, led by Hernan Cortes, began their invasion of Mexico in 1519, Aztec plant breeders already had developed dozens of cultivars within the species, including poblanos, jalapenos, and serranos, as well as other non-pungent chile plants. In its native South American home, the word for chile was *aji*. The Aztecs, however, used the Nahuatl term *chilli* to refer to various chile cultivars. Perhaps the most sophisticated chefs of their time, the Aztecs laid the foundation for modern Mexican and New Mexican foods by using chile in the preparation of *moles* (made also with the Mexican "spice," chocolate), tamales, salsas, pipian, and other dishes and sauces."

nation's favorite condiment. Now, native chiles, along with their fiery cousins in other parts of the world, figure prominently in the most sophisticated international culinary circles.

It's ironic, really, because, once upon a time, as New Mexico writer Marsha McEuen points out, "chile was humble food, working-class food. It grew in bad dirt and dry weather. And you could buy it for pennies and use it to flavor almost anything. It lent its liveliness to the cheapest cuts of meat and to huge stews of beans and dried vegetables. *Abuelas* loved it for its supposed curative powers and moms for its ability to stretch a budget. But, in the 1990s, the lowly chile pepper has gotten all dressed up in spangles and high heels and gone to dine with fancy friends like

Muscovy duck breast and rack of lamb in some of America's premier restaurants."

What you'll discover while traveling throughout the Southwest is both. You can dine happily on the unfancy but frequently spicy original, or seek out the culinary innovators in the region's metropolitan areas to sample the exciting tastes and textures of New Southwestern Cuisine.

CHILE-LACED DISHES

On the traditional side of the menu, foods – including the names they're given – vary widely of the southern Arizona border with northern Mexico owes its heritage to sturdy *ranchero* cooking, popular during the heyday of the sweeping 19th-century land grant ranches and haciendas that were home to powerful Mexican families. Enchiladas in southern Arizona, as in Sonora, are simple, hearty fare for big appetites, consisting of tortillas stuffed with meat and rolled into a tube, topped with cheese, and served with a choice of red or green chile. The chile has a softer edge and is milder than that of New Mexico.

Fiesta platter (chile con queso, guacamole, red chile ribs, and tortilla chips) at El Pinto Restaurant, Albuquerque.

even between Arizona and New Mexico. There are some dishes, like fajitas (a Mexican dish claimed by Texas as Tex-Mex), which is comprised of seared flank steak strips, onions, and mild peppers served with salsa, guacamole, and tortillas, that is essentially the same throughout the Southwest. The same is true of the flour tortilla and corn tortilla: one is an unleavened flatbread made of wheat flour and water; the other, a flatbread made of ground corn kernels (*masa*) processed with lime, mixed with water.

On the other hand, there are regional differences when it comes to a mainstream dish such as enchiladas – meat, veggie, or cheese stuffed corn tortillas covered in chile sauce and more cheese and baked. The border cooking

In New Mexico, enchiladas are more likely to be made with blue or yellow corn tortillas, which are stacked flat like pancakes and layered with a filling of choice (*carne adovada*, chicken, or ground beef). They're topped with either a blazing green chile, sharp-edged red chile, or a "Christmas" chile: red on one side, green on the other ("Red or green?" is the official New Mexico question). It is traditional to top with a fried egg in northern New Mexico if you are eating enchiladas at home; it is, however, a convention that you will find in few New Mexico restaurants.

HOME OF CHILES

Hatch, New Mexico is the famed capital of chile in America, so it's not surprising that in New

Mexico, chile is considered an essential part of any meal, and pops up in just about everything from burgers, pies, and ice cream to beer and mayonnaise. The green chile harvest starting in July, and even earlier in some places, is eagerly awaited by everyone in the Southwest; it is a bona fide cultural event, and you would be well advised to time your visit to coincide with chile season and indulge your senses.

On sale are usually the large specially developed Big Jim chiles from Hatch, a type of Anaheim that ranges between mild, medium, or

tap through the cold winters. Chiles are strung on *ristras*, or strings, and hung to dry on eaves in bright rows until the chiles turn into red pods that can be removed and ground into powder or reconstituted by blending smooth with water. Chimayo chile, grown in Chimayo in northern New Mexico, arrives a little later but is eagerly awaited as it is renowned for its sweet, complex, wine-like flavor.

To get round the heat of chile, be sure to order *sopaipillas* (little deep-fried pastry "pillows") to accompany your meal. Drizzled with honey, *sopaipillas* are a great antidote to chile's heat.

Red chile ristras hanging in the Plaza in Santa Fe.

hot. Be sure to ask and, better yet, sample chile before ordering, as chile varies in heat annually depending on the weather and conditions. Some years it will blow your head off.

Chile roasters set up all around New Mexico and Arizona and roast large sacks of chiles while you wait, manning their booths until the first frost or the chile runs out. The fragrant, vegetal smoke fills the air and is a sure sign that fall is around the corner. The first fresh green chile of the season is anticipated eagerly – warm from the roaster, smelling and tasting delectable. Locals warm tortillas in the pan, grate in some cheese, and add chopped green chile for the best quesadilla ever!

Ziplock bags of chile are placed in the freezer to last until the following year, ensuring chile on

⊙ A RICHTER SCALE FOR CHILES

A process known as liquid chromatography determines capsaicin – the chemical compound that produces the heat levels in chiles, and overall heat is measured in Scoville Heat Units (named after a pharmacist who devised the process). A bell pepper, for example, has 0 Scoville units; a jalapeño can have between 2.500 and 10.000 units. The hottest chile on record? A Red Savina habanero, which sizzled the scales at 577,000 Scovilles. And don't let anyone tell you that color determines heat in chiles: the heat is located in the seeds and in the placenta. The best rule of thumb is the thinner and smaller the pepper, the hotter it will be.

Once common only in New Mexico, *sopaipillas* are now on the menus of Mexican restaurants throughout the Southwest – but if they're not, you'll have to rely on a cold glass of milk or a packet of sugar to quell the fire.

TYPICAL DISHES IN THE SOUTHWEST

Burritos, like the small mules they're named for, carry within their flour tortilla "pack saddle" everything from beans and cheese, meats, and chile to breakfast staples like scrambled eggs, potatoes, sausage, and bacon, and in our

Zacatecas in Albuquerque, owned by Mark Kiffler of Santa Fe's famed The Compound and authentic Mexican to a fault.

Tamales, which consist of fillings inside masa steamed in a corn husk, are a particular treat deriving originally from ancient Aztec Mexico. Now commonly handmade and eaten at Christmas in New Mexico and Arizona, they pop up increasingly on nouveau Southwestern menus in all kinds of creative iterations. In Tucson, you'll find Café Poca Cosa, a restaurant run by Susan Davila that specializes in authen-

Chimichanga, or deep fried burritos.

modern era of "wraps," sandwiches made from rolled tortillas, all kinds of lunch meats, lettuce, tomato, and mayo. In New Mexico, you'll find some excellent breakfast burritos, often homemade, at backroads convenience stores and gas stations, as well as cafés. It's the classic handheld food to start the day.

Tacos are either soft or deep-fried and usually made from corn. They are filled with an amazing number of things, from fresh fish from the Gulf of Mexico to chicken and pork *al pastor* (shepherd style) – even dessert. They have become a popular staple, with numerous restaurants now specializing in serving them, including Taco Fundacion in Santa Fe, the latest venture from well-known restaurateur Brian Knox, and

> *The intense sensation of well-being one experiences when eating hot chiles comes from the release of morphine-like endorphins in the body, resulting in mild euphoria.*

tic Mexico City style tamales, complex mole sauces with many ingredients (including dark chocolate). The true sign of a good Mexican restaurant is fresh, flavorful, healthy food, livened with salsas made from roasted chiles, tomatoes, onions, and other vegetables. The heavy meat and cheese Mexican fare in the US may be popular, but it is far from authentic.

NATIVE CUISINE

Southwest native cuisine highlights fresh ingredients and is rooted in a seasonal, hunter-gatherer way of life that continues to inspire today's Indian chefs.

In Chris Eyre's 1998 film *Smoke Signals* – the first movie about American Indians to be written and directed by tribal members themselves – the mother of one of the two protagonists says to her son, while painfully kneading dough with arthritic hands: "People always tell me I make the best frybread in the world... but I don't make it myself, you know. I got the recipe from your grandmother, and she got it from hers. And I listen to people when they eat my bread."

Food made by the continent's first inhabitants is deliciously earthy and redolent of home and hearth. Usually accompanying a steaming bowl of hominy corn *posole*, green chile stew, or pork or mutton stew, frybread is the perfect utensil to soak up subtly seasoned sauces. In the Four Corners, frybread topped with beans, shredded lettuce, and tomato, meat, cheese, and salsa, is known as a Navajo, or Indian, taco.

As more American Indian chefs receive professional training, work in five-star restaurant kitchens, and head up their own restaurants in tribal casino-resorts and cultural centers, it is becoming increasingly possible to sample well-executed native dishes. Kai, the fine dining restaurant at the Wild Horse Pass Resort on the Gila River Indian reservation in Chandler, Arizona, exclusively sources native foods from reservations all over the United States, as well as supporting local growers on the reservation, including the local school. It wins awards for its elegant, flavorful dishes, showcasing game, wild salmon, locally raised shrimp and greens, berries, and corn. At the Indian Pueblo Cultural Center's onsite restaurant in Albuquerque, visitors can sample a variety of dishes and frybread. The Corn Maiden dinner restaurant at Santa Ana Pueblo's Tamaya Resort along the Rio Grande is famous for its native-inspired meat skewers and plates. And on Arizona's Tohono O'odham reservation, the tribe's cultural center in Sells includes the Desert Rain restaurant, featuring healthy, sustainable vegetarian and vegan Sonoran Desert foods, deliciously prepared.

Some of the more famous and visitor-friendly pueblos, such as Taos Pueblo, have small food stands built inside or outside family dwellings that sell satisfying bowls of *posole* with a side of frybread to adventurous tourists. If you're lucky, you may find

Red chile posole with avocados, cabbage, and lime.

homemade tamales being sold near a pueblo, with the meat fillings spiced with enough red or green chile to send you either to heaven or hell.

Also at Taos and other pueblos are the outdoor *hornos*, or beehive ovens, in which superb bread, cookies, and pies are baked. The round loaves, made and baked as nature sees fit, will remind you of a time when eating bread was a meal in itself. Emerging from these ovens are delectable thin pies with fillings of spiced pumpkin or fruit. Another way to sample pueblo foods is to attend the annual Santa Fe Indian Market in August, when stands on the Plaza sell everything from roast corn to frybread.

In Window Rock, Arizona – the tribal capital of the Navajo Nation – there's a good restaurant inside the Navajo-owned hotel where you can feast on lamb stews and posoles and other typical dishes. Don't refuse an invitation to dine in a pueblo home during one of the feast days open to the public. It will be an unforgettable culinary journey into the heart of a people where tradition has, thankfully, managed to transcend fast food culture.

The yellow flowers of the barrel cactus at Arizona-Sonora Desert Museum, Tucson.

FLORA AND FAUNA

The deserts of the Southwest demand that all who dwell there be perfectly adapted. The resulting ingenuity is fascinating.

Diverse though it is, all life in the Southwest is shaped by aridity. This is primarily a rain-shadow region of dry desert basins trapped between high peaks and plateaus, which capture what little Pacific storm moisture makes it over the 14,000-ft (4,300-meter) barrier of California's Sierra Nevada. Rain is much prayed for and received with thanks when it falls. It's no exaggeration to say that locating water, trying to hold onto it, and adapting to life without it are the main preoccupations of life.

Human squabbles over water rights are legendary, but when the going gets tough people can always leave. That's an option for birds and larger predators like mountain lions and coyotes which, although less visible, travel long distances to find water and prey and call most of the Southwest home. But those with smaller home ranges and specialized niches have to find other solutions.

ADAPTIVE LIFE

"The desert, the dry and sun-lashed desert, is a good school in which to observe the cleverness and the infinite variety of techniques of survival under pitiless opposition," wrote John Steinbeck in *Travels with Charley*. "Life could not change the sun or water the desert, so it changed itself."

And how! The most successful desert plant, cacti, take advantage of infrequent but hard rains by employing extensive root networks and conserving water in expandable, gelatinous tissues. Waxy trunks and paddles protected by spines are used for photosynthesis instead of leaves. The cacti lure moth and bat pollinators with bright flowers and produce tasty autumn fruits that are eaten and disseminated by many animals, from piglike Sonoran Desert javelinas

Plants in the desert, Monument Valley.

to humans. Some trees and shrubs shed their leaves and virtually shut down to conserve water; others close up or tilt fleshy, waxy leaves to keep cool. Most delightful of all are wildflowers, many of which bloom only if summer or early winter rain has been adequate, putting on wave after wave of brilliant Impressionistic color, starting in April in the low deserts and May and June at higher elevations.

The desert seems quiet in the daytime because three-quarters of animals are nocturnal. Take a walk at dusk or dawn to a local water hole if you want to glimpse coyotes, kit foxes, raccoons, bobcats, badgers, perhaps even a rare bighorn sheep. During the day, look skyward to see red-tailed hawks, golden eagles, peregrine falcons, and ravens patrolling the skies from cliff aeries in search of unsuspecting cottontails or ground squirrels in the bushes below. Smaller birds, such as tits, finches, vireos, tanagers, and a variety of hummingbirds, flock in huge numbers to riparian zones in sheltered canyons, with many Mexican species fraternizing with American cousins along US-Mexico borderlands.

Reptiles keep their body temperature down beneath bushes and rocks, becoming active on trails at twilight and leaving strange slither marks and delicate tracks in sandy soil.

Sonoran gila monster.

⊘ LOOK, BUT DON'T TOUCH

Venomous creatures are plentiful in the desert, but use venom only to immobilize prey and aid in digestion or to defend themselves. In fearsome-looking scorpions, size does not relate to potency. The giant desert hairy scorpion, more than 5 inches (13cm), long, is less poisonous than the inch-long bark scorpion, whose sting can be deadly. Gila monsters are rarely seen, move slowly, and will not bite unless they are cornered or picked up. In addition to rattlesnakes, coral and other snakes, poisonous desert dwellers include an 8-inch-long (20-cm) centipede, black widow and brown recluse spiders, cone nose bugs, tarantulas, ants, and wasps.

Collared lizards, whiptails, and chuckwallas are often seen, along with the huge and colorful Sonoran Gila monster, North America's only venomous lizard. Spadefoot toads simply bide their time, waiting in the bottom of dried-up potholes, or *tinajas*, for the drumbeat of rainfall to signal spawning time. Some animals, such as kangaroo rats and spadefoot toads, have lost the need to drink water at all, recycling it instead from seeds. The desert is certainly not short of miracles.

DESERTS

Not one but four types of desert are found here – the Chihuahuan, the Sonoran, the Mojave, and the Great Basin – with all four converging in Arizona, making the Grand Canyon State the most biologically rich of all desert Southwest states. Each desert has its own distinctive personality. The Chihuahuan Desert, two-thirds of which is in Mexico, stretches north as far as Albuquerque, New Mexico, and into parts of southeastern Arizona. At a mean 3,500–5,000ft (1,000–1,500 meters), it is quite high and has relatively long, chilly winters, with occasional snowfalls that disappear as quickly as they came. Summer temperatures often reach into the l00s Fahrenheit (upper 30s–40s Celsius), but are cooled by short, violent thunderstorms, which drop most of the 8–12ins (20–30cm) of annual rainfall for the area.

In Permian times, some 250 million years ago, this area lay under a warm, shallow sea, leaving a legacy of limestone and large cave systems such as those seen at Carlsbad, New Mexico, and Kartchner Caverns in southeastern Arizona. Carlsbad is famous for the half-million breeding Mexican free-tailed bats that summer just inside the entrance to the Natural Cave entrance and exit nightly to feed on cactus nectar that will, in the thrifty natural economy of the desert, also pollinate their cactus hosts for another season. Cactus such as prickly pear and cholla do well in these calcium-rich soils, along with creosote bush and grasses. Agaves such as lechuguilla are common and have tall, thick spikes rising from a rosette of fleshy, swordlike "leaves." Yuccas have been particularly useful to desert people, who use the roots for shampoo, the fibers for clothing, and the autumn fruits as a starchy food.

Another evaporite, gypsum, is washed out of surrounding highlands into the basins, where it is picked up by winds and built into dunes such as those seen at White Sands in the Tularosa Basin. Although they look bare, the dunes do support life. Plants like the soap tree yucca stabilize the dunes, growing fast enough and having long enough roots to avoid being buried. Fringe-toed lizards and western diamondback and desert massasauga rattlesnakes live here, along with the more ubiquitous coyote and cottontail, hunter and prey, which find ways to thrive in a variety of settings. Birds travel easily between mountains and dunes, with finches, doves, thrashers, and shrikes giving up the night skies to nighthawks and owls whose eerie hoots float across the dunes like strange echoes.

The Sonoran Desert, next door in Arizona, is relatively young, at only 10,000 years old, and spans the 3,000-ft (900-meter) lowlands and basins that start just north of Phoenix into Mexico. By a quirk of positioning, the Sonoran receives moisture twice a year from summer "monsoons," as they are known, and winter

Western coachwhip snake near Cerrillos Hills State Park.

⊙ WONDERFUL WETLANDS

Spring runoff promotes a last call to action for wildflowers in high altitude national parks and monuments like Cedar Breaks in Southern Utah, a veritable Monet painting of brightly splashed blooms roused from snowy sleep in early June, along with hibernating bears, pikas, and marmots. Townsend's nutcrackers make fast work of seeds as the season rolls on. Rushing mountain streams spilling to lowlands slow gradually to a trickle and ice up in places as winter arrives. Lack of rainfall and aggressive damming of major watercourses mean that many smaller southwestern rivers are dry arroyos for much of the year, flooded by seasonal runoff. But where mighty rivers such as the Colorado and the Rio

Grande run, they form green riparian corridors of cottonwood, boxelder, willow, exotic tamarisk, and other water-lovers that provide a respite from the heat and a habitat for many species. Deep, protected canyons offer cool, moist microclimates in which a Douglas fir might grow across from a prickly pear cactus. Groundwater here percolates through sandstone, attracting brightly colored monkeyflower, columbine, shooting stars, maidenhair fern, and other moisture-loving plants to form luxuriant hanging gardens in unexpected places. Also glorious is the song of the canyon wren: often heard, rarely glimpsed, and truly the top of the hit parade of southwestern crooners.

storms, making it by far the greenest of the deserts. Tough customers like mesquite, creosote bush, and blackbrush do well here, but most enchanting are the flame-tipped wandlike ocotillo, the green-barked palo verde with its rain of golden blossoms, and more than a hundred different kind of cactus, including organ pipe, cholla, prickly pear, beaver tail, pincushion, claret cup, hedgehog, and the most recognizable cactus in the world: the many-limbed saguaro.

Symbols of the Sonoran, saguaros are record-breakers in almost every way. They favor warm,

The Mojave is the hottest and most monotone of all the deserts in summer, but with the addition of a small amount of rainfall in winter it is transformed in early spring with stunning wildflower blooms. Some years there are "superblooms," something no one should miss.

Vegetation such as ironwood, desert holly, blackbrush, creosote, and bursage distributes itself to make the most of available moisture, with the indicator species the shaggy Joshua tree, a variety of yucca. In the Kofa Mountains southwest of Phoenix, relict palm trees have

Yellow palo verde trees and young saguaro cactus in the Sonoran Desert.

south-facing alluvial slopes, or *bajadas*, such as those found around Tucson and often get their start in the shelter of palo verde "nurse" trees. In spring, they sprout large, creamy topknots of blossoms to attract pollinating bats and moths, which, if they do their stuff, allow the saguaro to produce bright, globular fruits in late summer. Large cacti like the saguaro and the organ pipe (found in the Sonoran Desert) also provide nesting sites for birds such as elf owls and Harris hawks. Watch for Gambel quail at water holes and the road runner – state bird and cuckoo relative – along roads. The Mojave Desert is mainly found in California, extreme southwestern Utah, and Nevada but extends into the central and northern portions of Arizona.

⊘ WONDROUS CACTI

Though not indestructible, cacti can put up with almost anything except too little or too much water. Because cacti, like most plants, use sunlight to make energy, they thrive in the desert sun. And, like all plants, they "breathe" by opening their pores to exhale excess oxygen and inhale carbon dioxide to be used in photosynthesis. Cacti conserve moisture by holding their breath during daytime heat and opening their pores to exhale at night, when desert temperatures fall dramatically. This peculiar method of photosynthesis causes cacti to grow slowly, and while it enables adult plants to survive, seedlings need a series of wet summers to become established.

found a niche in a protected canyon along with a healthy number of endangered bighorn sheep, which are protected here and in Cabeza Prieta Preserve, farther south. Also endangered are desert tortoises, found between St George in southwest Utah and Las Vegas, Nevada, and heavily impacted by development and recreational use of their habitat.

The fourth desert type, the Great Basin, is found in the far northwest corner of Arizona and covers a far larger area than the others, extending all the way to eastern Utah and Oregon. At

> Some saguaros reach 150 years of age and beyond; they don't even begin sprouting their famous arms until they hit 75 – and then only if conditions are right.

elevations of 4,000ft (1,200 meters) and above, this is a cooler desert, once dominated by a mixture of lush native grasses that have been heavily grazed over the last century and crowded out by cheatgrass and vast quantities of sagebrush, saltbush, snakeweed, rabbitbrush, and other disturbance species.

THE SKY ISLANDS

The Southwest desert is by no means flat, although most newcomers think it is. In fact, elevations range from about 1,000ft (300 meters) to higher than 12,000ft (3,600 meters) atop the highest peaks, dubbed "sky islands" because, in the heat haze, they seem to float up from the lower deserts. The mountains of southern Arizona and New Mexico and western Utah and Nevada have been thrust up in typical basin-and-range fashion relatively recently, their craggy faces now softened by mixed evergreen-deciduous forests. In the sheltered canyons of the Mountains, on the Arizona–New Mexico–Mexico boundary, Arizona cypress and alligator juniper mingle with Mexican natives such as Mexican Chihuahua and Apache pine while at higher elevations, lush forests of Douglas fir, aspen, and ponderosa pine provide browse for white-tailed deer and cover for sulphur-bellied flycatchers, Mexican chickadees, and the elegant trogon – found on every birder's list.

The low basins between the mountains – what most of us think of as desert – are a tougher row to hoe for most desert dwellers. They are so hot that runoff evaporates, leaving behind dry salt flats, or *playas*, that attract only saltbush, iodine bush, pickleweed, and other salt-tolerant species. These lowlands often come into their own in winter, when they are flooded by rains and the resulting wetlands attract migratory fowl like sandhill cranes. Equally unpromising are the sprawling, angry-looking lava flows, some as young as only 1,000 years, that absorb

Meep meep! A roadrunner on its way.

the heat and reflect it into places like the Tularosa Basin's Jornada del Muerto. It may take a hundred years for a few hardy plants to colonize these flows – perhaps a thousand for anything substantial to grow. Ancient Jornada Mogollon people used the basalts as blank slates for remarkable petroglyphs, but like earlier Spanish travelers, today's visitors mostly hurry through, bound for the cooler climes of the high country.

THE COLORADO PLATEAU

Forming a distinct geologic province to the north is the Colorado Plateau, which covers 130,000 sq miles (337,000 sq km) of Arizona, New Mexico, Utah, and Colorado. The Colorado Plateau is a mile (1.6km) high and rising, a largely sedimentary monolith that was squeezed up beginning in the mid-Cretaceous period. It has been locally uplifted by volcanic forces into peaks, plateaus, and mesas and spectacularly eroded by the Colorado River and its tributaries.

Large, cheek-by-jowl elevation differences are particularly obvious in and around the Grand Canyon, which drops from 8,200ft (2,500 meters) at the North Rim to 1,300ft (400 meters) at the Colorado River. Along with these elevation changes are changes in plant types, from desert to montane. This piqued the interest of a young eastern naturalist called C. Hart Merriam, making studies in northern Arizona in 1889. In just 60 miles (100km), Merriam noted, one passed through landscapes more usually seen on a trip from Mexico to the Canadian Arctic. Merriam dubbed these Southwest zones: Lower Sonoran 2,000–5,000ft (600–1,500 meters), or desert scrub; Upper Sonoran 5,000–7,000ft (1,500–2,000 meters), or pinyon pine-juniper forest; Transition 7,000–8,000ft (2,000–2,400 meters), or ponderosa pine forest; Canadian 8,000–10,000ft

Elk feed near roadside in pine forest by the Grand Canyon.

☉ NATURE'S PAINT

Of the natural phenomena of the Southwest, among the loveliest are the dark curtains of desert varnish that stream down canyon walls and settle on desert boulders. Research shows this to be a biogeochemical process: colonies of bacteria living on the rock surface absorb manganese and iron from the atmosphere. In a process that takes thousands of years, the bacteria and minerals, along with clay particles form a one-hundredth-of-a-millimeter-thick coating. When manganese is dominant, the varnish is black; iron results in rusty red. When scientists find stone tools that have become covered with desert varnish, they know that they are ancient indeed.

(2,400–3,000 meters), or sub-alpine spruce-firaspen forest, and Hudsonian 10,000–12,000ft (3,000–3,600 meters), alpine to treeline.

Modern scientists have expanded on Merriam's ideas, now recognizing that slope angle, soil type, exposure to sun and wind, moisture, and other variables all contribute to local microclimates.

Great Basin-style vegetation extends onto the Colorado Plateau, covering large tracts of the Navajo Nation and providing enough rangeland for ranching to remain a popular lifestyle. Starting around 6,000 feet (1,800 meters) is the pinyon-juniper forest. Useful in a multitude of ways – for nuts, berries, firewood, posts, even insulating material – "P-J" is the friendliest of dwarf forests to camp under, offering views of the stars at night and adequate shelter at noon. Cedar gnats, or "no-see-ums," appear when temperatures warm up. Watch out. They give a mean bite.

FOREST INHABITANTS

At about 7,000 feet (2,000 meters), P-J gives way to ponderosa pine forest, which reaches its greatest density around Flagstaff. Sheltered against the cinnamon-smelling, platey trunks of ponderosa are stands of Gambel oak and

Watch for explosions of bluebells, lupines, columbines, Indian paintbrushes, gentians, primroses, penstemons, woolly mullein, and numerous asters and sunflowers. Above 8,000ft (2,400 meters), pioneer deciduous species like quaking aspen take over subalpine meadows in silvery profusion, but they will eventually be overshadowed by spruce, fir, and at higher elevations, lodgepole, limber, Jeffrey, and very occasionally bristlecone pines, the world's oldest tree, often reaching ages of 3,000 to 4,000 years.

Ponderosa pines in a meadow, Coconino National Forest, Arizona.

toothy maples that flare red and bronze in the dying days of fall. Mule deer are often seen here, twitching long ears and jumping away skittishly. The forest is often noisy with disputing Steller's jays and tassel-eared squirrels.

The native Abert squirrel is an interesting link in the ecosystem of the ponderosa forest. It lives on ponderosa pine cones and scrabbles among the roots of the ponderosa for fungi. The Abert's cousin, the Kaibab squirrel, lives only on the North Rim of the Grand Canyon and looks slightly different, having been separated in the past 6 million years by the great chasm of the canyon.

Snow is not uncommon in June on the plateau, so wildflowers are late bloomers here.

⊘ DELIGHTS OF THE FOREST

The pinyon-juniper forest (PJ) contains a gustatory treasure: the delectable pine nut. Birds and animals put it to good use, as do people. American Indians traditionally depended upon caches of nuts to see them through the lean winter months, and many tribal members still take time to gather nuts, which ripen in the fall. This is also true for traditional Hispanic residents of northern New Mexico who make gathering pinyon nuts a family social event each fall. Though corn is the "staff of life" for many southwesterners, pinyon nut protein is higher in amino acids essential for human growth. Gathering and shelling are labor-intensive, but the reward is in the taste.

New Mexico Museum of Art,
Santa Fe.

The goosenecks of the San Juan
River from Mulley Point.

Route 66 diner lit by neon at sunset, Albuquerque.

INTRODUCTION

A detailed guide to the entire region, with principal sites clearly cross-referenced by numbers on the maps.

Cacti and palm trees, Tucson.

The Southwest is an arid land of endless horizons and big skies, full-bore sunlight and lush riparian canyons, ancient dwellings and modern western cities. The traveler rushing from national park to natural spectacle can easily miss its secret treasures.

The Grand Canyon – Arizona's top attraction – is on everyone's bucket list, for example, but close by are Utah parks like Bryce Canyon and Zion, as spectacular as the Big Ditch but smaller, wilder, and awaiting discovery.

This Indian Country is home to the Navajo, Apache, and other tribes. The Hopi mesas of Arizona and the 19 Indian pueblos surrounding Albuquerque, Santa Fe, and Taos are Pueblo Country, but more besides. New Mexico awaits those who love history and culture, arts and nature. Explore Spanish Colonial church and adobe architecture and Indian and Hispanic arts and crafts in galleries and plazas, pueblos and villages. Become addicted to the best chile in the world.

Heading to a vortex site at Sedona.

Eastern and southern New Mexico, where Texas and Mexico meet the Land of Enchantment, offer sweeping western vistas, "sky island" mountains, and grassy plains, historic ranches and artsy old mining towns. The Border Country of Southern Arizona, La Frontera, is where American and Mexican cultures mingle. Here you'll find unique Sonoran Desert flora and fauna and Tucson, a city with easy Mexican charm, as well as award-winning wineries and superb bird-watching.

Phoenix is undergoing a surprising cultural renaissance of food, architecture, and arts, but its mountains lure outdoors lovers to dude ranches, preserves, and Apache lands. Neon-lit Las Vegas offers easy access to Grand Canyon West on the Hualapai Reservation, Lake Mead, and the Mojave Desert, but its main claim to fame is its big-name entertainment, luxury hotel-casinos, and fine dining.

Get ready for a special insider's tour, but expect to have an adventure. The Southwest is a place where dreams still trump reality.

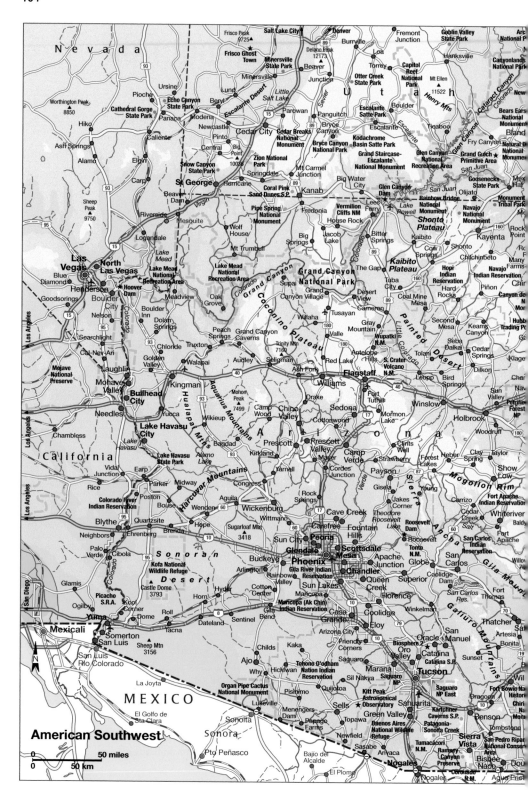

American Southwest

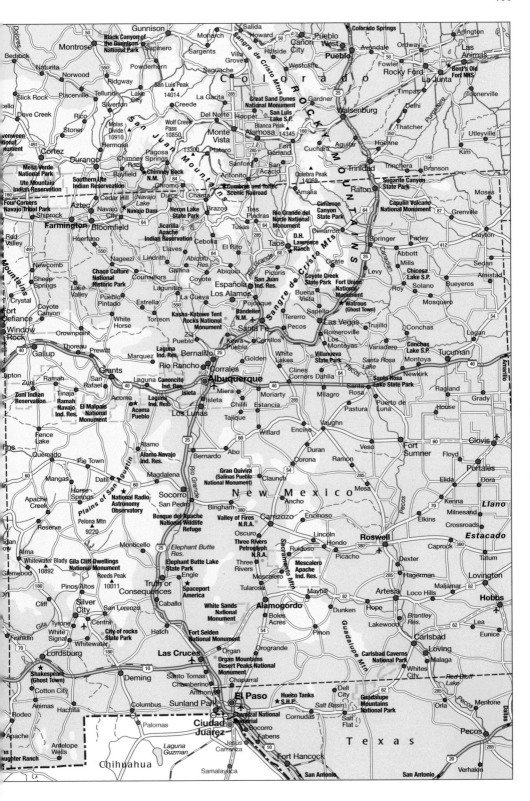

Senora desert near Rancho de
Los Caballeros.

THE BORDER

From stunning national parks and monuments, to mown lawns and skyscrapers, the Border region has it all.

Rider near Wickenburg.

People have made homes here for at least 2,500 years – the ancient Hohokam (who mastered the use of canals to bring water to their fields), the O'odham, and the Apache. The Spanish entered the region in the mid-1500s, and Jesuits established missions, ceding to Mexico in the early 1800s.

With American rule in the second half of the 1800s came miners, ranchers, and outlaws whose Western image is etched upon the silver screen. Snowbirds arrive each winter in droves, escaping colder climes.

The region is abundant in national and state parks, attractive ambassadors of the natural and cultural histories of a land that is beautiful but, in reality, harsh. Low levels of pollution make the border country a good place for astronomical observatories, and the Very Large Array Telescope of the National Radio Astronomy Observatory in New Mexico stands poised to receive communications from outer space. The wide-open spaces are also perfect for aircraft and weapons research and development. White Sands Missile Range occupies 3,200 sq miles (8,300 sq km) of southern New Mexico's Chihuahuan Desert.

Radio telescopes in New Mexico.

Phoenix, Arizona's bustling capital, may be in the Sonoran Desert but its golf courses, resorts, and Spanish-style homes luxuriate in lush green lawns and fountains – now fed by recycled water. Phoenix has now reduced its environmental footprint and expanded light rail and buses, walkable downtown boulevards, museums, farmers markets, and farm-to-table restaurants, and is now an attractive cultural destination. Tucson is catching up to Phoenix sprawl, but remains more northern Sonoran than southern Arizonan. It too has developed a light rail linking the east and west historic quarters and boosted cultural offerings, including a burgeoning nearby Wine Country.

Architectural jewels, from Spanish Colonial missions to organic architecture by Frank Lloyd Wright and Paolo Soleri, blend into the desert. Rustic frontier buildings and Victorian houses gracing Bisbee and other former mining towns are now popular art towns, escaping the fate of other ghost towns crumbling in the sun.

Golfing at at Phoenician Resort, Scottsdale.

PHOENIX

In summer, the dry heat of Phoenix can purge the mind of lucidity. But air conditioning and golf courses have made the Phoenix area one of America's fastest-growing metropolitan areas.

When Frank Lloyd Wright first saw the Salt River Valley in the late 1920s, it struck him as a "vast battleground of Titanic natural forces." Like a revelation to Wright were its "leopard spotted mountains... its great striated and stratified masses, noble and quiet," its patterns modeled on the "realism of the rattlesnake." Here, thought Wright, with the zeal of someone moving in, if Arizonans could avoid the "candymakers and cactus-hunters," a proper civilization could be created that would "allow man to become a godlike native part of Arizona."

Wright's architectural work in Arizona sought that lofty aim, though it has hardly happened. But aggressive irrigation – which has been in use both in ancient and modern times in this area – and air conditioning have nurtured a metro area of nearly 4.3 million people, with **Phoenix ❶** itself now ranking as America's fifth-largest city (and fastest-growing one), with a population of 1,615,017.

While the Valley of the Sun is still a sprawling metro area, linked by freeways and dependent on cars, it has recently taken major steps to refurbish its wasteful image. The communities in the valley are now linked by the 57-mile (92km) Metro Light Rail, which has been so successful, an extension is planned. As more young high tech

workers move to Phoenix – many from California's environmentally conscious Bay Area – green building, solar power, conservation, recycling, and all things locavore have been enthusiastically taken up. Phoenix's downtown has undergone a cultural renaissance, and it has now become hip to live and work in the urban core.

A citywide conservation education program has reduced water usage by 20 percent in the past 20 years. Today, Phoenix uses just 3 percent groundwater from its aquifer – down

⦿ Main Attractions
Arizona Science Center
Phoenix Art Museum
Heard Museum
Pueblo Grande
  Archaeological Museum
Desert Botanical Garden
Western Spirit:
  Scottsdale's Museum of
  the West
Musical Instrument
  Museum
Taliesin West

**Maps on pages
160, 184**

Robson House in Historic Heritage Square.

from a high of 35 percent in the 1980s; moreover, 90 percent of water greening its 200-plus golf courses, irrigating crops, and used in its award-winning riparian habitat restoration projects is reclaimed. Drought-tolerant xeriscaping and water catchment devices are, finally, the height of fashion.

PHOENIX'S HISTORY

As early as 500 BC, the Hohokam culture developed an intricate system of canals for irrigating fields of corn, beans, squash, and cotton. Remains of that ancient system were absorbed and expanded in 1868 by the Swilling Irrigation Canal Co, the first Anglo organization to stake claims in the long-deserted valley. The following year, their settlement was named Phoenix by an Englishman who saw a new civilization rising like the mythical bird from the ashes of the vanished Hohokam.

What rose from the ashes was an aggressive ranching community that catered to miners and military outposts. Canals were extended through the alluvial valley, watering fields of cotton and alfalfa, pastures for cattle, and rows of citrus to the horizon's edge. Water storage commenced on a grand scale with the construction, in 1911, of Roosevelt Dam, still the world's largest masonry dam, on the Salt River some 90 miles (145km) upstream from Phoenix. Three more dams on the Salt, and two on its major tributary, the Verde, allowed agriculturalists to send water where they liked. The Salt River became the driest place in the region.

Residents with long memories recall the 1930s as a Phoenician golden age. Those who couldn't afford the Arizona Biltmore found it too snobbish anyway and frequented the lively downtown, which still retained its Spanish-American flavor. In summer, when daytime temperatures spike to the 120s°F (50s°C) and stay above 100°F for months, locals complained less of the heat than they boasted of tricks to stay cool. It was common sport to be pulled on an aquaplane along the canals, holding a rope from a car.

Phoenix was transformed forever by World War II. The open desert was ideal

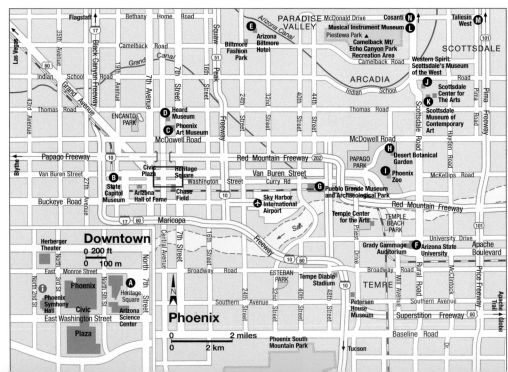

for aviation training, and much of Phoenix became something of an extension of nearby Luke Air Force Base. Aviation equipment companies moved into the valley, and even the cotton fields turned out silk for parachutes. It is less known that Phoenix had internment camps for German prisoners of war, and many of the prisoners, as susceptible to the desert's allure as anyone else, remained in the area after the war to become a part of the community.

The military revolutionized Phoenician life with a device called air conditioning. The city had previously seen minor use of the evaporative or "swamp" cooler, but now there was genuine refrigeration. Suddenly, Phoenix was a year-round possibility for those who couldn't stand the heat. The great migration was on. Camelback Mountain, at whose feet lay the most elegant dude ranches, was engulfed by suburbia. To the east, greater Phoenix swallowed up the once isolated communities of Scottsdale, Tempe, Mesa, and Apache Junction. Golf courses replaced dude ranches, and resort hotels sprouted like desert grass after a thunderstorm.

The stereotypical newcomer was once the snowbelt retiree, living in rule-bound planned communities of upscale houses such as Sun City or proletarian acres of mobile homes. That's no longer the case. The recent influx of career-oriented young people working for tech start-ups has so altered the population that the average resident within city limits, contrary to popular belief, is younger than the national average. With them has come a push for a more cohesive community, sustainable lifestyles, better urban infrastructure, and cultural offerings on a par with any major American city.

DOWNTOWN PHOENIX

The geographical setting of Phoenix is impressive, especially when the air is not veiled with smog. To the east soar the massive Four Peaks and the formal flank of the Superstition Mountains, while the Sierra Estrella, sacred to the Gila and Salt River Indian tribes, rides the southwest horizon in dorsales of blue silk. Hemming in the city north and south are young mountains of Precambrian gneiss and schist, framing the Phoenix trademark of Camelback Mountain – a freestanding, rosy, recumbent dromedary with a sedimentary head and granitic hump.

Like many young American cities, Phoenix has in the past lacked a strong local character or personality. That is rapidly changing. The improvement in downtown's infrastructure has made a real difference – from the construction of European-style light rail and attractively landscaped boulevards, city parks, community gardens, and farmers markets to the expansion of popular museums like the Heard and the Phoenix Art Museum. Downtown's Central Avenue has changed from anonymous high-rise glass buildings used only by office workers during the week to a vibrant place with a street scene, complete with new live-work spaces, residential towers,

Downtown Phoenix at sunset.

and gentrified adjoining areas like the Barrio, where hot new Mexican restaurants lure foodies and have brought back a needed Mexican influence.

Heritage Square Ⓐ (tel: 602-262-5070; www.heritagesquarephx.org; Wed–Sat 10am–4pm, Sun noon–4pm; free), a block east of the **Civic Plaza**, is what remains of this city's Victorian heritage and is part of downtown's **Heritage and Science Park**. Most striking of Heritage Square's 11 buildings – some of them, like the Lath House Pavilion, quite modern – is the **Rosson House** (tel 602-262-5070; http://heritagesquare phx.org/visit/the-rosen-house; Wed–Sat 10am–4pm, Sun noon–4pm, last tour one hour before closing, closed most public holidays; charge), built in 1895 and once one of the most prominent homes in Phoenix. Some of the other houses here, dating from the early 1900s, were moved from other locations to save them from demolition.

Also part of downtown's Copper Square and Heritage and Science Park is the **Arizona Science Center** (tel: 602-716-2000; www.azscience.org; daily 10am–5pm; charge), housed in a beautiful $50 million building designed by famed New Mexico architect Antoine Predock. Heritage Square is easily reached by the Valley Metro Rail Line, which stops here.

Several multi-million-dollar expansions have created a funhouse of hands-on science. The center has 300 exhibits in five themed galleries on four floors, where kids can explore the inside of a human body, understand networks and the digital world, learn how to create animation, experiment with solar power, and otherwise be "blinded by science." An immersion theater offers a thrilling virtual experience of different weather conditions and a flight simulator in an exhibit on aviation. Arizona's dominance as a center for astronomy is highlighted in the state-of-the-art planetarium, and an IMAX theater is a hit with kids.

Arizona's modest state capitol building is located 1.5 miles (2.5km) west of downtown, on Washington Street. The **Arizona State Capitol Museum** Ⓑ (tel. 602-926-3620; www.azlibrary.gov; Mon–Fri 9am–4pm, Sat 10am–2pm, Sept–May; free) uncovers some of the building's secrets. The capitol was constructed in 1899 to house the territorial government; in 1976, its dome was covered with 15 tons of copper donated by the state' mining interests. Atop the dome is Winged Victory, a quarter-ton statue dating from 1899 that turns with the wind. Much of today's governing is done in adjacent modern structures, but the restored Senate and House of Representatives chambers are open to visitors. Furnishings and ornamentation throughout the building date from 1912, when Arizona became a state.

MAJOR MUSEUMS

The largest art museum in the Southwest, the sophisticated **Phoenix Art Museum** Ⓒ (tel: 602-257-1880; www.phx art.org; Tue–Sat 10am–5pm, Wed until 9pm, first Fri until 10pm, Sun noon–5pm; charge), is located at Central Avenue and

Interactive exhibits at the Arizona Science Center.

McDowell Road, 1 mile (1.6km) north of Heritage Park, and easily reached by Valley Metro Light Rail (McDowell and Central station). In addition to hosting other major international exhibitions, the museum displays some 18,000 individual artworks by American and Asian artists, Southwest painters from the Taos Society of Artists, and recent Mexican artworks. Art of the American West includes works by Thomas Moran and Frederick Remington. There is an attractive sculpture garden, and the popular Palette restaurant offers casual American dining, featuring organic local produce from Phoenix farmers.

The nearby **Heard Museum** **D** (tel: 602-252 8848; www.heard.org; Mon–Sat 9.30am–5pm, Sun noon–5pm; charge) is one of the must-sees in Arizona, even for those travelers who are not particularly enamored of museums. It was founded in 1929 to house the Heard family's collection of American Indian art and artifacts, and it was – and is – an exceptional collection. Several huge expansions since 1999 have enhanced the visitor experience. The museum now occupies 13,000 sq ft (1,208 sq meters) with 11 galleries, and is a major presence on Central Avenue, a few blocks north of the Phoenix Art Museum. Aside from its famed museum store, which sells authentic Indian art of the highest caliber, it has a bookstore, a courtyard restaurant and coffee bar, and the Nichols Sculpture Garden.

The museum's signature exhibit, *Home: Native People in the Southwest*, is immediately to your right as you enter the museum. It tells the story of Arizona's Indian tribes, then and now, through multimedia, and includes 250 historic kachina dolls from the famous Barry Goldwater Collection. This is a very handsome exhibit room, which features blond bentwood exhibit cases that give the space a feeling of light and space. The central Crossroads Gallery and adjoining Sandra Day O'Connor Gallery display recent acquisitions from the Heard Museum Collection. To the left is the other permanent signature exhibit, *We Are! Arizona's First People*, in the Ullman Learning Center. Other permanent exhibits are located in the Lovena Ohl

Heard Museum.

Gallery and the Freeman Gallery on
the second floor and the Jack Steele
Parker Gallery on the upper level. Also
on the upper level is the East Gallery,
which has a moving permanent exhibit
on Indian boarding schools and pottery.

Phoenix feels positively European as
sidewalk cafés, such as the Courtyard
Café at the Heard Museum, take advantage of the warm weather and Spanish courtyard ambiance and more and
more visitors choose to ride the Valley
Metro Light Rail, which runs down the
center median of Central and along
nearby Camelback and McDowell.
Just east of Central Avenue, on 16th
Avenue, in the increasingly popular
and vibrant Barrio district, are some of
Phoenix's new wave of top-rated and
innovative Mexican restaurants for a
easy bite at the end of the day.

WRIGHT'S INFLUENCE

A great monument to another period
is the **Arizona Biltmore Hotel ❺** (tel:
602-955-6600; www.arizonbiltmore.com), 5
miles (8km) northeast of downtown and
Heritage Park. With a slack economy to

begin with, Phoenix hardly noticed the
Great Depression of the early 1930s, living off its own agriculture and catering
in fine style to those tourists who managed to hold onto their money. Built just
before the financial crash of 1929, the
Biltmore sailed in splendor through the
bleakest of times. It is to the Biltmore
that Phoenix owes the arrival of Frank
Lloyd Wright. The hotel was originally
designed by Albert Chase McArthur, a
former student of Wright, who found
himself in trouble and summoned the
master for help. Wright came, and then
stayed to create his home and architectural school in the organic architectural
style that was his hallmark at Taliesin
West in Scottsdale.

Wright probably gave more help than
required, for the result was a masterpiece of textile block construction from
Wright's middle period and is a delight
for the eye – geometrically tidy, quietly
whimsical, and aesthetically inspiring.
Gutted by fire in 1973, the interior was
refurnished with furniture and textile
designs from all periods of Wright's
career, overseen by Wright's widow

*The lobby of the
Arizona Biltmore.*

and the Taliesin West school. The visitor who enters no other building in Phoenix should make it to 24th Street and Missouri to inspect the Arizona Biltmore.

In the city of Tempe, part of the greater metropolitan area of Phoenix, is home to **Arizona State University** Ⓕ. This vibrant university community anchors the south side of Phoenix, with its lively downtown and postmodern buildings along the partially reclaimed Salt River. Of these, don't miss the beautifully designed **Tempe Center for the Arts**, a state-of-the-art community center housing two theaters, an art gallery, a restaurant with a view of Tempe Town Lake, an artificial lake impounded from the Salt River, and adjoining river walk and sculpture garden. The university campus is home to **ASU Gammage Auditorium**, also designed by Frank Lloyd Wright and renowned for its acoustics, and **Tempe Diablo Stadium**, used as a base for spring training by the Angels baseball team.

PUEBLO GRANDE

Pueblo Grande Museum and Archaeological Park Ⓖ (tel: 602-495 0901; www.phoenix.gov/parks/arts-culture-history/pueblo-grande; Mon–Sat 9am–4.45pm, Sun 1–4.45pm, closed Sun and Mon May–Sept) is located just outside downtown Phoenix, next to Sky Harbor International Airport. It is a confounding juxtaposition, but this ancient Hohokam pueblo site is worth a look. A wheelchair-accessible trail, just over half a mile long, encircles the ruins and has numerous, well-written interpretive displays. The visitor center has a museum displaying artifacts from the Hohokam culture and this pueblo site and a film about the Hohokam. It is the main location in Phoenix where you can find out more about the Valley of the Sun's first culture.

The Hohokam lived in southern Arizona until around AD 1450. Experts at cultivation, the Hohokam developed a complex system of irrigation canals extending hundreds of miles, some of which remain today. Archaeologists conjecture that drought, internal conflicts, and salinization of farmland from over-irrigation may have contributed to the abandonment of the Salt River Valley in the 1400s.

The Pueblo Grande mound is actually two smaller mounds dating from around AD 1150. Less than 200 years later, the two mounds were combined into a mound the size of a football field and about 30ft (9 meters) high. The public buildings constructed on top were probably used for ceremonial purposes. Immediately north of the mound, accessible by a walkway, is an excavated ball court similar to those found at ancient Mayan sites in Mexico.

BEYOND DOWNTOWN

East of downtown, increasingly surrounded by greater metropolitan Phoenix, is the **Desert Botanical Garden** Ⓗ (1201 N Galvin Parkway; tel: 480-941-1225; www.dbg.org; daily 7am–8pm; charge), is located on 50 acres (20 hectares) within Papago Park. It is home to

⊘ FRANK LLOYD WRIGHT

When Frank Lloyd Wright (1869–1959) was in his 60s, and at an age when other men are retiring, he was designing buildings that continued to revolutionize architecture, dismissing the stagnation found in much architectural design. Indeed, the older he got, the more innovative and revolutionary his designs became. His Guggenheim Museum in New York City, for example, was completed in 1959, the year he died aged 90. From his earliest days as an architectural student in the Chicago area in the 1890s, Wright remained true to his philosophy of "organic architecture," in which a building should rise from the nature of its natural surroundings.

"We must recognize the creative architect as poet and interpreter of life," he wrote. "This enrichment of life is the cause of architecture, as I see it," Wrote Lewis Mumford in 1929. "Wright has embodied in his work two qualities which will never permanently leave it – a sense of place and a rich feeling for materials."

Wright's works in Phoenix, including contributions to the Biltmore and his own home and studio, Taliesin West, revealed his deep belief that architecture should enhance both person and environment. Taliesin West, Wright's winter home and architectural studio from 1937 to 1959, was also a school that encouraged students' experimentation.

Giraffes at Phoenix Zoo.

Cacti at the Desert Botanical Garden.

139 rare, threatened, and endangered species of plants from around the world, as well as the Sonoran Desert, and is said to be the world's largest collection of desert plants living in a natural environment. Several trails lead through the beautifully conceived garden, which includes a fragrant Edible Plant Garden and the Desert Terrace Garden, home to aloe vera plants and the weird and wonderful Boojum, a plant usually only seen in Baja California. Huge cactus sculptures by glass artist Dale Chihuly adorn the entrance to the garden, art imitating and playing with nature.

The botanical garden has a popular onsite courtyard restaurant, **Gertrude's** (www.gertrudesrestaurant.net), which serves imaginative, locally sourced food at breakfast, lunch, and dinner. It is a destination in itself in the evening when it is cooler; make advance reservations.

Nearby, the **Phoenix Zoo ❶** (tel: 602-286-3800; www.phoenixzoo.com; daily 9am–5pm; charge) has been voted one of the nation's top five zoos. It contains more than 1,400 animals, including 30 species of endangered or threatened animals, all housed on 125 acres (50 hectares) accessed by 2.5 miles (4km) of trails. The Arizona Trail features the flora and fauna of the Southwest.

SCOTTSDALE

The Valley of the Sun's most liveable community is **Scottsdale.** It was once on the wild northeastern edge of Phoenix, home to lonesome cowboys like Lon Megargee, a commercial artist who fell in love with the West, built his adobe studio and home here in the 1930s, and reinvented himself as a popular cowboy artist. Megargee entertained guests in what is now the **Hermosa Inn** (5332 N Palo Cristi Road; tel: 602-955-8614; www.hermosainn.com), a boutique casita hotel set amid lush grounds in the peaceful residential neighborhood of Paradise Valley. Megargee's former studio retains his art and spirit and now houses Lon's, one of Phoenix's top dining restaurants.

An array of fine dining restaurants, elegant hotels, sprawling resorts, ritzy malls, and excellent museums have sprouted up in revitalized downtown Scottsdale, which welcomes visitors with the contemporary **Paolo Soleri Bridge** over the canal but plays up its Old West roots in a charming and very walkable Old Town.

Cowboy and Indian art can be found in a number of galleries here, as well as at the relatively new **Western Spirit: Scottsdale's Museum of the West ❷** (3830 Marshall Way; tel: 480-686-9539; www.scottsdalemuseumwest.org; Tue–Sat 9.30am–5pm, Sun 11am–5pm; charge), which tells the story of the Western states through art and is already one of the top Western museums in the nation.

Visitors to the green building (which meets high standards of LEED sustainable architecture) are greeted by Maynard Dixon's dramatic 1935 mural *Kit Carson with Mountain Men: A Visual Journey through the Early American West* and paintings by Taos artists, along with Kit Carson artifacts, Pueblo pottery, and iconic portraits by

photographer Edward S. Curtis. There are special sections dedicated to Frederick Remington and Charles Russell. A display of Western artists features works by Frank McCarthy, Howard Terpning, and Joe Beeler, among others.

In 2016, the museum partnered with ASU to take charge of the 5,000-piece Rennard Strickland Collection of Western Film History, the life's work of a Cherokee/Osage collector from Oklahoma. One hundred posters from the collection, dating from the late 1890s to the mid-1980s, are currently on display at the museum.

In addition to abundant Western art, there are permanent displays of saddles, cowboy chaps, spurs, and sheriff's badges, as well as interactive exhibits, which are sure to interest kids.

A few blocks east, the engaging **Scottsdale Museum of Contemporary Art (SMOCA) Ⓚ** (7374 E Second Street; www.smoca.org; tel: 480-874-4766; Wed, Fri, Sat 10am–5pm, Thu 10am–8pm; charge, but free Thu) is decidedly modern in its approach, and past exhibits include an installation by light artist James Turrell and James Marshall (aka Dalek). It is close to the **Scottsdale Center for Performing Arts** (7380 E Second Street; tel: 480-499-8589; www.scottsdaleperformingarts.org), a great place to catch a musical or concert.

The musically inclined will relish the **Musical Instrument Museum (MIM) Ⓛ** (4725 E Mayo Boulevard; tel: 480-478-6000; http://mim.org; Mon–Sat 9am–5pm, Sun 10am–5pm; charge), in northern Phoenix. Dreamed up by the energetic retired CEO of Target Stores, MIM tells the story of global music via a dizzying array of exhibits featuring musical instruments and videos of live performances (visitors wear headphones that are activated by sensors on each display). This place makes the Hard Rock Café's displays of rock musicians' instruments and paraphernalia look lame! It's no wonder that this place is a runaway hit with visitors and musicians alike, and was recently voted top museum in Phoenix in one poll. A Stratocaster played by Johnny Ramone, a guitar belonging to Eric Clapton, and the piano on which John Lennon

In downtown Scottsdale.

composed *Imagine* are among the thousands of instruments on display. This is a very big museum; plan on spending much of the day here. There is an onsite restaurant, and concerts take place regularly in a state-of-the-art theater.

Taliesin West  (tel: 480-627-5340; www.franklloydwright.org; daily for guided tours 9am–4pm, gift shop and grounds until 6pm, special evening tours available at certain times of year; charge), in the foothills of Scottsdale, is a highlight of any visit to this part of the city. It was architect Frank Lloyd Wright's personal residence and architectural school, and most of the buildings and facilities continue to be an ongoing, hands-on educational exercise for architectural and design students.

New techniques in the use of natural materials were developed here, often after the many failures considered part of the educational process by Wright. Rocks from the desert and sand from dry washes were melded into foundations, walls, and walkways, all the while following geometric proportions that stayed constant, from the smallest ornamental detail to the dimensions of the buildings themselves.

Some of Wright's trademark techniques, such as the squeeze-and-release of a cramped entranceway opening into an expansive room, are apparent here. But from a distance, the buildings merge so beautifully with the desert landscape, they almost disappear.

One of Arizona's best-known modern architects is Paolo Soleri, an Italian who lived in Arizona from 1956 until his death in 2013. Located in Paradise Valley, near Scottsdale, Soleri's home studio and gallery, **Cosanti**  (tel: 480-948 6145; https://arcosanti.org/cosanti; Mon–Sat 9am–5pm, Sun 11am–5pm; donation), offers an overview of the late architect's philosophy and of his grander site, Arcosanti, 65 miles (105km) north of Phoenix. Cactus and olive trees are scattered amid Cosanti's earth-formed concrete structures, designed and constructed to maximize both ecological efficiency and use of space. Many visitors like to purchase Cosanti's famed bronze bell wind chimes as a beautiful and ecological memento of their visit.

THE APACHE TRAIL

Of the desert drives outside Phoenix, the most spectacular is the **Apache Trail**.

One must endure the drive 25 miles (40km) eastward through trailer parks and roadside businesses to **Apache Junction ❷**, where the western flank of the Superstition Mountains rises. The road from there to **Roosevelt Dam ❸** weaves through 50 miles (80km) of volcanic ash spewed millions of years ago and settled into swirling rhyolite and tuff. Here and there, lakes of the dammed Salt River form blue calms in the riot of cactus and disordered stone. The Superstition Mountains themselves are protected by wilderness status and offer labyrinthine trails for hiking, horseback riding, and backpacking as well as several state and national parks protecting natural and cultural remains that are well worth visiting.

Taliesin West.

THE COLORADO RIVER

The river once known as the Grand, which less than 6 million years ago carved the mile-deep Grand Canyon, is now a managed resource, not the wild, churning, seasonally flooding great unknown it once was.

Too thick to drink, to thin to plow" – that's what they used to say about the Colorado River. Not anymore. The 1,450-mile (2,330km) -long Colorado, rising in the Rocky Mountains and draining an area the size of France, has been tamed – dammed, diverted for irrigation and power, and so heavily used by the states it flows through that it is no longer a river by the time it passes over the border with Mexico and into the Gulf of California.

Historically, the Colorado was a warm river that swelled into a red, silty, roaring froth when snow in the high country melted. Two thirds of its volume comes from the Green River, which confluences with the Colorado in what is now Canyonlands National Park. Twice mighty, the Colorado then rages in a series of whitewater rapids through the narrow confines of Cataract Canyon.

Plants and animals in the Grand Canyon, carved by the river, evolved to deal with seasonal surges in the river. Humpback chub appeared in the warm waters of the Colorado some 3-5 million years ago, when the river first cut through the layer-cake strata of the uplifted Colorado Plateau. Now, warm-water fish like the chub and razorback sucker struggle to survive in the colder waters exiting Glen Canyon Dam, which has created Lake Powell. The Grand Canyon is now a "naturalized" environment rather than a natural one, in the words of an environmental analyst, Stephen Corothers, meaning that the environment has changed to suit new conditions.

The greatest challenge today is to provide for the needs of a burgeoning Southwest population in the nation's fastest-growing region while conserving its natural habitats, such as those of the Grand Canyon. Daily surges in demand for power in large metropolitan centers like Phoenix once drove dam releases, creating damaging high- and low-river levels. This has been improved by the 1992 passage of the Grand Canyon Protection Act, which requires the dam's operators, the Bureau of Reclamation, to smooth out flows to ensure the natural habitat downstream is not subjected to extreme fluctuations.

On the other hand, infrequent great floods were once a feature of the Colorado and may have a place in the downstream environment. In 1996, the floodgates at Glen Canyon were opened to allow the river to run unchecked through the Grand Canyon. Beaches were quickly renewed, old vegetation whisked away and habitat improved in the week-long flood.

As Secretary of the Interior Bruce Babbitt put it, "When the dam was going up in the 1950s, it never occurred to anybody that they needed to think about what would happen a hundred miles downstream because we tended to see the landscape as fragments and each one of them independent. What we've learned is that nature doesn't operate that way."

Horseshoe Bend on the Colorado River.

TUCSON

Once perceived as a dusty town ringed by cacti and still air, Tucson is increasingly becoming Arizona's coolest city, grounded in Hispanic tradition and full of fun.

Tucson ④, or the Old Pueblo, as it is known locally, is a modern metropolis of a million souls spread across 500 sq miles (1,300 sq km) of southern Arizona's Sonoran Desert between five encircling mountain ranges. Warm winters, low year-round humidity, an unbeatable desert setting, hundred-mile vistas, and perhaps the easiest access to hiking, bicycling, camping, horseback riding, rock climbing, and skiing of any city in the nation have lured visitors and residents for decades. The historic campus of the high-ranked University of Arizona lies just east of El Presidio, the Barrio, and the lively, refurbished historic Downtown, linked by a free trolley. In the surrounding valley, four-star resorts, spas, dude ranches, historic inns, and gourmet restaurants nestle amid saguaro-clad foothills, nature parks, Wild West towns, Indian reservations, and to the south, Mexican border towns.

EARLY HISTORY OF TUCSON

Long before Europeans arrived, the Sonoran Desert was home to successive native cultures. Paleo-Indian hunters drifted through in search of mammoth during the Ice Age, but after the climate warmed and big game died out, Desert Archaic hunter-gatherers settled into a successful and sustainable nomadic lifestyle, moving with the seasons and

gathering an explosion of seasonal edible plants and hunting small game.

By AD 300, irrigation farmers from northern Mexico, the Hohokam culture, had arrived and were enjoying great success growing corn, beans, and squash along washes in what was then a lush valley watered by the Santa Cruz River. The Hohokam built a sophisticated system of canals to water their fields and prospered for 1200 years. Faint traces of their Mesoamerican-influenced culture linger, including compounds containing crumbling

Main Attractions

El Presidio Historic District
Barrio Historic District
Downtown Tucson
Arizona State Museum
Flandrau Science Center
Arizona-Sonora Desert
  Museum
Saguaro National Park
Titan Missile Museum
Biosphere 2
San Xavier del Bac Mission

Maps on pages
172, 184

Tucson from Sentinel Peak Park.

Pima County Court House.

caliche mud buildings with ceremonial structures atop mounds, ballcourts, beautifully etched shell jewelry and attractive pottery, and pecked petroglyphs on basaltic boulders on Signal Hill in Saguaro National Park West and other places.

By the time of the Spanish conquest, in 1540, the Hohokam had overstretched their resources and hunter-gatherers were again eking out a survivalist lifestyle in the desert. They were the ancestors of today's Tohono O'odham ("People of the Desert," formerly known as the Papago) and Akimel O'odham ("People of the Water, also known as the Pima) tribes, whose modern reservations adjoin Tucson.

O'odham people in Tucson lived in a *rancheria*, scattered huts constructed from mesquite limbs, saguaro ribs, and thorny ocotillo, on the now-dry Santa Cruz River at the base of "A" Mountain. The dark volcanic hill west of downtown with the whitewashed "A" (the work of University of Arizona students since 1915) was once used by Mexican soldiers as a lookout for

Apache raiders, when Tucson was under Mexican rule between 1821 and 1854 (hence its proper name, Sentinel Peak). It has breathtaking views of the city, nearby mountains, and basin-and-range topography all the way into Mexico, 65 miles (105km) away.

THE GOLD RUSH

Tucson became a US territory through the Gadsden Purchase, and the 1860s brought the first wave of American citizens to the Tucson area in search of gold. Although little gold was actually found, mountains of silver and copper were extracted, creating a frantic migration of miners, prostitutes, and their associates. The Akimel O'odham, or Pima, who remained skilled irrigation farmers, sold wheat and other supplies to miners and the US Army during the early American settlement period. However, Anglo settlers diverted water from the Santa Cruz River, cutting off the Pima from water used to irrigate crops and bringing destitution. A settlement in the 1980s finally returned water rights to the

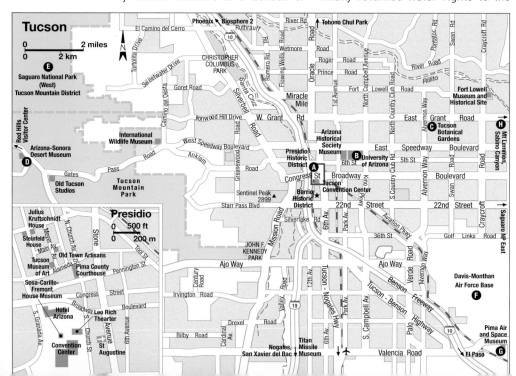

tribe, which today is successfully farming again and offering hospitality.

Tucson remained small until the military moved here and built Davis-Monthan Air Force Base in 1925. This brought thousands of military personnel, many of whom returned to Tucson as civilians following the end of World War II. The military presence is still strong, and numerous aircraft from the base criss-cross the skies above town.

A hot, dry climate has contributed to the most recent migration, mostly of retirees but also a great many young people attending the University of Arizona. All of these immigrants still contribute to Tucson's dynamic urban environment. Like few other cities, Tucson's historic populations still play a role in forming a culture that mixes Spanish, Mexican, American Indian, Old West, and New West peoples.

DOWNTOWN TUCSON

The most logical place to begin your visit is in the **Presidio Historic District Ⓐ**, where you can get a feel for Tucson's Spanish, Mexican, and Anglo

heritage. When O'Conor and his soldiers built the Presidio of San Augustin del Tucson in 1776, they surrounded it with adobe walls 12ft (4 meters) high and 750ft (230 meters) long to protect settlers from the Apache. A portion of the original Presidio wall can be seen in the distinctive Pima County Courthouse (115 N Church Street), which combines Spanish and Southwestern architecture in its columns, arches, decorated facade, and tiled dome, interior courtyard, and fountain. It sits on 10-acre (4-hectare) Presidio Park, a nice spot for a picnic.

Guided docent tours of the presidio are offered daily at 11am, but most people elect to do a self-guided walking tour, which takes you past some lovely historic buildings and cultural landmarks.

Begin at **Tucson Museum of Art** (tel: 520-624 2333; www.tucsonmuseum ofart.org; Tue–Sat 10am–5pm, first Thu until 8pm, Sun noon–5pm; charge), on the corner of Alameda and Main. The museum contains over 5,000 pieces of art, including Spanish Colonial paintings

Pima County Court House arches.

Ⓞ STJUKSHON TO TUCSON

O'odham people referred to their village as Stjukshon (*stjuk* means "black" and *shon* means "hill). This name was roughly translated as "Tucson" by Colonel Hugo O'Conor, an Irishman in the service of the Spanish Crown, when he was ordered to build a new garrison, or *presidio*, in Tucson in 1775, to protect San Xavier Mission (1690). El Presidio de San Agustin de Tucson, today's Old Pueblo, replaced the presidio at Tubac, adjoining the mission of Tumacacori (1691), after the former commander of the Tubac presidio, Juan Bautista de Anza, left to seek an overland route to Alta California.

San Xavier and Tumacacori were part of a string of missions in Pimeria Alta (the upper Sonoran Desert, including modern Mexico) established by a Jesuit missionary, Father Eusebio Francisco Kino, to attract Indian converts in the 1600s.

Tip

Every May, El Presidio hosts the Tucson Folk Festival, featuring American bluegrass, jazz, blues, celtic, country, zydeco, Latin, and Mexican folk music, on five stages around the historic downtown. More than 120 musicians perform at the festival, which attracts over 10,000 fans.

and furnishings and pre-Columbian artifacts from Latin America.

The museum's most interesting feature, however, is the five historic houses incorporated into its layout, which are all open during museum hours. One of the houses, the Hiram Stevens House, an adobe built by a politician in the 1860s, is home to a nice little café, **Café a la C'Art,** which has been voted one of the top 10 museum restaurants in the country. **La Casa Cordova**, built in 1848, is Tucson's oldest home. A classic Mexican adobe with traditional saguaro rib ceiling latillas and dirt floors, it has a central courtyard and dark interior rooms that have been restored to reflect early life in the Old Pueblo.

Privately owned **Old Town Artisans** (186 N Meyer; tel: 520-623-6024; www.oldtownartisans.com; daily), offers arts and crafts by more than 150 Western, Indian, and Mexican artists and occupies an adobe, parts of which date to between 1862 and 1875.

Stroll along Main and Court streets to view other houses in Snob Hollow,

as it was called. They include the 1886 American Territorial-style Julius Kruttschnidt House (297 N Main), now El Presidio Bed-and-Breakfast; the Owl's Club Mansion (378 Main), a men's club with an ornade facade; and nearby Steinfeld House (300 N Main), both designed by renowned architect Henry Trost in the Spanish Mission style that was in vogue in the early 1900s. The 1900 Jules Flein House (311 N Court) is home to **El Charro Café** (tel: 520-622-1922; www.elcharro.com), which claims to be the oldest Mexican restaurant in the country.

THE BARRIO HISTORIC DISTRICT

South of the Tucson Convention Center (260 S Church Street) and the Presidio is the 13-block **Barrio Historic District**, where crumbling adobes have been lovingly restored. You get a feel for Old Tucson's sleepy Mexican ambiance and lovely courtyard homes here, and it is a wonderful place to wander.

On South Main, **El Tiradito**, the Outcast's Wishing Shrine, is a memorial

Adobe building in Barrio Historic District.

to the unconsecrated burial spot of a young man killed in a love triangle with his mother-in-law and father-in-law. It is the only national historical landmark dedicated to a sinner. The tradition here, as in so many Catholic shrines in the Hispanic Southwest, is to light a candle for the soul of the departed. Also in the Barrio is the legendary **El Minuto Café** (354 S Main Street; tel: 520-882-4145; www.elminutotucson.com), which has been serving inexpensive and plentiful Sonoran food since the 1930s.

DOWNTOWN REGENERATION

North of El Presidio, the area around Congress Street has recently undergone regeneration and is now a popular destination for visitors. It's easy to explore. Just hop aboard one of the air-conditioned Sun Link Modern Streetcars, which travel a loop between downtown and the University of Arizona Medical Center on a 4-mile (6km) route with 19 stops along the way.

The legendary **Hotel Congress** (tel: 520-622 8848; www.hotelcongress.com), known for cheap sleeps, eats, and great live music within sight and sound of trains and highways, has attracted hipsters for years now and is at the heart of the downtown revival. Built in 1919 to serve the railroad, the hotel achieved notoriety in 1934 when police apprehended the outlaw John Dillinger and his gang.

The hotel's globally inspired **Cup Café** is a great place for a meal any time of the day or night, but particularly breakfast, if you have been up late in the on-site dance club. Other hip restaurants include the **Downtown Kitchen and Cocktails** (tel: 520-623-7000; www.downtownkitchen.com), the latest from famed restaurateur Janos Wilder, which rub shoulders with renovated vintage motels, live-work art spaces, and unique boutiques.

Also on Congress Street is the Ronstadt Transit Center. Federico Ronstadt, the grandfather of singer Linda Ronstadt, founded the F. Ronstadt Company in 1901, starting out as a manufacturer and repairer of wagons and carriages before evolving into an all-purpose hardware store, which closed in 1985.

AROUND THE UNIVERSITY

East of El Presidio, the **Arizona History Museum** (949 E 2nd Street; tel: 520-628-5774; Mon–Sat 10am–4pm, Fri until 8pm; charge) focuses on Tucson's Anglo history, with exhibits on 1870s Tucson, transportation, and mining. It has a full replica of a copper mine.

Several other must-see museums can be found across the street from AHS on the campus of the **University of Arizona ⑬**, which was founded in 1891 by the territorial legislature (in Old Main, the campus's oldest building) on land donated by a saloon keeper and two gamblers.

First stop should be the **Arizona State Museum** (Park and University; tel: 520-621-6302; www.statemuseum. arizona.edu; Mon–Sat 10am–5pm; charge), which occupies two buildings

University of Arizona campus.

just inside the west entrance. It was founded in 1893 to collect and preserve artifacts related to the native cultures of the Southwest and is the region's oldest anthropology and archaeology museum. An award-winning multimedia exhibit called *Paths of Life: American Indians of the Southwest* traces the origins, history, and contemporary life of the Seri, Tarahumara, Yaqui, O'odham, Colorado River Yumans, Southern Paiute, Pai, Western Apache, Navajo, and Hopi cultures. Displays on the vanished Hohokam, whose major community, Snaketown, was excavated by the university's Dr Emil Haury, are found in the South Building.

At the opposite end of campus is the **Flandrau Science Center** (tel: 520-621-4516; www.flandrau.org; science center and planetarium Mon–Thu 9am–5pm, Fri 9am–9pm, Sat 10am–10pm, Sun noon–5pm; observatory Wed–Sat 7–10pm; charge). It provides out-of-this-world fun for kids and adults alike, with hands-on science exhibits, night sky viewing through a 16-in (400mm) telescope, star shows that include an introduction to Arizona skies, American Indian skylore, and the demise of the dinosaurs, as well as evening laser light shows in the planetarium.

UA was the first university to partner with NASA on the Phoenix Mars Mission, which launched in 2007 to investigate water quality and habitability potential on Mars. The Phoenix Mars Lander landed on Mars in 2008 and transmitted photos back, before NASA eventually lost touch with the landing vehicle. The museum also has a world-class collection of meteorites, including a model of the Tucson Ring, a 1,400-lb (635-kg) chunk used unknowingly as an anvil in the 1860s, until scientists realized its extraterrestrial origins.

The University of Arizona is also home to the **Center for Creative Photography** (1030 N Olive Road; tel: 520-621-7968; www.creativephotography.org; Tue–Fri 9am–4pm, Sat 1–4pm; free). Conceived and co-founded by renowned landscape photographer Ansel Adams as a repository for his photographic archives, it is now one of the world's great photography and research centers, with over 50,000 photos by leading 20th-century photographers, such as Edward Weston, Paul Strand, and Alfred Stieglitz. One of the best reasons to stop here is to peruse the remarkable black-and-white images of Yosemite National Park and other parks by Ansel Adams. Exhibitions of the center's holdings are held year round.

URBAN OASES

When you tire of the city, head to the **Tucson Botanical Gardens** ⊙ (2150 N Alvernon Way; 520-326-9686; www.tucsonbotanical.org; daily 7.30am–4.30pm, Thu–Fri until 8pm; charge), northeast of downtown, where a collection of 17 residentially-scaled gardens represent various plants and is in bloom all year. Of particular note are the Native American Crops Garden and Tohono O'odham Path, which explore

The Center for Contemporary Photography.

the relationship between plants found in the Sonoran Desert and local Tohono O'odham people. Tucson's **Native Seeds/SEARCH** (www.nativeseeds.org), a local seed conservation program founded by ethnobotanist and writer Gary Nabhan in 1983, has banked 2,000 heritage seeds in an effort to preserve native foods. (Gardeners can buy these seeds in the garden or by mail order.) In October, the garden hosts La Fiesta de Los Chiles, a two-day festival celebrating the life-sustaining (at least for some) fire-hot chile.

A few miles north of downtown is **Tohono Chul** (7366 N Paseo del Note; tel: 520-742-6455, ext 0; www.tohono chulpark.org; daily 8am–5pm; charge). "Desert corner" in the Tohono O'odham language, the 49-acre (20-hectare) park was created to promote conservation of arid lands and has nature trails, a rock wall depicting the geology of the nearby Santa Catalina Mountains, and 500 plants from Sonora and the Southwest arranged by genus. Picnic here or enjoy breakfast, lunch, or refreshments in the popular Garden Bistro.

WEST OF DOWNTOWN

Desert animals are largely nocturnal, keeping cool in burrows or beneath rocks or shrubs during the day. Your best chance of seeing and learning about Sonoran Desert flora and fauna is to visit the world-famous **Arizona-Sonora Desert Museum** Ⓓ (2021 N Kinney Road; tel: 520-883-2702; www. desertmuseum.org; daily Mar–May and Sept 7.30am–5pm in winter, June–Aug Sun–Fri 7am–5pm and Sat 7.30am–10pm, Oct–Feb 8.30am–5pm; charge), located in Tucson Mountain Park.

This isn't a "museum" at all but a large outdoor zoo, botanical garden, and nature trail that so effectively re-creates the Sonoran Desert habitat, the 299 species of native animals and 1,400 species of native plants that live here are fooled into thinking they never left home.

You'll need good walking shoes, a hat, sunscreen, water, and at least half a day to see all the exhibits, which include a hummingbird aviary, where hummers buzz just inches from visitors' faces; a desert grassland with

Inspecting the cacti at the Arizona-Sonora Desert Museum.

a small but active prairie dog town; several "cat" canyons inhabited by bobcats, jaguarundis, and cougars; a plant-pollinator garden with humorous signs explaining why we need to be concerned about the birds and the bees; and javelina (also known as collared peccaries – they are not pigs) and coyotes, which roam freely behind "invisible" fences.

Continue north on Kinney Road to learn about the famous symbol of the Sonoran Desert, the saguaro cactus, in the Tucson Mountain District (West) unit of **Saguaro National Park** Ⓔ (tel: 520-733-5158; www.nps.gov/sagu; park daily 7am–sunset, Red Hills Visitor Center daily 9am–5pm; charge), one of two units of this 87,000-acre (35,000-hectare) national park bookending Tucson. This unit, located west of the Tucson Mountains, was added in 1961 for research purposes and contains stands of younger saguaros. The Rincon Mountain District (East) (tel: 520-733-5153), off Old Spanish Trail in the 8,400ft (2560-meter) Rincon Mountains was the first unit of the park to be set aside,

in 1933, to highlight the giant forest of mature saguaros.

Saguaros provide homes for numerous animals, including Gila woodpeckers, screech owls, and honey bees, while animals such as javelinas eat the fruit; native Tohono O'odham people harvest the fruit annually and process it into syrups and jams, which you will see on sale at the Arizona-Sonora Desert Museum and other locations.

Both park units have excellent visitor centers and scenic drives, as well as a variety of long and short hiking trails that wind among the saguaros, but if you choose only one unit to visit, choose Tucson Mountains. It is possible to enter from the north on Ina Road (exit 248 off Interstate 10), but the entry point from downtown, via narrow, winding Gates Pass, is really breathtaking, as the route summits the pass and starts to descend into Tucson Mountain Park, adjoining the national park. This is a lovely place to ride a bicycle through typical Sonoran Desert Arizona Upland vegetation of yellow-blossomed paloverde and mesquite trees, flame-tipped ocotillo, and

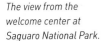
The view from the welcome center at Saguaro National Park.

ironwood. If you want to see the desert in bloom, be sure to visit in April.

EAST OF DOWNTOWN

Dedicated by aviator Charles Lindbergh in 1927, **Davis-Monthan Air Force Base** ⓕ (Kolb Road; tel: 520-228-8448; www.df.am.mil; AMARG tours Mon–Fri 9am–5pm) was a training ground for B-17 bombers during World War II and still trains pilots in combat aircraft. One of the base's tenants is the Aerospace Maintenance and Regeneration Group (AMARG), or "the boneyard," where the U.S. military takes advantage of the dry climate and hard ground surface to mothball an extraordinary 5,000 planes and helicopters before they are scrapped.

One-hour daily coach tours of AMARG are available through nearby **Pima Air and Space Museum** ⓖ (6000 E Valencia Road; tel: 520-574-0462; www.pimaair.org; Mon–Fri 9am–5pm; charge), which displays over 300 air- and spacecraft, the largest private collection in the world. Exhibits range from the 6ft (1.8-meter) wingspan Bumblebee

to replicas of President John F. Kennedy s *Air Force One* airplane and the *Kitty Hawk*, the Wright Brothers' plane. Children like the Challenger Learning Center, housed in the Aerospace Exploratorium, which has a mission briefing room, transportation room, mission control area, and space station.

Note: as of May 2017, there are new security procedures in place for those taking the AMARG tours. Please contact the museum for further information and allow extra time.

SANTA CATALINA MOUNTAINS

Northeast of Tucson, in the Coronado National Forest on the Santa Catalina Mountains, are the **Sabino Canyon Recreation Area** ⓗ (tel: 520-749-2861; 24 hours daily; www.sabinocanyon.com; charge and concessioner fees for tram, parking, and tours) and Mount Lemmon, at 9,157ft (2,791 meters), the highest peak in the area and a popular destination for skiing, hiking, camping, and scenic drives.

Sabino Canyon is a lush canyon cut by Sabino Creek, supporting cottonwood

Hiker in Saguaro National Park.

Sunset over the snow-capped Santa Catalina Mountains.

ⓞ SAGUARO NP

Access The Rincon Mountain District visitor center (Saguaro East) is on South Old Spanish Trail, about 2 miles (3km) east of Tucson. The Tucson Mountain District Red Hills Visitor Center (Saguaro West) is on Kinney Road in Tucson Mountain Park, west of Tucson.

Seasons & Hours Both park districts are open daily from sunrise to sunset. The visitor centers are open daily 9am–5pm; closed Christmas.

Entrance Fee Yes.

Handicapped Access Visitor centers, picnic areas, and trails.

Activities Scenic drive, backpacking, hiking, wildlife-watching, interpretive programs.

and willow bosque, deer, coyotes, javelinas, and numerous birds. This historic canyon is one of Tucson's most heavily used attractions, and over time has seen mammoths, Hohokam irrigation canals, and pony soldiers from the now-ruined Fort Lowell, who used to ride horses to the swimming hole. There's a bookstore and visitor center with exhibits on the natural and cultural history of the mountains, a butterfly and hummingbird sanctuary, a self-guided nature trail, and guided hikes.

From the parking area, you must either hike, ride horseback, or take one of the regular narrated tram tours up the 4-mile (6.5km) road that winds through the canyon. Popular trails include the 5.5-mile (9km) Seven Falls, which follows the flat floor of Bear Canyon to a waterfall. Allow at least a half-day here. No pets are allowed

The road up to **Mt Lemmon** (tel: 520-576-1321; www.skithelemmon.com; ski lift: Mon–Fri 10.30am–4.30pm, Sat, Sun 9am–5pm; charge for ski lift) begins a few miles from Sabino Canyon. The 40-mile (65km) drive up the

mountainside threads through five of the seven life zones in the United States – from cacti through oak woodlands to Douglas fir forests. The same visual result would require driving all the way to Canada from the desert. The temperature drops by 4°F for each 1,000ft (300 meters) of gain. Mount Lemmon is the southernmost ski area in the U.S. and annually receives over 120ins (3 meters) of snow. The tourist resort of Summer Haven offers food and lodging.

FARTHER AFIELD

Two other museums on the outskirts of Tucson offer entirely different visions of a space age future. **The Titan Missile Museum** (1580 W Duval Mine Road, Sahuarita; tel: 520-625-7736; www.titanmissilemuseum.org; May–Oct daily 9.45am–4pm, Nov–Apr Sun–Fri 9.45am–4pm, Sat 8.45am–5pm; charge), 20 miles south of Tucson, off Interstate 19, is a sobering reminder of Cold War politics and the only site in the United States with a disarmed US intercontinental ballistic missile

Biosphere 2.

(ICBM) still on its underground launch pad. One hour tours of this declassified subterranean museum allow visitors to hear a tape of an Air Force crew preparing to launch a nuclear missile, then see the missile itself – a 110ft (34-meter) -tall, 170-ton (154kg) (when fully loaded) monster contained behind 6,000lb (2,700kg) blast doors.

It's a far more positive experience at **Biosphere 2** (32540 S Biosphere Road, Oracle; tel: 520-8938-6200; www.b2 science.org; daily 9am–4pm; charge), in the town of Oracle, 35 miles (56km) north of Tucson. Biosphere was intended to study the zone in which all life exists when it opened in 1991. Glass-enclosed and isolated from the outside, this 3.5-acre (1.4-hectare) facility was intended to be completely self-sustaining in food, air, and water. Controversy involving the initial researchers tainted the experiment and led to accusations of hype, New Age cultism, poor science, and failed systems that endangered the health of the "bionauts" sealed inside it for two years. Biosphere 2 started down the road to credibility in 1996, when

Columbia University took over management. Today, it is owned by UA and now operates as the College of Science. Visitors are welcome.

Finally, don't miss the **San Xavier del Bac Mission** (tel: 520-294-2624; www. sanxaviermission.org; free), 9 miles (14km) southwest of Tucson, off Interstate 19 on the San Xavier Reservation. *Bac* is a corruption of the Piman word *wak*, which means "where the water emerges." The mission was founded in 1700 as a *visita* (satellite) parish of Tumacacori mission farther south, and construction of the church began in 1778, when Franciscan missionaries moved here after Tumacacori mission was abandoned. "The White Dove of the Desert," as San Xavier del Bac church is known, is considered the most beautiful of the Kino missions, with its classic white plaster and ornate facade. It is still the parish church for the San Xavier Reservation. In the 1990s, the tribe and members of a local friends group worked with an international team to restore the interior murals. Restoration of the exterior is now taking place.

In Mission San Xavier del Bac.

A US Border Patrol vehicle patrols the fence that separates the United States and Mexico in the Sonoran Desert.

ARIZONA'S BORDER COUNTRY

Southern Arizona's vast Sonoran Desert, scorching hot and lightly populated, forms the US-Mexican border, a natural and cultural frontier rich with history and diversity.

The US-Mexico border in Southern Arizona lies almost entirely within the Sonoran Desert, a border landscape that is far less empty than it seems to the casual eye. The combination of low intensity winter storms and violent, quick-burst monsoon summer thunderstorms fosters diverse plant and animal life and leads to a desert landscape that is remarkably green and filled with life at certain times of year. Add to this the young geology of the Basin and Range province, southern Arizona's famous "sky islands," once described as resembling a horde of "giant caterpillars marching northwest out of Mexico," and you have what may be the most beautiful desert region on the planet.

The convergence of four biotic communities – Rocky Mountain, Chihuahuan Desert, Sonoran Desert, and Mexican Sierra Madre – creates ideal habitat for the large numbers of specially adapted plants and animals that call it home. This is one of the premier birding regions in the country, and wildlife species that occur nowhere else in the United States can be found here.

Human beings may struggle with the 100–120°F (38–49°C) days that are the norm here in summer, but as residents like to point out – not always convincingly – it *is* a dry heat, meaning it is cooler in the shade and at night, temperatures can drop by 40°F. In a dry heat, you still sweat but don't notice as it evaporates immediately, and that can lead to severe heat exhaustion and hyponatremia, so monitor yourself and stay safe. Cover up in light, long-sleeved clothing and pants and a broad-brimmed hat, wear sunscreen, consume plenty of water and salty, nutritious snacks, and keep a water spray handy to cool down and stay comfortable.

Border country takes in the whole sweep of southern Arizona, from southwest to southeast, and remains in sight of Mexico most of the time.

Main Attractions

Kitt Peak Astronomical Observatory
Tubac
Ramsey Canyon Preserve
Amerind Foundation Museum
Kartchner Caverns State Park
Tombstone
Bisbee
Chiricahua National Monument

Map on page 184

View from Kitt Peak.

Southwestern Arizona is composed primarily of the Tohono O'odham Indian Reservation and vast public lands. Stark beauty is its main asset. Southeastern Arizona is a land of legends: Cochise and Geronimo, the Earps and Clantons. Fortunes were made in the late 1800s and early 1900s, but settlements faded quickly after the mining booms and languished until tourism started its own boom in the 1970s. Now there is a plethora of things to enjoy in this lovely area, from art towns, wineries, and outdoor pursuits to ghost towns, nature preserves, and mock gunfights.

SOUTHWEST OF TUCSON

Southwestern Arizona's lack of people and towns means lack of street lights – ideal for stargazing. The largest astronomical observatory in the world, **Kitt Peak Astronomical Observatory** ❺ (tel: 520-318-8826; www.noao.edu/outreach/kpvc; daily 9am–3.45pm, nights by reservation Sept–July only, tours 10am, 11.30am, and 1.30pm; charge for tours) sits atop the 6,875-ft (2,095-meter)

-high Quinlan Mountains, about 45 miles (72km), southwest of Tucson. Astronomers chose the site after a three-year-long investigation of 150 mountain ranges. The lack of artificial light combined with nearly 300 days and nights of cloud-free viewing make it the perfect choice. Nineteen optical and two radio telescopes, including the world's largest solar telescope and the 13ft (4-meter) Mayall Telescope, scan the heavens. A short self-guided tour takes you past the most state-of-the-art telescopes, and a visitor center offers exhibits and guided tours that will keep you fascinated for hours.

Kitt Peak also offers good views of the surrounding region, including spectacular 7,730ft (2,356-meter)-high **Baboquivari Peak** to the south. Baboquivari is sacred to the Tohono O'odham, as it is the home of I'itoi (Elder Brother), their creator god. The familiar motif of the Man in the Maze shows the path I'itoi took to his home beneath the mountain.

The observatory is located on the eastern edge of the **Tohono O'odham**

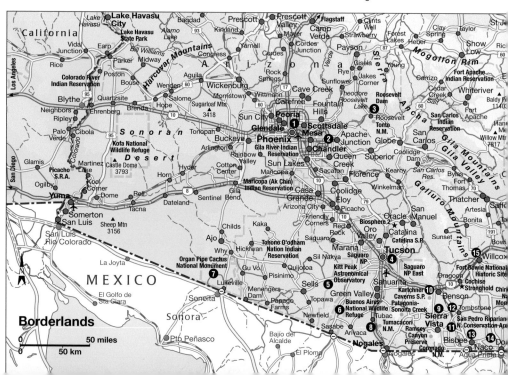

Indian Reservation, once called the Papago Indian Reservation. The O'odham, who at first objected to the observatory being built on their sacred land, lease the peak to the astronomers. Tribal elders changed their opinions after seeing the telescope at the University of Arizona. They call the astronomers "the people of the long eyes." The O'odham reservation, at nearly 2.8 million acres (1.1 million hectares), is the second-largest Indian reservation in the nation. About 28,000 people live on the mesquite- and cactus-covered land.

The attractive **Tohono O'odham Nation Cultural Center and Museum** (tel: 520-383-0200; www.tonation.nsn. gov; Mon–Fri 10am–4pm; free) can be found within sight of Baboquivari Peak, in the village of Topawa, 7 miles (11km) southeast of Sells, the tribal headquarters. The $15.2 million facility has a library, archive, classrooms, and in-depth exhibits on the history of the Tohono O'odham culture. A good time to visit is during the tribe's cultural celebration on June 11, which features a prayer run, the ancient stickball game

of *toka*, a film festival, *keihana* and *waila* music, and arts and crafts.

For years, the O'odham were called the Papago, which translates to "Bean People." In the past, native tepary beans were an important part of their diet, along with amaranth, mesquite, and cacti. They also used native plants such as creosote as a remedy for a variety of illnesses. A change in diet has had unfortunate effect on the O'odham: adult-onset diabetes. Ethnobotanists believe that changing to a diet of fast-food has altered the O'odham insulin metabolism, as well as made many overweight. This is a perfect combination for adult-onset diabetes, which in O'odham people is 15 times the rate found in Anglo-American communities.

Buenos Aires National Wildlife Refuge ⑥ (tel: 520-823-4251; www.fws.gov/ refuge/buenos_aires/; visitor center Nov– Apr Tue–Sun 9am–4pm; free, except some activities) is near **Arivaca**, southwest of Tucson, on US Route 286. More than 116,000 acres (50,000 hectares) of grasslands and *cienega*, a riparian system unique to the Southwest, were

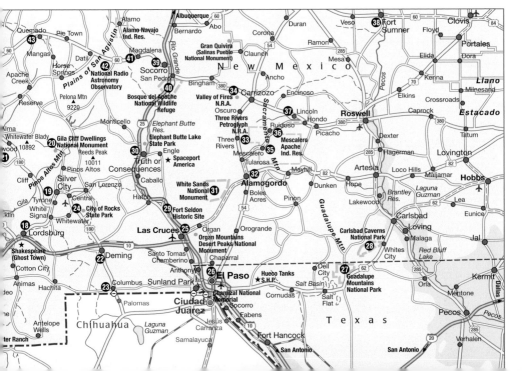

acquired in 1985 and are now protected in Altar Valley. Overgrazing in the late 1800s destroyed once-lush grasslands, which have slowly begun to return.

Ornithologists recognized that the grasslands would be an ideal location for the masked bobwhite quail, a bird thought to be on the verge of extinction until a small population was found in Mexico in 1964. Reintroduction began in the 1970s and continues to this day. Several hundred pairs now nest in the refuge. Pronghorn also range across the grasslands and may be encountered on 8-mile (l3km) -long Antelope Drive. The wildlife refuge also includes Arivaca Creek and Arivaca Cienega, home to gray hawks, vermilion flycatchers, and green kingfishers. Short trails wind through both areas.

About three hours southwest of Tucson, **Organ Pipe Cactus National Monument ❼** (tel: 520-387-6849; www.nps. gov/orpi; 24 hours; visitor center daily 8am–5pm; charge), borders Mexico and preserves species mainly found south of the border. The name refers to the many-limbed organ pipe cactus, which reaches its northern limit in the 516-sq-mile (1,336-sq-km) monument. Organ Pipe cactus can grow to 25ft (7.6 meters) in height and have more than a dozen arms. As with saguaros, in June and July, bats pollinate the abundant white blooms that open at night.

The 21-mile (34km) Ajo Scenic Drive circles the foothills of the Ajo range and provides glimpses of coyotes, desert tortoises, rattlesnakes, kit foxes, and the rarely seen desert critters. After a rain, brittlebush, desert marigolds, poppies, lupines, and other wildflowers burst into bloom. The drive takes about two hours but for those with more time, the 56-mile (90km) Puerto Blanco Scenic Drive winds deeper into the monument through the Puerto Blanco range and passes near the desert oasis of Quitobaquito. In the backcountry, you are likely to see more organ pipe cactus, rare Mexican elephant trees, limberbush, and senita cactus. Many dirt roads lead to historic ranches, mines, and prehistoric Indian sites; winter is the coolest time to visit.

Tumacacori Mission at Tumacacori National Historic Park.

In 2006, the National Park Service completed a 23-mile (37km) -long steel fence on its southern boundary, which has successfully prevented illegal cross-border vehicle crossings through the national monument. Even so, Homeland Security will be evident during your visit. Border Patrol officers patrol this area 24/7, and you will encounter checkpoints where you will be asked to show identification. Overnight stays in the backcountry are no longer permitted, but the park has a very nice campground.

SOUTH OF TUCSON

Less than an hour south of Tucson, on Interstate 19 and east of Buenos Aires National Wildlife Refuge, is the hamlet of **Tubac 8**. Its motto "Where Art and History Meet" is a fair description of the town. In 1691, the legendary Jesuit missionary Father Eusebio Francisco Kino was one of the first Europeans to enter the Santa Cruz Valley. The Spanish established the Tubac Presidio in 1752, a year after the Pima Revolt. Twenty-four years later, the Presidio was moved north to Tucson, leaving Tubac unprotected against Apache raiding and political turmoil, and by the time Tubac became American territory, in 1853, after the Gadsden Purchase, the presidio and nearby mission were both mostly in ruins.

Today, **Tubac Presidio State Historic Park** (tel: 520-398-2252; https://azstate parks.com/tupr; daily 9am–5pm; charge), operated by Tubac Historical Society, preserves part of the old garrison but the whole community is of interest to those intrigued by Arizona's early history

By 1859, Tubac had become a mining boomtown and home to Arizona first newspaper, the *Weekly Arizonan*, now on display in the Presidio museum. With the founding of an art school in 1948, Tubac morphed into an art colony, and thus it has remained. Popular with daytrippers, Tubac has about 100 art studios, galleries, and businesses and holds a popular annual Festival of the Arts in February. Santa Fe, this ain't, but it offers a pleasant day out, nevertheless.

Tubac makes a good jumping-off point for a visit to **Tumacacori National Historical Park** (tel: 520-377-5060; www. nps.gov/tuma; daily 9am–5pm; charge), 4 miles (6.5km) south, which preserves three Spanish missions established by Father Kino in the 1690s: Guevavi (11 miles/18km south), Calabazas (15 miles/ 24km south), and Tumacacori. Guevavi and Calabazas were abandoned in 1771, after Spain recalled its Jesuit missionaries. The last mission, **Tumacacori**, is the only one now open to the public.

The present church at Tumacacori was built by Franciscan missionaries between 1800 and 1822. It is a quiet place, dominated by the ruined church with its brick bell tower, white-domed sanctuary, and circular mortuary chapel. A peaceful self-guided trail leads through the church, which remains a remarkable testimony to the skills of Indian artisans.

If you are up for a hike, the **Juan Bautista de Anza National Historic**

Colorful pottery shop, Tubac.

Trail runs for 5 miles (8km) along the Santa Cruz River between Tumacacori and Tubac. This sandy route crosses the river three times. The trail commemorates Juan Bautista de Anza's 1775–76 expedition from Nogales, Mexico, to San Francisco. Three hundred immigrants and soldiers walked for 80 days with one death and three births. The goal is to eventually create a 600-mile (960km) -long trail following the old route. Only a few short sections are currently open.

Over the Santa Rita Mountains and into southeastern Arizona is **Patagonia-Sonoita Creek Preserve** (tel: 520-394-2400; www.nature.org; Wed–Sun Apr–Sept 6.30am–4pm, Oct–Mar 7.30–4pm, guided tours year-round Sat 9am; charge), owned and managed by The Nature Conservancy. Some of the tallest (over 100ft/30 meters) and oldest (130 years old) Fremont cottonwoods grow in the preserve. It is one of the last places to see a healthy cottonwood-willow ecosystem, as well as a good spot for finding Arizona black walnut, velvet mesquite, and velvet ash. Over 300 bird species, including northern beardless tyrannulet, rose-throated becard, and thick-billed kingbird, visit the area. Other animals include cougars, coatamundi, rattlesnakes, and toads.

As the name suggests, this preserve adjoins the former mining town of **Patagonia**, which make a good base for exploring this part of Arizona. Patagonia has several excellent little cafés serving delicious, healthy, local food and a great little bed-and-breakfast in a former miner's boarding house. It is also home to the Native Seeds/SEARCH experimental farm, on the edge of town.

One of the more important birding spots in southeastern Arizona is **Ramsey Canyon Preserve** (tel: 520-378-2785; www.nature.org; Thu–Mon Mar–Oct 8am–5pm, 9am–4pm Nov–Feb; tours Mar–Oct Mon, Thu, and Sat 9am; charge), located in the Huachuca Mountains just south of **Sierra Vista** ❾. Another Nature Conservancy preserve, 300-acre (120-hectare) Ramsey Canyon is pierced by a perennial stream that provides a habitat for many amphibians, including Chiricahua leopard frogs. Fourteen of the 19 species of hummingbird known to inhabit or visit the United States in the summer have been recorded in the canyon. It is also a splendid place to find butterflies, black bear, and excitingly, this area has had sightings of rare jaguars in these remote mountains, which provide a safe international crossing for wildlife from Mexico into the United States. The preserve has a delightful visitor center and bookstore, but parking is limited to just 27 first-come, first-serve spots; no pets allowed.

ARIZONA'S WINELANDS

Sonoita, and its neighbor **Elgin** can be found on Highway 82, heading east across the sweeping grasslands that are so distinctive in this part of Border Country. Today, the Sonoita-Elgin area is most famous for being one of three winemaking regions in Arizona's

Equestrians ride the Juan Bautista de Anza National Historic Trail.

increasingly popular Wine Country. It is the oldest of the three, and the only official AVA in Arizona.

Ten of the 11 wineries in the area are open for tastings and offer an excellent introduction to Arizona's award-winning wines. They include **Callaghan Winery** (tel: 520-455-5322; www.callaghanvineyards.com; Thu–Sun 11am–4pm) in Elgin, known for its wines made from Mediterranean grapes, and **Village of Elgin Winery** (tel: 520-455-9309; www.elginwines.com), which uses single varietals to make small-batch wines such as Tombstone Red and holds a harvest food-and-wine festival each September. **Dos Cabezas** (tel: 520-455-5141; www.doscabezaswinery.com; Thu–Sun 10.30am–4.30pm) in Sonoita saw its Red Vinefera win the Jefferson Cup Award in 2015. Its tasting room is right next to the highway. Other wineries can be found farther east, around Willcox, which has six tasting rooms in its historic downtown. Most are only open on weekends. For more information, visit www.arizonawine.org or www.azwinelifestyle.com.

EAST OF TUCSON

The quickest route to southeastern Arizona is to head east on Interstate 10 from Tucson. After about 40 miles (65km), you will arrive in **Benson ⑩**, home to one of the least commercial spots in the West, the **Singing Wind Bookshop** (700 W Singing Wind Road, Benson; tel: 520-586-2425; daily 9am–5pm). Located in the front couple of rooms of proprietor Win Bundy's ranch, the store contains an excellent collection of southwestern books on ancient and contemporary American Indian culture, geology, history, and mystery.

Across the interstate from Singing Wind at Dragoon, between Benson and Willcox, is the excellent **Amerind Foundation Museum** (tel: 520-586-3666; www.amerind.org; Tue–Sun 10am–4pm; charge). This is one of the Southwest's premier private archeological and ethnographic collections. The dream of the amateur archeologist William Fulton, who build this lovely hacienda-style ranch in 1937 to show off his artifacts, it should not be missed by archeology buffs. There are

Sonoita vineyards.

well-interpreted exhibits on the native peoples of the Americas and contemporary exhibits by some of the state's most talented native artists. This is an active research center. Important archeological studies are co-published with the University of Arizona.

From Benson follow Highway 90 south for 9 miles (14km) to one of Arizona's top visitor attractions, **Kartchner Caverns State Park** (tel: 520-586-2283 for reservations; 520-586-4100 for info; www.azstateparks.com/kartchner; daily 6m–10pm, visitor center/bookstore daily June–mid-Dec 9am–5pm, mid-Dec–May 8am–6pm, tours daily 9am–3pm, you must arrive 1 hour before your tour or forfeit your reservation; charge). Kartchner is a rare "wet cave," with more than 90 percent of its colorful Escabrosa limestone decorations still growing. It was discovered in 1974 by cavers potholing beneath the Whetstone Mountains and Kartchner Ranch. The 2.5-mile (4km) cave was kept secret for 14 years while the cavers, the Kartchner family, and state officials debated how best to develop the

caverns without destroying their delicate ecosystem.

State-of-the-art technology includes misting systems in the caves, double-lock doors to seal in moisture, and specially blasted entrance tunnels. Arizona State Parks has spared no expense in doing the job right.

Tours leave every 20 minutes from the Discovery Center, which has interactive exhibits that include a simulated cave crawl-through. Rangers offer entertaining and informative talks on the porch before accompanying the tram to the cave entrance. Inside, in the Rotunda and Throne Room and the Big Room, the temperature is a steady, steamy 68°F (20°C), with paved, barrier-free walkways leading past deep mud flats and unusual formations, such as colorful shields, streaky "bacon," "fried eggs," flowing draperies, "cave popcorn," wavy helectites, ceiling-hanging stalactites, and floor-growing stalagmites. Record-breakers here are the 58ft (18-meter) Kubla Khan column and a 21ft (6-meter) -long soda straw, the longest in the

Stagecoach in Tombstone.

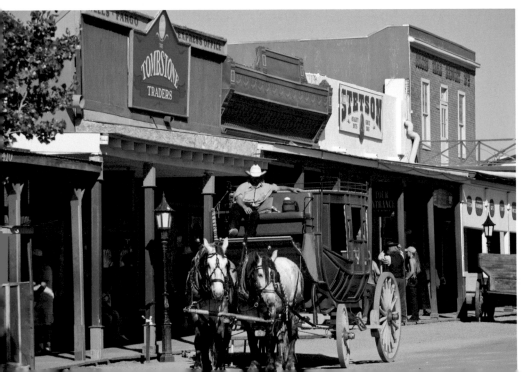

United States. Both the caves and the strong conservation message promoted here are impressive.

The **San Pedro Riparian National Conservation Area** ⓫ (tel: 520-439-6400; www.blm.gov/visit/san-pedro; visitor center daily 9.30am–4.30pm) protects 56,000 acres (22,600 hectares) of cottonwood-willow bosque along the San Pedro River, between Benson and St David, Arizona, on the US-Mexico border. Named a Globally Important Bird Area by the American Bird Conservancy, this perennial waterway managed by the Bureau of Land Management (BLM) in Hereford supports more than 80 species of mammals, 45 reptile and amphibian species, 100 species of breeding birds, and 250 species of resident birds, while an astonishing 4–10 million migratory birds lay over every winter, making this one of the most important birding sites in the region. Trails along the river lead to the historic **Little Boquillas Ranch**, the ghost towns of **Fairbank** and **Millville,** the ruined Spanish garrison of **El Presidio de Santa Cruz de Terrenate,** and **Lehner Mammoth Kill Site** and the **Murray Springs Clovis Site**, one of the oldest and most significant sites of the Clovis culture from 11,000 years ago. Bones found here include camels, mammoths, lion, and wolf. One exciting aspect of the Murray Spring site is that the tools and bones were found in situ, providing a wealth of information about the earliest culture known in North America.

TOMBSTONE

A few minutes southeast of the national conservation area, off Highway 80, is **Tombstone** ⓬ (tel: 520-457-9317, 888-457-3929; www.tombstonechamber. com). Originally known the "town too tough to die," a better modern appellation might be "the town too tacky to die." Tombstone has exploited the Hollywood image of the Old West like no other town. This is a place of costumed artifice that shamelessly takes its authentic history and turns it into a parody of itself. One is never far from an historic site or out of earshot of a reenacted shoot-out. Even if you have no desire to buy tombstone-shaped shot glasses, you will likely find yourself paying $1.50 to see the largest rose tree in existence (at the Rose Tree Inn) and be waited upon by waitresses dressed as 19th-century trollops in the Nellie Cashman Bar or one of the other joints. In Tombstone, it's what you do; go with it.

Most of the commercial action takes place on Allen Street, the town's main thoroughfare. The **OK Corral** (326 E Allen Street; tel: 520-457-3456; www. ok-corral.com; charge) is the best-known attraction on the block and commemorates authentic history. Cross into the restored grounds and see where, in October of 1881, US Marshall Wyatt Earp, his brothers Virgil and Morgan, and "Doc" Holliday battled the Clanton and McLaury boys, ranchers whose extracurricular activities included cattle rustling and

Actors in character in Tombstone.

Boot Hill Cemetary, garve stone with epitaph.

harboring stagecoach robbers. History was made in a scant 30 seconds after the Earp gang emerged victorious.

The same fee also includes an historic reenactment of the gunfight. If time is too short for the battle, mosey next door to the **Historama** and see a 26-minute multimedia presentation about the town, narrated by Vincent Price.

Farther down Allen Street are the **Bird Cage Theatre**, where working girls once plied their trade in 14 "cages," or "cribs," suspended from the ceiling; the **Oriental Saloon**, once part-owned by Wyatt Earp; and the **Crystal Palace Saloon**, still a fine location to find a cold drink in a dusty town. Allen Street is also a good place to see historical characters dressed in 19th-century clothes haunting the town. Striking up a conversation with them is a real treat, at least for the kids.

For a less commercial perspective, amble over to **Tombstone Courthouse State Historic Park** (tel: 520-457 3311; www.azstateparks.com/tombstone; daily 9am–5pm; charge), on Toughnut Street. Built in 1882, the brick Victorian structure houses the history of the town. Exhibits discuss the numerous lynchings and shootings that made the town famous and include a reconstructed gallows. The original courthouse is also visible, although one wonders how much more "justice" took place outside the building. The courthouse also has diagrammed exhibits addressing the two most popular theories about what actually happened on that legendary October day in 1881 at the OK Corral, when Virgil and Morgan Earp were wounded and three members of the Clanton gang were killed.

The Clantons and other victims of frontier justice are buried in **Boothill Graveyard**, just north of town, a cemetery so kitsch it's a must-see – complete with fake-looking headstones with cute epitaphs and piped-in Willie Nelson music. Characters interred here include Red River Tom and Dutch Annie, as well many other lesser-known victims of the vicissitudes of the Old West.

Tombstone is a resurrected mining town. To see what happens when boom leads to bust, take a little detour on a dirt road east from Tombstone to the dusty ghost towns of **Gleeson**, **Courtland**, and **Pearce**. Pearce hosted an 1894 gold rush and is now the only site with ruins (a two-story corner mercantile store, a post office, and the jail).

BISBEE AND THE OPEN-PIT MINES

About 25 miles (40km) south of Tombstone is the former mining town of **Bisbee** ⓭, now a popular arts center, spread out for 3 steep miles (5km) across Mule Pass Gulch and Tombstone Canyon in the 5,000ft (1,500 meter) Mule Mountains, just west of the border town of Douglas. After the discovery of copper in 1877, the town grew in a few years from a rowdy, cosmopolitan mining camp, where early mining claims were won and lost at

⊘ SHOOTOUT AT THE OK CORRAL

Hollywood likes to depict it as an epic shootout between good and evil, but the famous gunfight at the OK Corral in Tombstone was really little more than a small-town grudge match between two factions that wanted things their own way. On one side were the Earp brothers and their friend, dentist-turned-gambler John "Doc" Holliday. On the other side was a gang of cattle rustlers and thieves, including Ike and Billy Clanton, the McLaury brothers, and Billy Claiborne.

The Earps became one of the most powerful families in town after they arrived in Tombstone in 1879, soon making the town marshall and deputy jobs a family affair. The Earps, and friend Holliday, quickly made enemies, especially of the Clantons and McLaurys. After many months of bad blood, in 1881, the grudge turned violent at the OK Corral. The Earps got off the first shots. In all, the gunfight lasted half a minute. Billy Clanton and the McLaurys were dead or dying, two Earp brothers were badly wounded, Holliday barely scratched, and Wyatt untouched.

Holliday and Wyatt stood trial for the shootings and were exonerated. But the grudge – and killings – continued for years, and only Wyatt Earp died of old age, in Los Angeles in 1929 at the age of 81.

the faro table by hard-drinking miners and ex-soldiers, to a phenomenally rich, well-heeled town with Victorian brick buildings.

An air of respectability, as well as more money, came when Judge Dewitt Bisbee (who never saw the town named for him) and a group of San Francisco investors bought the Copper Queen Mine in 1880. But with underground copper seams running for miles into other claims, cooperation proved the only way for everyone to get rich, and the still-powerful Phelps Dodge Corporation was born, which basically controlled the town from that point forward.

This new concern built the **Copper Queen Hotel**, the town's most famous structure, in 1900, and the 1897 Phelps Dodge General Office Building, which now houses the impressive **Bisbee Mining and Historical Museum** (5 Copper Queen Plaza; tel: 520-432-7071; www.bisbeemuseum.org; daily 10am–4pm; charge), a satellite of the Smithsonian Institution. This museum is one of the Southwest's true gems, with terrific multimedia exhibits that capture the fascinating and storied history of Bisbee and real-life gems that stagger the imagination, alongside displays of enormous chunks of locally mined turquoise (typically found alongside copper and silver). A standout exhibit is the depiction of the Bisbee Deportation of 1917, when 1,000 striking miners of the Industrial Workers of the World – known as the Wobblies – were loaded at gunpoint into boxcars and shipped like cattle to Columbus, New Mexico, for "anti-government" activities during World War I.

Around the corner is Brewery Gulch, which once supported 50 saloons. Many buildings in the historic downtown, from the OK Jail to miner's boarding houses, have now been reborn as some of the Southwest's quaintest art galleries, museums, and offbeat lodgings. You can view them as part of a popular self-guided historic downtown walking tour, including the Muheim Block, where the Bisbee Stock Exchange was built. The original stock tote board is still in the bar. Structures

Main Street in Bisbee.

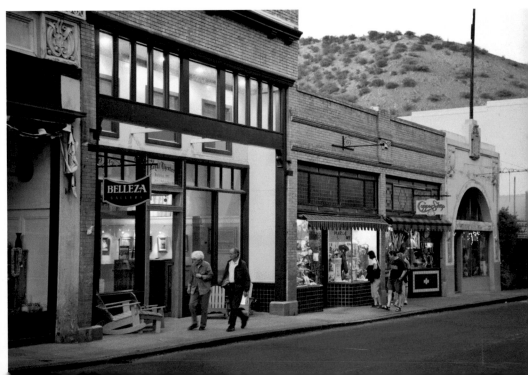

are built directly into the steep hills, so be prepared to exert yourself a little.

After yielding 8 billion lbs (3.6 billion kg) of copper, Bisbee's 33 mines (and an astonishing 2,500 miles/4,000km of tunnels) were all closed by 1975, including the yawning abyss of the **Lavender Open Pit Mine**, a 340-acre (137-hectare) and 900ft (275-meter) -deep hole on the edge of downtown, which long ago swallowed a whole mountain. Despite the pit's color, the name honors a former mining executive, Harrison Lavender.

The **Queen Mine Tour** (tel: 520-432-2071; www.queenminetour.com; daily tours; call for current times and reservations; charge) allows you to descend into the mine, and is the other unmissable attraction in Bisbee. Visitors are equipped with yellow slickers and miner's helmets and lamps and sit astride an old mine train for the chilly trip down the shaft with a flinty ex-miner – himself a mine of information about drilling, blasting, mining etiquette, and the cushy life of a sanitary engineer, or "s*** nipper."

Getting ready for the Queen Mine Tour.

When the Phelps Dodge Company decided the Bisbee smelter was too small, it built a new one in **Douglas** ⓮, 25 miles (40km) east of Bisbee and on the Mexican border, naming the town after the company president, Dr James Douglas. The twin smokestacks that loom over town stopped polluting in 1987. All that truly reveals the glory days of Douglas is the five-story 1907 **Gadsden Hotel** (tel: 520-364-4481; www.thegadsdenhotel.com), which bills itself as "the last of the grand hotels" and once hosted dignitaries such as President Theodore Roosevelt. Under new ownership since late 2016, the hotel is gradually being renovated and its attractive rooms are available to overnight guests at a very reasonable price. At the very least, step inside to view the impressive lobby, which features a white marble staircase and massive marble columns topped with 14-carat gold leaf and a vaulted ceiling with a 42ft (13-meter) -long Tiffany stained glass mural of desert scenes.

About 15 miles (24km) east of Douglas on the US side is the peaceful, 93,000-acre (38,000-hectare) **John Slaughter Ranch Museum** (tel: 520-678-7935; www.slaughterranch.com; Wed-Sun 9.30am–3.30pm; donation), a little slice of heaven once owned by former Texas Ranger and Cochise County Sheriff John Slaughter. His 1890s house, corral, and other buildings have been restored as an example of ranch life during Arizona's territorial years and are now run by volunteers for a local charity. This is a lovely spot to linger on the grass under shade trees and picnic, enjoy the views, and contemplate the frontier. A 2,330-acre (940-hectare) section is now protected as **San Bernardino National Wildlife Refuge.**

INTO CHIRICAHUA APACHE LANDS

Around 80 miles (128km) from Tucson, via Interstate 10, is **Willcox** ⓯, the fruit-and-nut-picking capital of

Arizona. In summer, one can pick apples, peaches, pecans, and pistachios, but in recent years, Willcox has become well known for its grapes and a burgeoning number of vineyards. Some 74 percent of grapes grown in Arizona are grown on the high-rise Willcox Bench, south of town, and 12 wineries now offer tastings and sales of award-winning wines onsite or at four tasting rooms in the historic downtown. **Rolling View Vineyard** (tel: 602-320-1722; www.bodegapierce.com) grows 20 different grape varietals and makes a nice Viognier under its Saeculum label. Its winemaker, Michael Pierce, is the director of enology at Yavapai College's Southwest Wine Center. **Keeling Schaefer Vineyards** (tel: 520-824-2500; www.keelingschaefervineyards.com) has a tasting room in downtown Willcox in a converted 1917 bank. Check out its Rhone wines, including a full-bodied Syrah. For more information about businesses and a wine tour map, visit www.willcoxwines.com. If you are a lover of Country and Western music, you'll want to mosey over to the **Rex Allen Cowboy Museum** (tel: 520-384-4583; www.rexallenmuseum.org; Mon 10am–1pm, Tue–Sat 11am–3pm; charge) and pay tribute to Willcox's native son.

In winter, nearby **Willcox Playa** and **White Water Draw** flood and become wetlands attracting 10,000 migratory sandhill cranes, Canada and snow geese, and other waterfowl, making these locations popular birding spots.

The final refuge for the Chiricahua Apache chief Cochise on his run from the US Army is about 25 miles (40km) south of Willcox in the Dragoon Mountains. He and his band of Apaches remained in the rocky confines of what is now called **Cochise Stronghold** for many years. A beautiful and quiet campground sheltered by oaks now marks Cochise's last hideout.

Fort Bowie National Historic Site ⑯ (tel: 520-847-2500; www.nps.gov/fobo; visitor center daily 8am–4pm; free) is a good location to learn more about the Apache. This ruined adobe outpost once consisted of US Army barracks, officer's quarters, storehouses, a trader's store, and a hospital. It was

Rex Allen Museum, Willcox.

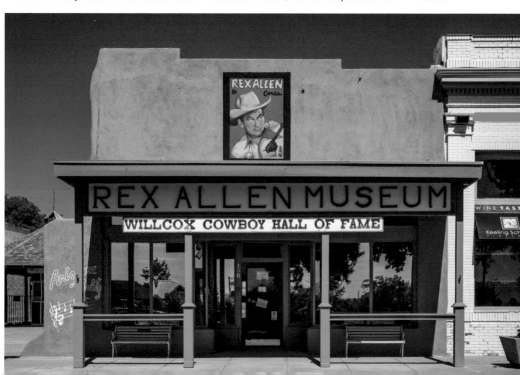

built to protect the Butterfield Overland Mail Stage and local residents from the Apache, who were falsely accused of theft. A 1.5-mile (2.5km) self-guided trail to the ruins leaves from Apache Pass Road.

Chiricahua National Monument ⑰ (tel: 520-824-3560; www.nps.gov/chir; visitor center daily 8.30am–4.30pm; free), on the western side of the Chiricahua Mountains, south of Willcox, was known as the Land of Standing Rocks by the Chiricahua Apaches who, led in later years by Geronimo and Cochise, used the mountains as a refuge. After the forced relocation of the Apache by the army in 1886, the Erickson family moved into the area. They lived at Faraway Ranch for nearly a century and were influential in obtaining National Park Service designation for the land they called a "wonderland of rocks." Visitors can still see the ranch house, located a few miles from the national monument's western entrance.

The land was set aside in 1924 to protect this fantasyland of rocks, which formed 25 million years ago when a nearby volcano exploded. Eruption of Turkey Creek caldera produced a 2,000ft (600-meter) -thick layer of fused ash volcanic rock, known as rhyolite. Subsequent erosion by water, ice, and wind sculpted the rhyolite into columns, balanced rocks, and strangely shaped hoodoos.

To view the rocks, follow the 6-mile (10km) **Bonita Canyon Scenic Drive**, which climbs from the visitor center through lush Bonita Canyon to Massai Point, the starting point for a short nature trail and longer trails among the rocks.

Like many ranges in southern Arizona, the Chiricahuas are called "sky islands." They receive significantly more precipitation and experience far cooler temperatures than the surrounding Sonoran Desert. Rocky Mountain and Sierra Madrean wildlife mingle in these sky islands via a natural corridor running through the Chiricahuas to Mexico. Mexican plants and animals such as rare Apache fox squirrels and Chihuahua and Apache pines live side by side with species more commonly found north of the border.

Of particular interest are the birds that summer in the **Cave Creek** area, near Portal, on the east side of the Chiricahuas. Top of the list is the trogon, a Mexican native bird with a long, coppery tail and bright feathers, sulphur-bellied flycatchers, tanagers, chickadees, warblers, and a variety of hummingbirds. Portal may be reached via a seasonal forest road from the national monument over the mountains into the Coronado National Forest and Chiricahua Wilderness in good weather and subject to wildfire closures. It's typically best to drive south on US Highway 80 from Interstate 10, then turn off toward Cave Creek, a very beautiful destination with a lovely campground, cabins, and bed-and-breakfasts beloved by birders.

Erosion of volcanic rocks at Chiricahua National Monument, Echo Canyon Trail.

GERONIMO

The life of Apache leader, Geronimo, continues to fascinate.

In 1905, while a prisoner of war at Fort Sill, Indian Territory, Geronimo recounted the Apache creation story: "In the beginning, the world was covered with darkness," he said. "There was no sun, no day. The perpetual night had no moon or stars. There were, however, all manner of beasts and birds. Among the beasts were many hideous, nameless monsters... Mankind could not prosper under such conditions, for the beasts and serpents destroyed all human offspring."

But there was one boy who was not eaten by the monsters, Geronimo said. His mother, White Painted Woman, hid him from a dragon who ate human children. When the boy grew up, he went hunting and met the dragon in the mountains. He shot three arrows into the dragon's scales, and then, with the fourth arrow, he pierced the dragon's heart. "This boy's name was Apache."

It must have seemed odd to the men who heard this tale that the old storyteller was once the most feared warrior in the American Southwest. Geronimo was a war leader of the Chiricahua Apaches, the most fearsome of the Apache bands. Between 1876 and 1886, Geronimo and his warriors terrorized settlers and frustrated soldiers with lightning raids, elusive retreats, and repeated escapes.

Geronimo's early life was subject to raids and warfare. As a young man he married and had children, but his entire family was wiped out by Mexican troopers. He launched bloody raids against the Mexicans in revenge, and emerged as a leading warrior. He later fought alongside Cochise and Mangas Colorado in engagements against American and Mexican soldiers.

Geronimo joined Cochise in 1874 on the newly created Chiricahua Indian Reservation, but when the reservation was dissolved two years later, he escaped and returned to raiding. He was captured in New Mexico in 1877 and brought to San Carlos, where many Arizona Apaches were being confined and encouraged to take up farming. It had no appeal for Geronimo. He broke out of San Carlos in 1881, and the raiding started again.

Twice more Geronimo agreed to return to San Carlos, and twice he bolted. Finally, in 1886, with some 5,000 soldiers and 500 Indian scouts chasing his band of 24 warriors, Geronimo surrendered for the last time.

Back home in Arizona, whites wanted him tried for murder and executed. Newspapers across the country painted him as a savage killer. Even President Grover Cleveland suggested that he be hanged. But Geronimo's punishment may have been worse. He and the Chiricahuas – even many who had served as army scouts – were shipped in chains to a prison camp in Florida, then, one year later, to another in Alabama. They were ravaged by tuberculosis, homesickness, despair. Within a few years, more than 100 died.

In 1894, after much lobbying by friends, Geronimo and his people were relocated to Fort Sill, Indian Territory. Throughout his imprisonment, Geronimo begged to go home, but his request was not granted. He died of pneumonia in 1909. He was still a prisoner of war at Fort Sill.

Geronimo, 1886.

Road in White Sands National Monument.

SOUTHERN NEW MEXICO

The south of New Mexico is home to top-secret military bases, vast dunes of white gypsum, one of the world's richest horse races, a mountain resort owned by the Mescalero Apache, and the shooting grounds of Billy the Kid.

Southern New Mexico is a study in opposites: snowcapped 11,000ft (3,400-meter) peaks abutting the torrid, 3,000ft (900-meter) -elevation Chihuahuan Desert; sleepy historic copper and ranching communities alongside Space Age towns, telescope arrays, and military installations; irrigated fields planted with corn, beans, squash, and chiles within sight of the empty barrens of Texas's Llano Estacado (Staked Plains) and dark lava flows; ruined Spanish missions poking up from lonely grasslands; and Indian dwellings in countryside so remote one wonders how anyone could make a living there.

People do make a living here – in agriculture, ranching, mining, aerospace, defense, and education – but feel unjustly neglected and maligned by the more glamorous northern part of the state. That's a shame. This is a great place for adventurous backroad drives and introspective walks, where the friendliness of the people is surpassed only by changing landscapes and the juxtaposition of the truly ancient with the world of tomorrow.

SOUTHWESTERN NEW MEXICO

A couple of miles south of **Lordsburg** ⓲, in the far southwestern corner of New Mexico, on Interstate 10, about 20 miles (30km) east of the Arizona–New

Mexico border, is the classic ghost town of **Shakespeare** (tel: 575-542-9034; www.shakespeareghosttown.com; open on some weekends for tours; charge), where Billy the Kid used to be a dishwasher. Now part of a family-owned working ranch, the town (originally named Mexican Springs) boomed and died through successive silver strikes and a great diamond hoax, witnessing its share of hangings and brothels. In 1879, it was bought by an Englishman who rechristened the town Shakespeare and its main street, Avon Avenue.

Main Attractions
Gila Cliff Dwellings National Monument
El Paso
Carlsbad Caverns National Park
White Sands National Monument
Mescalero Apache Indian Reservation
Lincoln
Bosque del Apache National Wildlife Refuge

Map on page 184

The Organ Mountains.

Also caught up in the silver boom, **Silver City**  was born in 1870 just 40 miles (65km) northeast of Lordsburg. Unlike most mining boomtowns, it never died. Like Bisbee, Arizona, it has transformed into an artists community of refurbished Victorian homes, bed-and-breakfasts, coffee houses, brewpubs, burgeoning new restaurants, art galleries, and boutiques. A nature lover's paradise, it's the gateway to Gila National Forest and Gila Wilderness, and also – remote as it is – the largest town in southwestern New Mexico.

To learn more about the local history, especially that of the Mogollon, visit the **Western New Mexico University Museum** (1000 W College; tel: 505-538-6386; www.wnmu.edu/univ/museum; Mon–Fri 9am–4.30pm, Sat–Sun 10am–4pm; donations) in Silver City, where there is a large exhibit of black-on-white pottery decorated with birds, snakes and other dramatic motifs, produced by the Mimbres branch of the Mogollon people between AD 900 and 1100.

Six miles (10km) north of Silver City is **Pinos Altos**, the oldest mining town in the district with a museum housed in the old school. Across the street is the **Buckhorn Saloon and Opera House** (tel: 575-538-9911; www.buckhornsaloonandoperahouse.com; Mon–Sat for dinner), with its whitewashed adobe walls, heavy-beamed ceiling, carved furniture, and velvet draperies adding a touch of elegance, Although not the original building, the Opera House has excellent exhibits of historic photographs and Mimbres pottery, and in the summer it often provides entertainment such as concerts, theatrical melodrama, or old movies.

Highway 15 winds slowly north through the Gila National Forest and mountains to **Gila Cliff Dwellings National Monument** ⑳ (tel: 505-536-9461; www.nps.gov/gicl; daily 9am–5pm, visitor center 8am–4.30pm; charge), where it dead-ends in a secluded canyon. The Mogollon people, influenced early on by contact with Mexico to the south, were resourceful mountain people who hunted, gathered, and lived in pithouses for many centuries prior to building cliff dwellings in these cliffs.

Taking photos at Gila Cliff Dwellings National Monument.

They were not unsophisticated, though, and were the first to make pottery in the Southwest, refining it over time to the collectable Mimbres pottery we know today. Branches of the Mogollon lived in southwest New Mexico for a thousand years before they were apparently enfolded by the greater Ancestral Pueblo culture to the north. A mile-long trail leads up the canyon and into the dwellings, 180ft (55 meters) above the canyon floor.

Other trails lead from the visitor center into the 790,000-acre (320,000-hectare) Gila, Aldo Leopold, and Blue Range wildernesses within 3.3 million-acre (1.3-million hectare) **Gila National Forest Wilderness**. The Gila Wilderness, established in 1924, was the first wilderness in the country. The Aldo Leopold Wilderness was named for the pioneering forester whose classic book *Sand Country Almanac* was one of the first to promote the idea of wilderness. Trips into the wilderness require backcountry permits and must be made on foot or horseback. The **Gila National Forest Wilderness Ranger Station** (tel: 575-536-2250; www.fs.usda.gov/detail/gila/about-forest/districts; Mon–Fri 8am–4.30pm) is located in Mimbres.

Sixty miles (100km) northwest of Silver City, on US 180, is the village of **Glenwood ㉑**, another headquarters for pack trips into the wilderness. Information and permits are available from the **Glenwood Ranger Station** (tel: 575-539-2481; www.fs.usda.gov/gila; Mon–Fri 8am–4.30pm). Glenwood is most famous for the **Catwalk,** a narrow, metal railed walkway that hugs the sheer rock wall of the gorge as it winds along the creek up the canyon for about 1 mile (0.6km) past the 100ft (30-meter) -deep gorge. The canyon walls are 1,400ft (427 meters) high, but the Catwalk is just 20ft (6 meters) above the river, so it is very dramatic and scenic, not to mention cool on a hot day. The Catwalk was built in 1893, when pipelines were laid through the canyon to provide water for a mill that serviced nearby gold and silver claims. Maintenance workers had to walk along the suspended pipes and referred to them as the catwalk. You can still see parts of the old pipelines. The Catwalk trailhead is at the end of Highway 174 in the national forest.

Three miles (5km) north of Glenwood, Highway 159 turns east toward the ghost town of **Mogollon**, 9 miles (14km) up in the mountains. Relics of mines, tailings dumps, and foundations on the hills show the prominence of gold and silver mining in this area from 1875 until World War I. About 15 people live in Mogollon now, mostly along Main Street, which follows Silver Creek. The buildings are weathered gray, the metal rusted red. Some were built years ago for a 1973 Henry Fonda movie called *My Name is Nobody*, but built so well most people can't tell the old from the new.

One Mogollon spot worth a special trip is **Silver Creek Inn** (tel: 866-276-4882; http://silvercreekinn.com; open May–Oct). Built in 1885 as a hotel and

☉ Tip

The Inner Loop, a paved, 100-mile (160km) scenic drive (state roads 15, 35, and 90), goes from Silver City to Gila Cliff Dwellings National Monument, then returns through the Mimbres Valley past lakes and farms.

Hiker on the Catwalk at Whitewater Canyon in the Mogollon Mountains.

general store, the bed-and-breakfast is owned by local food and hospitality mavens Stan King and Kathy Knapp of the Pie-O-Neer Cafe in Pie Town and has a lovely enclosed patio with waterfall and sweeping, curved exterior staircase. Four guest rooms are available by advance reservation. Guests may bring food to cook other meals in the kitchen and staff will do the cleanup for a $10 fee. The inn does not have TV or Wi-Fi, only accepts adults ages 21 and older, and has a no-pets policy. Note: Highway 159 is undergoing major repair until 2018; call the inn for an update.

TOWARD THE BORDER

Thirty-five miles (56km) south of **Deming ㉒**, the US–Mexico border is marked by the towns of **Columbus ㉓** on the American side and **Las Palomas** on the Mexican side. **Pancho Villa State Park** (tel: 575-531 2711; www.emnrd.state.nm.us/spd/panchovillastatepark.htm; daily 8am–6pm; charge) at Columbus commemorates much more than the revolutionary figure for whom it

Cinco de Mayo Fiesta in the historic village of Mesilla.

is named. In 1916, Pancho Villa led a band of rebels across the border in an attack that killed eight civilians and soldiers at Columbus and nearby Camp Furlong. This was the only time since the War of 1812 (against Britain) that the continental United States had been invaded by foreign troops. It is also the first time in American history that air power was used in war. General John J. "Black Jack" Pershing led a pursuit party into Mexico after Pancho Villa. Pershing's troops were given air cover by eight small single-engine planes from Fort Sam Houston in Texas.

Twenty-eight miles (45km) northwest of Deming is **City of Rocks State Park ㉔** (tel: 505-536-2800; www.emnrd.state.nm.us/prd/cityrocks; daily 7am–9pm; charge). Like a desert Stonehenge, the City of Rocks is made up of boulders that rise 40ft (12 meters) high – some with the appearance of skyscrapers, others tilting at crazy angles. In a state where prehistoric ruins are common, one might suppose these to be ruins, but they are actually the products of erosion on ancient volcanic rhyolite outcroppings, similar to the rocks found in the heart of southeastern Arizona's Chiricahua National Monument not far away.

This was a favorite lookout place for Apache waiting to ambush stagecoaches on the Butterfield stage route. Camping and picnic areas can be found among the rocks, sheltered from heat and wind by gnarled alligator juniper trees.

Fifty miles (80km) on Interstate 10, east of Deming, **Las Cruces ㉕** is New Mexico's second-largest and fastest-growing city with over 101,000 people. It took its name from a forlorn cluster of crosses that marked the place where Franciscan missionaries were killed by Apaches in the early 1800s. The town itself was not established until after the area became a US territory in 1849, but the Spanish El Camino Real (Royal Road) between Mexico City and Santa Fe passed through here. Today, it's an important transportation hub and agricultural center noted for its chiles, pecans, and cotton – a history that is examined in the **New Mexico Farm and Ranch Heritage Museum** (tel: 505-522-4100; www. nmfarmandranchmuseum.org; Mon–Sat 9am–5pm, Sun noon–5pm; charge).

Las Cruces is home to **New Mexico State University**, with a student population of over 25,000 and noted for its schools of engineering and agriculture. Sleepy little **Mesilla**, just south, was built about the same time as Las Cruces but has a lovely historic village feel. The Gadsden Purchase was signed here in 1853, fixing the boundary between the United States and Mexico and ceding the US vast areas of the Southwest that had once been Mexican territory.

South of Mesilla is the scenic **Oñate Trail** (Highway 28), named for Spanish explorer Don Juan de Oñate, founder of New Mexico. It traces part of the route that Oñate took into New Mexico more than 400 years ago. Stahmann Farms (http://stahmannpecan.com) began in 1932 and now boasts 168,000 pecan trees on 3,200 acres (1,295 hectares), making it one of the world's largest pecan groves. About 17 miles (27km) farther south, **La Viña Winery** (tel: 575-882-7632; http://lavina.wolfep.com; Thu–Tue noon–5pm; tours daily by appointment at 11.30am), is New Mexico's oldest winery, founded in 1977. The winery offers tastings and hosts a range of special seasonal events.

New Mexico's newest national monument, set aside by President Obama in May 2014 to protect significant historic, prehistoric, geologic, and biologic resources, is 496,330-acre (200,858-hectare) **Organ Mountains– Desert Peaks National Monument** (BLM Las Cruces office info, tel: 575-522-1219; www.organmountains.org). Managed by the BLM, it is divided into three main sections surrounding Las Cruces: the spectacular 9,000ft (2,743-meter) -high Organ Mountains, east of Las Cruces; the Desert Peaks, which comprise the Robledo Mountains, Sierra de las Uvas, and the Dona Ana Mountains,

The road to City of Rocks State Park.

northwest of Las Cruces, adjoining a smaller site containing a prehistoric trackway; and the Potrillo Mountains, southwest of Las Cruces, which contain volcanic features, including Kilbourne Hole Volcanic Crater National Historic Landmark, an 80,000-year-old volcanic maar crater used as a training ground by Apollo astronauts.

Dripping Springs Natural Area (tel: 575-522-1219; daily 8am–5pm; charge) is the main visitor-friendly section. Located in the Organ Mountains, off US 70, 10 miles (16km) east of Las Cruces, it has a visitor center, nicely developed campground, and trailheads. One of the trails leads past **La Cueva Rock Shelter,** which dates from the Desert Archaic period, 5,000 BC, to the historic period, when it was occupied by Apaches and later by an eccentric recluse named Giovanni Maria Agotino, known locally as "the Hermit." In the mid-1970s, approximately 100,000 artifacts were recovered here by the University of Texas at El Paso. Another trail leads to the ruins of **Dripping Springs Resort**, built in 1873 by

Colonel Eugene Patten and in 1917, converted to a sanitorium.

SLIPPING INTO TEXAS

South of Las Cruces about 50 miles (80km), over the state border in Texas, **El Paso ㉖** was originally a place where Spanish trails crossed the Rio Grande. Travelers called it El Paso del Norte, the Pass of the North. In 1659, a small colony was established on the south side of the river, and in 1827, another began on the northern side. After the war with Mexico, when the border was set, the two colonial villages became El Paso, on the north side of the river, and Ciudad Juarez, Mexico, on the south. The two today comprise an international city that is home to more than a million people.

You can learn more about the history of this international border at **Chamizal National Memorial** (800 S San Marcial Street, El Paso; tel: 915-532-7273; www.nps.gov/cham; grounds daily 7am–10pm, Cultural Center daily 10am–5pm, Art Gallery Mon–Fri 8am–4.30pm, Sat–Sun 10am–5pm; free), a 55-acre (22-hectare) national park

Mural at the Chamizal National Memorial, located in El Paso.

commemorating the peaceful settlement of the 100-year-old Chamizal boundary dispute over the Rio Grande between the US and Mexico. From here, you can walk across a bridge into Mexico, to a mirror friendship park unit on the other side of the border. Cultural events are often held here.

El Paso used to be a tough, gunslinging border town and a bit of that flavor persists in the number of cowboy boots and Stetson hats – strictly for fashion, in most cases – seen on the streets. In fact, five major cowboy-boot factories are located in El Paso.

During the Pueblo Revolt of 1680 in New Mexico, refugee Spaniards and non-hostile Indians fled to El Paso, where they established new villages on the Rio Grande. After the reconquest 12 years later, many chose to stay and these villages – Ysleta del Sur, Socorro, and San Elizario – are the vestiges of those settlements.

The Ysleta mission is still in use, as is the **Socorro Mission** (tel: 915-859-7718; Mon–Fri 8am–4pm; free), which was built in the same decade and is the oldest continuously active parish in the US. El Camino Real, the royal highway that once linked El Norte to the capital of New Spain in Mexico, is today a quiet farm road that connects the Ysleta and Socorro missions with the **San Elizario Presidio Chapel**. The presidio chapel was built in 1789, using a mixture of Spanish Colonial and native architectural styles, as a fortified base for the army. It was reconstructed in 1877.

El Paso Mission Trail Foundation (tel: 915-851-9997; http://visitelpasomis-siontrail.com; daily tours; charge) offers daily tours of El Paso's two restored Spanish missions and presidio chapel. They are located 9 miles (14km) apart. Across the border, in Ciudad Juárez, the even older (1668) **Guadalupe Mission** is famous for the legend that its shadows point to the Lost Padre Mine in the El Paso's Franklin Mountains, where Spanish gold is said to be hidden.

At 23,863 acres (9,657 hectares), **Franklin Mountains State Park** (1331 McKelligon Canyon Road; tel: 915-566-6441; http://tpwd.texas.gov/state-parks/franklin-mountains; early Apr–mid-Sept

The El Paso county symbol above the entrance to the city courthouse.

View of downtown El Paso.

Mon–Fri 8am–5pm, Sat–Sun 6.30am–8pm, rest of year daily 8am–5pm; charge) with its North Franklin Peak, at 7,192ft (2,192 meters), the highest peak in El Paso, is the largest urban city park in the US (no, it is *not* Central Park in Manhattan). It is home to ringtail cats, coyotes, and other wildlife, and offers numerous places to explore, picnic, and relax. Ride the **Wyler Aerial Tramway** (1700 McKinley Avenue; tel: 915-566-6622) to Ranger Peak (5,632ft/1,716 meters) for views of Mexico and New Mexico. Northwest of the city, scenic drives across the Franklin Mountains, and especially along **Transmountain Road** (exit off I-10 West), provide spectacular views.

CAVERNS AND CANYONS

One hundred miles (160km) east of El Paso, and still in Texas, is **Guadalupe Mountains National Park** ㉗ (tel: 915-828 3251; www.nps.gov/gumo; daily 8am–4.30pm; charge), where an ancient Permian Reef that built up 250 million years ago in a shallow sea has been uplifted, eroded, and exposed as limestone crags and deep canyons. Texas' highest mountain, 8,749ft (2,667-meter) **Guadalupe Peak**, towers at the center of the park, which also preserves Texas' largest wilderness. More than 80 miles (130km) of trails criss-cross the desert lowlands into the high country, and although there are no services here, there is a visitor center and small campground. Try to time a visit for early October and hike **McKittrick Canyon**, famous for the autumn brilliance of its Texas madrone, oak, and other deciduous trees, which cluster along the only year-round creek in the park. The trail leads to the quaint Pratt Cabin, built by oil-field geologist Wallace Pratt, who fell in love with the Guadalupes and helped establish it as a national park in 1972.

For surreal juxtapositions, it doesn't get much better than **Carlsbad Caverns National Park** ㉘ (tel: 575-785-2232; www.nps.gov/cave; charge), over the state line in New Mexico but adjoining Guadalupe Mountains and sharing its Permian era reef geology. The tour into the caverns descends into a strange, discreetly lit underground parallel universe, far from the harsh Chihuahuan Desert. The temperature remains a steady 56°F (13°C), and silence reigns, broken periodically by the drip-drip-drip of water. As your eyes adjust to the gloom, what emerges is a limestone fantasia, where popcorn flows across walls, soda-straw stalactite and helectite curtains drape from the ceiling, stalagmite pillars rear up from the floor as if holding up the earth, and you glide on slippery trails around pools filled with nets of calcite "pearls" and floating "lily pads."

You have to wonder: How did all of this get here? The process began 250 million years ago in a warm, shallow sea inhabited by marine sponges and calcareous algae, which died and piled up on the sea bottom, eventually forming a 400-mile (650km) -long limestone reef, long ago exposed by a receding sea.

McKittrick Canyon.

The oldest of the 80 known caves at Carlsbad Caverns (more are discovered all the time) formed 12 million years ago (and as recently as 200,000 years ago), when slightly acidic groundwater started percolating through the limestone reef, hollowing out caves. Corrosion was greatly accelerated by sulfuric acid from hydrogen sulfide gas seeping into the reef from the Permian Basin oil field in nearby western Texas. After the caves had formed, it was only a matter of time before groundwater exiting to air-filled caverns caused precipitation of limey water and calcareous formations.

If you only have a short time or cannot walk far, access the main cavern, the Big Room, via elevator from the visitor center. But the best approach is on foot, descending 830ft (250 meters) into the caves on the steep, 3-mile (5km) -long Natural Entrance trail. Far below, the Big Room opens up like some kind of great Hall of the Mountain King, 22 stories high, the size of 14 football fields and filled to the rafters with a weird assembly of limestone

formations that glow luminous in the low lights. Guided tours of caves leading off the Big Room, such as King's Palace, the Queen's Chamber, and the Papoose Room, offer a closer look at the eerie formations.

But it's the off-trail tours that offer the best caving introduction. The helmet-and-headlamp tour of Lower Cave and the easier candle-lit tour of Left Hand Tunnel are easily tackled by anyone of moderate fitness, while the popular Slaughter Canyon Cave tour (limit 25 people), 23 miles (37km) south of the visitor center, requires a strenuous one-mile hike to enter the undeveloped cave using flashlights. Experienced rangers make these tours safe, fun, and educational and always offer a few minutes of absolute darkness – definitely something everyone should experience once in a lifetime.

NORTH OF LAS CRUCES

Twelve miles (19km) north of Las Cruces lie the ruins of **Fort Selden Historic Site ㉙** (tel: 575-526 8911; www. nmhistoricsites.org/fort-selden; Wed–Sun

Trail among the striking stalagmites and stalactites at Carlsbad Caverns National Park.

⊙ CARLSBAD CAVERNS NATIONAL PARK

Access The park entrance is 23 miles (37km) southwest of Carlsbad, NM, and 150 miles (240km) east of El Paso, TX, via US 180/62.

Seasons & hours The park is open daily year-round, except Christmas. The visitor center is open daily 8am–5pm winter, 8am–7pm summer. Last time for visiting the caves is 3.30pm for walk-ins and 5pm for elevator in summer, 2.30pm for walk-ins and 3.30pm in winter.

Entrance fee Yes.

Handicapped access Visitor center, large section of Big Room cavern tour, a nature trail, and picnic sites.

Activities Main and off-trail cave tours, camping, hiking, bat viewing, wildlife-watching, night sky, and other interpretive programs. Experienced cavers may arrange permits for exploration of backcountry caves by contacting the Cave Resource Office, tel: 575-785-3107.

Note: You are advised to reserve all cave tours 48 hours in advance through www.recreation.gov (tel: 877-444-6777, 10am–10pm Mar–Oct; 10am–midnight Nov–Feb).

8.30am–5pm; charge), built in 1865. The fort played an important role in protecting the pioneers and miners who traveled along the overland trail to California. Continue north on Highway 195 or Interstate 25 and turn off at Hatch, which calls itself the Chile Capital of the World. The annual Hatch Chile Festival over Labor Day celebrates the year's crop of chiles.

The Rio Grande is dammed at **Truth or Consequences** ㉚ (known as T or C), north of Las Cruces, to form **Elephant Butte Lake State Park** (tel: 575-744-5923; www.emnrd.state.nm.us/spd/elephantbuttelakestatepark; charge), one of the state's most popular boating, fishing, and watersports spots. This small town on the central highlands changed its name from Hot Springs to T or C in 1948, in response to an offer from Ralph Edwards, who originated a popular radio show of the same name. As its old name implies, T or C is famous for its natural hot springs, and the quirky little town, increasingly a mecca for artists, is famed for its old-fashioned motels with onsite hot spring baths,

mild winter climate, and an increasing number of very good restaurants.

Thirty miles (48km) east of Truth or Consequences, on the desolate Jornado del Muerto Plain, is **Spaceport America**, the first spaceport in America. It was constructed by the State of New Mexico in partnership with several aerospace companies and Virgin Airlines founder Sir Richard Branson's Virgin Galactic, which plans to offer suborbital passenger tours into space at $250,000 a person. Temporary launch pads at the site have been used to launch prototype spacecraft and Spaceloft XL rockets since 2006, with 46 launches to date.

The facility is now open to the public for four-hour tours by advance reservation. Tours start at the **Spaceport America Visitor Center** (Foch Street, Truth or Consequences; tel: 575-267-8888; www.spaceportamerica.com), where you board a shuttle for the drive out to the Spaceport, during which time the driver offers background information on the project and its location. Visitors enter via the Astronaut Walk into the

Elephant Butte Lake.

Gateway Gallery, which has hands-on multimedia exhibits as well as a G-Shock Simulator that allows you to experience the same type of accelaration as astronauts do on launch into space. Spaceport personnel are also on hand to discuss their work in the Spaceport Operations Center. All in all, pretty exciting stuff – and not just for kids.

TULAROSA BASIN

Nestled between the Sacramento and San Andres mountains in the **Tularosa Basin** northeast of Las Cruces is **White Sands National Monument** ❸ (tel: 575-479 6124; www.nps.go/whsa; summer 8am–7pm, rest of year 8am–4.30pm; charge), off Highway 70, just outside Alamogordo. These white "sands" are really a 50-mile (80km) expanse of fine gypsum that has shed from the mountains and been picked up on the prevailing winds and dropped into dunes of many different types, some as high as 200ft (60 meters). Stop at the visitor center for an orientation and then take the 8-mile (13km) drive through the dunes. Interpretive signs and trails tell the story of their formation. You can also stop and picnic in the Heart of the Dunes for a dining experience in perhaps the world's strangest setting.

Surrounding White Sands are two giant military installations, **Holloman Air Force Base**, home to the B2 or Stealth bomber, and **White Sands Missile Range**, the latter best known for its Trinity Site, where the world's first atomic bomb was detonated in 1945. (The Trinity Site is open to visitors on the first Saturdays in April and October; for more information, contact Alamogordo Chamber of Commerce, tel: 800-826-0294).

The history of space exploration is the focus of the **New Mexico Museum of Space History** (tel: 575-437 2840; www.nmspacemuseum.org; daily 10am–5pm; charge) in **Alamogordo** ❷. Inside are exhibits on rockets, missiles, satellites, space programs such as the Apollo and Skylab missions, and milestones in astronomy. Former astronauts are inducted annually into the International Space Hall of Fame in a

White Sands National Monument.

special October ceremony. Outside the museum are actual rocket stages.

A 20-mile (32km) drive east of Alamogordo on US 82 takes you up into the lofty Sacramento Mountains to the mountain resort village of **Cloudcroft**, in Lincoln National Forest. The road climbs abruptly from 4,350ft (1,325 meters) to almost 9,000ft (2,750 meters) at Cloudcroft. Several pullouts offer panoramic views of White Sands National Monument to the west. Cloudcroft has a family-oriented ski area, Ski Cloudcroft (www.skicloudcroft.net), the southernmost ski area in New Mexico; old logging roads make good cross-country ski trails. In summer, visitors seek cool days and chilly nights away from the desert and flock to cabins, campgrounds, and the historic Lodge at Cloudcroft, a resort since the earliest days of Alamogordo's history. Located at an elevation of 9,000ft (2,750 meters), the golf course at the lodge is the nation's highest.

The **National Solar Observatory at Sacramento Peak** (tel: 575-434-7000; www.nso.edu/visit; visitor center Mar–Jan daily 9am–5pm; charge) in the village of **Sunspot** allows you to learn more about how astronomers study the sun. Tours of the observatory are currently suspended, but the observatory's visitor center (tel: 575-434-7190), a co-venture of NSO and Apache Point observatories and the US Forest Service, has astronomy exhibits and a gift shop, and the observatory grounds are open for self-guided tours from dawn to dusk. To get to Sunspot from Cloudcroft, take Highway 130 East to its junction with Highway 6563 (a designated scenic byway).

Combine a visit to the solar observatory with walking the grounds of nearby **Apache Point Observatory** (tel: 575-437-6822; http://apo.nmsu.edu), oriented toward nighttime astronomical observation. Owned by a private consortium and operated by New Mexico State University, the observatory is home to the Sloan Digital Sky Survey III, a project that is mapping 100 million celestial objects in one-quarter of the earth's sky using an 8ft (2.5-meter) telescope.

Heading north on Highway 54 from Alamogordo, turn off and drive 5 miles (8km) east to **Three Rivers Petroglyph National Recreation Area** ㉝ (tel: 575-525-4300; daily; charge), a BLM-managed site. The 0.75-mile (1.2km) -long trail leads past more than 21,000 petroglyphs carved on basaltic boulders by the prehistoric Jornada Mogollon branch of the Ancestral Pueblo culture between AD 900 and 1400. Rock art here is very diverse, including different inscriptions related to fertility, agriculture, and cultural symbols. It is clearly related to the symbols made by Mimbres Mogollon their famed black-and-white pottery. This is an exposed site; protect yourself from strong sun in summer.

Four miles (6km) west of **Carrizozo**, off Highway 380, is **Valley of Fires National Recreation Area** ㉞ (tel: 575-648-2241; www.blm.gov/nm/st/en/prog/recreation/roswell/valley_of_fires; daily;

Stick to the walkway through lava fields at Valley of Fires Recreation Area.

charge), which preserves one of the youngest and best lava fields in the United States. The thousand-year-old lava erupted from a small peak near the northern end of the *malpais* (badlands) and flowed 44 miles (70km) down into the valley. It offers a stark contrast with the shimmering white sands in the southern part of the Tularosa Basin.

These mountains, buttressing the eastern flank of Tularosa Basin, were the last stronghold of the Mescalero Apache before they were forced out by American westward expansion. The **Mescalero Apache Indian Reservation** (tel: 575-464 4494; www.mescalero apachetribe.com) occupies almost a half-million acres (200,000 hectares) in the Sacramento Mountains. The wealthy tribe makes a good living in cattle ranching, lumber, and tourism. A popular annual powwow is held every July 3–4 in the town of **Mescalero ㉟**, the location of the **Mescalero Apache Cultural Center and Museum** (Mon–Fri 8am–4.30pm; free), with exhibits on the history and culture of the Mescalero Apache. At the northern end of the

reservation is the tribal-owned **Inn of the Mountain Gods** (tel: 575-464-7059; www.innofthemountaingods.com), a luxury resort and casino, complete with golf course, of course. The grounds are located at the base of 11,973ft (3,649-meter) Sierra Blanca, the tribe's sacred mountain. The Ski Apache Resort in Lincoln National Forest draws skiers from Texas and the Midwest.

Just northeast of the Mescalero reservation is **Ruidoso ㊱** (Spanish for "noisy," referring to its lively stream), a year-round vacation town favored by West Texans. With horse races every weekend from May through Labor Day, **Ruidoso Downs** is one of the most popular racetracks in the Southwest. World-class quarterhorses are bought, sold and raced here, and the world's richest quarterhorse race – the multimillion-dollar All-American Futurity – is run here each Labor Day.

Equines are also the focus of the **Hubbard Museum of the American Southwest** (841 US 70 West; tel: 575-378-4142; www.hubbardmuseum.org; daily 10am–5pm; charge), which has 10,000

⊙ Tip

The Inn of the Mountain Gods is in a beautiful setting, high in the mountains of the Mescalero Apache Indian Reservation, one of the most economically successful – not counting gambling – reservations in the country.

Horses in action at Ruidoso Downs racetrack.

Billy the Kid's grave in Old Fort Sumner.

horse-related exhibits, including a horse-drawn fire truck, an 1860 stagecoach, and paintings and sculptures by famed Western artists.

BILLY THE KID'S TURF

Over the mountains, 37 miles (60km) northeast of Ruidoso, is **Lincoln 37**. A hundred years ago this was the scene of the so-called Lincoln County War, a brief but bloody battle pitting ranchers, merchants, cowboys, and politicians against each other – with the outlaw Billy the Kid gunning on the side of the good guys. The entire town (pop. 100) is now preserved as **Lincoln State Monument** (tel: 505-6534372; charge), with six buildings open to the public, including the Old Courthouse, the site of a daring jailbreak by the Kid; the bullet holes from that breakout remain. During the first weekend in August, the citizens of Lincoln stage a colorful "Last Escape of Billy the Kid" as part of Old Lincoln Day, which features arts, crafts, and an authentic Pony Express race from the ghost town of White Oaks to Lincoln, with the riders carrying mail specially cancelled to mark the event. There are several nice little bed-and-breakfast inns and restaurants in historic buildings in Lincoln, most of them with some connection to the Kid.

Billy the Kid was eventually killed by Sheriff Pat Garrett in **Fort Sumner 38**, northeast of Lincoln off Highway 285, where you can visit the Billy the Kid Grave in Old Fort Sumner Cemetery, which has been so often robbed of its tombstone it is now caged in with a steel fence. **The Old Fort Sumner Museum** (tel: 575-355-2942; daily 9am–4pm; charge) has Billy the Kid's chaps and spurs as well as letters from the Kid and Pat Garrett and other memorabilia, including an interesting barbed wire collection.

If you're a true Kid fanatic, you will enjoy the privately owned **Billy the Kid Museum** (1435 E Sumner Avenue; tel: 575-355-2380; www.billythekidmuseum-fortsumner.com; daily 8.30am–5pm May 15–October 1, Mon–Sat Nov–May 14, closed Sun; charge but free for ages 6 or under), open since the Fifties, with more than 60,000 relics collected

☉ BILLY THE KID, AKA HENRY

Whatever he was like as a real kid in the Irish slums of New York City is lost to history, but his bloody exploits as a teenager in New Mexico are infamous. Billy the Kid was born Patrick Henry McCarty in 1859, in lower Manhattan. A childhood in Wichita, Kansas, was followed by a move to Santa Fe for his mother's tuberculosis, then Silver City, where his mother died. Henry was 15.

A year after his mother died, the Kid was arrested for stealing clothes from a Chinese laundry. He escaped by climbing up a chimney and heading to Arizona, where he stole livestock and killed his first man in a saloon fight. He fled back to New Mexico, where he joined a gang of thieves near Silver City and took the name William Bonney. He moved to Lincoln County to gain notoriety during the Lincoln County War, a violent clash of commercial and political interests. The Kid was later captured by Lincoln County Sheriff Pat Garrett, convicted of murdering a sheriff, and sentenced to be hanged.

The Kid shot two deputies and escaped. Two months later in the early morning and in a dark bedroom in Fort Sumner, Billy awoke to the shadow of a man – Garrett – who then put a bullet into Billy the Kid's chest, killing him.

by Ed Sweet, former owner of the museum, and his wife, Jewel. Kid artifacts include his guns, a jail-cell door, locks of his hair saved by a Las Cruces barber, and an original Billy the Kid wanted poster, signed by territorial New Mexico governor Lew Wallace (a Civil War general and author of the novel *Ben Hur*).

Bosque Redondo Memorial at Fort Sumner State Monument (tel: 575-355-2573; www.nmmonuments.org/bosque-redondo; http://bosqueredondomemorial.com; charge) commemorates the end of a sadder and longer trail that led thousands of Navajos and Mescalero Apaches to federal internment here, at Bosque Redondo, in the 1860s. Particularly cruel was the 400-mile (650km) enforced march of Navajos (Dineh) from their homeland in 1864, dubbed "The Long Walk." Nine thousand Navajo and Apache were held here, with 3,000 dying from exposure, starvation, alkaline water, and diseases. It was a miracle that anyone was still alive when the experiment was finally deemed a failure and the Mescalero Apache and Dineh allowed to return to designated reservations in 1868.

TO THE NORTH

Socorro ㊴ ("help" in Spanish) received its name by early Spaniards for its helpful Indian pueblo residents, who would eventually decline to take part in the Pueblo Revolt and left with the Spanish to live in El Paso in 1680. The first church was built in 1628, but the village was abandoned during the Pueblo Revolt and not resettled until 1815. Socorro is in the middle of a rich mining district and was a boom town during the last two decades of the 19th century. When the railroad arrived in 1880, Socorro quickly grew into a ranching headquarters town. The original plaza is a block off the main street, and several buildings around it are designated historic landmarks.

Socorro's premier institution is the **New Mexico Institute of Mining and Technology** (tel: 575-835-5434; www.nmt.edu), a few blocks west of the town plaza, which has been training geologists and engineers since 1889. The

An Old West street in Lincoln.

Mineral Museum (tel: 505-835-5140; www.nmt.edu/museum; Mon–Fri 8am–5pm, Sat–Sun 10am–3pm; free) houses the largest geological collection in the state, with samples of ore and minerals from the Magdalena and San Mateo mountains. The college also serves as the administrative center for the Very Large Array (VLA), a cluster of 27 radio telescopes on the Plains of San Agustin, about 50 miles (80km) west on US 60.

Continue north along the Rio Grande Valley, where old Spanish settlements, small farms, and wildlife refuges cluster along the river. Twenty miles (30km) south of Socorro, on old US 85 (which parallels Interstate 25), is the 57,000-acre (23,000-hectare) **Bosque del Apache National Wildlife Refuge ⓴** (NM1; tel: 575-835-1828; www.fws.gov/refuge/bosque_del_apache; Mon–Fri 7.30am–4pm, Sat–Sun 8am–4.30pm; charge), one of the wildlife jewels of the Land of Enchantment. From November through February, thousands of waterfowl – most spectacularly snow geese, 15,000 sandhill cranes, and a small number of endangered whooping cranes – make a winter home here, and their spectacular dawn and dusk massings over the wetlands are truly one of the wonders of the natural world. Information about birding tours, photography workshops, lectures, and the annual Festival of the Cranes in late November is available at the visitor center.

Thirty miles (50km) west of Socorro, along US 60, is **Magdalena ⓵**, railhead for the old Magdalena Livestock Driveway. Cattle were driven here from Arizona and western New Mexico to be shipped to market as late as the 1950s. A few remnants of wooden windmills mark the famous cattle driveway.

The highway continues west across the Plains of San Agustin, the setting of Conrad Richter's novel *Sea of Grass*. In the middle of this ancient sea-floor valley, completely encircled by mountains, is where you will find the Very Large Array Telescope of the **National Radio Astronomy Observatory ⓶** (tel: 505-835-7000; www.vla.nrao.edu; daily 8.30am–sunset; free), where 27 huge antennae mounted on a Y-shaped railroad track probe the skies in search of

Dishes pointing skywards at the National Radio Astronomy Observatory.

intelligent life, work that was fictionalized in the 1997 film *Contact*, based on Carl Sagan's book.

Catron County, in west-central New Mexico, is the least populated part of the state – about 3 sq miles (8 sq km) for every person. The county seat and largest town is **Reserve**, population 279. About 80 miles (130km) west of Magdalena is the county's second-largest town, **Quemado** ⓭, with a population of 228.

About 30 miles (50km) north of Quemado is **The Lightning Field,** a work of land art that is the essence of isolation. In 1970, American artist Walter de la Maria won a commission from the Dia Center for the Arts in New York City to create the installation, which is made of 400 thin, pointed stainless-steel poles, 15–20ft (4.5–6 meters) long, arranged in a grid 1 mile by 3,330ft (0.6km by 1,015 meters), 16 rows by 25. In the flat light of midday, the poles almost disappear, but in late afternoon, early morning and even by full moonlight light catches on the poles like spots of gold or silver shining in perfect symmetry to a diminishing point that seems to vanish into eternity.

Visitors may experience The Lightning Field, but only six people at a time during summer. Leaving cars and cameras behind, they are driven by pickup truck from the foundation's office in Quemado to an old homesteader's cabin in the field, which becomes home for the next 24 hours until the manager reappears to drive guests back to Quemado. Visiting season is May through October, and reservations are taken from March on. For more information and to check available dates, call 575-898-3335 in Corrales. For comprehensive information and to make reservations online, visit Dia Center's website at www.diaart.org/visit/visit/walter-de-la-maria-the-lightning-field.

Just east of Quemado is **Pie Town**, famous for – you guessed it – delectable homemade pies. As early as the 1920s, a general store owner began baking pies to sell to miners in the area, and the name Pie Town stuck. During the Dust Bowl years, it came to the attention of Texas photographer Russell Lee, who, like Dorothea Lange and others, was documenting conditions in rural areas during FDR's New Deal era. Those 600 or so extraordinary black-and-white photos now housed in the Library of Congress brought wider public attention to Pie Town, and it is still going strong.

Several cafes offer pie, opening at different times to serve travelers. The **Pie-O-Neer Café** (tel: 575-772-2711; www.pieoneer.com; Mar 14–Nov 25, Thu–Sat, 11.30am–4pm) is renowned for its sunny Pie Lady, Kathy Knapp. Kathy and her partner Stan personally greet you and make time for a sit-down and a photo. A Pie Bar showcases the many daily choices, including strawberry-rhubarb pie, peach-green chile, chocolate chess pie with red chile, and many others. If you call ahead, Kathy will make your favorite pie and save you a slice or the whole thing to eat in or take home. A Pie Festival is held every September, a good time for a visit to this little one-horse town.

Tuck in at Pie Town.

:camera: LIFE IN A DRY LAND

Perhaps somewhat surprisingly, the lack of water has not hampered the Southwest's wildlife but shows us how truly adaptable nature can be.

The Southwest's landscape is extremely varied – grass and shrublands, high and low mountains, high and low deserts, mesas, arroyos, and deeply cut canyons. In one particular way, these features are similar: all are bereft of moisture. Everything that lives here, whether it has feet, wings, roots, or crawls on its belly, must get by on what little there is. Their methods go right to the basics of existence. Roadrunners' breeding corresponds with seasonal rains when food is plentiful. In the Sonoran Desert, which has both summer and winter rains, they often breed twice. Kangaroo rats do without water altogether, getting all the moisture they need from their food. To retain burrow humidity, they seal the entrances. Burrowing owls will take up residence in abandoned rat burrows, and astonishingly, will join prairie dogs in theirs, keeping watch outside, bobbing up and down. Living underground makes it easy for predators to visit, so young burrowing owls try to throw them off with a call that sounds like a rattlesnake.

When temperatures are high, rattlesnakes become more active at night. They cannot control their body temperature, so they remain underground during the day hidden in burrows, under rocks, or in the shade of shrubs. When it cools down, they can be seen sunbathing on rocks or hunting for food during daylight hours.

Rattlesnakes, generally heavy and slow, rely on menacing sounds to protect themselves and warn potential predators of their presence with an unmistakable rattle.

Desert coyotes have made physical adaptations for survival. They have shorter, thinner, paler fur, and weigh about half as much as other coyotes.

The roadrunner, a member of the cuckoo family, has special ways of coping with the heat and cold. It warms up by spreading its wings and exposing its black skin to the sun's rays – and pants for evaporative cooling.

Saguaro cacti in the Sonoran Desert.

Symbol of the desert

Although we may see the saguaro as being representative of all deserts, they grow only in the Sonoran Desert. They can grow up to 50ft (15 meters) tall, weigh several tons, and live for 175 years, given warm exposures and sufficient rain on Arizona's mountain slopes, or *bajadas*. They do not even begin to sprout "arms" until they are almost 70 years old. Their shallow roots suck up moisture into barrel-like torsos that swell like an accordion, storing up to 200 gallons (760 liters) of water after a heavy but infrequent rain, and can live several years on that supply, if necessary. In late spring, creamy white blossoms appear on top of the cactus. The light color allows them to be seen by Brazilian free-tail bats, which visit and pollinate the flowers. Later in summer, they develop beautiful, juicy red fruits with sharp spines. Each ripened fruit splits to reveal about 4,000 tiny black seeds. The few that survive predation by hungry animals such as javelinas will root and develop into baby saguaros, forming new sentry posts in the desert.

A burrowing owl often colonizes burrows previously made by ground squirrels.

A gila monster can live several years on fat stored in its tail if drought limits the availability and number of small animals that usually make up its diet.

A gilded flicker male at its nest cavity in a cactus.

Hundreds of small paper lanterns known as luminaria illuminate the ruins of the San Jose de los Jemez Mission to celebrate the holiday season.

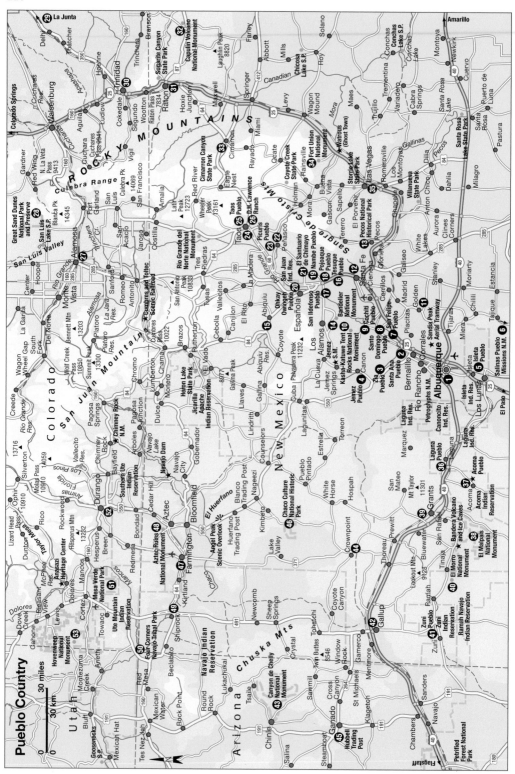

Pueblo Country

PUEBLO COUNTRY

Echoes of Spain persist in this ancient volcanic region, mingling with those of American Indian cultures whose artistry is of the highest caliber.

Primal landscapes and ancient cultures are the main attractions for travelers to Pueblo Country. Ancestral Puebloans lived here long before the Spanish came in search of wealth and converts, but the Hispanic influence remains everywhere. Central plaza gathering places; brightly painted historic Catholic churches; mud and saltillo tile floors; carved wooden Spanish Colonial furniture and viga-and-latilla ceilings; sprawling, flat-roofed adobe hacienda homes with walled courtyards; and hearty, chile-infused cuisine centered on marinated meats and the Three Sisters of corn, beans, and squash – these are just some of the echoes of Spain and Mexico to be found in the Four Corners.

When Spanish adventurers beheld the Zuni pueblo of Hawikuh in the setting sun in the early 1500s, they were convinced they had discovered the fabled Seven Cities of Cibola, the cities of gold. Truth, disappointment, and fury came soon enough, but Spaniards settled anyway and discovered other treasures – cotton, salt, silver, and turquoise.

Pueblo Country includes 19 pueblos in New Mexico and the Hopi Pueblos in northern Arizona, each with its own strong identity. Mission churches dating back to Spanish times still hold regular services, but Pueblo people retain their old spiritual ways. Living here, too, are the Dineh, the Navajo, whose 27,425-sq mile (71,030-sq km) reservation is the largest in the US, with a population of 173,667. Tribal headquarters are in Window Rock, Arizona, and landmarks and mountains sacred to the Navajo encircle the reservation, keeping the Dineh safe within their Center Place. National park units throughout the Four Corners interpret Indian culture, including rock art, which at places like Petroglyph National Monument in Albuquerque and El Morro National Monument near Zuni, is on display on both a grand and intimate scale.

The dramatic land forms here, many of them, such as Ship Rock, volcanic in origin, are associated with the origin stories of Indian tribes. Millennia of geological history, interpreted from both scientific and cultural angles, is on vivid display no matter where you go, whether climbing atop youthful volcanic lava flows or hiking a sandstone mesa that was once beneath an ancient sea. The very land here is alive – laid down in shallow seas, sandy beaches, or riverine mudflats, and exposed by uplift, erosion, and ongoing seismic activity across the Colorado Plateau and the Rio Grande Rift Zone, the ancient beating heart of Pueblo Country.

ALBUQUERQUE

New Mexico's largest city is not the state's capital, but it retains some of its Spanish heritage, dating from 1598, while embracing high-tech industries and Pueblo cultures and arts.

It all began in 1706 as a cluster of mud huts near a simple mud chapel, where the Rio Grande makes a wide bend, leaving rich bottomlands for settlers to plant corn and orchards. The provincial governor of New Mexico named the small outpost in honor of the Viceroy of New Spain (modern-day Mexico), the Duke of Alburquerque. (In the early 19th century the first "r" disappeared from the spelling of the city.) For a century and a half, **Albuquerque** was Spanish farming community and military outpost on El Camino Real, the administrative and trading road from Santa Fe to Chihuahua and on to Mexico City.

For over a century and a half, Albuquerque's center was what today is called Old Town. But when the railroad arrived in 1880, Albuquerque's commercial center moved 2 miles (3km) east, where downtown is today, leaving Old Town to enjoy a long siesta – but without losing any of its identity. In the four centuries since the Spanish first arrived, four flags have flown over Albuquerque's old plaza: Spain, from 1598 to 1821; Mexico, 1821 to 1846; the Confederacy, in 1862; and finally that of the United States.

Today, Albuquerque is the largest city in the state of New Mexico, with a population of 545,852 in 2016. Its growth has been phenomenal, like many cities in the American Southwest: in 1860

there were less than 2,000 people, and in 1950 less than 100,000.

It is the trade center of the state, headquarters for regional governmental agencies, a medical center of some renown, home of the state university and, since World War II, a center for space-age research and development. (Contrary to expectations, Albuquerque is not the state capital; Santa Fe, to the northeast, is the government center.) Slightly more than a mile above sea level, it has a warm, dry desert climate and a relaxed lifestyle.

⊙ Main Attractions
Old Town
Indian Pueblo Cultural Center
Albuquerque Biological Park
Petroglyph National Monument
Jemez Pueblo
Salt Trail
Kasha-Katuwe Tent Rocks National Monument
Turquoise Trail

Maps on pages 221, 224

Folklorico dancers in Old Town.

⊙ Tip

Although historically significant, remember that Albuquerque's plaza, like those of Santa Fe and Taos, is increasingly a place for extracting money from tourists – gift shops, schlock shops, and "art" galleries abound in the area.

OLD TOWN

Any visit to Albuquerque begins with **Old Town Plaza Ⓐ**, a community focus since 1706. Galleries here (and in other parts of town) represent some of the most prestigious artists in the state. Jewelry, pottery, rugs, and weavings are good buys and of dependable quality. In the plaza are the replicas of cannons left behind by Confederate troops in 1862; they buried them behind the church before retreating from Albuquerque. The original cannons are in the Albuquerque Museum.

Most activity in Old Town revolves around **San Felipe de Neri Church**, which hasn't missed a Sunday service in more than 275 years. The church was originally erected on the plaza's west side but was moved to its present north-of-the-plaza spot in 1793. In May, the church is the scene of the Blessing of the Animals and, in April, the Old Town Fiesta, celebrating the city's founding. For nine days before Christmas, Las Posadas processions circle the plaza in candlelit reverence, reminding the faithful how Mary and Joseph sought shelter for the birth of baby Jesus. On Christmas Eve, the plaza glows with thousands of *luminarias*, an Old Spanish custom to light the pilgrim's way to the Christ Child.

Originally, *luminarias* were small bonfires of crossed sticks (this is what they are still called in northern New Mexico, when they are lit on Christmas Eve on the Canyon Road carol walk and at pueblos like Taos). Today, *luminarias* in central and southern New Mexico consist of small brown paper bags with lit votive candles inside, held steady by a fairly thick layer of sand in the bottom. These brown bag illuminations are known as *farolitos*, or "little lanterns," in northern New Mexico, an anomaly you will notice as you travel around.

Some of Albuquerque's best cultural museums sit close to one another in Old Town, on Mountain Road, opposite Tiguex Park, making visiting easy and enjoyable.

Start with **Albuquerque Museum** (2000 Mountain Road NW; tel: 505-243-7255; www.albuquerquemuseum.org; Tue–Sun 9am–5pm; charge) two

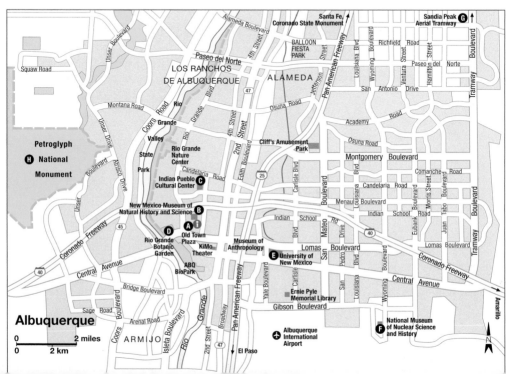

blocks north of the plaza, directly west of Tiguex Park, is a modernistic, solar-heated adobe building with changing exhibits of art, history, and science. The major permanent exhibit covers 400 years of New Mexican history. The museum is kid-friendly, with hands-on exhibits ranging from weaving to old-fashioned toys.

Two blocks east is the **New Mexico Museum of Natural History and Science ❸** (1801 Mountain Road NW; tel: 505-841-2800; www.nmnaturalhistory.org; daily 9am–5pm; charge), another favorite with kids but positively entertaining – and educational – for adults, too. The route through the museum leads through the geological and natural history of New Mexico, from tropical times to the ice ages to recent volcanism. There is a working fossil research facility where one can watch scientists identify and preserve actual fossils, many of which are beautifully displayed. A naturalist's center allows children to learn hands on some of the techniques that biologists and naturalists use to explore and identify the world.

Explora Science Center and Children's Museum (1701 Mountain Road NW; tel: 505-224-8300; www.explora.us; Mon–Sat 10am–6pm, Sun noon–6pm; charge) has all kinds of fun bells and whistles for kids of all ages who want to learn how the world works. Explore the properties of electricity, light gravity, and water through fun exhibits, including a miniature power station. There are 250 exhibits in all. Highlights include a kinetic sculpture and a series of exhibits where kids can experiment with motion, force, and energy.

Just south of the plaza is the dubiously named **American International Rattlesnake Museum** (202 San Felipe Street NW; tel: 505-242-6569; Sept–May Mon–Fri 11.30am–5.30pm, Sat 10am–6pm, Sun 1pm–5pm, Jun–Aug Mon–Sat 10am–6pm, Sun 1–5pm; www.rattlesnakes.com; charge). Strictly a commercial effort to empty your wallet in its overwhelming gift shop, it is still interesting if you're keen on snakes. It claims to have the largest collection of rattlesnake species in the world. True or false, the cramped displays reveal a lot about rattlesnakes.

San Felipe de Neri Church.

You'll learn everything you need to know about the Southwest's most precious stone turquoise, including how to tell real from fake, at the by-reservation-only privately run **Turquoise Museum** (2107 Central Ave; tel: 505-247-8650; www.turquoisemuseum.com; expert-led 90-minute small tours by reservation Mon–Sat 11am and 1pm; charge) not far from Old Town. Gorgeous examples of turquoise are on display, nicely interpreted with plaques, and there is a working lapidary workshop.

The **Indian Pueblo Cultural Center** Ⓒ (2401 12th St NW; tel: 505-843-7270, 800-766-4405; www.indianpueblo.org; daily 9am–5pm; charge), a few blocks north of Old Town and just north of Interstate 40, is owned by the 19 pueblos of New Mexico, each of which has an exhibit area showing its own unique arts and crafts. It is a good place, for example, to see the difference between Zuni and Acoma ceramics. One floor is devoted to the history of the Pueblo Indians, and there is a shop and popular restaurant serving well-prepared native foods. On summer weekends,

members of different tribes perform dance on the patio, between 11am and 4pm; demonstrations take place at 10am. Photography is permitted free here and may be your best chance of photographing Indian dancers as many Indian villages ban cameras.

To the south is **Albuquerque Biological Park** (or ABQ BioPark) (903 10th Street SW; tel: 505-764-6200; www.cabq.gov/culturalservices/biopark; daily 9am–5pm, Jun–Aug Sat–Sun until 6pm; charge). The park entrance opens onto a main plaza, with café and outdoor seating.

To the right is the entrance of the **Rio Grande Botanic Garden** Ⓓ. The botanic garden offers unfettered strolling paths through a number of gardens, including one of Spanish-Moorish design. Also within the grounds are two enclosed conservatories one with Mediterranean flora and the other with a comprehensive collection of desert flora. To the left from the main plaza is the **Albuquerque Aquarium**, an aquarium with a 285,000-gallon (1,078,842-litre) tank and environments containing salt marshes, the Gulf Coast, coastal

A White Mountain Apache dance performance at the Indian Pueblo Cultural Center.

zones, and the open ocean, all beautifully represented in the aquarium. You will see coral reefs, eels, jellyfish, sharks, stingrays, and sea turtles among other marine life. Outside is an actual shrimping boat, the *Candy M*.

Part of Albuquerque Biological Park but on separate grounds south a bit along the Rio Grande, the **Rio Grande Zoo** is a pleasant place for both animals and people. In addition to the expected menagerie, all of it displayed with the idea that zoos are for animals first and human visitors next, the zoo has special displays of lions, Asian elephants, Komodo dragons from Indonesia, and Australian wildlife, including the popular koala, to name just a few. Of particular note is the $2.2 million exhibit where polar bears cavort in an 11ft (3.3-meter) -deep pool, lounge by a stream, play under four waterfalls, slip down a waterslide, and enjoy an air-conditioned ice cave.

CONTEMPORARY ALBUQUERQUE

Route 66 bisects Albuquerque, running past the University of New Mexico at Nob Hill on what is now Central Avenue. The Civic Center, the tourist office (www.visitalbuquerque.org), and a handful of vintage buildings lie across the Atchison, Topeka, and Santa Fe railroad tracks just past Second Street in downtown Albuquerque. A multimillion-dollar revitalization of the route has transformed this stretch into a vibrant Downtown scene with neon signs and street lighting, theaters, nightclubs, hotels, and restaurants. A notable landmark is the KiMo Theater (www.kimotickets.com), built in 1927 in a fusion of Pueblo Revival and Art Deco styles, known as Pueblo Deco. This is a great place to see live music.

On the other side of Interstate 25, in the university district, the architecture at the **University of New Mexico** **E** shows how adaptable the basic Pueblo architectural style is. Traditional

buttressed walls with protruding *vigas* (beams) sit happily beside modern angular lines with lots of glass. In the center of the campus are the seven-story library and the president's home, both outstanding examples of Pueblo architecture. Also on campus are the **Maxwell Museum of Anthropology**, with one of the best displays of Mimbres pottery outside Silver City; the **Fine Arts Museum**; and **Popejoy Hall**, which has a full schedule of symphony, light opera, Broadway shows, and many other forms of live entertainment. This attractive part of town, **Nob Hill**, is your best bet for a good meal in one of the city's best-rated restaurants or to do a spot of shopping in a quirky boutique.

Six blocks south of Central, off Interstate 40, **the National Museum of Nuclear Science and History** **F** (601 Eubank SE; tel: 505-245-2137; www.nuclearmuseum.org; daily 9am–5pm; charge), a Smithsonian affiliate, is the only Albuquerque museum to be congressionally chartered and now has its own purpose-built warehouse. Hands-on exhibits include the development of

The National Musuem of Nuclear Science and History.

x-rays, radiation, Hiroshima and Naga-saki, the Cold War, the Uranium Cycle, and the development of nuclear technology. The museum's collection of nuclear hardware is on display in Heritage Park.

ALBUQUERQUE ENVIRONS

The Sandia Mountains, named for their watermelon (*sandia*) hue at sunset and made of uplifted granite topped with marine limestone, a tipoff to the area's oceanic origins, lie hard against the east side of Albuquerque, dominating the region aesthetically, recreationally, and climatically. The mountainsides facing the city are rugged and steep; the other side is gentler, with forested slopes (you can experience this sudden shift flying into Albuquerque from the east from the Plains, when the Rio Grande Valley rift zone suddenly drops away below as you come in to land at the airport – always a thrilling sight). Both sides of the Sandias offer miles of hiking trails in the national forest.

Take in spectacular views from the Sandia Peak Tramway.

The best way to access the Sandias from the west side is to head to **Sandia Pueblo**, 14 miles (22km) north of Albuquerque, exit 234 off Interstate 25, which has fertile river bottomland for farming (and a small herd of bison) as well as lands that extend to the top of the mountains. This strategy helped the pueblo to rebound in AD 1300, and in modern times, has allowed it to capitalize on tourism, with its attractive Pueblo-style Sandia Resort; Bien Mur Arts and Crafts Center offering artwork by artists from many different tribes; and a popular travel center.

Just past the pueblo, on Tramway Road is **Sandia Peak Aerial Tramway** ❻ (tel: 505-856-7325; www.sandiapeak.com; daily 9am–9pm, until 8pm in winter, Tue 5–8pm in winter; charge), the longest aerial tram in North America, which ascends the west (city) side of the mountains. By day, one can see mountain ranges a hundred miles to the north, west and south. At night, eat at a restaurant at the summit while the lights of Albuquerque, Santa Fe, and Los Alamos twinkle like stars below. In winter, skiers take the tram to the top to access Sandia Peak Ski Area or drive up the other side from SR 14.

Built in 1966 by a Swiss company, the double-reversible, jigback aerial tramway spans 2.7 miles (4.4km) along two towers between the terminals. Climbing 3,819ft (1,164 meters) to the top terminal, which is at an elevation of 10,378ft (3,163 meters), the tram moves 20ft (6 meters) a second to cover the distance in about 15 minutes. The land is rugged directly beneath the tramway, especially along the 7,720ft (2,353 meters) of free space between the second of the two towers and the top.

On Albuquerque's west side, you'll find **Petroglyph National Monument** ❼ (6001 Unser Boulevard NW; tel: 505-899-0205; www.nps.gov/petr; visitor center daily 8am–5pm; charge). Established in 1990, this 11-sq-mile (28-sq-km) national monument preserves some 350 archaeological sites and one of the largest collections of petroglyphs in the country, with more than 35,000

petroglyphs, some dating back 3,000 years, etched on the dark volcanic rock of 17-mile (27km) West Mesa. Ninety percent of the petroglyphs display the Rio Grande style of rock art carved between AD 1300 and 1650 by Ancestral Pueblo people who flooded into the Rio Grande region. The rock art may have been used in ceremonies.

Three main units are managed by the NPS: Boca Negra Canyon, Rinconada Canyon, and Volcanoes Day Use Area, which is accessed on the opposite side of the monument; a fourth unit, Piedras Marcadas, is managed by the City of Albuquerque Open Space Division. Las Imagines Visitor Center is located in a 1948 adobe building adjoining Boca Negra Canyon that was home to one of Albuquerque's most important archaeologists, Dr. Sophie Eberle. The units have hiking trails to the different petroglyph panels.

PUEBLOS NORTH OF ALBUQUERQUE

Of special interest geologically and historically is a drive through the Jemez Mountains northwest of Albuquerque, via US 550 and Highway 4. The sights on this tour range from red and saffron cliffs to mountain streams, from forested slopes and alpine meadows to Indian pueblos. It covers 200 miles (320km) and can be done in a day, but two would be better, allowing you to overnight in the mountains.

The first stop is **Coronado Historic Site** (US 550; tel: 505-867-5351; www.nmhistoricsites.org/coronado; Wed–Mon 8.30am–5pm; charge), 20 miles (30km) northwest of town. These are the ruins of a mighty Tiwa-speaking pueblo, Kuaua, built in AD 1300 on the Rio Grande and thought to be the spot commandeered by the Coronado expedition as winter headquarters in 1540. The experience was clearly traumatic, and the pueblo was never reoccupied. The attractive 1930s visitor center was designed by famed Santa Fe Style architect John Gaw Meem; exhibits here help you visualize what the pueblo once looked like, as there is little but an outline here now. Of particular interest are the kachina mural panels that

Ancient Native American rock art along the Rinconada Trail at Petroglyph National Monument.

were taken from the Great Kiva during the 1940 excavation by the Civilian Conservation Corps to mark the 400th anniversary of Coronado's Entrada. They are now on display in a separate room.

Santa Ana Pueblo ❷, just west of the Rio Grande, operates high-visibility businesses along US 550, including a large casino and golf course with a popular restaurant and the elegant **Hyatt Regency Tamaya Resort**, a mile off US 550, on 500 acres (202 hectares) of the pueblo's hauntingly beautiful ancestral lands along the river, which offers cultural tours; nature tours, horseback riding, and other outdoor activities; 350 restful guestrooms; a spa; and a fine dining restaurant.

Traditional polychrome pottery and inlaid straw art such as crosses are associated with Santa Ana pueblo artisans. The beautiful polished pottery almost became a lost art until Endora Montoya undertook teaching the younger women. You will see a great deal of art on display in the hotel's public spaces, in its small onsite cultural museum; and over the river at

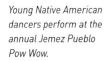

Young Native American dancers perform at the annual Jemez Pueblo Pow Wow.

the Coronado National Monument's museum. The pueblo of Kuaua is considered an ancestral home of Santa Ana Pueblo; the main ancestral pueblo of Tamaya is 9 miles away (14.5km) and is closed to visitors.

Zia Pueblo ❸, 36 miles (58km) northwest of Albuquerque, sits on a volcanic mesa, its mud-plastered houses blending so well with the landscape that they are easily missed. Zia pottery, usually earth tones painted with stylized figures of birds and flowers, and well fired, is sought by collectors; especially prized are the pots made by Candelaria Gauchpin. Zia is a small pueblo and conservative; photography is not allowed. Watercolor paintings by Zia artists are also prized. The ancient Zia sun symbol appears on New Mexico's state flag as a symbol of "perfect friendship." The pueblo's feast day is August 15, marked with a corn dance.

Jemez Pueblo ❹, located 48 miles (77km) northwest of Albuquerque, is a Towa-speaking pueblo picturesquely set among the red and ocher cliffs of San Diego Canyon in the Jemez

Mountains. The people of Jemez migrated into this canyon from Mesa Verde in the 1100s and built several pueblos, eventually coalescing into two large pueblos as conditions became more challenging under Spanish rule in the 1600s. They eventually abandoned the northernmost pueblo, Guisewa, and came to live here, at Walotowa. They were one of the last pueblos to capitulate to Spanish Reconquest in 1592, when many of its people went west to live with the Navajo. Even today, at any feast day in Jemez, a surprising number of Navajo will be present.

The pueblo has a strong arts tradition and has produced internationally known artists such as sculptor Cliff Fragua and writer Scott Momaday. Jemez Pueblo used to produce black-on-white pottery but stopped making this pottery during the Pueblo Revolt; on their return to Walotowa, potters started to make black-on-red and black-on-tan pottery, similar to Santa Ana. **Walotowa Visitor Center** (US 550; tel: 575-834-7235; www.jemezpueblo.com; daily 8am–5pm summer, 10am–4pm winter, guided tours at 11am and 1pm; charge) offers information and exhibits. A popular arts and crafts show takes place at the visitor center each year, where you can see a lot of traditional and contemporary artwork.

Just beyond Jemez Springs, you can tour the ruins of the large ancestral Jemez pueblo of Guisewa and its 1670 mission church at **Jemez Historic Site** (tel: 575-829-3530; http://nmhistoricsites.org/jemez; Wed–Sun 8.30am–5pm; charge). It's hard to imagine how big this pueblo once was, stretching from the cliffs to the river. It was gutted during the 1680 Pueblo Revolt and never rebuilt. Jemez celebrates its patron saint, San Diego, on November 12, and in August, the Pecos Bull Dance is performed to honor the Pecos people who moved in with the Jemez in 1838. The little museum here has some fine examples of ancestral black-on-white

Jemez pottery and activities for kids, such as grinding corn.

The highway follows the Jemez River past campgrounds, picnic areas, and hiking trails in the Santa Fe National Forest, including one trail that goes to undeveloped hot springs. The little rustic resort village of Jemez Springs has abundant opportunities to enjoy hot springs, whether in the Jemez River, in developed tubs at quaint inns, or the town's 1870 **Jemez Springs Bath House** (tel: 575-829-3303; www.jemezspringsbathhouse.com; daily; charge), where you can soak in hot mineral water in cement tubs, receive a massage after a day of hiking or skiing, then enjoy live honky tonk music and a burger at the Los Ojos Restaurant and Saloon, before slipping into sleep. This is a great place to relax.

PUEBLOS SOUTH OF ALBUQUERQUE

Isleta Pueblo ❺ is only 13 miles (21km) south of Albuquerque on Interstate 25, but it manages to retain a strong identity nevertheless. Its people farm the

⊙ RETURNING TO AN ANCIENT HOME

After nearly 75 years of study and storage at Harvard University, the bones of almost 2,000 Pueblo Indians were returned to New Mexico in 1999. The bones were met by 200 Indians from the Jemez Pueblo (see page 230) who had walked three days for the private rendezvous and mass reburial of the bones, which had been taken from an excavation at Pecos Pueblo (Cicuye) in Pecos Valley. Pete Toya of the Jemez Pueblo said: "When I walked into that room (at Harvard University) and got together with our ancestors, that was emotionally disturbing. I shed some tears. And then, being there for a couple of hours ... they told me that they were going back home."

For 500 years, Cicuye had been a regional trade center and was thought by the early Spaniards to be one of the sought-after cities of gold. In 1838, the remaining residents of Pecos Pueblo joined Jemez Pueblo.

Excavation of Cicuye was a touchstone in modern archeology, setting standards for archeological dating techniques, particularly ceramics, which are known as the Pecos Classification, and an excavation technique called stratigraphy, digging carefully through successive layers of deposition to unearth artifacts and structures. A Pecos conference for archeologists is still held annually at what is now Pecos National Historical Park.

bottomlands along the river, hold jobs in Albuquerque, and work in the large Isleta casino-resort, golf course, and recreational lake complex. Founded in 1300, the Tanoan-speaking people of Isleta Pueblo have taken in refugees and been refugees themselves itself during their history. Many Isletans fled to the Hopi Mesas during the 1680 Pueblo Revolt and intermarried with the Hopi, returning to their pueblo after the Reconquest with their Hopi relatives; others followed the Spanish to El Paso and stayed loyal to the Spanish, returning with them following the Reconquest.

Isleta took in starving refugees from the nearby Salinas Pueblo Missions in the late 1600s. In the 1800s, Acoma and Laguna people joined the pueblo, but friction led to separation into three separate villages: Oraibi (named for the Hopi pueblo), Chicale, and the main pueblo of Isleta. Their magnificent mission church, built in 1612, was gutted during the Pueblo Revolt and restored on their return. It is still in use, one of the most venerable in New Mexico. San Agustin, the patron saint, is honored

Quarai Ruins at Salinas National Monument.

on September 4, but other dances are held in fall and summer.

THE SALT TRAIL

Driving east of Albuquerque on Interstate 40, then turn south on State 14 to follow the road down the east side of the Manzano Mountains, known as the Salt Trail because of the precious saltbeds, or *salinas*, found here in the Estancia Basin. In the early 1600s, the Spanish built missions to serve the Pueblo Indians on the eastern face of the mountains, but within 50 years, Spanish demands on the pueblos, poor crops and starvation, and raids from the fierce Plains Indians became unbearable and the Pueblos abandoned their mountain homes for the Rio Grande Valley and pueblos like Isleta.

Together three of these Salt Missions make up **Salinas Pueblo Missions National Monument** ❻ (102 S Ripley Street, Mountainair; tel: 505-847-2585; www.nps.gov/sapu; daily 9am–5pm, until 6pm in summer; charge), headquartered at **Mountainair,** a ranching and bean-growing community at the intersection of US 60 and State 14. At the missions of **Quarai** (built in 1626 and located north of Mountainair off State 14) and **Abo** (built in 1622 and located west of Mountainair, on US 60), carefully laid red sandstone walls mark the location of the silent mission churches, now open to the heavens.

South of Mountainair on State 14, **Gran Quivira** (also known as Pueblo de las Humanas, "Pueblo of the People with the Striped Faces," likely a reference to Apaches) is by far the largest of the pueblos and has a more complex history. From its founding in the 1400s, it was an important trading pueblo and served as the southernmost gateway between the Rio Grande pueblos to the west, the Plains Indians to the east, the Pacific cultures to the far west, and the Mesoamerican cultures to the south. Built of local gray limestone, in contrast to the sandstone found in the other missions, the pueblo is interesting for its different types of architecture, including unusual Mogollon-style rectangular kivas, and the ruins of two large Spanish Colonial mission churches, one of which was abandoned before it was finished. There are onsite visitor centers at all three pueblos.

PUEBLOS NORTH OF ALBUQUERQUE

Twenty-eight miles (45km) north of Albuquerque, on Interstate 25, the Keres-speaking **San Felipe Pueblo ➐**, or Katishtya, is one of the most conservative and traditional pueblos; its main daily connection to the outside world is its travel center and Casino Hollywood. The pueblo itself is only open a few times a year. During the May 1 feast day of San Felipe, the dramatic Green Corn Dance is performed by hundreds of dancers in its sunken plaza; in October, the pueblo holds an arts festival; and on Christmas Eve, its lovely mission church is open for midnight mass.

Dances following Christmas Eve Midnight Mass are beautiful to witness.

Spirits of the animal kingdom pay homage to Jesus as dancers representing deer or buffalo. Elaborately dressed women dancers enter the church. In hushed closeness, onlookers await the arrival of the procession. No one is supposed to be around to see the dancers emerge from their kiva. Buffalo dancers wear the dark fur and horned headdress of the buffalo, with their exposed skin darkened, and stomp on the floor. Deer dancers, their headdresses bedecked with antlers, move more lightly. One by one, the dancers move to the altar to greet the figure of the holy infant.

One enters and leaves pueblo lands one after the other in New Mexico, and just north of San Felipe is **Santo Domingo Pueblo ➑**, or Kewa, the largest and most traditional pueblo and also Keresan speaking. Its proximity to the Cerrillos turquoise mines and its inhabitants' skill in making turquoise jewelry and heishi (turquoise disks) made it an important ancient pueblo. It is probably the best place to see the Corn Dance, which is performed several times a year, including

Santo Domingo Pueblo.

on New Year's Day and at Easter, on the huge plaza. A Labor Day arts and crafts market takes pace at the pueblo, which features dances and more than 350 stands selling food and jewelry. A few artisans sell their wares next to the tribe's main travel center on the Cochiti Road off Interstate 25.

Continue on the Cochiti Road to reach **Cochiti Pueblo** , the northernmost Keresan pueblo. The 1,100-member tribe has a diverse modern economic base, which includes farming, ranching, commerce, and recreation. Cochiti artisans are known for their aspens drums and unusual ceramic figurines, the most famous of which are the Storyteller dolls, revived and popularized by potter Helen Cordero in 1964, and depicting a woman with children climbing all over her.

Dances take place in June, July, and August here, with the most important on the tribe's feast day, on July 14. The tribe operates a golf course, Cochiti Lake and Dam, and spectacular **Kasha-Katuwe Tent Rocks National Monument ⑩** (tel: 505-761-8700; www.

blm.gov/visit/kktr; daily Apr–Oct 7am–7pm, Nov–Mar 8am–5pm; charge), which sits on tribal land but is managed by the BLM as a primitive landscape monument with no visitor center or campground. The tent rocks are actually hoodoos weathered out of volcanic pumice into pointy rocks and strange formations. You may also find black volcanic glass pearls, known as Apache Tears. Note: do not take rocks from this protected site.

Santa Feans like to take out-of-town guests hiking here when it is too cold and snowy to hike in northern New Mexico. The monument sits right below La Bajada, the steep uplift that separates the north from the south in the state. Be careful if traveling over La Bajada on Interstate 25 in winter; it can get very slippery.

THE TURQUOISE TRAIL

An alternative scenic route to Santa Fe from Albuquerque takes you north on the Turquoise Trail on SR 14, around the back (the east side) of the Sandia Mountains, through ghost towns and

Kasha-Katuwe Tent Rocks National Monument.

Hispanic villages. It is basically the northern extension of the same road known as the Salt Trail to the south.

To get there, drive east over the mountains on Interstate 40, take the Tijeras–Cedar Crest exit, then drive north on State Route 14. The first town you come to, **Cedar Crest**, is the main gateway to **Sandia Peak Ski Area** (SR 536; tel: 505-242-9052; www.sandiapeak. com), a popular destination for skiers in winter and a nice scenic drive into the mountains and national forest for hikers in summer.

Cedar Crest is also home to a quirkier attraction that is pure Americana: **Tinkertown Museum** (SR 536; tel: 505-281-5233; www.tinkertown.com; Apr–Oct 9am–6pm; charge), the life's work of the late painter Ross Ward and still run as a private family museum. The main exhibit here is a delightful three-ring circus and miniature Wild West town, which Ward carved over many years as a hobby. The entrance wall is made of 50,000 bottles.

Just north is the ghost town of **Golden ⑪**, the oldest gold mining town in the West. The first gold strike west of the Mississippi was made nearby in 1826 (look closely and you'll see the ruins of foundations in the narrow canyon). You can still see the remains of the general store, two 14th-century pueblos, and St Francis Mission Church, built in 1830 and restored in 1958 by famed New Mexico historian Fray Angelico Chavez. The church and cemetery still serve the parish. The gate is usually locked, but one can drive up to the gate.

Eleven miles (18km) farther is **Madrid** (pronounced MAD-rid), which was a major coal mining town from the 1850s on, connected by a railyard spur to the main Santa Fe Railroad, for which it supplied coal. By 1892, 2,500 people lived in Madrid and in the 20th century, it became a company town, complete with schools, hospitals, a company store, a tavern, and an employees club. The company was famous for its Madrid Christmas illuminations, which were powered by 500,000 kilowatts of electricity from coal-fired generators.

Exhibits at Tinkertown.

Madrid's days were numbered in 1952 when diesel fuel started to replace coal on the railroads, but it got a reprieve in the 1970s, when the town's then owner, the son of the former mine superintendent, virtually gave away the old miner's shacks to anyone with an interest and the town came back to life. Today, Madrid is known for its funky galleries, bed-and-breakfasts, cafés, and eclectic boutiques. Attractions include the Old Coal Mine Museum, the Mine Shaft Tavern, and the Engine House Theatre next door, which puts on a melodrama between Memorial Day and mid-October. The movie *Wild Hogs* (2007) was filmed here, a star vehicle featuring John Travolta and other big names.

The turquoise mines of **Cerrillos**, the final stop on the Turquoise Trail, are what give this backroad its name. In the ancient Pueblo world, turquoise was hugely important to trade and found its way across the Southwest, North America, and south to Mesoamerica, where it was used in ceremonies. Turquoise's economic value was what attracted the first Spanish settlers to this area, including the founder of New Mexico, Don Diego de Vargas, and turquoise was sent back down El Camino Real to Mexico City under the Spanish as it had been under earlier prehistoric cultures. As you might imagine, quite a few movie and television series have been filmed in the Cerrillos area, including *The Hi-Lo Country* (1998) and *Young Guns* (1988). The main attraction here, if you don't have much time, is **Cerrillos Hills State Park** (37 Main Street, Cerrillos; tel: 505-474-0196; www.cerrillos hills.org; daily sunrise–sunset; free if arriving on foot or by bicycle, charge otherwise), which protects a number of Cerrillos's 221 historic mines and has 5 miles (8km) of trails to explore.

Cerrillos turquoise is a rare and expensive collector's item today. You can find out more about turquoise – and a lot else besides – at **Casa Grande Trading Post**, **Cerrillos Turquoise Mining Museum**, and **Cerrillos Petting Zoo** (17 Waldo Street; tel: 505-438-3008; www.casagrandetradingpost.com; daily 9am–5pm; free), a classic family-run roadside attraction in a 28-room handmade adobe, featuring collections of everything you can imagine, from glass bottles to railroad paraphernalia to precious stones and chunks of rock. An onsite petting zoo, with llamas, chickens, goats, and other small animals, will be a draw for kids.

Just north of Cerrillos, before you get to Santa Fe, SR 14 comes to an end through a very scenic area of hills, arroyos, and colorful rock formations called **Garden of the Gods,** the northernmost margin of the Galisteo Basin. Rife with ancient ruins and rock art, it's a quiet reminder of a time in Pueblo history in the 1400s, when drought, starvation, and unrest led to the abandonment of numerous pueblos in this once overpopulated area, with surviving pueblos being those that relocated to the Rio Grande and other more reliable resources.

Pick up souvenirs at Casa Grande Trading Post in Cerrillos.

A local gallery in the old mining town of Madrid.

Pueblo artists selling jewelry at
the Palace of the Governors.

SANTA FE AND ABIQUIU

Historic Santa Fe and nearby Georgia O'Keeffe country enchant visitors with their unique mountains-meet-redrocks beauty, multicultural arts and crafts, and nearby Indian pueblos.

Officially established in 1610 as the capital of the Spanish province of New Mexico, **Santa Fe** is one of the trendiest addresses in the West. This has been a mixed blessing in New Mexico, one of the poorest states in the country. Driven by money from southern California and other higher-income origins, land values in Santa Fe have reached the point where most locals can't afford to buy land in their hometown, where some families have lived for tens of generations.

To the first-time visitor, the preserved historic downtown seems to verge on self-parody, an adobe theme park of high-priced real estate with photo-op local characters dressed in Wild West dusters or full "Santa Fe Style" – bolero, stetson, broom skirt, velvet blouse, concha belt, and dripping with silver and turquoise, all of it against a backdrop of carefully curated museums, historic buildings, trendy boutiques, souvenir shops, and art galleries. It's a carefully established veneer, of course – a protective shield. The real Santa Fe is far richer and more interesting than the postcard views and cultural cliches can convey.

Historic downtown Santa Fe is anchored by its central plaza. The Palace of the Governors and official buildings of the Spanish era are on the north side of the Plaza, now part

of the Museum of New Mexico's history museum. Spanish colonization in the New World left a ruling triumverate of clergy, military, and aristocracy, which often resulted in intrigue of epic proportions. In the early days of Santa Fe, there was much internal bickering between secular and civic officials, with Pueblo Indians caught in the middle.

In 1680, the Pueblos of New Mexico rebelled against heavy-handed missionaries and *encomienda*, or tribute demanded by settlers, which had brought the pueblos to the point

◎ Main Attractions

Santa Fe
Pecos National Historical Park
Bandelier National Monument
Abiquiu
San Ildefonso Pueblo

◉ Maps on pages 220, 240

Route US 84 near Abiquiu.

of starvation with their onerous demands. In an astonishingly well-orchestrated coup, they took back their homeland, burning administrative records, books, and churches; smashing church bells and religious accoutrements; and expelling the Spaniards, who fled over the border to El Paso with a few Pueblo allies.

The Pueblo Revolt, a milestone in the history of the Southwest, kept the Spanish out of New Mexico for 12 years, before Diego de Vargas carried out a successful Reconquest in 1692, still celebrated today in Santa Fe's famous Fiesta Days in early September. The Spaniards learned that the Pueblos could not be bullied, and on their return, they permitted kivas to be built at missions where kiva societies continued to hold traditional rites. The king of Spain enshrined the sovereignty of each New Mexican pueblo in a revered charter recognized by all successive governments. This pragmatism allowed Pueblo people to retain their individual identities, cultural traits, and sovereignty and is in large part why

New Mexico is an authentically multicultural place today.

Santa Fe is the oldest capital city in the United States and remained so through the short-lived Mexican period (1821–46), US Territorial period (1846–1912), and US statehood. Located at 7,000ft (2,100 meters) at the base of the Sangre de Cristo Mountains – the southernmost extension of the Rockies – Santa Fe today is home to an estimated 71,000 people (more than double that if you include Santa Fe County). This population swells considerably when you add in second-home owners, temporary residents, and the thousands of international visitors who come for the many cultural events and holidays.

AROUND THE PLAZA

Santa Fe Plaza remains a popular community gathering place for locals and visitors alike, the setting for free music on hot summer evenings and other events. Traces of all three historic periods remain in buildings surrounding the plaza. Of these the most important is the historic **Palace of the**

Santa Fe Plaza.

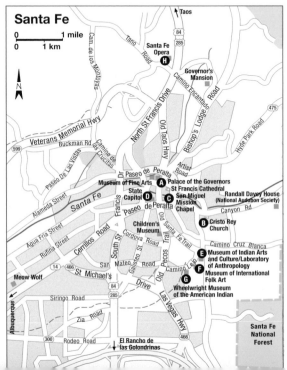

Governors ⓐ (105 W Palace Avenue; tel: 505-476-5100; www.palaceofthe governors.org; May–Oct daily 10am–5pm, until 8pm on Fri, Nov–Apr Tue–Sun 10am–5pm, until 8pm on first Fri; charge), part of the four-unit **Museum of New Mexico** (www.museumofnew mexico.org), which anchors the north side of the Plaza. Under its entry portal, Pueblo artists sell high-quality jewelry, pottery, and other crafts from blankets spread on the ground. They are an official "exhibit" of the museum and competition for spots is fierce among Native artists; you can be sure that any arts and crafts you buy here (or in the Museum of New Mexico gift shops) is of the highest caliber.

Exhibits inside relate to the history of New Mexico's Indian, Spanish, Mexican, and American Territorial periods, although much of the Indian artifact collection is now at the Museum of Indian Arts and Culture on Museum Hill (see box). In one area, the original walls of the palace are exposed under glass, showing adobe over 400 years old. Excavations have uncovered pits beneath the floor that were dug in the 1680s by Pueblos as food storage during their short time in control at the palace. The Spanish later used the excavated holes for trash dumps.

The Palace of the Governors has been in continuous public use longer than any public building in the United States. It was nearly pulled down at the beginning of the 20th century, but was saved at the last minute by the School of American Archaeology, which in 1909 moved its headquarters into the palace, restored it, and converted it into the New Mexico History Museum.

In 2009, a century later, a new state-of-the-art **New Mexico History Museum** (113 Lincoln Avenue; tel: 505-476-5200; www.nmhistorymuseum.org; May–Oct daily 10am–5pm, until 8pm Fri, Nov–Apr Tue–Sun 10am–5pm, until 8pm on first Fri; charge) opened behind the governors' palace in a former stables and parade ground. This is a great place to get a sense of the sweep of New Mexico history, from Paleo-Indian times 12,000 years ago to New Mexico's unique role in World War II and beyond. Special

Welcome to the Museum of Indian Arts and Culture/Laboratory of Anthropology.

⊘ NM CULTURE PASS

New Mexico History Museum/Governors Palace is the main unit of the **Museum of New Mexico** (http://museumofnewmexico.org), which, in Santa Fe, includes this site and the neighboring New Mexico Museum of Art, the Museum of International Folk Art, and Museum of Indian Arts and Culture/Laboratory of Anthropology on Museum Hill. Statewide, the Museum of New Mexico runs seven state museums and seven state monuments. If you plan to visit three of the four state museums in Santa Fe, and other state-run history museums and monuments in the state, you are urged to buy the **New Mexico Culture Pass**, which, for $30, offers admission to each of the Museum of New Mexico sites and is valid for 12 months. It is available from any of the 14 sites run by MNM for immediate use, or you can purchase online ahead of time.

exhibitions touch on uniquely New Mexican and Southwest historical topics such as early 20th-century hotel and restaurant entrepreneur Fred Harvey and New Mexico's celebrated lowriders, the tricked-out, low-slung cars that "paseo" in downtowns throughout northern New Mexico.

On the other side of the street is the elegant Santa Fe-style building housing the **New Mexico Museum of Art** (107 W Palace Avenue; tel: 505-476-5072; www.nmartmuseum.org; May–mid-Sept daily 10am–5pm, Fri until 7pm, Nov–Apr Tue–Sun 10am–5pm; charge). Built in 1917, this branch of the state museum is a classic example of Pueblo Revival architecture. The permanent collection features artists whose work has been synonymous with New Mexico for more than half a century, including Georgia O'Keeffe and Ernest Blumenschein. Other exhibits change frequently as a showcase for outstanding New Mexican artists.

The **Georgia O'Keeffe Museum** (217 Johnson Street; tel: 505-946-2000; www.okeeffemuseum.org; daily 9am–5pm, until 7pm Fri; charge), housed in a renovated adobe church a block and a half from the Plaza, has more than 80 works by the artist on permanent display. O'Keeffe was seduced by the New Mexican desert on her first visit in 1917 and returned regularly, staying in an old adobe cabin at Ghost Ranch, just north of Abiquiu in the Chama River valley northwest of Santa Fe, the dude ranch owned by Arthur Pack and later donated to the Presbyterian Church as a retreat center. She settled in New Mexico permanently in 1949, following the death of her husband, photographer/gallery owner Arthur Stieglitz, fixing up an old adobe in Abiquiu and living there for four decades before moving to Santa Fe and passing away, aged 98 years, in 1986.

Some of the best people-watching in Santa Fe takes place at the historic **La Fonda** (100 E San Francisco Street; tel: 505-982-5511; www.lafondasantafe.com), the famed inn on the southeastern corner of the Plaza. Sit in the ornate Pueblo Deco-style lobby and you are likely to see movie stars, politicians, musicians, Indian artisans, artists, poets – and other tourists. There has been a *fonda*, or inn, at this location from the first days of Spanish settlement.

The present establishment was built in 1922 in the style of a multi-storied Indian pueblo, with protruding vigas, smooth, flowing adobe lines, flagstone floors, interior patios, colored glass, carved corbels, and furniture. It has had a number of updates since then, but retains its authentic Santa Fe style ambiance. The lounge is a place to sit in comfortable dimness, listen to classical guitar, sip margaritas, and crunch nachos.

The **Cathedral Basilica of St Francis** (tel: 505-982-5619; www.cbsfa.org; daily) stands in Romanesque grandeur a block east of the Plaza, on Cathedral Place. Constructed between 1869 and 1886 by French-born Archbishop Lamy, the cathedral has a decidedly European

The adobe building of the New Mexico Museum of Art.

look and was built on the spot where Santa Fe's original church was erected in 1610. It is clearly a statement building, designed to inspire awe in Pueblo people. Willa Cather's novel, *Death Comes for the Archbishop*, immortalizes Lamy's work in the Southwest.

On the opposite side of Cathedral Place is the **IAIA Museum of Contemporary Native Arts** (tel: 888-922 4242; https://iaia.edu/iaia-museum-of-contemporary-native-arts; Mon and Wed–Sat 10am–5pm, Sun noon–5pm; charge), the nation's leading museum for collecting, exhibiting, and interpreting the most progressive work by contemporary American Indian artists. It is associated with Santa Fe's famed Institute of American Indian Arts on the outskirts of Santa Fe, the alma mater of some of the top Native artists in the country. The museum downtown is housed in the old adobe post office and displays the nation's top collection of contemporary Indian art, about 7,500 pieces dating from 1962. It has galleries dedicated to IAIA co-founder Lloyd Kiva New, a Cherokee artist; Santa

Clara Pueblo artist Helen Hardin, Luiseño tribal artist Fritz Scholder, and an attractive sculpture garden of works by celebrated Chiricahua Apache artist Allan Houser, whose son Bob Haozous is also a well-known sculptor.

Immediately south of the cathedral, on Old Santa Fe Trail, is the **Loretto Chapel** (tel: 505-982-0092; www.loretto chapel.com; Mon–Sat 9am–4.30pm, Sun 10am–5pm; charge), also known as Our Lady of Light, housing a locally famous spiral staircase built without visible support. Legend says an itinerant carpenter appeared at the convent of the Sisters of Loretto in 1878 in answer to a novena and built the circular, freestanding stairway. The carpenter disappeared, but the sisters believed he was St Joseph.

CANYON ROAD

A few blocks east of the Plaza is **Canyon Road**, Santa Fe's celebrated historic arts district. Originally a narrow, winding Indian trail through the mountains from Pecos Pueblo to the east to Santa Fe, it was later used by Hispanic

The Cathedral Basilica of St Francis of Assisi.

Pueblo revival-style buildings on Canyon Road house the city's arts quarter.

In the Canyon Road art gallery area.

farmers to haul firewood, beans, and other crops to market. The Acequia Madre, or Mother Ditch, was used by local people to irrigate their fields and remains a working *acequia*, or irrigation ditch, carrying water through Santa Fe's tony east side. In the early 1900s, it was a popular place for penniless artists to rent old adobe houses for $10 a month. How times have changed! It is now one of the best-known art streets in the country, with a string of interesting galleries on either side of the road between Paseo de Peralta and Camino Cabra, and artist compounds and nature reserves on the its more remote side, dead-ending at Cerro Gordo, the Santa Fe Reservoir, and trails into the Santa Fe National Forest.

Cristo Rey Church Ⓑ (tel: 505-983-8528; www.cristoreyparish.org) at the upper end of Lower Canyon Road, where it meets Camino Cabra, was designed by famed Santa Fe Style architect John Gaw Meem, constructed in 1939, and is still a parish church today. It holds the most remarkable piece of Spanish Colonial art in the country – a huge stone altar screen, or *reredos*, carved with saints and intricate designs. Measuring 40ft (12 meters) wide and 18ft (5.5 meters) high, and weighing many tons, it was made in 1760 at the order of the then-governor of New Mexico by Mexican artisans. It was intended for the military chapel on the Plaza, but proved far too big, so was kept in storage for over 200 years before a church large enough to hold it was built.

Just south of Canyon Road is the **School for Advanced Research** (660 Garcia Street; tel: 505-954-7200, tours: 505-954-7205; www.sarweb.org; Indian Arts Research Center (IARC) tours Fri 2pm and Wed in Jun–Sept, call to book; charge), the former School of American Archaeology, which moved from the Palace of the Governors to this historic property. SAA's first director, educator Edgar Lee Hewett, was one of the most important early archeologists in the country, not just New Mexico. Spurred on by looting at Chaco Canyon among other problems, Hewett was responsible for drafting the now-controversial

Antiquities Act, which in 1906 allowed US Presidents to unilaterally set aside national monuments for protection of public lands of scientific, natural, and cultural merit, without the approval of Congress. You can tour SAR's outstanding prehistory pottery collection in the Institute of Indian Arts Research Center a couple of afternoons a week by reservation.

BARRIO ANALCO

San Miguel Mission Chapel (tel: 505-983-3974; www.sanmiguelchapel.org; daily), farther down Old Santa Fe Trail on the other side of the Santa Fe River, is sometimes called "the oldest church in America." It isn't, but it stands over the foundations of a church built around 1636 and burned during the Pueblo Revolt. It has been rebuilt and remodeled five times since then, most recently in 1955. This part of old Santa Fe was known as the Barrio Analco and was settled in the 1600s by Tlaxcalan Indians from Mexico, while Spanish colonists settled north of the river, where the Plaza is today. The original chapel

at the San Miguel Mission was built by the Tlaxcalans, who were for a long time important allies for the Spaniards – they helped Cortes conquer Mexico – and who had accompanied them to New Mexico in 1598. The Spaniards had no church of their own at first, so they too celebrated mass in San Miguel Chapel.

While Santa Fe is the oldest capital in the United States, the **State Capitol** (tel: 505-986-4589; www.nmlegis. gov/visitors; daily for self-guided tours 7am–6pm, Sat and holidays 9am–5pm; free) is perhaps one of the newest state buildings. Dedicated in 1966, it is in the New Mexico territorial style, an adaptation of the Greek Revival style with Pueblo influences. Known locally as the Roundhouse, the building is in the shape of a Zia Pueblo sun symbol, also found on the state's red-on-yellow flag. In the floor of the rotunda is the Great Seal of the State of New Mexico, done in brass and turquoise. You can visit the Roundhouse for a self-guided tour daily and to view the state art collection. The state legislature is in session every January and convenes for

Cristo Rey Church.

60 days on odd-numbered years and 30 days on even-numbered years.

RAILYARD DISTRICT

From the Capitol, wander a few blocks west toward Guadalupe Street, a gentrified warehouse area beside an extension of the Santa Fe Railyard, which, after a decade of planning and construction, opened as **Railyard Park and Plaza** in 2008. This is Santa Fe's newest gathering area and features a large children's play area landscaped with boulders for climbing and a playground of wood beams and ropes, an open-air concert area, restaurants, two arthouse movie theaters, and art galleries.

A central feature is **Santa Fe Farmers' Market Pavilion** (tel: 505-983-4098), which houses one of the largest and oldest farmers' markets in the country, gift shops, and a popular local microbrewery. As many as 200 small organic farmers sell their produce here year round. The Railyard is the main Santa Fe depot for the state-run **New Mexico Rail Runner Express** (tel: 866-795-RAIL; www.riometro.org). The

Crowds at Santa Fe Railyard Farmers' Market.

big red-and-gray passenger train with a roadrunner painted on its side began service to Santa Fe in December 2009. It was designed to serve commuters between Albuquerque and points north and south, but has proved enormously popular with tourists. It runs daily.

MUSEUM HILL

To reach Santa Fe's other main museum complex, drive south on Old Santa Fe Trail to Museum Hill on Camino Lejo. Three important cultural museums are located here – two of them units of the Museum of New Mexico – so it's worth a special trip.

The 1929 **Museum of Indian Arts and Culture/Laboratory of Anthropology** ❸ (tel: 505-476-1269; www.miaclab.org; May–Oct daily 10am–5pm, Oct–Apr Tue–Sun 10am–5pm; charge) has excellent modern exhibits interpreting pottery, kachinas, and other American Indian artifacts. Videos of storytellers sharing creation stories and a walk-through Navajo hogan enrich one's knowledge of the Southwest. The lab next door, in a former archeologist's

historic adobe home, is the repository for artifacts from excavations throughout the region.

The **Museum of International Folk Art** G (tel: 505-476-1200; www.internationalfolkart.org; May–Sept daily 10am–5pm, Oct–Apr Tue–Sun 10am–5pm; charge) is one of Santa Fe's most popular and unique museums. Founded by Alexander Girard, it exhibits religious and other folk art, highlighted by the Girard Exhibit, a collection of 120,000 pieces from around the world.

The small **Wheelwright Museum of the American Indian** G (tel: 505-982-4636; www.wheelwright.org; daily 10am–5pm; charge, free first Sun of month) is just around the corner on Museum Hill, so be careful not to miss it. A privately endowed museum once devoted exclusively to Navajo ceremonial art but now including culture and art from other tribes, it often features exhibitions of one particular artist or craftsperson's work. Its Case Trading Post downstairs sells authentic Indian-made items, including a good selection of Navajo folk art. Note: this museum is open Mondays year round, so if you happen to be in Santa Fe off season, when most museums are closed on Mondays, this museum is your ticket!

SILER DISTRICT

The gentrifying industrial zones on Second Street and farther south between Siler Road and Cerrillos (known as SIDI, or Siler District) are rapidly becoming Santa Fe's most creative and interesting modern arts districts. Live-work warehouses and old commercial buildings are now home to artists, entrepreneurs, coffee shops, breweries, galleries, art studios, and other local businesses – and, as of March 2016, Santa Fe's biggest new arts attraction: Meow Wolf.

The brain child of a group of artists, **Meow Wolf** (1352 Rufina Circle; tel: 505-395-6369; http://meowwolf.com; Mon, Wed, Thu, Sun 10am–8pm. Fri,

Sat 10am–10pm; charge) – look for the huge iron sculpture of a robot – consists of The House of Eternal Return, a futuristic version of a Victorian haunted fun house-cum-immersive art experience-cum-children's museum, with colorful, clever, artful, and interactive experience rooms that engage the senses and disorientate you. With the financial support of *Game of Thrones* author George R.R. Martin, who purchased the old 20,000-sq-ft (1,858-sq-meter) bowling alley complex as a home for the project, Meow Wolf has been a runaway success with locals and visitors alike from day one, making $6 million in its first year. It's a bit of a trek, but, seriously, you won't want to miss this.

SANTA FE ENVIRONS

Over 25 years, the **Santa Fe Opera** (tel: 505-280-4654; www.santafeopera.org), located just north of Santa Fe near the village of Tesuque, has built a worldwide reputation for excellence. The season is July and August, and performances are usually sold out. Those without reservations can try at the gate

Colorful interactive art installation inside Meow Wolf.

A performance by the Los Matachines de San Lorenzo, a traditional dance troupe, at the Fall Harvest Festival at El Rancho de las Golondrinas.

for standing room. The open-air Opera House is a spectacularly impressive structure set amid the badlands and foothills. With the sides and part of the roof open to the stars, the setting is part of the performances.

El Rancho de las Golondrinas (334 Los Pinos Rd, La Cienega, exit 276 off I-25; tel: 505-471 2261; www.golondrinas. org; June–Sept Wed–Sun 10am–4pm; charge), 10 miles (16km) southwest of town, is a reconstructed 200-acre (80-hectare) living history museum featuring a Spanish colonial village of the 18th and 19th centuries, once the final stopping place on El Camino Real before Santa Fe. You'll find working blacksmiths, wheelwrights, a winery and molasses mill, a schoolhouse, and chapels. Spring and fall festivals are held on the first weekends of June and October, respectively, with colonial folk art demonstrations and activities. The village of La Cienega grew up around the *hacienda*.

Spanish records from Coronado's 1540 expedition mentioned stopping at a large Indian pueblo east of

Santa Fe. Located on a pass between the Rio Grande Valley and the Pecos River Valley, the great trading pueblo of Cicuye had communal dwellings four or five stories high with over 700 rooms. There were five separate plazas and 23 kivas, attesting to the size and importance of the pueblo. Around 1620, Spanish missionaries built a large mission church there, with thick adobe walls, mortared and solidly buttressed, with fine carved corbels. In 1680, the residents of Cicuye joined the Pueblo Revolt and burned the church. The pueblo was resettled after the 1692 Reconquest, and a smaller adobe church built inside the burnt foundation, but Pecos Pueblo, as it now was, never regained its importance and life proved unsustainable. In 1838, the last two dozen inhabitants went west to join Jemez Pueblo, the only other pueblo that spoke their language.

The ruins of both churches and the pueblo are preserved at **Pecos National Historical Park** ⓭ (tel: 505-757-2421; www.nps.gov/peco; summer daily 8am–6pm, winter 8am–4.30pm; free), where you'll find the attractive E.E. Fogelson Visitor Center (named for the husband of actress Greer Garson, who donated land for the new park) with exhibits of the nearly 80,000 artifacts excavated at the pueblo by archaeologist A.V. Kidder in the early 1900s. Kidder's work led to the ceramics dating system known as the Pecos Classification. A one-mile trail leads through the ruins of the pueblo and the lovely church. Special van tours on weekends visit Garson's historic 100,000-acre Lightning Fork Ranch and the 1862 Glorieta Pass Battlefield Site, where an important Civil War battle turned back Confederate soldiers and saved the Colorado goldfields. Tours begin at Kozlowski's Santa Fe Trail Trading Post, the last stop on the historic Santa Fe Trail.

The drive to Pecos from Santa Fe on Interstate 25 follows the old Santa Fe Trail. State Route 63 goes north from

the monument through Pecos Canyon for 20 miles (32km) until it dead-ends at Cowles, a summer home area and trailhead for horse and backpacking trips into Santa Fe National Forest and Pecos Wilderness.

You can continue east on Interstate 25 past the Pecos turnoff for another 15 miles (24km) to State Route 3, which goes through several villages as pastoral and quiet as they were a hundred years ago. At **San Miguel**, 3 miles (5km) south of Interstate 25, you can still see where travelers on the Santa Fe Trail forded the Pecos River. In the Mexican period (1821–46), San Miguel was the portal to New Mexico, where wagon trains stopped to pay duty. **Villanueva State Park** (tel: 505-421-2957; www.emnrd.state.nm.us/spd/villanuevastatepark; Apr–Oct daily 7am–9pm, Nov–Mar daily 7am–7pm; free), 9 miles (14km) south of San Miguel, has picnic and camping amenities on the Pecos River. This narrow valley, where the stream is bordered with small fields and villages, lies at the heart of rural Hispanic New Mexico.

Northwest of Santa Fe, **Los Alamos** is a true company town, built secretly during World War II for scientists on the Manhattan Project developing the atomic bomb. It now welcomes visitors with attractive residential and business areas, a museum on its history, in addition to the still-secret nuclear research laboratories, which include development of nuclear weapons. The lab's original mission has changed from designing weapons of mass destruction to maintaining existing ones and preventing an escalation of nuclear arms. In addition, top scientists researching space exploration, renewable energy, medicine, and climate change work at the lab now.

You can find out more at the **Bradbury Science Museum** (1350 Central Avenue; tel: 505 667-4444; www.lanl.gov/museum; Tue–Sat 10am–5pm, Sun, Mon 1–5pm; free) in the Museum Park Complex, which chronicles the atomic age by focusing on achievements in weapons development, alternative energy sources, and biomedical research.

Where the road turns east through the Jemez Mountains you'll find **Valles Caldera National Preserve** (mile marker 39.2 on SR 4; tel: 575-829-4100; www.nps.gov/vall; daily summer 8am–6pm, winter 9am–5pm; free), a lush, grassy valley 12 miles (19km) across, cupped in high mountains, now protected as a unit of the National Park System. A few million years ago this was the seething innards of a volcano that, layer by layer, gradually built up the entire 50-mile (80km) -long mountain range. Finally, 1.25 million years ago, the caldera of the volcano collapsed, creating this wide valley, known as Valle Grande. The volcanic ash and dust from the cataclysmic event added another 1,500ft (450 meters) to the Pajarito Plateau. Erosion cut the plateau into deep canyons, and where layer of volcanic ash were exposed, natural caves were hollowed out by the wind.

Eons later, Ancestral Puebloans migrating into Frijoles Canyon from

In Bradbury Science Museum.

Mesa Verde scooped out caveate homes in the canyon walls for cliff dwellings and built a large circular pueblo on the canyon floor. These dwellings are now a highlight of spectacular **Bandelier National Monument** ⑭ (SR 4; tel: 575-672-3861, ext. 517; www.nps.gov/band; park: daily dawn–dusk, visitor center: daily 8am–6pm, 9am–5pm winter; charge), which was designated a national monument in 1916 to protect one of the largest concentrations of archeological sites in the Southwest. It contains more than 70 miles (113km) of backcountry trails and 23,000 acres (9,308 hectares) of designated wilderness.

The 50-sq-mile (129-sq-km) monument is named for Adolph Bandelier, a Swiss-American scholar who extensively surveyed the prehistoric ruins in the region and studied the Pueblo Indians around Santa Fe in the 1880s.

The easiest way to experience Bandelier is to orient yourself at the attractive visitor center, which dates to the WPA era in the Thirties and has a film to watch, a museum, and handouts,

then walk the Main Ruins Trail, a 1-mile (1.6km) paved loop that takes about 45 minutes. One highlight can be reached by continuing up the canyon to the base of Alcove House (formerly Ceremonial Cave). The pueblo and kiva in this cave are accessible only by climbing four steep ladders, a total of 140ft (43 meters) high. There is a pleasant campground on the mesa above the park. Note: Between May and November, visitors are required to park and ride a shuttle bus (included in cost of park entrance) to Frijoles Canyon from the gateway community of White Rock; you may drive in the rest of the year or outside the shuttle bus's hours of operation (9am–3pm).

O'KEEFFE COUNTRY

Beyond the crossroads of Española, north of Ohkay Owingeh Pueblo, US 84 follows the Chama River valley into a gorgeously eroded red rock landscape dubbed O'Keeffe Country, for its most famous fan: painter Georgia O'Keeffe. It took 10 years for O'Keeffe to talk the Catholic Church into selling her

On the main trail through Frijules Canyon, Bandelier National Monument.

a ruined adobe in **Abiquiu** ⑮, parts of which date to 1760, and four years to remodel it for her use. Today, it's a beautiful walled oasis with stripped-down interiors suited to O'Keeffe's thrifty Midwesterner aesthetic and familiar views across the Rio Chama to an area of badlands in the cliffs known as The White Place, where O'Keeffe wandered and picked up bones. **O'Keeffe Home & Studio Tours** (tel: 505-946-1000; www.okeeffemuseum.org/tickets-and-tours) are available seasonally by reservation. Tours begin at the Georgia O'Keeffe Foundation offices adjoining the **Abiquiu Inn** (tel: 505-685-4328; www.abiquiuinn.com), a good place for lodging and a meal. Hearty New Mexican food on the go, such as homemade breakfast burritos and burgers, can be found nearby at **Bode's Store** (tel: 505-685-4422; www.bodes.com), a gas station/hardware/café/gift shop across from the village, where O'Keeffe herself used to shop.

Those with more refined sensibilities may wish to stop at the lovely seasonal **Purple Adobe Lavender Farm** (www.purpleadobelavenderfarm.com), off US 84, to stroll among the lavender, buy lavender products, and even enjoy lavender scones, gelato, and tea in the little teahouse. Abiquiu Inn, the lavender farm, and numerous artist's studios take part in a popular self-guided annual November **Abiquiu Studio Tour** (www.abiquiu studiotour.org), which visits many beautiful artists' homes in the valley.

Twelve miles (19km) northwest of Abiquiu is **Ghost Ranch Conference Center** (tel: 877-804-4678; www.ghostranch.org). Started as a dude ranch by publisher Arthur Pack, who gave O'Keeffe her first home in the valley and later donated the property to the Presbyterian Church, Ghost Ranch is a wonderful destination in itself. Visitors can take a workshop, hike into the canyons, stay in the pretty campground, take a tour of O'Keefe's favorite locations, and enjoy lodging and meals in a peaceful atmosphere. Two excellent museums are on the property. The Florence Hawley Ellis Anthropology Museum traces the human history of the area, while the Ruth Hall Paleontology Museum has information about the colorful rock formations behind Ghost ranch where dinosaurs have been unearthed.

From Ghost Ranch, you have a good view of **Pedernal**, the flat-topped volcanic plug above NM 96 and US 84, near **Abiquiu Lake**. O'Keeffe painted it so often, she exclaimed, "God told me that if I painted Pedernal often enough, I could have it." In a way she was right. She is now buried there.

This is spectacular high country, where you leave the Rio Grande Valley behind and enter the scenic Colorado Plateau country and encounter brightly colored sandstone hoodoos and amphitheaters similar to those found in southern Utah. One of them, **Echo Canyon Amphitheater** (tel: 575-758-6200), is right off US 84 about 3 miles (5km) north of Ghost Ranch. It has a sweet little unmanned campground

Desert views made famous by Georgia O'Keeffe's paintings at the Ghost Ranch Conference Center.

run by the forest service that offers inexpensive camping and killer views down the whole Chama River valley.

Highway 84 continues on through the historic **Tierra Amarilla Valley** to **Chama,** where lush meadows, grazing sheep and cattle, and the looming San Juan Mountains take the breath away and indicate you are close to the Colorado state line. If you visit in fall, be sure to ride the 1880 narrow-gauge **Cumbres and Toltec Scenic Railroad** (tel: 888-286-2737; www.cumbrestoltec.com) into the mountains to Antonito, Colorado. The turning aspens are breathtaking.

SANTA FE TO TAOS

The road north from Santa Fe to Taos is peppered with pueblos. **Tesuque Pueblo** ⓰, 10 miles (16km) north of Santa Fe, is a small pueblo but has some excellent potters, usually working with earth-colored clay in animal figures. Its patron saint day, November 12, celebrates San Diego. The pueblo residents perform animal dances in winter.

San Ildefonso Pueblo ⓱, 20 miles (32km) northwest of Santa Fe, just east of the Rio Grande, is best known as the home of the famous potter Maria Martinez. Inspired by Ancestral Puebloan pottery excavated by archaeologist Edgar Lee Hewett, Martinez and her husband, Julian, developed San Ildefonso's trademark black-on-black ware and sparked a new interest in Pueblo pottery of every style. Julian died in 1943 and Maria's son, Popovi Da, took up the painting chores. His son, Tony Da, also an artist, became well known for integrating turquoise incising techniques and unconventional shapes into his pottery designs. Examples of the Martinez ceramics can be seen at the Millicent Rogers Museum, in Taos (see page 260). San Ildefonso has a large plaza used for dances at key times of year, including Christmas Day, when the Buffalo or Deer Dance is performed.

Pojoaque Pueblo ⓲, 16 miles (26km) north of Santa Fe, shrank almost to extinction. It was reorganized and now has a tribal structure and many successful businesses. On December 12, it holds a tribute to Our Lady of

Native American residents of San Ildefonso Pueblo participate in the Eagle Dance.

Guadalupe, patron saint of New Mexico and Mexico. The tribe has a large complex at the junction of US 285 and NM 54, consisting of a casino-hotel, stores, restaurants, apartments, a health center, and other businesses. Its flagship business is its elegant Pueblo-style Hilton Santa Fe **Buffalo Thunder** (tel: 505-455-5555; www.buffalothunder resort.com), off US 285 to the south. Managed by Hilton, it offers attractive guest rooms, gourmet dining, a conference center, and golf.

Nambe Pueblo ⑲ (tel: 505-455-2036; www.nambepueblo.org), 21 miles (34km) northeast of Santa Fe, has been largely Hispanicized but its impressive mission church is well maintained and dominates the area. San Francisco is celebrated on October 4, and on July 4 there's a popular festival at the foot of Nambe Falls, where dances are performed and photography is permitted. A campground is near the falls.

Thirty miles (48km) northwest of Santa Fe, **Santa Clara Pueblo** (www. santaclaran.com) has several outstanding potters, including the well-known Lonewolf and Medicine Flower, members of the Naranjo family. Red or black ware is polished and incised with intricately carved designs.

The tribe's ancestral home is protected at **Puye Cliff Dwellings** (SR5; tel: 505-917-6650 (tribal headquarters) or 888-320-5008 (tours); www.san-taclaran.com/attractions; Apr–Sept daily 9am–6pm, Oct–Mar daily 9am–4pm; charge) across the highway. Four different guided tours of the 1 mile (1.6km)-long ruins are offered. Basic entrance admits you to the Harvey House, a late 19th-century bed-and-breakfast built by the famous railroad entrepreneur Fred Harvey at the foot of the cliffs; it is the only one built on an Indian reservation. It now serves as an interpretive center and museum and allows you to take photos of the cliff dwellings from below.

Across the river from the place chosen by Juan de Oñate as the first capital of New Mexico, in 1598, Tewa-speaking **Ohkay Owingeh Pueblo ⑳** (tel: 505-852-4400; www.ohkay.com), or Ohkay Owingeh, is 46 miles (75km) north of Santa Fe. Only a cross on the mound of an unexcavated pueblo marks the spot of the old pueblo today, but the modern pueblo is large (6,748 members) and headquarters for the Eight Northern Pueblos. Its feast day is June 24; on Christmas Day pueblo members perform the Matachines Dance, an adaptation of a Spanish morality play.

The Poeh Cultural Center at Pojoaque Pueblo.

THE HIGH ROAD TO TAOS

The High Road to Taos, SR 76, winds through colonial New Mexico and isolated historic mountain villages like Chimayo, Las Trampas, and Peñasco. From Santa Fe, go north on US 84/285 to **Santa Cruz** (home to America's largest Sikh community, founded by Yogi Bhajan), then turn onto SR 76. Holy Cross Church in Santa Cruz was built in the 1740s and is one of the largest of the old mission churches. Its buttressed walls are 3ft (1 meter) thick

The view from Route 503, north of Sante Fe.

and sheltered the villagers when Plains Indians came through the mountains to steal crops, women, and children.

El Santuario de Chimayo ㉑ (tel: 505-351-9961; www.elsantuariodechimayo.us) in the traditional village of Chimayo is called the Lourdes of America. During Holy Week (the week before Easter), pilgrims from miles around drive, walk, even crawl toward the santuario to offer prayers, give thanks, and receive blessings there. The altar screen and Stations of the Cross are fine examples of religious folk art. To the left of the altar, a room is hung with crutches, poems, letters, and other offerings from the devout. In a small adjoining room is a hole in the dirt floor (*el pozo*), where pilgrims get a pinch of the holy earth of Chimayo, said to have healing powers.

Chimayo is famous for its sweet, complex red chile, which is available in several gift shops near the santuario, along with Mexican tin charms called *milagros*, or miracles; candles; and other religious items. Several families of Chimayo weavers have achieved national fame for their tightly woven, brightly colored blankets. Weaving shops can be found in the pretty traditional village of Chimayo, including the famed family-run **Ortegas Weaving Shop** (53 Plaza del Cerro; tel: 505-351-4215; www.ortegasweaving.com; Mon–Sat 9am–5pm), open since the 1700s, and **Centinela Traditional Arts** (946 SR 76; tel: 505-351-2180; www.chimayoweavers.com; daily 9am–6pm), run by the Trujillo family.

The tiny village of **Truchas** sits high on a forested plateau beneath the snow-covered Truchas Peaks (*truchas* means trout, a reference to the good fishing here). On the main street are a *morada* (a small church associated with the Penitente sect, common in rural northern New Mexico) and a plastic-roofed Pentecostal church. Truchas has several art galleries worth browsing. This is a great place to enjoy high country views and fresh mountain air. The setting is superb.

A few miles on is **Las Trampas**, best known for its church, said to be the finest example of pueblo architecture in the state. The village was founded in 1760 as a buffer for Santa Cruz and Santa Fe against marauding Comanches. The church, San Jose de Gracia, is on the state and national historic registers. Many visitors travel this road to photograph its churches, and you will certainly not be disappointed.

Peñasco ㉒ is a crossroads village, with a popular café, Sugar Nymphs Bistro, which serves a mean green chile burger. The high road doesn't have a lot of places to eat, so you might want to stop. The route divides here. Turning right 6 miles (10km) to SR 3 takes you through the mountain into Taos, passing **Sipapu Ski and Summer Resort** (tel: 800-587-2240; www.sipapu nm.com), which has gentle slopes and is popular with families. Alternatively, turning left onto SR 75 leads to SR 68, the main road to Taos.

If choosing the second route, stop

Buy blankets at Ortegas Weaving Shop.

at **Picuris Pueblo ㉓**, 20 miles (32km) southwest of Taos. This pueblo is believed to have been founded around 1250 by a group from Taos Pueblo – the two tribes speak the same language (Tiwa); there are six distinct Pueblo languages. The annual feast day at Picuris is August 10, at which time a Corn Dance is performed in honor of San Lorenzo. Women potters produce utilitarian cooking pottery that is reddish brown, with highlights of mica and is not decorated. The pueblo's restored church is worth viewing; ask the custodian to let you in.

Picuris was once much larger than it is today, but being on the eastern edge of the pueblo world, it was subject to attack by Plains Indians more than any other pueblo. Pueblo ranchers raise bison here, and you will see the herd on the reservation. The tribe's main income comes from its majority share in Hotel Santa Fe in Santa Fe, which is filled with art from this and other pueblos. Bison from the tribe's herd is served in the excellent hotel restaurant, Amaya.

San Francisco de Asis Church at **Ranchos de Taos** (tel: 575-758-2754; daily 10am–4pm), on US 68, just south of Taos, is not one of the oldest churches in New Mexico – it was built in 1850 – but it is probably the best known and most photographed church exterior because of its classic pueblo architecture. Georgia O'Keeffe and other artists have captured the flowing lines that seem to be part of the earth.

Also in Ranchos de Taos, on the banks of the Rio Pueblo, is the 200-year-old **Hacienda de los Martinez** (708 Hacienda Road, off SR 240; tel: 575-758-1000; Mon–Sat 10am–5pm, Sun noon–5pm; charge), the sprawling, 21-room home of Don Antonio Severino Martinez, a trader at the northern end of El Camino Real. The hacienda encloses 2 *placitas* (courtyard-type areas), has no exterior windows, and was fortified against Apache and Comanche raids. On view are a blacksmith shop, tack room, granary, weaving room, and living quarters with period furnishings.

El Santuario de Chimayo.

TAOS AND THE SANTA FE TRAIL

Iconoclastic Taos is Santa Fe's artsy little sister, the first stop on a spectacular high country drive through mountains, plains, the Rio Grande, historic land grant ranches, and stops along the Santa Fe Trail.

The light glows with a physical radiance, white sunlight and lavender shadows, blue distance and golden earth. In 1912, this light drew to **Taos** ㉔ eight young artists from the East Coast who formed the Taos Society of Artists. Whether the spell lies in the physical beauty, the legends or the history of the area, few people visit Taos without feeling its magic.

Taos was settled by the Spaniards in the early 1600s, close to Taos Pueblo. **Taos Plaza** has seen a lot of history – Indians, Spanish conquistadors, mountain men, and merchants. The American flag flies 24 hours a day on the plaza. It's a special honor commemorating the bravery of Taos resident Kit Carson and other frontiersmen during the Civil War. When Confederate sympathizers tried to replace the American flag with the Confederate flag, Carson and friends nailed the stars and stripes to the tallest pine tree they could find and stood armed guard until the Confederates had been driven back to Texas.

The first American governor of New Mexico, Charles Bent, was murdered in his Taos home in 1847 during an Indian rebellion a few months after the American occupation. His family escaped by tunneling through the adobe wall to the next-door house. Bent Street commemorates this first governor in Taos; the home is now a privately run museum.

El Santero mural on a building in the plaza.

Better known and represented in Taos is Kit Carson, the Kentucky-born legendary trapper, mountain man, Indian scout, translator, and army officer who lived in Taos with his Mexican wife for 25 years. Their house is now the **Kit Carson Home** and **Museum** (113 Kit Carson Road; tel: 575-758-4945; www.kitcarsonmuseum.org; daily 10am–5pm, except Nov–Feb 10am–4pm; charge). Carson bought this 12-room adobe home as a wedding gift for his bride, Maria Josefa Jaramillo, in 1843, and the couple raised seven children here. Individual rooms in

⊙ Main Attractions

Taos Pueblo
Rio Grande del Norte
  National Monument
Great Sand Dunes
  National Park and
  Preserve
Cimarron
Las Vegas

Map on page 220

the 1825 home have exhibits depicting Taos's colorful history and celebrating the trappings of Carson's adventurous life. Kids will enjoy walking through a typical mountain man camp and viewing historic guns. Carson's grave is in nearby Kit Carson Park.

TAOS MUSEUMS

Taos (pop. 5,700) has a plethora of worthwhile museums that explore the groundbreaking artists and visionaries who put this small town on the map. All can be easily visited in a day or two, and provide insights into what drew people here in the 1800s and early 1900s.

The **Blumenschein Home and Museum** (222 Ledoux Street, tel: 575-758-0505; daily 9am–5pm; charge). In 1912, Ernest Blumenschein and five other artists founded the Taos Society of Artists, dedicated to helping its members exhibit their art in galleries throughout the country. Although Phillips moved to Taos immediately, it took a bit longer for Blumenschein, who had commitments and a young family back east in New York City. However, in 1919, after spending many summers in Taos, Blumenschein and his wife and daughter moved from New York to Taos and purchased this adobe home. It has the intimate feel of an artist's home gallery.

Nearby is the **Harwood Museum of Art** (238 Ledoux Street; tel: 575-758-9826; www.harwoodmuseum.org; Wed–Fri 10am–5pm, Sat–Sun noon–5pm; charge), founded in 1923 and operated by the University of New Mexico since 1936. This is a great place to see paintings, drawings, prints, sculpture, and photographs by Taos artists from 1898 to the present. One room has 19th-century *retablos* (religious paintings on wood) that were given to the foundation by local arts patron and writer Mabel Dodge Luhan. Special exhibitions of Taos artists and works from the University of New Mexico's collections are also displayed during the year.

Also downtown is the **Taos Art Museum at Fechin House** (227 Paseo del Pueblo Norte; tel: 575-758-2690; www.taosartmuseum.org; Tue–Sun 10am–5pm; charge), located in the former home of

In the Dorothy and Jack Brandenburg Gallery of Early 20th Century Art at Harwood Museum of Art.

Russian artist Nicolai Fechin. Fechin excelled in woodworking and his small but light-filled home, remodeled from an old adobe home between 1924 and 1927, is almost completely made of carved wood, from bed, chests, and chairs to posts and corbels. Fechins's vibrant portraits are on display downstairs, while upstairs rooms contain some 300 pieces of art by 50 Taos artists.

The newest museum in downtown Taos is only open to the public for tours by appointment in summer, but for anyone interested in the Taos Society of Artists, it's a necessity. The **Couse-Sharpe Historic Site** (146 Kit Carson Road; tel: 575-751-0369; www. couse-sharp.org; tours by appointment May–Oct Mon–Fri 10am–5pm, Nov–Apr Fri 10am–4pm; charge) preserves the home and studios of two of the six founding members of the Taos Society of Artists: E.I. Couse and Joseph Henry Sharp. The property includes the Couse home, studio, and gardens; the workshops of Couse's son; and the two neighboring studios of fellow artist Joseph Henry Sharp.

TAOS PUEBLO

Two miles (3km) north of the town of Taos, **Taos Pueblo** ㉕ (tel: 575-758 1028; www.taospueblo.com; Mon–Sat 8am–4.30pm, Sun 8.30am–4.30pm; separate charge for entrance and photography fees) is the most photographed and familiar of all Indian pueblos, with its large, multistoried structures facing each other across the plaza. While the pueblo is home for many members, it is also now clearly a commercial commodity and source of income.

Taos marked the northern frontier of Spanish colonial control, and it was here that the Comanche and other Plains Indians came to trade with the Spaniards and Pueblo Indians. Most of the year, the Plains people often raided and plundered the Pueblo tribes, but during the trade period a truce prevailed.

Even today, Taos Indians show traits of their Plains contemporaries: long braids, beaded moccasins, aquiline noses, high cheekbones. The Plains war dances sometimes performed at Taos are unlike the traditionally quieter dances of the other pueblos. Taos

Taos Pueblo.

Native American Wedding Vase from Taos Pueblo.

View over the Rio Grande near Taos.

potters produce a good red-brown micaceous pottery, like that at Picuris, not ornamental but useful.

NORTH FROM TAOS

An important stop for those interested in American Indian arts – weaving, ceramics, jewelry and painting – is in El Prado, 4 miles (6.5km) north of Taos, at the **Millicent Rogers Museum** (tel: 505-758-2462; www.millicentrogers.org; Apr–Oct daily 10am–5pm, Nov–Mar closed Mon; charge). The collection is more extensive than can be displayed at one time: *colcha* embroideries, Hispanic *santos* (religious icons), Navajo and Pueblo jewelry, contemporary works, Hopi and Zuni kachina dolls, basketry and, for the knowledgeable, a large display of ceramics by San Ildefonso potter Maria Martinez. As for Millicent Rogers, she came from a notable New York family and lived in Europe for years, socializing with the likes of Ayn Rand and Noel Coward. She came to Taos in 1947, where she lived until her death. During her time in Taos, she gathered one of the best collections anywhere of Southwestern aesthetic creativity. Time in this museum is time superbly spent.

A few miles west of Taos, the **Rio Grande** flows through an 800ft (244-meter) -deep gorge cut by the river in the volcanic plateau. In 2013, President Barack Obama designated the 48-mile (77km) stretch of "wild and scenic river" in northern New Mexico, which includes the 18,000-acre (7,284-hectare) Wild Rivers Recreation Area, as the expanded 242,500-acre (98,136-hectare) **Rio Grande del Norte National Monument**. It is managed by the Bureau of Land Management (BLM), which operates two visitor centers in the monument: Rio Grande Gorge Visitor Center at Orilla Verde Recreation Area, south of Taos, and Wild Rivers Visitor Center in Cerro, 20 miles (32km) northwest of Questa, north of Taos. Each offers information and permits for outdoor recreation. This is the place to view exhibits on the fascinating Rio Grande rift zone geology of the area, as well as learn about the rock art and other American Indian artifacts in the monument, the traditional homeland of

⊘ SAN GERONIMO DAYS

On September 30 and October 1, Taos Indians pay homage to San Geronimo with dances. At dawn, male members of North House race against those of South House; at the end of the race the teams are showered with Crackerjacks and oranges by Taoseños from the stepped roofs of North House. The *chifonetti* are male clowns painted with black-and-white stripes and adorned with corn husks in their hair who cavort among onlookers, cart off children, and tease the crowd. Their joking has a moral purpose – chastising miscreants and warning others. Immediately after the races, an intertribal trade fair begins. Selected artisans show their wares in booths set up on the wide plaza between North House and the stream that divides the pueblo. A visitor center at the entrance collects fees and issue permits.

the Jicarilla Apache and Utes, as well as Taos and Picuris pueblos.

Wild Rivers Backcountry Byway follows the rim for 22 miles (35km) and offers great scenery and photograph and wildlife-viewing opportunities, as well as access to developed campgrounds, primitive hike-in campsites within the gorge, and hiking and mountain-biking rim and river trails. Guided hikes and regular campfire presentations are offered during summer. To get to the visitor center (1120 Cerro Road, Cerro; tel: 575-586-1150; http://blm.gov; daily 9am–6pm; charge), head 3 miles (5km) north of Questa on SR 522, then go west on SR 538 for 17 miles (27km).

In May and June, whitewater rafters find this part of the Rio Grande a real challenge, with some rapids classed Grade VI, the most dangerous kind of whitewater. Nine miles (14km) west of Taos on US Highway 64, a dramatic bridge spans the green-and-white ribbon flowing between black basalt walls 650ft (200 meters) below. South of town at Pilar, a road leads down to the river, a favorite spot for trout fishing.

During the 1920s, the flamboyant Mabel Dodge Luhan brought many artists to Taos, including D.H. Lawrence. She married a Taos Pueblo Indian and built a rambling adobe home (now Mabel Dodge Luhan Inn) on the edge of Taos Pueblo, where she entertained talented and famous people in great style. She gave the Lawrences a ranch at San Cristobal in the Sangre de Cristo Mountains, north of Taos. After Lawrence's death in France, Lawrence's German wife Frieda brought his ashes back to the ranch and built a shrine for him on a hill with an unrestricted view of the Taos Plateau. Frieda herself was buried outside the simple white shrine built by her third husband, Angelo Ravagli, and the ranch was willed to the University of New Mexico in perpetuity.

Today, the **D.H. Lawrence Ranch** ㉖ (tel: 575-776-2245; www.dhlawrencetaos.org; Thu, Fri 10am–2pm, Sat 10am–4pm; free) remains in UNM hands. In 2014, the university reached an agreement with the D.H. Lawrence Alliance to restore and reopen the ranch to visitors, which occurred in 2015. A grant

The Homesteader's Cabin at the D.H. Lawrence Ranch.

has allowed for a docent program and tours of the property, as well as restoration of certain buildings, including the Lawrence cabin and the cabin belonging to their friend, artist Dorothy "Brett."

To reach the ranch, head north of Taos on SR 522 for about 12 miles (19km). A directional sign and historical marker at San Cristobal mark the turnoff. The ranch and memorial are about 7 miles (11km) off the highway, at the end of a dirt road that climbs into the mountains.

SKIING IN TAOS

Taos Ski Valley (tel: 800-776-1111; www.taosskivalley.com), 20 miles (32km) northeast of town, is the best known of New Mexico's 12 ski areas. The runs are on the slopes of Wheeler Peak – at over 13,000ft (4,000 meters) high, New Mexico's tallest peak – and the ski area has dozens of powder bowls, glades, and chutes. The season usually lasts from at least early November into April. Ernie Blake, a Swiss transplant known as The Godfather of the Slopes, developed Taos Ski Valley over many years, earning a reputation for high standards. Miles of hiking trails lead from the ski valley into the forests and wilderness areas fringing Taos.

Alamosa ㉗ is in the San Luis Valley of Colorado, a productive farmland 50 miles (80km) wide between the San Juan Mountains to the west and the Sangre de Cristo Mountains to the east. **Great Sand Dunes National Park and Preserve** ㉘ (11999 SR 150, Mosca, CO; tel: 719-378-6395; www.nps.gov/grsa; park daily 24 hours, visitor center daily Memorial Day–Labor Day 8.30am–5pm, Oct–May 9am–4.30pm; charge) lies 35 miles (56km) northeast of Alamosa against the base of the Sangre de Cristos like piles of soft brown velvet, protecting the tallest sand dunes in America. Prevailing winds blow across the valley from the west, picking up particles of sand and dust and dropping them when they reach the solid barrier of the mountains. The dunes are over 700ft (200 meters) high and 10 miles (16km) long. A visitor center has exhibits describing the history, plants and animals of the area. There are no trails on the dunes, so you walk where you

Family on a ski lift in Taos Ski Valley.

please. When storms sweep in from the northeast, the winds reverse the pattern of the ridges.

SANTA FE TRAIL COUNTRY

Starting in 1821, the Santa Fe Trail was the channel of commerce and communication between the Spanish Rio Grande and the United States. Because of the social and business relationships that had already been established, commerce made victory easy when the United States took the Southwest in the Mexican War (1846–48). Forts protected settlers, pioneers, and miners as they fulfilled the nation's "manifest destiny." The main branch of the trail came across southeast Colorado into New Mexico over Raton Pass, through Cimarron, Las Vegas, and then around the southern end of the Rocky Mountains to Santa Fe.

You can still see parts of the Santa Fe Trail in northeastern New Mexico. Wherever the ground has not been plowed, as in the areas north of Las Vegas and Fort Union, ruts are plainly visible from the train or from Interstate 25 in Apache Canyon. **Bent's Old Fort National Historic Site** (35110 SR 194, La Junta, CO; tel: 719-383-5010; www.nps.gov/beol; daily Jun–Aug 8am–5.30pm, 9am–4pm rest of the year; charge), 8 miles (13km) east of **La Junta** ㉙ in southeastern Colorado, is a reconstruction of the fort that was built by the Bent brothers in 1833. It became one of the most famous forts and trading posts in the West, doing brisk business with both pioneers and Indians. Living history exhibits help bring the fort to life today, and offer a lot of fun for kids.

THE FUR TRAPPERS

Bent's Old Fort was the meeting place for fur trappers from all over the Rockies, the most famous of whom was Kit Carson. Military and government surveying parties, wagon freighters, and stagecoaches stopped for supplies, food, and rest. Indians came to trade buffalo hides and furs for food and tobacco.

Another stopping place on the Santa Fe Trail was on El Rio de las Animas Perdidas en Purgatorio (River of Lost Souls in Purgatory) – generally shortened to Purgatory or Purgatoire – just before it crossed the mountains into New Mexico. Today the town of **Trinidad** ㉚, just over the border in Colorado, is on that spot, a coal mining and trade center with many brick buildings dating back to the last century. **Trinidad History Museum** (312 E Main Street; tel: 719-846-7217; www.historycolorado.org/museums/trinidad-history-museum-0; Tue–Sat 10am–4pm; free) preserves several historic homes on one block in downtown Trinidad. **Baca House,** built of adobe in 1869, was purchased by prominent rancher and merchant Felipe Baca in 1873 as a home. **Bloom Mansion** was built in 1882 in the Second Empire style by a pioneer merchant, cattleman, and banker. **The Santa Fe Trail Museum** is in a 12-room adobe building behind the Baca House and includes local history exhibits as well as a fringed buckskin coat given to the mayor of Trinidad by Kit Carson.

Bent's Old Fort.

Main Street in Trinidad.

Across Raton Pass from Trinidad, in extreme northeastern New Mexico, a good spring provided another stopping place on the trail, and here the railroad town of **Raton** ㉛ grew. A historic district on First Street preserves several old buildings that now house specialty shops, a coffee house, a theater museum, and the Palace Hotel, which does not rent rooms but has a fine steakhouse restaurant.

One of the colorful men in Raton's past, Uncle Dick Wootton, trapped beaver, and hunted and scouted for the Fremont Expedition with his close friend Kit Carson. He is best remembered for his toll road over Raton Pass. He moved boulders and trees from 27 miles (43km) of extremely rough terrain to make what was, for the time, a fair wagon road. He built a home and way station at the summit, and not many people argued with this 6.6ft (1.98-meter) -tall frontiersman, when he stood at his toll gate and asked $1.50 a wagon, or a nickel or dime a head for livestock. Anyone who chose not to pay could go around the mountains, a detour of more than 100 miles (160km). He never charged Indians. He sold his road to the railroad, and the site is marked today. The Santa Fe Railway still follows the same route, and Interstate 25 is on the hillside just above it.

Capulin Volcano National Monument ㉜ (tel: 575-278-2201; www.nps.gov/cavo; Memorial Day–Labor Day daily 8.30am–5pm, rest of year 8am–4.30pm; charge), 34 miles (55km) south of Raton on US 64/87, is a perfectly shaped 1,000ft (300-meter) volcanic cone that erupted 60,000 years ago and served as a landmark on one of the branches of the Santa Fe Trail. It is part of the extensive Raton-Clayton Volcanic Field and has many interesting volcanic features. At the base there is a visitor center with picnic area, and a historic road winds up to the summit, where views extend all the way to Colorado, Oklahoma, Texas, and Kansas. A 1-mile (1.6km) trail circles the caldera, and another short trail leads down into the crater, a rare chance to enter a dormant volcano.

Cimarron ㉝, 35 miles (56km) southwest of Raton, was another stop on the Santa Fe Trail. Cimarron was founded by Lucien Maxwell, another trapper-trader-scout-freighter friend of Kit Carson. Through inheritance and purchase he became sole owner of the 1.7 million-acre (694,500-hectare) Maxwell Land Grant which covered most of northeastern New Mexico and some of southern Colorado. Maxwell became a legend of the Santa Fe Trail, entertaining lavishly in his baronial adobe mansion in Cimarron. Weary stagecoach travelers were drawn into gambling at card games or on horse racing when they stopped at Cimarron. Maxwell paid his rare losses from a chest of gold coins. He sold the grant in 1870 and it was subsequently broken up into ranches and town sites.

THE PAST IN MUSEUMS

The **Old Aztec Mill Museum** (tel: 575-376-2417; May–Sept daily 1–4pm, call

Capulin Volcano National Monument.

to confirm) is the four-story gristmill Maxwell built in Cimarron in 1865 to supply his ranch and the Jicarilla Apache Indian Reservation. The **St James Hotel** (617 S Collison Avenue, Cimarron; tel: 575-376-2664) was built around 1872 by a French chef from Lincoln's White House and has guest rooms that have plenty of tales to tell as well as a dining room. The tin ceiling of the original bar, now the dining room, is pierced by 30 bullet holes, reminders of Cimarron's wild past.

Four miles (6km) south of Cimarron on State Highway 21 is **Philmont Scout Ranch** (tel: 575-376-2281; www.philmontscoutranch.org; daily 8am–5pm; free), where every summer for many decades as many as 17,000 Boy Scouts and their leaders visit for their famous Scout Jamboree. The 127,000-acre (51,000-hectare) ranch was given to the Scouts by the wealthy oil baron Waite Phillips. It contains grassy valleys, timbered mountains, streams, and a mansion with a 14-room guest house. An expansion of the ranch is being built to house the National Scouting Museum and Seton Memorial Library and Education Center at present.

Visitors are welcome at Philmont, especially to visit its museums. The **Kit Carson Museum** at Rayado is in the home Carson rebuilt and enlarged in the 1850s. **Philmont Museum** (tel: 575-375-1136; Mon–Fri 9am–5pm) houses the Seton Memorial Library, containing much of the work of the famous naturalist, Ernest Thompson Seton, one of the founders of scouting. Visitors can also take tours of **Villa Philmonte**, the glorious 1920s Italianate summer home of Waite and Genevieve Phillips. Call the Philmont Museum for information.

Fort Union National Monument ㉞ (Watrous; tel: 505-425-8025; www.nps.gov/foun; daily Memorial Day–Labor Day 8am–5pm, Oct–May 8am–4pm; charge), 9 miles (14km) off Interstate 25 and 19 miles (30km) northeast of Las Vegas, was one of the largest and most important forts in the West. Built in 1851 (two replacements were built during the next 30 years), it was a supply depot for other forts throughout

⊘ Where

The entire downtown of Las Vegas is a designated historic district with more than 900 listed structures. Call 505-425-8803 for a historic walking tour booklet. Many historic buildings surround the lovely Plaza, including the nicely restored 1882 **Plaza Hotel** (tel: 505-425-3591; www.plazahotellvnm.com), now owned by the same artist partnership as La Posada in Winslow, Arizona.

Old wagons and adobe ruins at Fort Union National Monument.

the Southwest. Almost at the end of the Santa Fe Trail, many a Conestoga wagon thundered through its protecting walls barely ahead of the Comanche. Fort Union was closed in 1891 after the railroad arrived in New Mexico. Rangers offer daily guided tours between 10am and 1pm in summer. A 1.6-mile (2.5km) self-guided trail with interpretive plaques and push-button audio leads through the ruins of all structures at the fort; a shorter half-mile (1km) trail offers an overview.

LAS VEGAS VICTORIANA

Las Vegas ❸ (not to be confused with the Nevada gambling town) was founded in 1835 at the edge of the Great Plains and was the capital of New Mexico for two months during the Civil War when the Confederates held Santa Fe.

The town boomed when the railroad arrived, outpacing Santa Fe in population growth by 1900. Wealthy Easterners traveled by rail to Las Vegas to summer at **Montezuma Castle**, a luxury resort just north of Las Vegas

at the mouth of Gallinas Canyon built by entrepreneur Fred Harvey around natural hot springs. The historic hotel is now **United World College** (tel: 505-454-4252; http://uwc-usa.org), a private international school.

On campus, you may enjoy visiting the **Dwan Light Sanctuary**, created by Virginia Dwan, artist Charles Ross, and architect Laban Wingert. The project grew out of Dwan's dream of creating a quiet space for contemplation for people of all beliefs. The Light Sanctuary incorporates 12 angles of light within its circular space, and 12 large prisms in the apses and ceiling create a progression throughout the year of unique spectrum events. Visitors to the campus must first stop at Moore Welcome Center to register and be accompanied around campus by a UWC guide.

During the 1898 Spanish-American War, Teddy Roosevelt recruited his Rough Riders from the Spanish-speaking population of Las Vegas. The small **City of Las Vegas and Rough Riders Memorial Collection** (727 Grand Avenue; tel: 505-426-3205; www.lasvegas museum.org; Tue–Sat 10am–4pm; donation) includes a small museum with Rough Rider exhibits.

The natural springs in Las Vegas made it an important stop for travelers on the Santa Fe Trail and later the railroad, as well as for wildlife. The name refers to its well-watered "meadows," a haven for migratory birds and other wildlife in winter. Several wildlife refuges are located in the shortgrass prairie grasslands between Las Vegas and Raton, including **Las Vegas National Wildlife Refuge** (Rt. 1; tel: 505-425-3581; www.fws.gov/refuge/las_vegas; trails daily sunrise–sunset, visitor center Mon–Thu 8am–4.30pm, Fri 8am–3.30pm; free), 7 miles (11km) southeast of town, which attracts 270 species of birds, including neotropical migrants. Watch for herds of pronghorn antelope and bison, a familiar sight on New Mexico's grassy plains.

Bridge Street, Las Vegas (not that one).

ORIGINS OF THE SANTA FE TRAIL

The Santa Fe Trail emerged as a vital trade connection between the isolated Southwest and the East in the 19th century.

It's amazing how far a man will travel to find his pot of gold. Take one William Becknell, an Indian fighter and war veteran from Missouri with a pile of debt and not much to lose. When Mexico threw off two centuries of oppressive Spanish colonial rule in 1821 and began courting foreign trade, Becknell was well positioned to take advantage. Directly out of Franklin, Missouri, was an 800-mile (1,300km) -long overland trail leading to Santa Fe – a route that crossed rivers, endless prairie, and rugged mountains. Buffalo and elk were plentiful enough to keep a man alive, but grizzlies, hostile Indians, violent prairie storms, and rock slides could put him six feet under. The risks were great, the potential profits greater. Undeterred, Becknell loaded his wagons and set off.

The journey took two and a half months and passed without serious incident. Any reservations Becknell had about his reception in New Mexico evaporated when the caravan pulled into Santa Fe (whose adobe buildings, one later trader said, reminded him more of "a prairie dog town" than a capital city). Citizens swarmed around the wagons, and the governor himself welcomed Becknell, expressing "a desire that the Americans would keep up an intercourse with that country." Becknell sold all his goods and returned the following fall, bringing with him 22 men driving wagons loaded with trade items. They blazed a southern desert route that was hot, dry and liable to flash flood, with hostile Comanches threatening at every turn, but shorter than the mountain route.

Becknell and other traders formed large caravans of 100 wagons. One 1824 wagon train left with $35,000 in merchandise and returned with $180,000 in gold and silver. It was said New Mexico nearly ran out of silver pesos in the 1820s, so many went east. Each "prairie schooner" was heavily laden with soap, cloth, shawls, pots, pans, wallpaper, ribbons, molasses, shoes, cider, coffee, flour, sugar, whiskey, cured meats, tools, farm implements, even window glass. There seemed to be nothing the Americans couldn't sell to a Southwest long isolated from the rest of the world.

In 1833, the Bent brothers and Ceran Verain built Bent's Old Fort, near La Junta, Colorado, along the northern (mountain) route of the Santa Fe Trail, and the fort quickly became a major rendezvous for Plains tribes, mountain men, traders, and travelers.

Exotic though it was, New Mexico could not long remain unaffected by America's plans for the West. In 1846, the US war with Mexico led to the bloodless handover of New Mexico, and just two years later, Mexico ceded vast tracts of the West to the US. Citizens of the Southwest were now American, and traffic along the Santa Fe Trail increased, peaking with the California Gold Rush in 1849 and the Civil War in the 1860s. Soldiers stationed at forts along the route protected settlers, traders, and travelers from Indian attack.

After the Civil War, the trail remained an important link, with stagecoaches carrying mail from Missouri to Santa Fe, but by 1880, the railroad replaced the Santa Fe Trail, signaling its demise.

Engraving of a wagon train, circa 1840.

FOUR CORNERS

Where the states of Utah, Arizona, New Mexico, and Colorado meet is a region of astounding geological grace, ancient Pueblo cultures and dwellings, and breathing space.

The desert people are bonded fast to their dry land, and these ties are sacred and as old as the Hopi people themselves. Two stories demonstrate these facts. The first story is from the dark night when the Hopi emerged from the underworld in what is now northern Arizona. The people who emerged from the womb of the Earth were greeted by Maasaw, deity of this Fourth World. "You are welcome," Maasaw said. "But know this land offers scant food or water. Living here will not be easy." The Hopi still chose to stay.

The second story is set at Bosque Redondo, in New Mexico, in 1868 and is taken from the record of the Peace Commission named to establish a reservation for the Navajo. General William Tecumseh Sherman offered the Navajo three options: the tribe could remain at Bosque Redondo (Fort Sumner, where the Army was holding the Navajo), move to fertile river-bottom land in Oklahoma, or return to their homeland – the arid canyon country on the borders between Arizona and New Mexico. Sherman said he doubted that this wasteland could support the tribe but that since it was worthless, the Navajo should be safe there from the greed of white men. It was, Sherman told President Andrew Johnson, "far from our possible future wants."

It was the same choice the Hopi faced in their ancient myth. The Navajo spokesman that day was Barboncito, a noted fighter and not an orator, who replied to Sherman: "If we are taken back to our own country we will call you our father and mother. If there was only a single goat there, we would all live off it. I hope to God you will not ask us to go to any other country but our own. When the Navajo were first created, four mountains and four rivers were pointed out to us, outside of which we should not live ... Changing

Main Attractions

Acoma Pueblo
El Morro National Monument
Canyon de Chelly National Monument
Navajo Nation
Mesa Verde National Park
San Juan Mountains
Hovenweep National Monument

Map on page 220

Spider Rock in Canyon de Chelly.

Woman gave us this land. Our God created it for us."

The 7,300 Navajo who were being held by Sherman at Bosque Redondo voted unanimously to turn down the relatively lush Oklahoma reservation and return to their desert. It was, as Barboncito told Sherman, "the very heart of our country." It is still the very heart of America's Indian country, this high, dry southeastern side of the Colorado Plateau known informally as the Four Corners, in the only place in the United States where the boundaries of four states (in this case, Colorado, Utah, Arizona, and New Mexico) meet at a common point.

WEST FROM ALBUQUERQUE

West from Albuquerque, about 45 miles (75km) along Interstate 40, is **Laguna Pueblo** ③. A turnout (where several Laguna artists sell pottery and jewelry) gives travelers a good view of the pueblo – a church and some squat, square adobe homes on a low hill a few hundred yards away. For a better view, drive into the pueblo. The pueblo is currently home to 1,241 members living in seven villages. Uranium mines provided employment there for a long time. Now, cattle ranching, arts and crafts sales, and jobs in Albuquerque and in the tribe's **Route 66 Casino Hotel** on Interstate 40 offer a modest livelihood.

Known as Sky City, **Acoma** ③ is 65 miles (105km) west of Albuquerque off Interstate 40. Perched on a 400ft (125-meter) -high rock mesa, the old pueblo had a strong defensive position. Most Acoma people today live in two newer villages below, raising cattle and sheep, operating highway businesses, or working at the tribe's **Sky City Casino Resort** (tel: 888-759-2489; www.skycity.com) on Interstate 40. Some Acoma are chosen each year to live on top of the rock and keep the old village and church in good repair. Most of the tribe returns to the hilltop for special feast days each year.

An overwhelming sense of history pervades Acoma's church, **San Esteban del Rey**, built in 1629 of flagstone and adobe mud. Every timber had to be carried from the distant mountains, and water and mud for the adobe

The Acoma Pueblo sits on a mesa 365 ft (111 meters) above the desert floor.

were carried up the steep trail to the mesa top. The high ceiling, hand-hewn beams, thick walls, square towers, and adjoining priests' quarters are a masterpiece of Pueblo architecture.

The tribe's attractive modern Pueblo-style **Sky City Cultural Center and Ha'aku Museum** (tel: 800-747-0181; www.acomaskycity.org; Mar–Oct daily 8am–5pm; charge for museum and tour) sits at the base of the mesa. It includes exhibits on tribal history and arts and crafts, gift shops, and a café serving native foods. Guided tours of Acoma – the only way outsiders can view the pueblo – are offered half-hourly between 8.30am and 3.30pm starting from the center, with the exception of private ceremonial periods. The mesa-top pueblo provides stunning views of the surrounding area, including spectacular 400ft (121-meter) -high Enchanted Mesa, ancestral home of the Acoma people. Acoma pottery is thin, well-fired, and watertight. It is usually white or off-white and painted with black geometric designs; a newer style is all white with fingernail marks pressed into the wet clay.

West of Albuquerque is a black and angry river of frozen lava now protected as **El Malpais National Monument** ❸ (1900 E Santa Fe Avenue, Grants; tel: 505-876-2783; www.nps.gov/elma; free). The *malpais* (badlands), pronounced locally *mal-pie*, are composed of five distinct lava flows, which began erupting in the vicinity of 11,300ft (3,400-meter) -high **Mount Taylor** around a million years ago. The last eruption, more than 500 years ago, was apparently witnessed by local Zuni and Acoma people, whose legends tell of rivers of fire in the region.

The monument is co-managed by the National Park Service and Bureau of Land Management. By far the best place to get information is at the attractive and informative multiagency **El Malpais Visitor Center** (tel: 505-876-2783; www.nps.gov/elma; daily 8am–5pm), just off I-40 at exit 85 in Grants. The visitor center is staffed by rangers and offers comprehensive information on the region, as well as stunning views of the badlands through its huge picture windows. El **Malpais Information Center** (summer 9am–6pm, spring/fall 10am–5pm; closed winter) run by the National Park Service, has information and exhibits about 23 miles (37km) south of Grants on SR 53.

At the western edge of **Grants** ❸, SR 53 turns south on the west side of the Malpais. More timber and grass grow on this side, and one or two dirt roads go to the edge of the flow. Twelve miles (19km) down SR 53, signs point to **Bandera Volcano and Ice Caves** (tel: 888-423-2283; www.icecaves.com; daily 9am–5pm, closed Nov–Mar; charge), which are privately owned but an integral part of the Malpais. Bandera Volcano, a perfect cinder cone, was one of the sources of the lava flow. Trails go to the top of Bandera and steps lead into the ice caves.

Just under 43 miles (69km) from Grants on SR 53 is **El Morro National Monument** ❹ (tel: 505-783-4226; www.

Looking down on the old lavaflows of El Malpais National Monument.

⊙ Fact

Sheep, along with horses and cows, were brought to the Southwest by the Spanish in the 1600s. Today, Navajo sheepherders mix goats in with their flocks, as the smarter goats make good leaders.

A Pueblo woman balances a pot on her head in a ceremony in Gallup.

nps.gov/elmo; Memorial Day–Labor Day trails daily 9am–5pm, visitor center 9am–6pm, both close one hour earlier in winter; free), a sandstone mesa that juts up from the plateau like the prow of a ship. Also known as Inscription Rock, El Morro has a precious pool of fresh water at its base and was an oasis used by the residents of Atsinna Pueblo atop the rock. Starting in 1605, with the earliest Spanish arrivals, the oasis become a magnet for Spanish, Mexican, and American travelers crossing this parched landscape. They slaked their thirst and rested, and – inspired by earlier graffiti writers – many left their own inscriptions in the soft sandstone. El Morro is one of the oldest national monuments in the US, set aside for protection by Teddy Roosevelt within months of the signing of the Antiquities Act in 1906. A flat 1-mile (1.5km) trail goes around the base of the rock past inscriptions, and another climbs up to the ruins of the pueblo. The park has a nice little first-come, first-served free campground, and you'll find a good restaurant next door at the trading post.

Zuni Pueblo ㊶, in the far western part of New Mexico, 40 miles (64km) south of Gallup, was the first New Mexican pueblo seen by Spaniards. In 1539, soldiers and priests leading an advance party for Coronado's expedition saw the cluster of flat-roofed adobe buildings and immediately went back to report that they had seen the "Seven Cities of Gold," long sought by the Spanish. Although gold cities were lacking, today the Zunis are superb jewelry and pottery craftsmen. The silver inlay jewelry is usually made with small pieces of turquoise, jet, coral, mother-of-pearl, and tortoiseshell set in intricate patterns. Their crafts are available at a cooperative store and trading posts just outside the old village.

The most famous Indian dance in the Southwest is the Shalako Dance at Zuni, held in late November or early December but sadly, no longer open to outsiders. Beginning at sundown, towering, grotesque figures come into the village to dance and sing all night at certain designated homes. The costly costumes are draped over a wooden framework with pulleys to move parts like a puppeteer. The covering is of feathers, paint, animal skins and other materials. The head is bird-like, the body is conical. To be chosen as a Shalako is an honor, and the role demands training, both physical and spiritual. As Zuni is at an elevation of over 7,000ft (2,000 meters), the night of the Shalako is almost always bitterly cold and snowy.

CANYON DE CHELLY

Gallup ㊷, New Mexico, calls itself the "Indian Capital of the World," and it is America's most Indian off-reservation town, the trading center for the eastern Navajo and Zuni reservations. Along downtown Gallop's Railroad Avenue walk Hopi, Laguna, Acoma, and possibly Jicarilla Apache. It's a ramshackle, unkempt, and lively town, a good place to prowl the pawnshops for Zuni jewelry Navajo silver, rugs, and other artifacts, and enjoy driving on a long segment of Route 66. But first there is an essential and highly recommended side trip into eastern Arizona.

Thirty miles (50km) north of Ganado is **Canyon de Chelly National Monument** ❸ (tel: 928-674-5500; www.nps. gov/cach; monument daily sunrise–sunset, vistor center daily 8am–5pm; free), where three great gorges, part of Tsegi Canyon, slice through the plateau under the Chuska Mountains. Generations of Ancestral Pueblo people and Navajo have lived along the sandy bottoms of these washes, under cliffs that, in places, tower 1,000ft (300 meters) high. Access to the canyon is permitted by guided vehicle tours from Thunderbird Lodge, either in a large "shake-and-bake," as the big-tired tour vehicles are called, or with a hired Navajo guide in your own vehicle; you may also hike down the cliff on the White House Ruin trail.

It is believed that the earliest dwellers here, the Pueblo, settled 1,000 years ago; only later did the Navajo replace them. Some of the more than 60 ruins protected in the monument today date from AD 300. The more spectacular ruins have been given names – Mummy Cave, White House, and Antelope House. Other than White House Ruin, the only ruin accessible to visitors by trail from the clifftop, the Pueblo ruins are off limits to visitors. To see most of them, you will need to drive the scenic road along the clifftops and stop at viewpoints or take a backcountry tour within the canyon itself.

In a way, these canyons sum up the heartland of America's Indian country. They offer not only spectacular sculptured stone but a sense of the silence, space, and great beauty that encouraged Navajo and Pueblo people to choose this hard, inhospitable land as the heart of their country.

From Gallup, head into the Checkerboard Reservation, so named because the Navajo once owned only alternate square miles – an oddity now partially corrected. **Crownpoint** ❹ has a school, medical center, Navajo tribal police station, and the offices of the Navajo bureaucrats who administer 3-4 million acres (1.5 million hectares) of the tribe's eastern territory. Like all Navajo communities, it has a temporary, government-built look as if tomorrow the tumbleweeds will again reclaim it. Crownpoint is the site of a well-known rug auction that, six times a year, attracts scores of Navajo weavers and hundreds of buyers for the sale of the fruit of Navajo looms.

SR 264 winds back to Gallup via the old Hopi government town of Keams Canyon and through Ganado, where a trader named John Hubbell, known to the Navajo as "Double Glasses," opened his historic **Hubbell Trading Post** ❺ (tel: 928-755-3475; www.nps.gov/hutr; May–Oct daily 8am–6pm, until 5pm rest of the year; free) in 1870 to serve the Navajo people, for whom he became an important go-between and confidant. The home and trading post are now a national historic site with exhibits and

White House ruins at Canyon de Chelly National Monument.

> **Tip**

Window Rock is the site of Navajo powwows. These events renew and sustain Indian pride with feasting, dancing, and sometimes rodeos. Dancers from all around compete for prize money.

demonstrations of weaving. This is still a working trading post run by Western Parks Association, and if you are in the market for a high-quality rug, you won't go wrong buying one here.

WINDOW ROCK AND NORTH

On the way back, be sure to stop in **Window Rock**, Arizona, capital of the Navajo Nation. Attractions in Window Rock include **Window Rock Tribal Park and Veterans Memorial** (tel: 928-871-6647; http://navajonationparks.org/navajo-tribal-parks/window-rock-navajo-tribal-park/), a good place to view the famed hole in the rock and enjoy a picnic; the modern hogan-style **Navajo Nation Museum** (SR 264/Post Office Loop; tel: 928-871-7941; www.navajonationmuseum.org; daily 9am–5pm; charge), where you can immerse yourself in the Navajo culture and view exceptional historic arts and crafts; and the **Navajo Nation Zoo** (SR 264; tel: 928-871-6573; www.navajozoo.org; charge), which interprets wildlife found on the reservation from a Navajo viewpoint, including mountain lions and coyotes. You can see Mexican

wolves here, which are being slowly reintroduced.

From Crownpoint, SR 57 jogs northeast 37 miles (60km) to lead to the mysteries of **Chaco Culture National Historical Park** (tel: 505-786-7014; www.nps.gov/chcu/planyourvisit/basicinfo.htm). In this shallow canyon, a great civilization flourished and fell between the 10th and 12th centuries, leaving the ruins of its multistoried houses and myriad unsolved anthropological puzzles. Satellite photography has confirmed that Chaco Canyon was the center of a network of at least 250 miles (400km) of what appear to be "roadways," arousing speculation that the Chaco pueblos housed a religious and administrative center for outlying pueblos across the San Juan Basin and beyond. The visitor center and the ruins in the main canyon and along back-country trails over the cliffs offer a rare look into America's ancient past.

Thirty miles (48km) north, SR 57 joins US 550 at Blanco Trading Post. Two miles up the highway toward Farmington is Dzilth-Na-O-Dithle, with its Navajo health clinic and boarding school, and beyond it rises **Huerfano Mesa**. This great mesa is home of First Man and First Woman and other Navajo Holy People. From it one can see other landmarks of the Navajo Genesis.

The blue shape of **Mount Taylor**, one of the highest peaks in New Mexico, looms on the horizon 50 miles (80km) to the south. It is Tsoodzil, the Turquoise Mountain, one of the four sacred peaks that First Man built as corner posts of the Navajo universe.

Northeast of Mount Taylor, the basalt thumb jutting into the sky is **Cabezon Knob**. In a cloud covering its crest one mythical day, First Man and First Woman found the infant White Shell Girl. According to the traditions of the eastern Navajo clans, it was somewhere on the rolling sagebrush hills north of El Huerfano where Talking God, Black God, and the other Holy People held the first

Visitors explore the ruins of Pueblo Bonito at Chaco Culture National Historical Park.

puberty ceremonial, converting While Shell Girl into Changing Woman.

Eight miles (13km) northeast of El Huerfano, on US 550, a right turn leads to **Angel Peak Scenic Overlook**, managed by the BLM and offering a spectacular view across the wilderness formed by the Blanco Wash and Canyon Largo. Here, the Holy People hung out the stars, and Changing Woman, made pregnant by sunbeams and mist from the San Juan River, bore Monster Slayer and Born for Water, the Hero Twins who were to purge this "Glittering World" of its monsters.

Just before US 550 drops into the San Juan River Valley, it passes one of the West's most spectacular examples of the human power to modify nature. The endless silver-gray of sage and rabbitbrush abruptly gives way to the dark green of corn, potatoes, and alfalfa – 44,000 acres (18,000 hectares) of the Navajo Irrigation Project, or NAPI.

INTO THE NAVAJO NATION

North of the Navajo Nation and the San Juan River on US 64, **Farmington** ⑰ is the main Anglo business and trading center for the area. Its economy is based on oil, gas, farming, and coal, with tourism and Indian trading secondary. About 35 miles (56km) up the river is Navajo Dam at **Navajo Lake State Park** (tel: 505-632-2278; www.emnrd.state.nm.us/spd/navajolakestatepark.html; daily 24hrs; free), which forms a blue-water lake in a network of drowned canyons backed across the Colorado border. The lake is popular with trout and coho salmon fishermen, and on several miles of the river below the dam is the best fly fishing in New Mexico.

Aztec, 13 miles (21km) east of Bloomfield on US 550, is the site of **Aztec Ruins National Monument** ⑱ (tel: 505-334-6174 ext. 0; www.nps.gov/azru; daily 8am–5pm, summer until 6pm; charge), an "outlier" pueblo – one of a number radiating out from Chaco Canyon – built by Chacoans in their characteristic style and adopted as a new center of power after they left Chaco Canyon in the 1100s in search of reliable water for farming along the San Juan and Animas rivers. Later occupation by Pueblos from

Angel Peak Scenic Overlook.

⊘ CHACO CULTURE NP

Access The park is about 65 miles (105km) north of Thoreau in northwest New Mexico via Routes 371 and 57. The last 21 miles (34km) are unpaved road and may be impassable in bad weather. From the north, the park is about 70 miles (113km) from Bloomfield via Routes 44 and 57. The last 16 miles (26km) are unpaved and may be impassable in bad weather.

Seasons & Hours The park is open daily year-round. The sites and trails are open sunrise–sunset. The visitor center is open 8am–5pm; closed Christmas and New Year's Day.

Entrance Fee Yes.

Handicapped Access Two campsites and some trails, with assistance.

Activities Camping, hiking, guided and self-guided tours, interpretive programs.

Tourists on a Balcony House Tour in Mesa Verde National Park.

Exploring a cliff house at Mesa Verde National Park.

Mesa Verde is evident in the rougher stonework in the walls and distinctive Mesa Verdean black-on-white pottery found here. A trail leads through ruins displaying both Chacoan and Mesa Verdean style architecture, and you have the unique opportunity to enter a reconstructed Great Kiva, used for ceremonies by Ancestral Pueblo people.

Farmington and the nearby Navajo town of Shiprock are the northern gateways to the Navajo Nation, or the "Big Rez," a term that requires explanation. With more than 300,000 members, the Navajo Tribe, the nation's largest, controls 27,425 sq miles (71,030 sq km), an area larger than New England. The biggest chunk is on the borders between New Mexico, Arizona, and Utah, in an area the size of West Virginia. This includes the "Checkerboard Reservation" and the smaller Alamo, Ramah, and Canoncito Navajo reservations. On the Navajo Nation, an elected tribal council operates its own courts, police force, and other services. More than 1,100 miles (1,770km) of paved road, and another thousand, which range from quality gravel to tracks impassible in wet weather, tie the reservation together. The lowest Navajo deserts get only a few inches of rainfall annually, while the forested slopes of the Chuska Mountains at 10,416ft (3,175 meters) get 25 inches (63cm).

Surrounded by these Navajo lands is the 2,532-sq-mile (6,558-sq-km) Hopi Reservation. It's a huge place, and one of the best ways to visit its interior is by driving west out of Farmington to **Shiprock** ⓯, which, like Crownpoint, is a Navajo bureaucrats' town. Driving west on US 64, the sky over the San Juan is smudged with plumes of whitish smoke. The pollution (sharply reduced by millions of dollars worth of soot precipitators in the towering stacks) is from the **Four Corners Generating Plant**.

Coal from the adjoining Navajo Mine, the nation's largest open-pit operation, rolls directly into the furnaces, and thence over electrical transmission lines to warm Californian swimming pools. Only the ashes and pollution veiling the previously pristine air are left behind. A side trip through the farming town of **Kirtland** offers a look at this mind-boggling operation. Pollution from this plant is also blamed for the considerable degradation of visibility at the Grand Canyon.

Four Corners Navajo Tribal Park ⓾ (www.navajonationparks.org), north of US 64, has virtually nothing going for it except for the thought that one might stand in four states at once. There's a parking lot and a slab on the ground where the state boundaries of Utah, Colorado, New Mexico, and Arizona intersect. It's good for a photo, though, and to purchase arts and crafts and snacks from Navajo and Southern Ute vendors.

A short drive north of Farmington to Cortez, Colorado, leads to nearby **Mesa Verde National Park** ⓾ (tel: 970-529-4465; www.nps.gov/meve; daily 8am–5pm; charge), one of the most famous archeological sites in the

ancient Pueblo world. The numerous cliff dwellings snugged into canyons here are deservedly among the West's most popular visitor attractions – and also the most visited, so plan carefully.

Most visitors focus on Cliff Palace, the ruin that was first glimpsed by local cowboys Richard and John Wetherill back in the late 1800s, leading internationally renowned archeologists to this site. Cliff Palace and nearby Balcony House can only be visited on a guided ranger tour (tickets available at the visitor center; leave plenty of time to drive to locations). A few ruins, such as Far View, may be explored on a self-guided tour on the scenic drive. If you are short on time and just want to take a quick look, **Chapin Mesa Archeological Museum** (early Apr–mid-Oct 8am–6.30pm, early Mar-early Apr and early Nov–late Dec 9am–5pm, mid-Oct–early Nov 8am–5pm, Jan–early Mar 9am–4.30pm) is a good place to learn about the Mesa Verde culture and view artifacts, and to look down at Spruce Tree House, a 114-room ruin below. This ruin was once open for self-guided tours – a

lovely experience – but is now, unfortunately, closed due to unstable ground.

The sight of numerous, myriad smaller houses in cracks and crevices leads you to wonder why the Mesa Verdeans – and other Pueblo people in the Four Corners region – placed their homes in such dizzying places, and how they raised children where a toddler's misstep meant death.

East of Mesa Verde, **Durango** ⑤ makes a good base for visiting the national park. It was once described by Will Rogers as "out of the way and glad of it." No longer. In the 1990s, Durango came into its own and is now a favored destination year round. Once an 1879 railroad town frequented by miners and cowboys – and skiers in winter – Durango is now a popular college town with tourism on its mind and beginning to display touches of Aspen chic, with gourmet coffee shops, natural foods markets, elegant farm-to-table restaurants, smart boutiques, and renovated historic hotels. One of its most popular attractions is the **Durango and Silverton Narrow Gauge Railroad** (www.

A Durango and Silverton Narrow Gauge Railroad steam train.

durangotrain.com), an historic steam train that puffs out from the downtown depot daily and winds its way up along the steep sides of the spectacular San Juan Mountains to the quaint mining town of Silverton. The views are simply breathtaking, especially in fall, when the colors start to change. The San Juans are a magnificent destination for hiking, Jeeping, camping, and scenic drives.

Heading west on US 64, consider taking US 491 south for 16 miles (26km) for an upclose look at *Tse Bit A'i* ("the Rock with Wings"). Better known as Ship Rock, the ragged blue shape of this distinctive formation on the Navajo Nation on the other side of the San Juan River is visible for miles but only when you get closer is its size apparent. It is the core of a volcano, the cinder cone cut away by 15 million years of wind and rain. This core towers 1,450ft (440 meters) above the grassy prairie – 20 stories taller than the Empire State Building – suggesting an immense black Gothic cathedral. In Navajo mythology, it was the home of the Winged Monster slain by the Hero Twins with the help of Spider

Ruins at Hovenweep National Monument.

Woman. Ship Rock may be viewed from the road, but climbing it is both illegal and dangerous.

Chinese-style walls of basalt radiate for miles from its base, 20 to 30ft (6 to 9 meters) high in places but only 3 or 4ft (1 meter) thick. They formed when volcanic pressure cracked the earth and molten lava squeezed upward like toothpaste.

One of the most out-of-the-way places to visit in the Four Corners region is also one of the numerous ruins that pepper the area. **Hovenweep National Monument** ⓾ (tel: 970-562-4282 ext.10; www.nps.gov/hove; trails daily sunrise–sunset, visitor center daily 9am–5pm; free) established in 1923 and straddling the Colorado-Utah border, requires travel over substandard roads, but the journey is worthwhile. These dry lands north of the San Juan River were once home to the Pueblo people until the 1300s, when they moved on. Six major groupings of ruins are included in the monument's 780 acres (315 hectares), with walls 20ft (6 meters) high and towers overlooking the desert. The most famous of these towers is **Square Tower**, the best preserved and accessible by car. Information is available at the attractive visitor center; a nice little campground with great views is located nearby.

Adjoining Hovenweep, and part of the same greater Mesa Verde prehistoric communities, is 178,000-acre (72,034-hectare) **Canyons of the Ancients National Monument** (https://www.blm.gov/programs/national-conservation-lands/colorado/canyons-of-the-ancients), which preserves one of the richest collections of archeological artifacts in the country. The only accessible recreational site at the monument is 40-room **Lowry Pueblo National Historic Landmark**, off Highway 491 and County Road CC. For more information, stop at the terrific **Anasazi Heritage Center** (27501 Highway 84, Dolores, CO; tel: 970-882-5600; daily 9am–5pm) to view multimedia exhibits and plan your trip.

ADOBE'S MAGIC

Adobe, unbaked clay bricks made from earth, has long been the traditional building material of the Southwest.

Structures made from adobe are undulating and sculptural in nature, yet their mass lends them a sense of permanence and timelessness. In New Mexico, archeologists have discovered remnants of adobe walls built by Pueblos that date back to AD 1200, 400 years before the Spanish arrived. There is evidence of two types of earthen wall built between the 13th and 15th centuries. One was coursed adobe, using a stiff mixture of mud blended with anything from stones to pottery shards. The mud was applied by the handful, course on top of course, until the desired height was reached. A more sophisticated method made use of hand-formed, unbaked clay bricks. Mud mortar cemented the bricks.

The word *adobe* comes from Arabic. Spanish colonists brought a new way of working with adobe to North America at the end of the 15th century, introducing a new brick-making method. Wooden bottomless molds were made with a handle on each end that could hold from one to eight bricks. The molds were set on the ground and filled with a mixture of mud and straw. The straw helped dry the bricks by conducting moisture from the center of the adobe and kept the bricks from cracking as they dried. When the bricks were dry enough not to sag, the forms were lifted, moved to a new spot and the process repeated.

These were the two primary methods of building with adobe until the coming of the railroad in the 1880s, which almost eliminated the use of adobe for several decades with the introduction of new technology. Redfired brick, board and batten, concrete block, and frame-stucco were just a few of the construction materials and methods that dominated the Southwest landscape. Elaborate ornamentation and new rooflines gave the simple, flat-roofed buildings a facelift.

Not until after World War I was there any significant reemergence of adobe architecture. Decreasing natural building materials and excellent passive solar properties made adobe a viable material once again.

Adobe has the ability, when properly oriented to the sun, to retain its temperature for long periods of time.

With the reemergence of adobe came commercial adobe yards, which are now producing a stabilized adobe block. As the word implies, a stabilizer is an additive, such as an asphalt emulsion, that when mixed with mud produces an unbaked clay brick that resists moisture penetration, adobe's worst enemy. A traditional adobe structure must be readobed every so often because of erosion.

Unfortunately, the amount of labor required in adobe construction often makes it too expensive for the average home buyer, though its use by owner-builders hand constructing homes is steadily increasing. Solutions are slowly being found. Recently architects and builders have been looking for more innovative methods that will increase productivity and decrease the dollar margin between adobe and conventional building materials.

Adobe house in Santa Fe.

Hikers at Angels Landing Trail at the final ascent near Scout Lookout, Zion National Park.

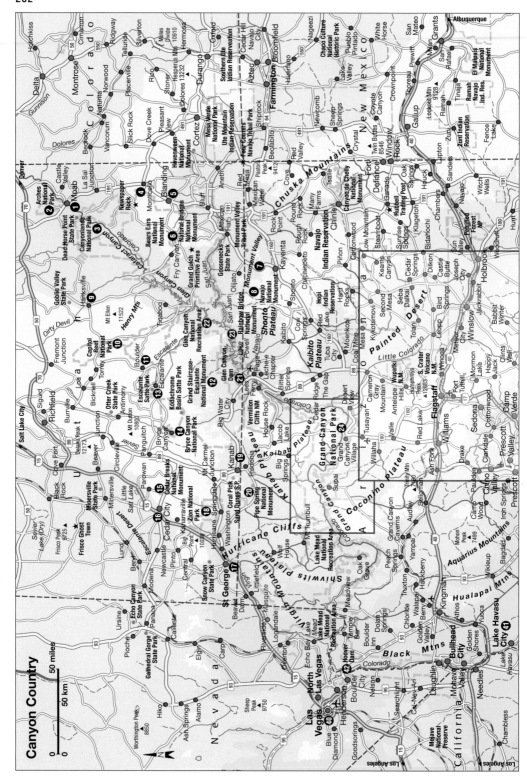

Canyon Country

CANYON COUNTRY

The weather has sculpted the sedimentary rocks in this region into magnificent shapes, from Monument Valley to the Grand Canyon.

Zebra Canyon, Grand Staircase-Escalante National Monument.

High desert for the most part, the Southwest's canyon country almost defies description, but that doesn't keep anyone from trying. The slickrock and gray-green desert scrub blend with pinyon-juniper forests as elevation rises and falls. Heated by relentless sun, gusts of wind gather sand and Russian thistle into swirling dust devils and tumbleweeds that dance across the sparsely vegetated countryside, while winter brings dustings of snow. This is a land of subtle shifts and stark contrasts that challenge preconceptions.

You'll find arches and natural bridges, hoodoos and rock fins, and more gulches and gullies than can be numbered. There are also magnificent mesas and mountain ranges. For sheer Wild West spectacle in its distinctively shaped red rocks, Monument Valley is in a class by itself. The population is sparse, the few towns many miles apart.

This is country where the getting there can be more exciting than the destination. One outstanding scene leads to another and natural spectacles are too numerous to list. State and national parks showcase the most spectacular of these treasures in a never-ended hit parade of sights.

The Coconino National Forest, the country's largest ponderosa pine forest, spreads like a green ocean across northern Arizona around Flagstaff and the high San Francisco Peaks and north to the South Rim of the Grand Canyon. South of Flagstaff, off Interstate 17, Highway 89A delivers you, in an exciting 2,000ft (600-meter) drop in elevation, to Sedona's red-rock country and on to the Verde Valley, with its ancient American Indian and US military history. The Colorado River carries its tributary waters

Helicopter tour over Grand Canyon West.

into Lake Powell, behind Glen Canyon Dam, flows through the Grand Canyon and is again trapped, this time by the Hoover Dam and Lake Mead. Both dams are spectacles of engineering. The canyons channeling the river, made less wild and natural by dams, lead right to the most unnatural place of all: Las Vegas in the Mojave Desert. In casinos where the sun neither rises nor sets, you might strike it rich or lose every cent, but the people-watching is free and fabulous, and if you want to escape, national parks and other natural attractions are just a couple of hours away.

Sunset view from Hunts Mesa in Monument Valley Navajo Tribal Park.

SOUTHERN UTAH

Arguably one of the country's most spectacular regions, southern Utah offers ethereal light, spellbinding colors, a look into ancient geological history, and some of America's finest national parks.

In 1869, after a two-month journey down the Green River from Wyoming, an expedition led by explorer Major John Wesley Powell reached the confluence of the Green and Colorado rivers, one of the most inaccessible spots on the North American continent. Here, in the heart of what Powell called "the Great Unknown," both rivers lay deep within the earth, imprisoned by sheer cliffs of their own making. Climbing to the rim, Powell was amazed by what he saw. "What a world of grandeur is spread before us!" he wrote. "Wherever we look there is but a wilderness of rocks; deep gorges, where the rivers are lost below cliffs and towers and pinnacles; and ten thousand strangely carved forms in every direction; and beyond them, mountains blending with the clouds."

Today, travelers can drive across southern Utah in a matter of hours on paved roads, but there remains no fast route to appreciating the beauty and scope of the geography Powell described: you simply need time, and plenty of it – anywhere from a week to a year to a lifetime. Nature, pure and simple, rules here in a continually metamorphosing landscape whose predominant feature is bare sedimentary rock rearranged by volcanism along deep-seated faults and erosion by water, weather, and time.

A 4x4 on the Onion Creek Trail.

MOAB AND ARCHES NATIONAL PARK

Few towns in the Southwest have as beautiful and dramatic a setting as **Moab ❶**, southeastern Utah's commercial center and a logical place to begin a trip. Sheer red rock cliffs form fortress-like walls on all sides, enclosing the town in a private world of sandstone, verdant riverbanks, and tidy houses fronted by ditches irrigating colorful gardens. Moab has a typically Mormon, grid-like layout in its quaint historic downtown but has burst its confines to

Main Attractions

Arches National Park
Canyonlands National Park
Bears Ears National Monument
Monument Valley Navajo Tribal Park
Grand Staircase-Escalante National Monument
Bryce Canyon National Park
Zion National Park
Glen Canyon Natural Recreation Area

Maps on pages 282, 287

the south, spilling into Spanish Valley and other farmlands near the turnoff for the La Sal Mountain Loop.

The town's history is unusual. Members of the Elk Mountain Mission – one of many colonizing efforts in southern Utah in the 1850s and 1860s by the Church of Jesus Christ of Latter Day Saints (or the Mormons) – briefly built a settlement here in 1855 but were driven out by hostile Utes. By the time another group of Mormons succeeded in founding the town in the 1870s, a motley crew of homesteaders, ranchers, rustlers, drifters, and grifters had settled.

Moab became a sleepy hamlet, miles from nowhere. And it might have stayed that way if it hadn't been for the atomic bomb. At the onset of the Cold War after World War II, the former US Atomic Energy Commission (AEC), as part of a nationwide search for uranium, established a generous fixed price for the ore as an incentive to miners.

The first big strike was Charlie Steen's. In an area south of Moab that the AEC had deemed "barren of possibilities," Steen discovered his Mi Vida mine, from which he was able to ship $100 million of uranium-235. Overnight, Moab became the "Uranium Capital of the World."

Mining today takes a very different form: that of mining for tourist dollars, following the huge recreational boom of the post-war years that saw surplus army rafts converted to river-running boats, four-wheel-drives to recreational vehicles, then in the 1980s the mounting popularity of mountain biking on slickrock trails around town. This boom appears to be here to stay. Between 1995 and 2017, the resident population of Moab doubled to more than 5,000 – with thousands more descending on the town from spring break all the way through October.

Moabites, always free with their opinions, grouse that with real estate prices and property taxes what they now are, they can barely afford to live there anymore. And the growing number of motels, fast-food outlets, overpriced eateries, microbrew pubs, espresso joints, and T-shirt boutiques that have sprung up in town certainly

The North and South Windows at Arches National Park.

signals major changes. But one can't argue with success.

Moab is perfectly located for trips to Canyonlands and Arches national parks, the Manti-La Sal National Forest, and Bureau of Land Management–administered lands nearby. For books and maps, stop in at the multiagency **Moab Information Center** (Center Street and Main; tel: 435-259-8825; www.discovermoab.com/visitorcenter; Mon–Fri 8am–5pm), or the MIC, as it's known locally, for help with trip planning and a good selection of books and maps on sale. A new HD film offers plenty of inspiration, and free lectures by regional experts are given weekly April through November at 6pm.

Then head to the enjoyable little **Dan O'Laurie Museum** (118 E Center Street; tel: 435-259-7985; www.moab museum.org; mid-Apr–mid-Oct Mon–Sat 10am–6pm, rest of year Mon–Sat noon–5pm; charge) to learn more about the history of the area.

For most folks, a trip to **Arches National Park ❷** (tel: 435-719-2299; www.nps.gov/arch; park daily 24 hours, visitor center daily 9pm–5.30pm, until 4pm in winter; charge), a few miles northwest of town, is *de rigueur*. Nowhere in the world are there as many natural arches – some 2,000 at the last count – all clustered together in a setting of such glorious whimsy, satisfying to both geologists and casual sightseers. Moreover, would you believe that all this was caused by salt?

Arches National Park sits in the northern corner of the huge Paradox Basin, an ancient faulted depression that formed here 300 million years ago below the Uncompahgre Uplift (in the vicinity of the present-day La Sal Mountains). In Permian times, a warm inland sea was trapped in the basin, then when the climate dried, the sea evaporated, leaving behind huge quantities of salt, gypsum, and other evaporites, which were then buried beneath sediments carried down into the basin by high-country rivers. Thousands of feet of sediments put pressure on the underlying salt, which became plastic and flowed away from the overburden. As it encountered deep fault blocks, it

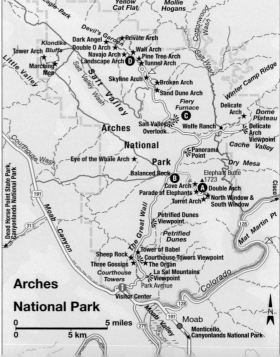

was forced upward into salt domes that eventually cracked, allowing groundwater to enter joints and dissolving the sail. Erosion then began widening the joints, leaving deep red Entrada Sandstone fins that weathered into arches. You can see their linear nature, if you look closely. They seem to dance in formation like chorus lines of bandy-legged showgirls on a tilted stage of sandstone.

Many arches are visible along the paved scenic drive, which begins at the visitor center, 5 miles (8km) north or Moab, or within easy walking distance along well-maintained trails. If pressed for time, visit the **Windows Section** to view **Double Arch** Ⓐ and **Balanced Rock** Ⓑ. On the other side of Salt Valley, a mile-long trail winds into the **Fiery Furnace** Ⓒ, a spectacular jumble of fins separated by sandy corridors that radiate vast amounts of heat in the late afternoon. For safety reasons, visitors can only enter the Fiery Furnace with a backcountry permit or on ranger-led tours, available twice a day between April and October. Tickets and permits are first come, first serve and only

available from the visitor center; they sell out fast, so purchase as far ahead as you can, up to a week in advance.

Popular Devil's Garden Campground, 18 miles (29km) north of the visitor center, has 50 campsites that *must* be reserved ahead between May 1 and October 31. Reservations may be made online at www.recreation.gov or by calling tel: 877-444-6777, 518-885-3639 (international); reservations may be made no less than four days and more than one year ahead of time. Between November 1 and February 28, campsites 1–24 are available on a first-come, first-served basis in addition to reserved sites. Get to the visitor center early to register for a site.

From the campground, a 6-mile (9.6-km) loop trail leads to seven different arches, including 291ft (89-meter) **Landscape Arch** Ⓓ, the second-longest known arch; 310ft (94-meter) Kolob Arch in Zion National Park is the longest. Midsummer temperatures often exceed 105°F (41°C) throughout southern Utah, so it's essential to wear sunscreen, polarized sunglasses, a broad-brimmed hat, and long-sleeved shirts and pants, and to eat salty, nutritious snacks and drink a gallon of water a day, especially when hiking.

CANYONLANDS NATIONAL PARK

If you think Arches is spectacular, wait until you meet its neighbor, **Canyonlands National Park** ❸ (tel: 435-719-2313; www.nps.gov/cany; daily 24 hours, visitor center hours vary: Island in the Sky 8am–5pm Apr–late Oct, late Oct–Dec and early Mar–mid-Apr 9am–4pm, closed Jan–early-Mar; Needles Mar–mid-Apr, July–Aug, and early–late Nov 9am–4pm, Apr–June 8am–4.30pm; early Sept–early Nov 8am–5pm, closed winter; Hans Flat year round 8am–4.30pm; charge). This 527-sq-mile (1,365-sq-km) park is the *piece de resistance* of Canyon Country and should not be missed. Planning is

Double Arch in Arches National Park.

everything here, as each section of the park is a long way from the others and there are no roads across the canyon abyss that divides them.

There are three main districts: Island in the Sky, a 2,000ft (600-meter) headland cut by the confluencing Green and Colorado rivers, and closest to Moab; the Needles District, southwest of Moab on US 191, near Monticello; and the remote, undeveloped Maze on the east side of the river, south of the town of Green River. The Colorado and Green rivers make up a fourth, unofficial River District. River trips above and below the confluence of the Colorado and Green rivers allow access to the three primary units from below.

For a raven's-eye view of Canyonlands, head to **Island in the Sky**, 40 miles (64km) from Moab. Grand View Point offers l00-mile (160km) views of the entire basin, including the Needles directly ahead, Cedar Mesa and Comb Ridge, the Bear's Ears, Navajo Mountain, and the encircling La Sal, Abajo, and Henry mountains. Immediately below is the 100-mile (160km) -long White Rim Trail on the White Rim Sandstone slickrock, halfway up from the river, which offers thrills and spills for off-road vehicles, mountain bikers, and hikers and is accessed by the precipitous dirt Shafer Trail. (Four-wheel-drive tours and rentals can be arranged in Moab.) Scenic hiking trails here are short and enjoyable and lead to overlooks and natural features such as elegant Mesa Arch and the unusual Upheaval Dome, once thought to be a collapsed salt dome but now generally believed to be a meteor impact crater, where salt has domed up and broken the surface. A 12-site first-come, first-served campground (no water) is available next to the scenic Green River Overlook.

You can camp for free on surrounding BLM lands at the Island in the Sky but for a developed campground, you'll need to head to nearby **Dead Horse Point State Park** (tel: 435-259-2614; www.stateparks.utah.gov/parks/dead-horse; daily 8am–10pm; charge), the only place up here where you can see the Colorado River, trapped in a huge hairpin bend, more properly known as an

Green River in Canyonlands National Park.

⊙ CANYONLANDS NP

Access The Island in the Sky District is 32 miles (51km) from Moab via US 191 and SR 313. The Needles District is 80 miles (129km) from Moab via US 191 and SR 211; the Maze District is 2.5 hours from Green River, Utah. Take SR 24 south from I-70 for 24 miles (39km), then make a left onto a dirt road just beyond Goblin Valley State Park and drive for 46 miles (74km) to Hans Flat Ranger Station.

Seasons & hours The park is open daily year-round, except Thanksgiving, Christmas, and New Year's Day.

Entrance fee Yes.

Handicapped access Visitor centers, some campsites, and some overlooks.

Activities Scenic and four-wheel driving, Jeeping, camping, hiking, biking, river-running, horseback riding, rock-climbing, wildlife-watching, interpretive programs.

Fact

Newspaper Rock contains images of horses, indicating that these particular petroglyphs were made after the late 16th century, when the Spanish introduced them to North America.

entrenched meander. Stories tell of historic ranchers using this point and the neck of land leading to Island in the Sky to corral horses, which starved when their captors were themselves detained in distant parts.

Allow more time to visit the Needles. Return to Moab on US 191, load up on gas, food, and water, then head south, turning off just north of **Monticello** and west across BLM-administrated rangelands. The road drops into shady Indian Creek and passes **Newspaper Rock**, a well-preserved rock art panel close to the road with petroglyphs from Archaic, Ancestral Pueblo, Navajo, Ute, and pioneer times. Just beyond is the historic **Dugout Ranch**, which once stretched from the San Juan River to the Colorado border continues to be run by the historic Redd family under the aegis of The Nature Conservancy.

You'll need to camp at the Needles, so arrive early to snag a campsite at Squaw Flat, the jumping-off point for several trails. Sites in Loop A may be reserved in spring and fall. To make a reservation up to six months ahead,

visit www.recreation.gov, or call tel: 877-444-6777, 518-885-3639 (international). Supplies, gas, campsites, and most importantly, showers are available at **Needles Outpost** (tel: 435-459-0777; www.needlesoutpost.com; Apr–Oct), just outside the park boundary. Dispersed primitive camping is allowed on BLM-managed Canyon Rims National Recreation Area lands surrounding the Needles. Remember: the desert ecosystem is fragile and takes a long time to mend. Pack out what you pack in, and leave no trace of your passage.

The **Needles** themselves are 500ft (150-meter) -high eroded cream-and-red-banded pinnacles of Cedar Mesa Sandstone, a rock composed of 250-million-year-old white beach sand and reddish river sediments. When the park was set aside in 1964, the lush meadows of gramma, Indian rice, and other native grasses among the rocks were mainly used by ranchers and cowboys for grazing, and a number of old cowboy camps can be seen in this area. Much earlier occupation by Ancestral Pueblo people is evident in the many small cliff dwellings, granaries and rock art found in four canyons – Davis, Lavender, Salt, and Horse. Deep within Salt Canyon is Angel Arch, perhaps the most sublime arch in Canyonlands, with its humorous sidekick, Molar Rock.

The best day hike in the Needles is the 7-mile (11km) Chesler Park Trail, which leaves from Elephant Hill. This moderately strenuous trail heads into the Needles, with side hikes to Druid Arch and the Joint Trail. Longer backcountry treks head along Lower Red Canyon Trail to the river via the Grabens – down-faulted valleys shaped like shoe boxes that have slumped due to salt movement and erosion – directly across from the Maze. The Grabens may also be accessed via four-wheel-drive vehicle over Elephant Hill, the most challenging off-road route in the park. Drivers must at one point turn around completely while perched on a rock fin teetering on the edge of a cliff

Newspaper Rock, Canyonlands National Park.

and negotiate a 30-degree switchback – in reverse! Not surprisingly, passengers often decide to forsake the vehicle in favor of their feet.

The undeveloped **Maze District**, 250 road miles (400km) from the Needles, is best left for a later visit when you're comfortable driving difficult four-wheel-drive tracks and hiking over and into unbelievably confusing slickrock canyons. For a taste, though, sign on with one of the raft companies in Green River or Moab for a four-to-seven-day whitewater trip through 14-mile (22km) Cataract Canyon; on most trips time is set aside for hiking into the Maze.

Green River trips begin at the town of the same name. Don't pass up one of the town's famous melons, if you're here in summer. They're delicious. Nor should you miss the **John Wesley Powell River History Museum** (1765 Main Street; tel: 435-564-3427; www.johnwesleypowell.com; summer Mon–Sat 9am–7pm, Sun noon–5pm, winter Tue–Sat 9am–5pm; charge), a huge modern facility on the riverbank with terrific exhibits bringing to life epic river trips

of the past. If you decide to drive into the Maze, stop at Hans Flat Ranger Station (tel: 435-259-2652; https://www.nps.gov/cany/planyourvisit/maze.htm; daily 8am–4.30pm) for more information and route planning. Shortly before getting there, you'll pass **Robber's Roost Ranch**, the remote 19th-century hideout of two of the West's most famous outlaws, Butch Cassidy and the Sundance Kid, and their gang, the Wild Bunch.

TO THE SOUTH

South from Moab is the small pioneer town of **Monticello** ❹ on the flanks of the snowclad Abajo (Blue) Mountains. The Abajos provide a pleasing counterpoint to the slickrock country – and an escape from the summer heat. A quiet back route into the Needles district of Canyonlands leads through the mountains from the center of town, then drops down onto BLM land outside the park.

Learn more about the Ancestral Pueblo and later Ute, Navajo, and Anglo cultures of the area at the **Edge of the Cedars State Park** (660 W 400 N; tel: 435-678-2238; www.stateparks.utah.gov/

A rafting group taking to the Colorado River below the Maze District.

parks/edge-of-the-cedars; Apr–Oct Mon–Sat 9am–5pm, Sun noon–4pm, Mar Mon–Sat 9am–5pm, Nov–Feb Mon–Sat noon–5pm; charge), in **Blanding** ❺, site of a large pueblo occupied between AD 770 and 1200. The museum's innovative displays include a superb pottery collection excavated from the area. This is a wonderful small museum; don't miss it.

South of Blanding, Monticello is BLM headquarters for the recently-designated 1.35-million-acre (546,326-hectare) **Bears Ears National Monument** (tel: 435-587-1500; www.blm.gov/programs/national-conservation-lands/Utah/bears-ears-national-monument; field office Mon–Fri 8am–4pm, backcountry permits tel: 435-587-1510 8am–noon), which was set aside by President Obama on December 28, 2016 to prevent resource extraction on public lands of natural, scientific, and cultural value around the distinctive mesas known as the Bear's Ears, sacred to the Ute, Navajo, and Paiute tribes. At the time of writing in mid-2017, Bears Ears is one of the main national monuments being immediately reassessed by the Trump administration, with the express intention of shrinking boundaries and opening up lands for oil and gas exploration.

The undeveloped monument offers a wealth of attractions – some easily seen from the highway, others requiring backpacking into the wilderness. It's bounded on the north by the Abajos and Manti-La Sal National Forest, Dark Canyon Wilderness, Canyon Rims, and Canyonlands National Park; on the east by US 191 and Monticello and Blanding; on the south by the San Juan River, Bluff, Mexican Hat, SR 261 to Ceda Mesa, and US 163 to Valley of the Gods and Monument Valley on the Navajo Nation; and on the west by the Colorado River, Grand Staircase-Escalante National Monument, Glen Canyon NRA, Grand Gulch Primitive Area, White Canyon, and Buckhorn Canyon. Natural Bridges National Monument is a separate park unit in the center of the monument and may be accessed via SR 95.

From Blanding, a right turn on paved SR 95 (which figures so prominently in Ed Abbey's novel, *The Monkey Wrench Gang*) takes you directly to the

Bears Ears plateaus seen from Moki Dugway at Cedar Mesa near Natural Bridges National Monument.

distinctive geological formation known as **Comb Ridge** and several significant Ancestral Puebloan ruins at **Butler Wash** and **Mule Canyon**.

Due west is delightful **Natural Bridges National Monument** ⑥ (tel: 435-692-1234 ext. 16; www.nps.gov/nabr; 24 hours, visitor center daily 9am–5pm; charge). Although bridges and arches are similar in appearance, only the former have been carved by a stream, in this case by a tributary of the Colorado River in White Canyon. Each of the three bridges in the monument – Sipapu, Kachina Bridge, and Owachomo – can be seen from a paved loop road that originates from the visitor center and by making a 10-minute hike to the base of any of the three.

This small park has great views, a 13-site, first-come, first-serve campground with well-screened campsites, and good ranger campfire programs on astronomy, herpetology, and other interesting topics. If you want to explore the area, it makes a good base. Be sure to bring food with you; the nearest restaurants are in Blanding, 40 miles (64km) away.

Just before the turnoff for Natural Bridges, scenic SR 261 drops south across **Cedar Mesa** down to US 163, the route to Monument Valley. **Grand Gulch Primitive Area** off Cedar Mesa is another major area of archeological sites, including Moon House Ruin. Access is via Kane Gulch Ranger Station, about 4 miles (6.5km) south of the junction with SR 95, where you will find the main Grand Gulch trailhead, a paved parking lot, and a restroom. You will need a day-use permit (available at the ranger station) to hike these primitive trails and explore the four-wheel-drive dirt roads; overnight permits may be reserved through the Monticello BLM office up to 90 days ahead of time.

Farther south on SR 261, the breathtaking **Moki Dugway** (Moki and Moqui are pioneer variants of Hopi) offers extraordinary views to the Navajo Nation. At US 163, you won't want to miss viewing the

world-class entrenched meanders at **Goosenecks State Park** on the San Juan River, where the **Muley Point** viewpoint above the hairpin bend in the river offers the classic Canyon Country photo op. River runners floating the San Juan far below look tiny. Bluff and Mexican Hat are the main put-ins for river trips.

In the winter of 1879–80, this corner of southeastern Utah witnessed a remarkable journey by Mormon colonists "called" to settle the San Juan River. Believing the southern route the most direct, more than 200 pioneers left Escalante in the autumn for southeastern Utah. They soon ran into difficulties negotiating the unforgiving, broken landscape of these rugged canyons and cliffs. What had started out as a six-week journey took six months as colonists labored over what is now dubbed Hole-in-the-Rock Road in Grand Staircase-Escalante National Monument. They were forced to spend the winter near Dance Hall Rock and blast a route out of sheer, 500ft (150-meter) cliffs to let their wagons down to the Colorado River.

In Bears Ears National Monument's Cedar Mesa.

Exhausted, they founded a settlement at the first suitable spot on the San Juan River, which they named **Bluff,** and planted crops and began building homes, many of which can still be seen on a historic loop through the village. After persistent flooding ruined the harvest, some Hole-in-the-Rock pioneers moved north and founded Blanding and then Monticello, towns that retain strong associations to these early colonists.

MONUMENT VALLEY AND NAVAJO NATIONAL MONUMENT

Encompassing 30,000 acres (12,000 hectares) on the Arizona-Utah border, south of Blanding, **Monument Valley Navajo Tribal Park** (NR 42, Oljato, UT; tel: 435-727-5870; www.navajonationparks.org; daily 6am–8pm Apr–Sep, 8am–5pm Oct–Mar; charge) embraces the truly monumental **Monument Valley** ❼ and its punctuated horizon of graceful mesas, spires, and red buttes. Monument Valley, familiar to those who've watched director John Ford's many Western movies, may be viewed from a scenic drive that winds through the spectacular rock formations, such as Rain God Mesa, the Totem Pole, the Mittens, and Yei-Bi-Chai. If you want to go off the main road, hire a Navajo guide at the visitor center, famed Goulding's Lodge, or Navajo-owned The View hotel. You'll learn a lot driving this traditional Navajo area with a native guide.

Just south of nearby Kayenta, **Navajo National Monument** ❽ (SR 564, Shonto; tel: 928-672-2700; www.nps.gov/nava; Memorial Day–Labor Day daily 8am–5.30pm, rest of year 9am–5pm; free) contains three of the largest prehistoric, pueblo-type cliff dwellings in Arizona, in three different areas. The most accessible of the three is **Betatakin**; access to the pueblo ruins is only via guided tours, which are available on a first-come, first-served basis. The 5-mile (8km) hike is not easy and can be tiring in summer's heat. A short trail leads from the visitor center to an overlook where you can view Betatakin ruin, which nestles in a huge alcove in the Tsegi Canyon.

⊙ WHEELS IN THE BACKCOUNTRY

Mountain biking is popular with both Southwest residents and visitors. "The self-powered thing is cool," says Lou Warner, who runs a bike-touring company in Moab, Utah, which is considered by freewheelers to be the mountain bike capital of the world. Located in the redrock country of southeastern Utah, the area is crosshatched with thousands of miles of dirt roads left behind by miners and rangers, giving bikers plenty of spare room. "The riding is excellent because the scenery is excellent," Warner says. "It can go from an elevation of 4,000ft (1,200 meters) at the Colorado River to almost 14,000ft (more than 4,000 meters) on the snow-capped peaks of the La Sal Mountains."

Mountain biking combines the best aspects of hiking and skiing – access to the hills and downhill speed – and leaves behind slow travel. In national parks, biking is allowed only on paved roads and a few designated and marked trails. Although knobby treads on mountain-bike tires can eat up soft earth and cause considerable erosion, on the correct surface it can allow visitors to reach remote locations that might otherwise be missed, and without noise or pollution.

CAPITOL REEF PARK

Back in southeastern Utah, the tiny town of **Hanksville ❾**, at the western end of SR 95, is the access for the remote Henry Mountains, the last discovered, named, and explored mountain range in the continental United States. These mountains offer solitude aplenty, and you may even glimpse the large herd of bison that lives there, but don't head off without first checking in with the BLM's Henry Mountains Field Station (380 S 100 W; tel: 435-542-3461; Mon–Fri 8am–4.45pm).

Forty miles (65km) west of Hanksville is **Capitol Reef National Park ❿** (tel: 435-425-3791; www.nps.gov/care; daily 8am–6pm summer, until 4.30pm rest of the year; charge), whose central attraction is the Waterpocket Fold, a 100-mile (160km) -long flexure in the earth's crust. It was dubbed a "reef" by fanciful Mormons who fled here in the 1880s to avoid prosecution by federal agents for their polygamous lifestyle. After it was uplifted about 65 million years ago, the reef was eroded into narrow canyons interspersed with giant domes of creamy Navajo Sandstone. Perhaps residents had government on their minds when they said the domes reminded them of the US Capitol in Washington, DC. Either way, the name stuck.

The northern portion of the fold is transected by scenic US 24, which runs beneath soaring cliffs of red Wingate Sandstone alongside the Fremont River. This was the home of the Fremont culture, people who had much in common with Ancestral Pueblo neighbors like the Kayenta and Virgin River cultures but who continued to live in pithouses and hunt and gather. They fashioned unique moccasins of hide heeled with a deer claw and created clay figurines, perhaps for use in rituals. Most distinctive, though, were the huge red pictographs they left on the rocks, displaying large triangular anthropomorphs with ear bobs, headdresses, and other unusual adornments.

Because the Waterpocket Fold is nowhere more than 15 miles (24km) wide, most of the hikes in the park are short, around 2–4 miles (3–6km) long. Grand Wash Narrows passes through

Explaining Anasazi cliff dwellings at Navajo Monument National Park.

500ft (150-meter) -high canyon walls less than 20ft (6 meters) apart, where inscriptions left by early settlers, including Butch Cassidy, are visible. Chimney Rock Trail, just inside the west end of the park, is another great day hike particularly if you walk a mile or two into the upper reaches of Spring Canyon. Be careful here in summer. This extremely rugged terrain sizzles under extreme heat and water can be found in only a few places. Inquire at the visitor center for information on hiking Hall's Creek or Muley Twist Canyon in the southern section of the park, off the Burr Trail, an old ranch trail with switchbacks that wind precipitously over the southern section of the fold between Boulder and the Notom-Bullfrog Road.

GRAND STAIRCASE-ESCALANTE NATIONAL MONUMENT

After leaving Capitol Reef, continue west on US 24, then drop south on US 12 and cross 10,000ft (3,000-meter) Boulder Mountain, exiting near the little ranching community of **Boulder** ⑪, at the start of the Burr Trail, a scenic drive over the middle of the Waterpocket Fold. Boulder is a great place to stop and relax at the famed **Boulder Mountain Lodge** and its award-winning onsite **Hell's Backbone Grill** organic farm-to-table restaurant. Nearby **Anasazi State Park Museum** (tel: 435-335-7308; www.stateparks.utah.gov/parks/anasazi; daily 8am–6pm mid-Mar–end Oct, 8am–4pm winter; charge), which preserves a 12th-century pueblo with 87 rooms, the largest such site found west of the Colorado River.

Boulder offers access to **Grand Staircase–Escalante National Monument** ⑫ (tel: 435-644-1300; www.blm.gov/programs/national-conservation-lands/utah/grand-staircase-escalante-national-monument; daily; free), set aside in 1996 by President Bill Clinton to protect 1.9 million acres (769,000 hectares) of spectacular Utah wilderness from coal mining on the Kaiparowits Plateau. As with all recent national monuments set aside in Utah and managed as undeveloped landscape conservation monuments by the BLM, Grand Staircase-Escalante remains controversial locally. Traditional Mormon ranching and farming communities concerned about losing their way of life have fought the national monument since its inception, and have now won a review of boundaries under the Trump administration. In fact, though, the local community has greatly benefited economically from tourism, and a number of lodges, bed-and-breakfasts, motels, restaurants, and outfitters now serve travelers' needs in Boulder, Escalante, Torrey, and elsewhere.

This large national monument is split roughly into three units: Grand Staircase, Kaiparowits Plateau, and Escalante Canyons. Stop at the **Escalante Interagency Visitor Center** (755 W Main Street, Escalante; tel: 435-826-5499; www.fs.usda.gov/recarea/dixie/recarea/?recid=24978; daily Mar–Oct

Calf Creek Falls cutting through the Navajo Sandstone in Grand Staircase Escalante National Monument.

7.30am–5.30pm, Nov–Feb 8am–4.30pm) to plan your trip with a ranger. This is truly a wild place, with almost no developed trails and only two modest campgrounds. The BLM deliberately emphasizes personal discovery, so you need to take the initiative on where you want to go and ask for help planning your route.

It's not that hard to get into the outlying areas of the monument off US 12 and 89, using the Burr Trail (paved to Capitol Reef National Park), Hole-in-the-Rock Road, the Cottonwood Road, Johnson Canyon, and Wolverine Loop Road. It's a lot harder once you park the car and start hiking. Start with hikes along known routes and major river canyons like the Escalante, and don't hike cross-country unless familiar with route finding through narrow, winding desert canyons and rim country. High-clearance, four-wheel-drive vehicles are advised on many unpaved roads, which shouldn't be attempted during inclement weather when the road turns to gumbo mud, stranding vehicles for days at a time.

BRYCE CANYON NATIONAL PARK

The drive from Boulder to **Escalante** ⓭ along the hogbacks of US 12 above the Escalante Canyons is one of the region's most scenic drives, taking in swirling knobs and buttes of pale Navajo Sandstone slickrock, pierced by labyrinthine canyons flaring green with cottonwoods, willows, and other deciduous trees that warm to autumn hues in October.

Crossing the Escalante River and its trailhead, the road climbs out of the canyon, with the lonely, remote Kaiparowits Plateau off to the south. An equally dramatic graded road travels 40 miles (64km) over Hells Backbone Road to Escalante, climbing to 11,000ft (3,400 meters), and crossing Box–Death Hollow Wilderness via a narrow 1930s bridge near two glorious alpine campgrounds before dropping into Escalante. Until 1929, Boulder got its mail by pack mule over this route – a feat readily appreciated by anyone driving along it.

From Escalante, it's a couple of hours to **Bryce Canyon National Park** ⓮ (tel: 435-834-5322; www.nps.gov/brca; daily

The Gulch on Burr Trail, Grand Staircase-Escalante National Monument.

8am–8pm May–Sept, 8am–6pm Apr and Oct, 8am–4.30pm Nov–Mar; charge). The Paiute made their home in the region called Bryce, the place where "red rocks stand like men in a bowl-shaped canyon." An apocryphal story has Mormon settler Ebenezer Bryce complaining that the canyon was "a hell of a place to lose a cow!" If not looking for cows, you can afford to be charmed by Bryce Canyon, with its Fantasia of pastel-washed hoodoo limestone marching off the east side of the 9,000ft (2,700-meter) -high Paunsaugunt Plateau. Technically, Bryce is not a canyon but a series of 14 amphitheaters eroded into an escarpment whose beauty can best be appreciated from overlooks along its 17-mile (27-km) scenic drive. A free shuttle runs along the drive in summer.

But why stay on the rim when a variety of colorful and unusual hikes among the hoodoos beckon? One of the easiest is Navajo Loop Trail, which passes Douglas firs that have found a protected spot in narrow corridors of shifting Wasatch Formation. Save your energy to hike out – you're climbing a hill in reverse.

Fairyland Loop Trail or a horseback trip on the Peekaboo Loop offer more strenuous outings, but visitors can just as easily stroll the Rim Trail between any two viewing points, return by shuttle, then relax at historic **Bryce Canyon Lodge** (tel: 877-386-4383 or 435-834-8700; www.brycecanyonforever.com; year round, fewer lodging options in winter; reserve at least 13 months ahead).

On a clear day from Yovimpa Point, visibility is over 100 miles (160km) to the Grand Canyon, where the rocks are 160 million years older, forming the top "step" in a "grand staircase" with the gray, white, and vermilion cliffs below. Leaving Bryce, head west on US through Red Canyon, Bryce's pretty little sister, then south at the junction with US 89.

CEDAR BREAKS NATIONAL MONUMENT

Twenty miles (32km) ahead, turn west onto SR 14, a scenic high country route across the Markagunt Plateau above Zion National Park that leads to **Cedar Breaks National Monument** Ⓑ (SR 143; tel: 435-586-9451; www.nps.gov/cebr;

The amphitheatre at Bryce Canyon.

Ⓞ BRYCE CANYON NP

Access The park is 80 miles (129km) east of Cedar City via SR 14, UT 89, and SR 12, and 26 miles (42km) southeast of Panguitch via US 89 and SR12.

Seasons & hours The park is open daily year-round, see above for details; closed Thanksgiving, Christmas, and New Year's Day.

Entrance fee Yes.

Handicapped access Visitor center, some campsites, and a section of Sunset-Sunrise Point Trail.

Activities Scenic drive, camping, hiking, backpacking, horseback riding, wildlife-watching, interpretive programs.

daily June–late Sept; charge), a higher, steeper, and more pristine eroded amphitheater of Wasatch Formation rocks surrounded by basaltic flows barely one million years old. Between June and September, when snows in the high country have melted, visit Cedar Breaks for its spectacular wildflower shows, then descend a scenic back route across the Markagunt Plateau onto the Kolob Terrace section of Zion National Park, picking up SR 9 to Zion National Park via the hamlet of Virgin, in the Virgin River valley. Some of the park's most interesting and challenging backcountry trails begin or cross at Kolob Terrace, offering a unique bird's-eye view of the tops of Zion's 2,000ft (600-meter) cliffs, buttes, and natural temples. The west side of the Markagunt Plateau marks the edge of the Colorado Plateau and the beginning of the Great Basin Desert, 6,000ft (1,800 meters) below.

Continuing on SR 14, the road descends sharply to **Cedar City ⑯**, home to Southern Utah University and the popular nine-week summer Utah Shakespeare Festival, and a good overnight stop. Founded in 1852 as part of the Iron Mission, it's also headquarters of the Cedar City Paiute, one of several bands of Southern Paiutes living on small reservations in Utah and Nevada. Beautiful examples of Paiute basketry, collected by a Mormon in the early 20th century, are on display at **Southern Utah University**. The tribe also holds an annual Paiute Restoration Gathering (open to the public) to celebrate its 1980 official reinstatement.

The **Daughters of Utah Pioneers Museum** (145 N 100 E, St George; tel: 435-628-7274; www.dupstgeorge.org; Mon, Tue, Thu–Sat 10am–5pm; free) is a good place to start a historic walking tour of **St George ⑰**, home of the historic Cotton Mission and the largest town in southern Utah. Known as Utah's Dixie for its moderate winters, St George was chosen by Brigham Young as the site of his winter home.

Here, Young oversaw the construction of the dazzling white **St George Mormon Temple** (490 S 300 E, St George; tel: 435-673-5181; www.stgeorge templevisitorscenter.info; visitor center

St George Mormon Temple.

Fact

Zion's Virgin River can carry away more than one million tons of sediment and rock each year en route to the Colorado River, at Lake Mead.

daily 9am–9pm; free) and the sandstone **Mormon Tabernacle** (tel: 435-628 4072; daily for guided tours 9am–6pm; free), both completed in the 1870s. Note: only Mormons in good standing may enter the temple, but non-Mormons may visit the adjoining visitor center; the Tabernacle, however, is open to all. The historic buildings are within easy walking distance of **Ancestor Square** in the heart of downtown, which also houses excellent restaurants serving Greek, Chinese, and other foods. Located on the northern edge of the Mojave Desert (with its characteristic Joshua trees), St George gets pretty hot in summer but it's a good base for explorations of the surrounding region.

ZION NATIONAL PARK

Drive west to Santa Clara, known for its fruit, and take a tour of the **Jacob Hamblin** House (3324 Hamblin Drive; tel: 435-673-2161; www.lds.org/locations/jacob-hamblin-home; early Apr–early Oct Mon–Sat 9am–7pm, Sun 1–7pm, early Oct–early Apr Mon–Sat 9am–5pm, Sun 1–5pm; free), built in 1862 by Mormon

missionary Jacob Hamblin, a friend of John Wesley Powell, who explored the Colorado River. Continue north to **Snow Canyon State Park** (tel: 435-628-2255; www.stateparks.utah.gov/parks/snow-canyon; daily 6am–10pm; charge) for some dramatic lava-and-sandstone scenery and terrific hiking, camping, and horseback riding in an area used as a backdrop in a number of John Wayne cowboy movies.

St George is just 40 miles (64km) from **Zion National Park ⑱** (tel: 435-772-3256; www.nps.gov/zion; daily 24 hours, visitor center: Memorial Day–Labor Day daily 8am–7pm, early Sept–early Oct 8am–6pm, early Oct–Late Nov 8am–5pm; charge) via SR 9. Here, in narrow Zion Canyon, is the most dramatic exposure of Navajo Sandstone in the West – some 2,400ft (730 meters) at the Temple of Sinawava below the Zion Narrows – carved into a stunning array of sheer cliffs, twisting buttes, and craggy temples by the busy little North Fork of the Virgin River.

One of the classic hikes in Zion leads from the canyon floor at the Grotto Picnic

A hike up through Zion Narrows, Zion National Park.

Area, up 1,500ft (450 meters) of cliff and side canyon, to the vertiginous precipice of Angel's Landing, using only cables and nerves to steady you. For those wanting to keep their feet firmly on the ground, shady trails on the flat floor of the canyon lead to the Gateway to the Narrows, Weeping Rock, and Emerald Pools. Most memorable along these shady trails are seeps, where water percolating down through Navajo Sandstone meets impervious Kayenta shale and is forced out of the rock as horizontal springlines, fostering hanging gardens of yellow columbine, red monkeyflower, acid-green maidenhair fern, and purple shooting stars. It is truly spectacular.

SR 9, which passes through the park, is especially beautiful in spring, when cottonwood, oak, and other deciduous trees leaf out along the Virgin River and its tributaries, and again in fall, when the golden rain of turning leaves becomes breathtaking against ruddy sandstone. The road climbs from the valley floor via a series of dramatic switchbacks, then continues through the 1-mile (1.6km) -long Zion–Mt Carmel Tunnel, built by the Civilian Conservation Corps in 1930 to provide a faster roadlink to parks east of Zion. On the higher, cooler, moister east side of the park is the best evidence of the dune-formed 175-million-year-old Navajo Sandstone in the strangely cross-hatched surface of Checkerboard Mesa, the whirling surfaces of barely petrified sand dunes.

Turn south at Mount Carmel and head to the historic town of **Kanab ⑲**, at the intersection of US 89 and 89A. Kanab is a fine place to find overnight lodging, have a meal, and explore spectacular redrock canyons surrounding the town. Pick up information and permits for the Grand Staircase–Escalante National Monument (see page296) from the BLM's Kanab Field Office (669 S Highway 89A, Kanab; tel: 435-644-1300; www.blm.gov/programs/national-conservation-lands/utah/grand-staircase-escalante-national-monument; Mon–Fri 8am–4.30pm). Most vehicles can reach the historic Pareah Townsite and movie set off Highway 89 (but avoid it in the rain when the dirt road through the colorful Chinle badlands turns to mud).

Road through Zion National Park.

⊘ ZION NP

Access Zion Canyon Visitor Center is 46 miles (74km) east of St George via I-15 and SR 9. Kolob Canyons Visitor Center is 18 miles (29km) south of Cedar City via Exit 40 from I-15.

Seasons & hours Open daily year-round. See above for visitor center hours.

Entrance fee Yes.

Handicapped access Visitor centers, Zion Lodge, three trails, Riverside Walk (with assistance) and some campsites at the South Campground.

Activities Scenic drive, camping, hiking, biking, backpacking, backroad driving, horseback riding, rock climbing, wildlife-watching, interpretive programs.

A different experience can be had by heading south of Kanab to Fredonia, Arizona, then east through the Arizona Strip toward Hurricane, Utah. This remote area, a section of Arizona between the North Rim of the Grand Canyon and the Vermilion Cliffs, offers a hypnotically beautiful drive through quiet rangelands, ranches and tiny, old-style Mormon communities that have barely changed in a century.

Don't bypass the lovely little **Pipe Spring National Monument** ⓴ (406 Pipe Springs Road, Fredonia; tel: 928-643-7105; www.nps.gov/pisp; daily 8.30am–4.30pm, extended hours in summer; charge), 14 miles (23km) southeast of Kanab. Surrounded by the Kaibab Paiute Indian Reservation, this monument preserves the beautifully maintained building of an historic 1870s-period, fortified Mormon tithed cattle ranch and dairy built over a perennial spring and adjoining an ancient Indian pueblo. Fortified to prevent federal government agents discovering Mormon polygamists, it was a stopping place for Mormon couples being sealed at the St George Temple and for explorers like John Wesley Powell, who used local Paiute guides and lived in one of the cabins here while surveying the region. The first telegraph in the region was located here.

LAKE POWELL AND GLEN CANYON

At 180 miles (290km) long, **Lake Powell** – named for the explorer – is the second-largest and most spectacular reservoir in the United States. The lake was created by Colorado River waters impounded behind the 710ft (216-meter) -high **Glen Canyon Dam** ㉑, downstream at **Page**, which generates 1,200 megawatts of hydroelectricity for the megalopolises of Phoenix and environs – and ample controversy. When it was begun in 1956, the dam had the blessing of almost everyone concerned. By the time it was finished in 1963, conservationists had belatedly recognized that Glen Canyon, "the place no one knew," was comparable in grandeur to anything – including the Grand Canyon – on the Colorado

Lake Mead Marina in Glen Canyon National Recreation Area.

Plateau. Today, many people believe that the drowning of Glen Canyon was an unspeakable ecological tragedy, and are working to eventually dismantle the dam and use generated power from Hoover Dam in Nevada. An ongoing drought has, in fact, been doing much of the work for activists, drying out the lake and its far marinas and exposing archeological sites long ago drowned under the lake.

That said, Lake Powell, administered by the National Park Service as **Glen Canyon National Recreation Area** ㉒ (4304 Bullfrog; tel: tel: 928-608-6200; www.nps.gov/glca; daily 24 hours, visitor center hours vary; charge) is a stunning place to waterski, fish, boat, camp, and explore. At Page, the dramatic Carl Hayden Visitor Center at Glen Canyon Dam **r** (tel: 928-608-6200, tours: 928-608-6072; mid-May–mid-Sept 8am–6pm, Nov–Feb daily 8am–4pm, rest of year daily 8am–5pm, call for days; charge) offers frequent tours of the facility (note: heightened security is currently in place, and you will not be able to bring purses and other personal items onto the property) and the small **John Wesley Powell Memorial Museum** (tel: 928-645-9496; www.powellmuseum.org; daily 9am–5pm; donation) has information about the lake's namesake and local history. Miles of blue water and a shoreline of carved cliffs make the lake a photographer's dream. Houseboats, popular with vacationers, may be rented at any of the four marinas, along with fishing tackle and powerboats.

Don't miss visiting 290ft (88-meter) -high **Rainbow Bridge National Monument** ㉓ (tel: 928-608-6200; www.nps.gov/rabr; daily sunrise–sunset; free), the tallest natural bridge on the planet and a site sacred to the Navajo, whose reservation adjoins the area. Overland horseback tours of the reservation to Rainbow Bridge are available through the Navajo Nation. Daily guided boat tours to Rainbow Bridge are available through the park concessioner, Aramark (tel: 800-528-6154; www.lakepowell.com), leaving from Wahweap and Bullfrog marinas. Boats may not moor at Rainbow Bridge and camping is not permitted.

Rainbow Bridge National Monument.

GRAND CANYON

Words, images, music, even film cannot convey the experience of time and space that accompanies a pilgrimage to the Grand Canyon, Arizona's top visitor attraction.

The **Grand Canyon** is considered one of the seven natural wonders of the world. Every year, people arrive at its edge and gaze into this deep gash in the earth, drawn by its reputation but completely unprepared for its scale and complexity. The approach to the canyon across northern Arizona's Coconino Plateau gives no hint of what awaits. US 180 crosses a sweeping land of sagebrush, grass, and dwarf pinyon-juniper (P-J) woodlands and enters fragrant forests of tall ponderosa pines sighing in the wind. Then suddenly, the earth falls away and below you yawns an immensity of carved buttes, terraces, side canyons, and layered rocks that the mind simply can't take in. It is thrilling, unnerving, confusing, literally ungrounding – an encounter with raw nature everyone should experience at least once in their lives.

Looking below, there appears to be a tiny stream. Though it looks small from this distance, it is in fact the Colorado River, one of the great rivers of the West. Unbelievable as it may seem, it is the chisel that carved the Grand Canyon. The river rushes through the canyon for 277 miles (446km) wild and undammed. Over several million years it's been doing what rivers do – slowly but surely eroding the canyon to its present depth of 1 mile (1.6km).

To the east, the scalloped skyline of the **Palisades of the Desert** defines the

canyon rim. To the north, about 10 miles (16km) as the hawk flies, is the flat-lying forested **North Rim** on the Kaibab Plateau. To the west, the canyon's cliffs and ledges, cusps, and curves extend as far as the eye can see, taking in the Havasupai Reservation and adjoining Hualapai Reservation, home to the famous Skywalk, with only distant indigo mountains breaking the horizon. **Grand Canyon National Park** (tel: 928-638-7888; www.nps.gov/grca), set aside by President Theodore Roosevelt as a national monument in 1908, and later upgraded to a

Main Attractions

Grand Canyon Village
Hermits Road
Bright Angel Trail
South Kaibab Trail
Hermit Trail
Havasu Canyon
Grand Canyon West
The North Rim

Maps on pages
282, 306

Horses on the South Kaibab Trail.

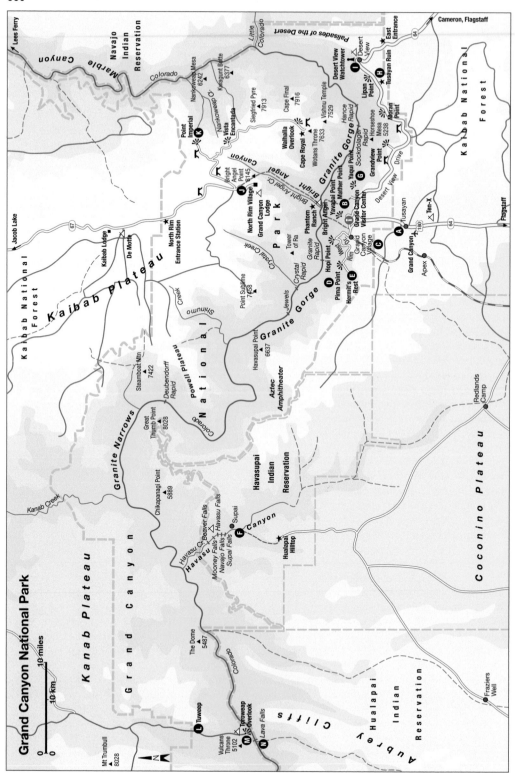

Grand Canyon National Park

national park, encompasses more than a million acres (400,000 hectares), and this view takes in only a quarter of the entire canyon.

A GEOLOGIC IMMENSITY

The ancient rock strata that form the Grand Canyon represent geological time on a scale incomprehensible to human experience. The upper layers of Kaibab and Toroweap limestone, for example, were formed by ancient oceans, while the lower layers of sandstone were created even earlier, by a desert covering more than 32,000 sq miles (82,880 sq km). A desert preceded by an ocean preceded by yet an earlier desert. And beneath all that, volcanoes that erupted with lava at the very beginning of life on earth, nearly 2 billion years ago.

That 5 million visitors would eventually come from all over the world to experience this marvel of geology, and even hike down inside it, would never have occurred to early explorers. "The region is, of course, altogether valueless," wrote US Army surveyor Joseph Ives in his report after being led into the western section of Grand Canyon by local Hualapai Indians in 1857. "Ours has been the first, and will doubtless be the last, party of whites to visit this profitless locality."

Famous last words.

THE SOUTH RIM

Most visitors to the Grand Canyon see it from the more developed 7,000ft-elevation (2,134-meter) South Rim, which remains open year round and offers the bulk of food, lodging, and visitor amenities in its historic village. The South Rim is easily accessible from Flagstaff to the south, Williams from the southwest, and US 89A on the Navajo Nation to the east – a journey of about an hour.

Grand Canyon Railway (tel: 303-843-8724; www.thetrain.com; daily) runs a steam train into the heart of Grand Canyon Village from the historic depot in tiny Williams, off Interstate 40, and offers an easy way of visiting the South Rim. If you're driving, expect long lines to get into the park in summer. Park the car as soon as you can, and take one of the free

Keeping the sun off at Eagle Point overlook on Grand Canyon West.

GRAND CANYON NATIONAL PARK

Access Grand Canyon Village and Grand Canyon Visitor Center at the South Rim are about 85 miles (137km) from Flagstaff, Arizona, via US 180/64. Although only 10 miles (16km) across the canyon, the North Rim is about 215 miles (346km) by road from Grand Canyon Village. Take SR 64 east to Cameron, US 89/89A north to Jacob Lake, then SR 67 south to the North Rim. Visitors can also arrive by air at the Grand Canyon National Park Airport, just outside the park in Tusayan, or by rail from Williams, Arizona, on the historic Grand Canyon Railway.

Seasons & Hours The South Rim is open year-round; the visitor center is open daily 9am–7pm in summer. (Note: Arizona does not observe Daylight Savings Time.) The lightly visited North Rim is open mid-May–mid-October and has a visitor center, historic cabins and lodge, campground, and trails.

Entrance Fee Yes.

Handicapped Access South Rim Visitor Center and some shuttle buses. Contact park for free Accessibility Guide.

Activities Scenic drive, backpacking, wildlife-watching, river trips, mule packing, fishing.

Note: Grand Canyon is heavily visited most of the year, so apply well in advance for permits, accommodations, and car parking.

shuttle buses and/or walk. In summer, a free shuttle (Purple Route) runs from **Tusayan** 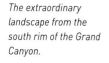, the gateway village near the park entrance, to **Grand Canyon Visitor Center** (daily 8am–5pm; plaza exhibits 24 hours) near **Mather Point** ⑧ just inside the park, where you will also find a spacious pedestrian plaza with interpretive boards, and car and bus parking.

The bus terminal is just east of the visitor center and has free shuttle buses running at frequent intervals all day along the main park routes: Grand Canyon Village (Blue Route), the Kaibab/East Rim (Orange Route), and Hermits Road/West Rim (Red Route). By extending the public transportation system, and providing more park-and-ride opportunities, the National Park Service aims to get people out of their cars and restore that invigorating sense of discovery we all seek in a national park. Now the ravens (and a good number of reintroduced condors, which congregate at the Kolb brothers' historic photographic **Lookout Studio** on the Rim Trail just west of the Village) are taking back their rightful place soaring over the dizzying abyss and croaking their calls of greeting.

The paved Rim Trail, extending from Mather Point all the way to Grand Canyon Village and then in both directions on the East and West Rims, offers a nice flat surface for walking and taking in the extraordinary sights at your own pace. The historic buildings on the rim, most of them built from native stone and timber, are an attraction in themselves. One is **Yavapai Point and Geology Museum** (daily 8am–7pm), the next point west of Mather Point on the Rim Trail. One entire wall of this museum and bookstore is glass, affording a stupendous view into the heart of the canyon – slices of the Colorado River, a 1928 suspension bridge, and **Bright Angel Campground** and **Phantom Ranch** tucked at the very bottom.

GRAND CANYON VILLAGE

A mile west of Mather Point is **Grand Canyon Village** ⓒ, tourism central for the park. Across the road from park headquarters and the Shrine of the Ages Auditorium are Yavapai Lodge,

The extraordinary landscape from the south rim of the Grand Canyon.

Mather Campground, Babbitt's General Store, and Market Plaza, which has restaurants, a gas station, a post office, a bank, public showers, and a laundromat. Most of the park's lodges are located just west of here, including the venerable **El Tovar Hotel,** designed by Charles Whittlesey, and Southwest-style **Bright Angel Lodge**, designed by famed architect Mary Jane Colter. All were built at the turn of the 20th century, at a time when most visitors arrived by train and were treated to elegant lodgings and service-oriented restaurants provided by concessioner Fred Harvey.

BELOW THE RIM

Immediately adjacent to Bright Angel Lodge is **Bright Angel Trailhead**. Since the Bright Angel and the South Kaibab are the only two maintained trails into the Grand Canyon, the National Park Service recommends hiking one of them before venturing onto any of the unmaintained trails. There is no water along the more exposed South Kaibab, so most visitors choose to take their introductory hike on the Bright Angel, which

has water in three places. Because of the heat and exposure – temperatures routinely exceed 105°F (41°C) in summer – hikers must wear suitable clothing, including hiking boots and socks or sturdy, supportive river sandals; a broadbrimmed hat, sunglasses, sunscreen, and long-sleeved shirts and pants to cover exposed skin; and most important: carry salty, nutritious snacks and plenty of water – at least a gallon per person per day, preferably lightly salted to keep electrolytes balanced and prevent hyponatremia (low salt).

Stepping below the rim of the Grand Canyon changes the experience of it – the quiet and the grandeur of the landscape are measured against each descending footstep. A logical destination for an all-day hike is **Indian Gardens**, a verdant oasis about 4 miles (7km) and 3,100 vertical feet (945 meters) below the rim. Follow the example of avid hikers by rising very early; the colors are most radiant and the heat most merciful shortly after dawn.

Day hikes will satisfy most people, but others will want to stay overnight,

⊘ **Fact**

Once colored by silt – the name Colorado is Spanish for "reddish colored" – the Colorado River is often clear and blue-green, the silt retained by the Glen Canyon Dam upstream of the Grand Canyon.

perhaps on a hike to the Colorado River and back (do not attempt to do the round trip in one day; even the fittest person will get into trouble that way). Backpacking in the Grand Canyon is hard but rewarding work. Consider joining a mule train. To stay overnight below the rim, you must have a reservation at either Phantom Ranch or a designated campground. It's necessary to make arrangements for camping and mule rides several months in advance, particularly in the summer. Travelers visiting the Grand Canyon in autumn or early spring will have an easier time, though it will also be a cooler one. For more information, contact the **Backcountry Information Office** at the South Rim.

WEST RIM DRIVE

From Grand Canyon Village, Hermits Road (also called West Rim Drive) extends west for 8 miles (13km). Constructed in 1912 as a scenic drive, it offers several overlooks along the way. During the summer, the 8-mile (13km) West Rim Drive is closed to

Smokey the Bear, at Tusayan Ranger Station.

private vehicles, so you must take the free shuttle bus. You can get on or off the bus at a half-dozen viewpoints; this makes it possible to take the 10-minute hike between **Pima Point ⓓ**, which offers one of the best views of the Grand Canyon and the Colorado River, and **Hermit's Rest ⓔ**, where you'll find an historic stone building with a gift shop, concession stand, and restrooms.

The hermit was a Canadian prospector named Louis Boucher, a charming character with a long, flowing white beard and a white mule named Calamity Jane who settled at an idyllic spot called Dripping Springs off the Hermit Trail. Boucher was one of many prospectors who arrived in the late 1800s, Deposits of copper, asbestos, lead, and silver were found, but the costs of transporting ore by mule train were so astronomical that none of the ventures, including those of Boucher, proved profitable. Most miners quickly turned instead to prospecting for tourist gold, escorting visitors on trails, feeding them and selling them homegrown produce, or like John Hance, another well-known

⊘ THE POWELL EXPEDITION

John Wesley Powell and his party of Anglo explorers were the first to run the Colorado River through the Grand Canyon in 1869. By the time they drifted out of Glen Canyon, they were 10 gaunt men in three battered boats who were glad to be alive. Ten weeks earlier, they had left Green River, Wyoming, 500 miles (800km) to the northeast, with four boats and 10 months of supplies, but after repeatedly capsizing in the rapids, they were now down to rancid bacon, musty flour, dried apples, and coffee. The men were getting mutinous, but Powell was unperturbed. "If he can only study geology," grumbled one of the hands, George Bradley, "he will be happy without food or shelter, but the rest of us are not afflicted with it to an alarming extent." For three months, Powell and his expedition traveled 1,000 miles (1,600km) down the Colorado River, which in this region threads 277 miles (446km) through a continuous gorge, from Lees Ferry to the Grand Wash Cliffs. The final 215 miles (346km) are within the Grand Canyon itself. Years later, as the head of the US Geological Survey and the Bureau of Ethnology, Powell would become one of the most influential men in Washington, DC. At the time of the expedition, however, he was unknown, simply a one-armed Civil War veteran and self-taught scientist who, with his inherent curiosity, intuition, and discipline, would make fundamental contributions to the budding sciences of geology and anthropology

character, telling tall tales that have gone down in Grand Canyon lore.

We have the miners to thank for most of the unmaintained trails that enter the canyon, including the 8-mile (13km) **Hermit Trail**. There are two good day hikes from Hermit's Rest: the 5-mile (8km) round-trip hike to **Santa Maria Springs** and the 6-mile (10km) round-trip hike to the less frequently visited **Dripping Springs**. Constructed in 1912 for mule riders staying at El Tovar Hotel, the trail is in good condition, though unmaintained, and rarely congested. Nearly 15 miles (24km) later, the trail reaches the Colorado River.

Several viewpoints along West Rim Drive offer vistas of different isolated buttes and "temples." The **Battleship** is best seen from **Maricopa Point**, while **Isis, Shiva**, and **Brahma** are temples that were named by Clarence Dutton, a classically educated geologist with the early US Geological Survey and a protégé of Major John Wesley Powell (see box).

VENTURING WEST

The paved road ends at Hermit's Rest, but it is possible, via the Rowe's Well road, to venture farther west along the rim, although a topographical map and a few gallons of water are essential. The Bass Trailhead is beautifully located on a narrow peninsula jutting into the canyon and is one possible destination. Backpackers find the Bass one of the most scenic and easy-to-follow of the unmaintained trails, and the trailhead itself makes a fine picnic or camping site for anyone anxious to escape the relative pandemonium of Grand Canyon Village.

Even farther west is the Topocoba Hilltop Trail, which leads 8 miles (13km) to **Havasu Canyon ❻**, home of the Havasupai Indians – "people of the blue-green water" – since AD 1300 and now the Havasupai Reservation, with a population of around 500. Tourism sustains the people. Until this century, the Havasupai, in addition to tilling their fields, spent part of each year roaming throughout the canyon in search of game and edible plants. At one time a rarely visited Shangri-La, Havasu Canyon is now visited by an average of 100 people daily, though in actuality the numbers are considerably larger in summer (and fewer in winter).

Thirty miles (50km) west of Grand Canyon Village, Havasu Canyon's lure is **Havasu Creek**, a blue-green stream tinted by algae that plunges over three stunning waterfalls, one of which, Mooney Falls, is almost 200ft (60 meters) high. These waterfalls spill over rippled dams made from travertine, formed by calcium carbonate that has been deposited over the centuries. (Calcium carbonate is the same stuff from which a limestone cave's stalactites and stalagmites are formed.) While the area receives less than 10ins (25cm) of precipitation each year, Havasu Creek is the drainage for thousands of square miles. In 1990 and 1993, flash floods surged through Havasu Creek. Boulders and

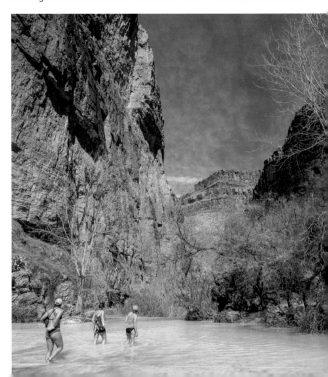

Exlporing the majestic river at Havasu Falls.

Murals in Desert View watchtower.

Skywalk is located at Grand Canyon West.

silt-thickened water caused residents of Supai to climb to safety.

Havasu is the most stunning of the side canyons that drain into the Colorado, and despite the crowds, it is worth visiting – particularly during the off season, late September through early April. Access is difficult (most travelers to Havasu Canyon arrive by boat on river trips), and the canyon is subject to severe flash flooding, sometimes causing evacuations and extensive damage. There is a small lodge in the tribal headquarters village of **Supai**, as well as a trading post, post office school, and tribal museum; most visitors stay at a campground. For more information, contact the Havasupai Tourist Office (tel: 928-448-2127).

From the rim, you must hike or ride horseback down the 8-mile (13-km) trail from Hualapai Hilltop, 67 miles (108km) northeast of Peach Springs, headquarters of the Hualapai Reservation, on Old Route 66. Unlike the remote Havasupai, the Hualapai Tribe has elected to develop its section of the canyon into **Grand Canyon West** (daily 7am–7pm; charge) (see page 305), creating a spectacular see-through "Skywalk" viewing deck high above the Grand Canyon and offering other activities, including helicopter rides and river rafting. Grand Canyon West is reached by car from Kingman, Arizona, off Interstate 40, and is your best bet for a quick look at the canyon in its remote western end.

EAST RIM DRIVE

Heading east from Grand Canyon Village through fragrant forests of ponderosa pine on the 23-mile (37km) **East Rim Drive**, via car or shuttle, the scenic drive passes the South Kaibab Trailhead, near **Yaqui Point G**, and after 20 miles (32km) arrives at **Tusayan Ruin H** and Tusayan Museum. Anthropologists believe that the Ancestral Puebloans who built this small pueblo came to the canyon around AD 500. They were not the ancestors of the Havasupai, but rather lived a similar life, raising corn, squash, and beans on the rim during the summer and moving down to the warmer canyon floor in the winter. These Ancestral Pueblo people abandoned Tusayan Pueblo and a number of other sites around AD 1150, possibly as a result of a long period of drought.

But the Ancestral Puebloans were not the first people to inhabit the canyon. Anthropologists have discovered split-twig willow figurines pierced by small spears that date to 2000 BC, a period when nomadic Desert Archaic people wandered through the canyon, hunting and gathering. What, one wonders, did these people think of the Grand Canyon? Perhaps Hopi religion offers a clue. Each year, Hopi holy men make a pilgrimage to a sacred site in the canyon, from whence they believe their ancestors emerged from the underworld.

The last viewpoint on East Rim Drive within the park is **Desert View I**. Here, the **Desert View Watchtower**, a beautiful Ancestral Pueblo–style stone lookout tower designed in 1932 by Mary

Jane Colter, rises 67ft (20 meters) high and offers excellent views of the Colorado River 4,000ft (1,200 meters) below; inside are spectacular murals by Hopi artist Fred Kabotie. There is a campground at Desert View, as well as a little-known road that soon deteriorates to a trail leading to Comanche Point. This secluded spot, with its marvelous views, is ideal for seekers of solitude. Here, the canyon opens out into the wide Marble Platform and east to the huge Navajo Nation.

THE NORTH RIM

From Desert View, continue east on SR 64 to **Cameron Trading Post** on the Navajo Nation. Stop for gas and what connoisseurs say is a "respectable Navajo taco," a local dish that is a hybrid of Indian fry bread smothered with refried beans, lettuce, and cheese. The Little Colorado River meets the main Colorado River here. Views of the Little Colorado can be had at an overlook on the Navajo reservation just before the junction between SR 64 and US 89, and at the road bridge at Cameron Trading

Post, which also has a trading post selling rugs, a gift shop, and a lodge. At the US 89 junction, the highway turns south back to Flagstaff or north to Page, the route to the North Rim.

It doesn't look very far, but the North Rim is actually 220 miles (354km) from the South Rim by highway. Allow plenty of time on this 55mph (88kph) road, which takes you into a remote and beautiful part of northern Arizona across the Navajo Nation and part of the Painted Desert. At the Page turnoff, continue on US 89A, cross the bridge over the Colorado River at Marble Canyon (watch for released condors circling above and river rafters below at this historic bridge). Allow time for the 5-mile (8km) detour to **Lees Ferry**, the put-in for river trips and a historic spot developed by famed Mormon pioneer John D. Lee. This is the only place for nearly 300 miles (480km) where you can get down to the river, sit on the shore, and marvel that this is the same insignicant river you saw from the rim.

Highway 89A continues west through the wide, lonesome stretch of historic

Desert View Watchtower, designed by Mary Jane Colter.

House Rock Valley, access for the **Vermilion Cliffs National Monument** (tel: 435-688-3200; www.blm.gov/visit/virmillion-cliffs), which includes the highly photogenic Paria Plateau, Vermilion Cliffs, Coyote Buttes, and Paria Canyon. Permits are required to hike the narrow canyons and spectacular land formations in this rugged landscape, and trips take planning. Information boards at the entry point offer information about the condor release program here and you may be lucky to glimpse the resident bison herd in House Rock Valley, which has been here for decades.

From here, the road climbs up the east flank of the Kaibab Plateau, reentering first P-J woodlands then ponderosa pine forest. At Jacob Lake, SR 67 turns south and winds 45 miles (72km) through the forest to the North Rim. The North Rim is 1,000ft (300 meters) higher than the South Rim and is closed by snow from late October to late May due to snow. But during summer and fall, it offers a cooler and less crowded alternative. Free dispersed camping is permitted in the national forest.

Drive south through lush forests of ponderosa pine, spruce, fir and aspen trees, interspersed with wide meadows edged by lingering snow banks and dotted with duck-filled ponds. After 45 miles (72km) you'll reach **North Rim Village** ❶, whose centerpiece is **Grand Canyon Lodge**, which perches on the canyon's edge. This handsome structure, a masterpiece created in beams and stonework, was built by hand in 1928 and is best appreciated while eating a piece of pie in the lodge restaurant or sitting in one of the old-fashioned wooden rocking chairs on the veranda and staring into space. Because of the short season and isolation the North Rim has never been as fully developed as the South Rim. In addition to the lodge, there is a nice campground, small cabins, a visitor center, and a cafeteria. A couple of lodges offer food and lodging just outside the park.

Drive to **Point Imperial** ❶, offering views of the eastern Grand Canyon and the Painted Desert, and to Cape

The Wave at Coyote Buttes, Vermilion Cliffs National Monument.

Royal. Day hikes along the rim include the Widforss Trail and the Ken Patrick Trail. The only maintained trail into the canyon from the North Rim is the North Kaibab Trail. Allow a full day to hike to **Roaring Springs** and back, a 9-mile (14km) round-trip. More experienced hikers might want to backpack the Thunder River Trail to Deer and Tapeats creeks, gorgeous trout streams that plunge full-born from springs at the base of the Redwell Limestone.

West of the North Rim is the least visited section of Grand Canyon National Park – **Tuweep ❶**, reached over 60 miles (100km) of rough, dirt roads from the isolated Mormon communities of either Fredonia on US 89A or Colorado City, via UT 153 in the remote Arizona Strip. The roads to the isolated unit of Tuweep cross **Grand Canyon-Parashant National Monument** (345 E Riverside Drive, St George, UT; tel: 435-688-3200; www.nps.gov/para), which protects the western Grand Canyon and Virgin River Gorge, a tributary of the Colorado. Don't attempt roads like this in winter or during the summer

monsoon season, which turn the dirt to gumbo. Heed the Park Service's advice: "A trip into this area, one of the most remote in northern Arizona, should not be attempted without ample gasoline, water, and food."

Despite restricted access, it's surprising that Tuweep is so rarely visited. Research suggests that within the last million years the Colorado has been damned 11 times by molten lava. The largest lava dam was 550ft (168 meters) high and backed water 180 miles (290km) upstream. "What a conflict of water and fire there must have been here!" wrote John Wesley Powell on his pioneer voyage. "Just imagine a river of molten rock running down into a river of melted snow. What a seething and boiling of the waters; what clouds of steam rolled into the heavens!"

There are two points of interest at Tuweep. **Toroweap Overlook ⓜ** offers unrivalled views of the lava flows that cascaded into the canyon. Then there's a short but extraordinarily rugged trail to **Lava Falls ⓝ**, the most violent rapid in the canyon.

Grand Canyon and Colorado River seen from Toroweap Overlook.

📷 RAFTING THE COLORADO RIVER

On its 277-mile (446km) course through the Grand Canyon, the Colorado River provides a world-class rafting adventure

From its headwaters in the state of Colorado to the Gulf of California, the Colorado River is 1,440 miles (2,300km) long. Through the Grand Canyon, the Colorado River averages 300ft (90 meters) wide and 40ft (12 meters) deep. It is famous for its whitewater rapids.

Rapids form where the canyon narrows, forcing the same volume of water to pass through a restricted channel, where debris from side canyons has tumbled into the riverbed, or where elevation drops abruptly. From Lees Ferry to the Grand Wash Cliffs, the Grand Canyon portion of the river, it loses almost 2,000ft (600 meters) in elevation. In that stretch, rapids account for 90 percent of the river's elevational drop, but only 10 percent of its length. The river is a heart-stopping 3,000ft (900 meters) below Toroweap Overlook. And from that lofty perch, the river looks pretty tame, except that Lava Falls Rapid's thunder still reaches your ears.

Summer is prime time for running the 277 miles (446km) of the "Grand." While private individuals with the proper gear and expertise may make private trips, a Park Service permit can take years to obtain. That's why most of the 22,000 people who raft the Colorado each year go as paying passengers with one of the river concessioners licensed by the Park Service.

Guides on the Colorado must have superb skills to negotiate often-treacherous rapids.

Rowing the Upper Granite Gorge on the Colorado River, in the Grand Canyon.

Seen more often these days than in years gone by, bighorn are entirely unhindered by terrifyingly rough terrain and sometimes peer at boaters from rocky overlooks.

Glen Canyon Dam from the river.

The dam on a desert river

Glen Canyon Dam, which impounds Colorado River waters in Lake Powell above Grand Canyon, generates as much controversy as hydroelectric power. It may have given us the "world's most beautiful reservoir," but it has altered the river's character, and the ripple effect upon the environment has been weighty. From this strange new river many native species fled or died; odd plants grew; riverbanks eroded. People who knew and respected the old river raised the alarm, and in 1992, George W. Bush signed the Grand Canyon Protection Act, which mandates that the dam be managed to enhance the natural environment in regions both upstream and downstream of the dam. On several occasions since then, the Bureau of Reclamation has opened the dam gates for a week at a time to allow high-flow releases of river water through the Grand Canyon, renewing beaches, whisking away old vegetation, and improving habitat for native species. More such releases are needed, but there are so many demands for Colorado River water officials have shown little political will to fulfill the mandate of the GCPA.

Whitewater rafting lava rapids on the Colorado river in the Grand Canyon National Park.

Ancestral Puebloans farmed this river delta and stored corn in granaries high above the river.

A group paddling a whitewater raft through rapids on the Colorado River.

NORTHERN ARIZONA

Centered around the university town of Flagstaff, nestled below the highest mountains in Arizona, the northland is the gateway to the spectacular Colorado Plateau.

The journey from Phoenix up to the high country of northern Arizona, often called the Northland, offers a rare combination for the traveler: an easy two-hour drive along a well-maintained freeway (Interstate 17) and a dramatic introduction to Arizona's changing geology and natural history. The road climbs out of the searing lowlands of the Sonoran Desert, up over the 2.000ft (600-meter) -high barrier of the Mogollon Rim that transects Arizona and onto the mile-high Colorado Plateau, a 130,000 sq mile (340,000 sq km) geological province spanning parts of Arizona, New Mexico, Utah, and Colorado, also known as the Four Corners (see page 269).

Leaving the overheated desert basin of Phoenix to the south, the landscape changes from cactus and desert vegetation to sagebrush range bordered by mountains and narrow valleys, dotted with ranches and roads leading to colorfully named places like Bloody Basin. The highway crosses the broad Verde River valley and on through pale limestone road sections that stand out against the dark volcanic escarpment of the Mogollon Rim. In no time, you are up on the Rim itself, motoring through a verdant ocean of pygmy pinyon-juniper forest. Off to the west, the red rocks of Sedona appear, and the road ascends into the cool, fragrant

domain of the Coconino National Forest, the largest ponderosa pine forest in the Lower 48, at an elevation of 7,000ft (2,000 meters). Up ahead, lit by a subtle sunset glow, are the San Francisco Mountains and 12,633ft (3,850-meter) **Humphreys Peak**, Arizona's highest point. Wrapped around the base of the mountains is Flagstaff, the northland's main commercial center.

Flagstaff is not only surrounded by strong contemporary Indian cultures but the preserved remains of those who preceded them – Ancestral

⊙ **Main Attractions**

Flagstaff
Sedona
Sharlot Hall Museum, Prescott
Walnut Canyon National Monument
La Posada, Winslow
Petrified Forest National Park
Wupatki National Monument

Maps on pages 282, 320

The road to Humphreys Peak.

Puebloans like the Kayenta and the Sinagua, the Cohonina to the west, and the Mogollon, whose culture was centered in southwestern New Mexico but which spread into the White Mountains of Arizona. Flagstaff and environs, as far south as Verde Valley, were primarily home to the Sinagua (Spanish for "without water"), pueblo-building farmers who made fine, red-hued pottery.

FLAGSTAFF

In the 1990s, **Flagstaff** ㉕ earned city status when it reached 50,000 residents; by 2015, the population of this increasingly popular university town topped 70,000, with a combined metropolitan population of 139,000. Sheepman Thomas McMillan was the first official settler in 1876, a few months after a group of colonists from Boston passed through and stripped a pine to serve as a flagpole for the July 4th centennial celebration, giving the town its name in 1881. The arrival of the railroad in 1882 allowed meat as well as wool to be sold to markets back east, giving Flagstaff the boost it needed to grow into a lively boardwalk town next to the tracks. Businessmen joined sheepherders, railroad workers, and cattle ranchers making (and losing) small fortunes financing business ventures and opening banks, saloons, hotels, stores, restaurants, and other services.

By the turn of the century, Flagstaff had turned from a town with Wild West leanings into a settled Victorian community dependent on natural resources. Nowadays, although the railroad continues to be a lively presence, lumber and livestock have declined, replaced by jobs linked mainly to the university; federal, state, and local governments; construction; and tourism.

Start with a visit to the **Flagstaff Visitor Center** (tel: 928-213-2951; www.flagstaffarizona.com/visitors; Mon–Sat 8am–5pm), located in the 1926 railroad depot on Route 66. From here, stroll across the street and visit the funky diners, bars, and newer breweries and boutiques in what was once called New

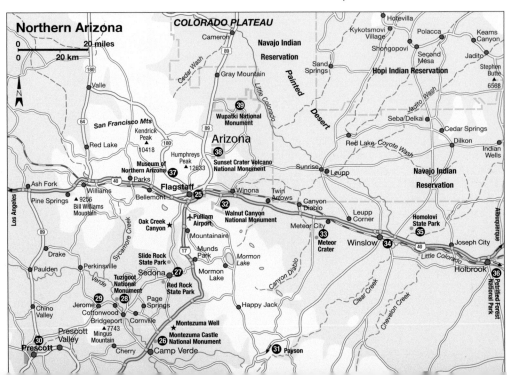

Town. Continue north on San Francisco Street for a walking tour of downtown's many refurbished brick buildings.

On the corner of San Francisco and Aspen streets is the 1887 **Babbitt Building**, still owned by a descendant of the Babbitt brothers who came here to ranch in 1886 and opened so many businesses in Flagstaff that it was said even the sheep said "Baa-bbitt." Just west, where Aspen and Leroux streets meet, is the 1900 **Weatherford Hotel**, which once hosted travelers like Theodore Roosevelt, William Randolph Hearst, and writer Zane Grey, who wrote *Call of the Canyon* while staying here.

Flagstaff is unusually rich in cultural institutions for such a small city. One of the most famous is **Lowell Observatory** (tel: 928-774-3358; www.lowell.edu; Mon–Sat 10am–10pm, Sun 10am–5pm; charge) atop Mars Hill, easily reached on foot or by car just west of downtown. Evening telescope viewing is available; call for hours. The observatory was founded in 1894 by Percival Lowell, an astronomer who used his family fortune to search for signs of intelligent life on Mars. His work also led him to predict the existence of the dwarf planet Pluto, although it was not actually located until after his death, in 1930. In 1993, the observatory made news when the late astronomer and geologist Eugene Shoemaker and his wife Caroline were the first to identify the Shoemaker-Levy comet. Shoemaker made his home in Flagstaff, attracted by the fellowship of many scientists in the area, including those at the US Geological Survey here.

Just south of downtown is **Northern Arizona University** (tel: 928-523-9011; www.nau.edu), the center of Flagstaff learning, with a student population of 29,000. Founded in 1899 as the Normal School, the university still turns out many of the state's teachers and is also known for its anthropology and forestry schools. Cultural events abound here, many of which are held at Ardrey Auditorium, home to the Flagstaff Symphony. The university also hosts a busy series of public lectures by visiting authors, scientists, and others.

⊙ Fact

Percival Lowell believed in Martian life, based on his observations of lines radiating from the planet's surface, which thought was a network of canals. He suggested that Mars had an atmosphere, thin and cloudless but adequate to support life.

Historic Flagstaff.

"Red Rocks and the Cowboy Artist" is a tribute both to Sedona's red rocks and to the Sedona artist, Joe Beeler.

Red Rock State Park, Sedona.

Next to the campus is **Riordan Mansion State Historic Park** (tel: 928-779-4395; www.azstateparks.com/riordan-mansion; daily tours May–Oct 10am–4pm, Nov–Feb 11am–4pm; charge), which preserves the elegant 1904 log-and-stone home of Flagstaff's most successful lumbermen, Timothy and Michael Riordan. Designed by Charles Whittlesey, architect of El Tovar Hotel at the South Rim of the Grand Canyon it sits just off Milton Road, Flag's busy commercial artery. This area was once called Mill Town, a separate community for millworkers.

Another terrific place to learn about local lore is the **Arizona Historical Society Pioneer Historical Museum** (2340 N Fort Valley Road.; tel: 928-774-6272; www.arizonahistoricalsociety.org/museums/welcome-to-pioneer-museum-flagstaff; Memorial Day–Labor Day Mon–Sat 9am–5pm, Sun 10am–4pm, early Sept–end Oct Mon–Sat 9am–5pm, Nov–Apr Mon–Sat 10am–4pm; charge), a few miles north of downtown on US 180. Built as the community hospital in 1908 and now the home of the Arizona Historical Society, it houses artifacts dug up from Old Town (now known as Plaza Vieja and located on Coconino Avenue, west of downtown), as well as pioneer Ben Doney's cabin.

SOUTH OF FLAGSTAFF

For a further look at late-period Sinagua ruins, head south from Flagstaff on Interstate 17 for about 50 miles (80km) to the retirement haven of Verde Valley to view the dramatic remains of a 12th-century cliff pueblo at **Montezuma Castle National Monument** ㉖ (tel: 520-567-3322; www.nps.gov/moca; daily 8am–5pm; charge), so named by early explorers who thought it the work of Aztecs, not northerners moving into areas vacated by earlier farmers of the Hohokam culture. For an early Hohokam pithouse, visit **Montezuma Well**, 11 miles (18km) north.

These ruins are one of the main reasons to visit **Sedona** ㉗, a former fruit-growing center amid spectacular red rocks. Sedona has become the overhyped New Age Santa Fe of Arizona, with high prices and overpriced

⊘ FLAGSTAFF ARTS AND CRAFTS

Northern Arizona University has an exciting program of dance performances, readings, lectures, plays, and concerts by the Flagstaff Symphony, as well as art shows in the NAU Art Museum. Coconino Center for the Arts, showcases local and regional artists and musicians, and stages a variety of events. During the popular First Friday Art Walk, when galleries stay open 6–9pm, visitors can meet local artists producing fine art and crafts in glass, wood, cloth, and other media. Heritage Square is a good place to meet. Live music concerts are offered every Thursday in summer, and almost nightly in the nearby historic Orpheum Theater.

March's Arizona Archeology and Heritage Awareness Month and September's Festival of Science bring archeology enthusiasts and science lovers of all ages to dig at Elden Pueblo; view Mars, Jupiter, and other planets at Lowell Observatory; and attend talks and lectures at the Museum of Northern Arizona, Northern Arizona University, and the United States Geological Survey. In summer, a Labor Day county fair and horse races and many different types of arts and crafts festivals are held at the huge Fort Tuthill County Park, south of town, while the Zuni, Hopi, and Navajo juried shows at the Museum of Northern Arizona attract international connoisseurs and collectors of Indian arts and crafts.

art as common as millionaire mansions and four-wheel-drive tours to UFO and power-vortex meditation sites. More down to earth, Sedona is where the Cowboy Artists of America was founded, and the arts are still vital here, with many world-class artists and musicians resident or visiting.

There's no denying the area's great beauty and pleasant climate, though, and no visitor to northern Arizona should miss the breathtaking scenic drive down Oak Creek Canyon on US 89A, which drops from 7,000ft (2,100 meters) to 5,000ft (1,500 meters) in a series of dramatic, shady switchbacks backed by sheer cliff walls. National forest, redrock vistas, and recreational and historic sites can be found on either side of the road. You will need to purchase a Sedona Red Rock Pass at one of the Forest Service visitor centers or onsite kiosks if you want to park and hike. This is strictly enforced.

Continue southwest of Sedona for 17 miles (27km) to **Cottonwood**, a little town that is starting to attract residents who work in Sedona but can't afford the rent, as well as river runners and tourists. Its historic downtown is gradually gentrifying and is sprouting several popular local farm-to-table restaurants and wineries such as Arizona Stronghold, Merkin Vineyards and Caduceus Cellars (owned by Tool frontman and wine enthusiast Maynard James Keenan), and Pillsbury Vineyard, who grow grapes in the Verde Valley and Willcox area and produce award-winning Arizona wines. Old Town Cottonwood has several excellent tasting rooms/restaurants. For more information, call 928-340-2740 or visit www.oldtown.org/wineries.

Nearby is **Tuzigoot National Monument** ㉘ (tel: 928-634-5564; www.nps.gov/tuzi; daily 8am–5pm; charge), a large pueblo in a clearly defensive setting above the Verde River and built around the same time as Montezuma Castle. More Sinagua ruins can be seen in the valley of Sedona to the north, where cliff sites such as **Palatki** and **Hananki** are hidden among the glorious red rock canyons on national forest land surrounding Sedona and Oak Creek.

Hilltop dwellings of the Victorian era can be seen at the old copper-mining town of **Jerome** ㉙, off US 89A, where fading "painted lady" homes clinging to the slopes of Cleopatra Hill high on 7,743ft (2,360-meter) Mingus Mountain have been rescued and fixed up by artists. To learn about copper mining and the wealth it brought Arizona, visit **Jerome State Historic Park** (tel: 928-634-5381; www.azstateparks.com/parks/jero; daily 8.30am–5pm; charge), located in the 8,000-sq-ft (750-sq-meter) 1916 home of "Rawhide Jimmy" Douglas above his Little Daisy Mine. It has a model of the mines, an assay office, old photos, mining tools, and mineral displays. It's a great place to find unusual artwork and kick back with views nearly to infinity.

Much more sedate is **Prescott** ㉚, about 75 miles (120km) southwest

Jerome State Historic Park.

Tip

What's billed as "the world's oldest rodeo" takes place in Prescott in early July and the popular Arizona Cowboy Poet's Gathering attracts saddlestruck bards to the town in September.

of Flagstaff, a little town cradled in a forested basin beneath the Bradshaw Mountains, south of Jerome. The historic town of Prescott has a population of just under 50,000, but mushrooming subdivisions have pushed the Prescott metro area population much higher, and the total Yavapai County population, of which metro Prescott is the center, is now over 222,000, the third largest in the state after Phoenix and Tucson!

Prescott (PRESS-cut) became Arizona's first territorial capital in 1864 and remained the state's seat of government until the capital moved to Phoenix. Tree-shaded streets, solid Victorian buildings, a stately courthouse, and several historic hotels grace the town center, which also attracts local cowboys to the saloon bars along Gurley Street on Saturday nights and to the world's oldest rodeo, held each July.

Prescott offers a window on Arizona history through its superb **Sharlot Hall Museum** (415 W Gurley Street; tel: 928-445-3122; www.sharlot.org;

Mon–Sat 10am–4pm, Sun noon–4pm; charge), housed in the 1864 Governor's Mansion and 11 other buildings. It was founded in 1928 by former territorial historian Sharlot Hall, a pioneer Prescott rancher, travel writer, and not incidentally, cowboy poet. Six miles north of Prescott, just north of US 89A, **the Phippen Museum of Western Art** (tel: 928-778-1385; www.phippenartmuseum.org; Tue–Sat 10am–4pm, Sun 1–4pm; charge) honors Western artist George Phippen, founder of the Cowboy Artists of America. The museum has a lovely selection of paintings, sketches, and bronzes.

Central Arizona's most spellbinding drive begins east of Camp Verde, along the 200-mile (320km) -long **Mogollon Rim**, the great volcanic escarpment that towers over the Verde Valley. Take SR 260 east then pick up Forest Road 300, a 45-mile (70km) -long gravel road that twists and turns along the limestone cliff edge and offers lakes, picnic areas, trailheads, and campgrounds.

At the intersection with US 87 (the main highway between Interstate 40

The wide open road along Route 66, near Winslow.

to the north and the Mogollon Rim and points south), drop down through the quaint little western backwaters of **Strawberry** and **Pine** and continue to the busy little town of **Payson** ㉛, at an elevation of 5,000ft (1,500 meters). Payson is known for its guest ranches, rodeo, and long association with Zane Grey, who built a cabin nearby and set many of his novels in this rugged Tonto country. The charming **Rim Country Museum** (tel: 928-474 3483; https://rimcountrymuseum.org; Mon, Wed–Sat 10am–4pm, Sun 1–4pm; charge) has a replica of Zane Grey Lodge, the author's hunting cabin in Payson, which burned to the ground in the 1990 Dude Fire. The museum, housed in a 1907 forest ranger's house, has a marvelous display of Grey memorabilia that survived the fire, including the author's tooled saddlebags, first editions of several of his books and an embroidered waistcoat, as well as exhibits on the area's forests and Indians.

EAST OF FLAGSTAFF

In the 13th century, cultural pressures and a long drought led the Sinagua to move to **Walnut Canyon National Monument** ㉜ (tel: 928-526-3367; www.nps.gov/waca; daily 8am–5pm; charge), a few miles east of Flagstaff off Interstate 40. The people once living here built snug cliff homes in sheltered alcoves above a stream, farmed mesa-top fields, and constructed what appear to be forts, perhaps as a defense against interlopers.

    Meteor Crater ㉝ (tel: 928-289-2362; www.meteorcrater.com; daily 7am–7pm summer, 8am–5pm off-season; charge), 37 miles (60km) east of Flagstaff, was formed approximately 50,000 years ago by an iron meteor 100ft (30 meters) in diameter and weighing 60,000 tons. Hitting the earth at 45,000mph (72,000kph), it left a crater 4,000ft wide (1,200 meters) and 570ft (173 meters) deep. Nearly 85 percent of the meteor melted on impact. The remainder was spread far and wide as grain-size particles now called Canyon Diablo meteorites.

    Another 25 miles (40km) beyod Meteor Crater is the railroad town of **Winslow** ㉞, once a bustling Indian Country destination accessed by rail, plane, and Route 66. Beside the tracks stands **La Posada** (303 E Second Street; tel: 928-289-4366; www.laposada.org), a grand hotel that was the last of the Harvey Houses designed by architect Mary Jane Colter in 1930. The Mission-style structure has been restored by hands-on owners and artists, and it is worth stopping in Winslow just to tour the public spaces, galleries, and grounds (or arrive by train), as well as dine in the award-winning Turquoise Room restaurant; a night here is delightful.

    La Posada is the linchpin of a visionary arts scene that is revivifying this western town. Artists like California's Ed Ruscha are moving here, taking over empty buildings for studios, opening galleries, and banding together to promote the arts. A new **Route 66 Art**

La Posada is worth stopping by, even if you're not staying there.

Museum is planned for the 1930 former Fred Harvey train station waiting room adjoining La Posada. It will also function as the official visitor center for tours of light artist James Turrell's nearby **Roden Crater** landscape art installation. For more information, visit http://winslowartstrust.org.

A few miles north of town is **Homolovi State Park** ㉟ (tel: 928-289-4106; www.azstateparks.com/horu; charge). Located atop high mounds overlooking the Painted Desert are 14th-century pueblos. Certain Hopi clans claim Homolovi as the home of their ancestors, the Hisatsinom, who made this their last stop before arriving at their present homes on the mesas about 60 miles (100km) to the north. Homolovi sites I and II are accessible to visitors. Hiking trails, a campground, picnic areas and a chance to watch archeologists at work are features of the park.

Scenic drives and outdoor activities abound in the densely forested White Mountains, but since more than 1.6 million acres (650,000 hectares) of the area belong to the White Mountain

aApache Tribe, you'll need to get permits (tel: 520-338-4346; www.wmat.nsn. us) for fishing, hunting, and camping when on reservation land. For solitude, head to **Greer** or **Alpine**, where travelers can rent a log cabin for a romantic weekend getaway or walk for miles in the forest.

Head back through the primarily Mormon communities of **Show Low** and **Snowflake** and turn east on US 180 to access the southern section of **Petrified Forest National Park** ㊱ (tel: 928-524-6228; www.nps.gov/pefo; daily mid-May–early Aug 7am–7.30pm, early Mar–mid-May and early Aug–early Sept 7am–7pm, early Sept–late Oct 7am–6pm, Nov–early Mar 8am–5pm; charge). Some 200 million years ago, this was the province of dinosaurs wandering amid equatorial swamps populated by giant cycads and other large flora and fauna. Trees falling into the swamp were quickly entombed by mud mixed with thick ash from highly active volcanoes in the region. Cut off from oxygen, the trees, woody cells were replaced by crystalline structures of many hues – today's petrified wood – which were then buried by encroaching streams, rivers, and seas over millions of years. Later, Pueblo people living along the Rio Puerco found the "wood" eroding out of the crumbly Chinle Formation and used it to build structures like Agate House.

NORTH OF FLAGSTAFF

The geological, natural, and cultural history of the Colorado Plateau is beautifully presented through permanent and revolving exhibits at the outstanding **Museum of Northern Arizona** ㊲ (3101 N Fort Valley Road; tel: 928-774-5213; www.musnaz; Mon–Sat 10am–5pm, Sun noon–5pm, Memorial Day–Labor Day Thu until 8pm for concerts; charge), a few miles up US 180. Even if you're just driving through town en route to the Grand Canyon, try to stop at this respected research

A Hopi Kiva mural and ladder at the Museum of Northern Arizona.

and educational institution standing amid the ponderosas beside the Rio de Flag. It was founded by Harold Colton, a wealthy intellectual from the eastern US who fell in love with the area's rich archeology in the 1920s and stayed. Colton's wife, Mary, was drawn to the arts and crafts of the surrounding Indian reservations – principally the Navajo and Hopi to the northeast – and encouraged artisans to improve the quality of their offerings through juried shows at the museum. This tradition continues, with annual summer shows that include high-quality rugs, jewelry, pottery, sculpture, and other crafts by the Navajo, Hopi, Zuni, Paiute, and other regional tribes, with authenticated items for sale in the museum store.

Two places with strong Sinagua connections are **Sunset Crater Volcano National Monument** ❸❽ (tel: 928-526-0502; www.nps.gov/sucr; daily sunrise–sunset; charge), 12 miles (19km) northeast of Flagstaff on US 89, and **Wupatki National Monument** ❸❾ (tel: 928-679-2365; www.nps.gov/wupa; daily 9am–5pm; charge), a bit farther on US 89, at 22 miles (35km) northwest of Flagstaff.

Sunset Crater Volcano, a 1,000ft (300-meter) -high cinder cone named by explorer John Wesley Powell, is part of the extensive San Francisco Volcanic Field, which includes the San Francisco Mountains and Kachina Peaks Wilderness. Eruptions in this active volcanic field formed the cone starting in 1065 and ending in the 1200s, witnessed by Sinagua farmers who fled but later returned to soil made fertile by the volcanic ash.

A loop drive passes huge lava flows that still look remarkably fresh and continues to Wupatki National Monument, with views to the Painted Desert and the Hopi mesas in the east, and the San Francisco Mountains to the west. The monument preserves a number of major pueblos, with the largest, Wupatki, showing strong signs of having been the northernmost great house on a vast trading route that took in Chaco Canyon to the east and Mesoamerica to the south.

⊙ Fact

Sunset Crater Volcano is one of 600 cinder cones that are part of the young, active San Francisco volcanic field on the grassy plain surrounding Flagstaff.

Wupatki National Monument.

LAS VEGAS

Leave any ambivalence at home. This town demands a response to its completely over-the-top extravagance and assault on the mind and pocketbook. Still, it can be seductive and fun.

Reputedly Lady Luck's favorite piece of real estate, **Las Vegas** is a neon valley of round-the-clock risk-taking and, increasingly, endless theme park extravagance intended to make the town primarily a family, not a gambler's, destination. The ultimate urban extrovert, Las Vegas serves little purpose except to entertain and vacuum in immense amounts of cash, enough to fund most of the State of Nevada's operating budget from gambling taxes alone. At one time, the casino-hotels came with motherload names like the Nugget and Frontier. Then more extravagant places took on names suggesting venues, like Circus Circus. Then came the ancient icons like Luxor. But even that wasn't enough for Las Vegas, and more recent hotels reflect entire cities in both name and contrived ambience, like New York and Venice.

Las Vegas is improbably centered in a desert valley ringed by treeless mountains. The sky seems endless, especially to big-city eyes. Gaming and glitter in the middle of nowhere creates a fantasyland atmosphere.

ROOTS OF LAS VEGAS

The earliest white people in the area were Anglo traders traveling from Santa Fe to California on the Old Spanish Trail. They found Las Vegas to be an oasis of refreshing springs and grassy fields, a discovery reflected in the Spanish meaning of *Las Vegas*: "The Meadows." Although explorers like Jedediah Smith and Captain John C. Fremont noted this oasis in their travels, the area remained largely uninhabited until 1855, when Mormon leader Brigham Young sent a band of 30 Mormon men from Utah to Las Vegas to mine for lead in the mountains and, of course, to convert the Indians.

They did not stay long, discouraged by their lack of success in converting the Indians and in smelting the ore

Main Attractions
Las Vegas Strip
Neon Museum
Stratosphere Las Vegas
Downtown/Fremont Street
Mob Museum
Lake Havasu City
Hoover Dam
Lake Mead National
  Recreation Area
Red Rock National
  Conservation Area

Maps on pages 282, 330

Gambling at the JW Marriott Resort.

they found here. They could not have known it then, but the unsatisfactory lead was, in fact, silver. When the fabled Comstock Lode, a rich vein of gold and silver, was discovered in 1849, Nevada came into its own.

Towns sprang up all around. Nevada became a territory in 1861 and was rushed into statehood in 1864 – the Union needed the wealth of the Comstock Lode to win the Civil War. In time, the area around the abandoned Mormon settlement became the property of a succession of ranchers, who provided a way station for California bound travelers. One of these ranchers, Helen Stewart, remained a rancher – and a lone woman with several children – after her husband was mysteriously shot and killed. She ran the 1,800-acre (730-hectare) ranch, cooked meals for travelers, and offered lodging for boarders until the coming of the railroad.

In 1902, Stewart sold her property to the forerunner of the Union Pacific Railroad, which had come to link the West with the East – Las Vegas was to be a division point depot. The town was born on May 15, 1905, when the railroad auctioned off some 1,200 lots to high-bidding speculators. In two days, all the lots were sold and a boomtown of tents and shacks soon appeared on the scene.

Las Vegas stayed a small and sleepy railroad town until the 1930s, when the immense Boulder (Hoover) Dam project on the Colorado River brought in workers from all over the country. In 1931, gambling was legalized in Nevada to funnel revenue into the state. Liberal marriage and divorce laws were also enacted in 1931 and Las Vegas became an easy option for a quick Nevada divorce. In some counties, prostitution was, and still is, legalized.

THE LAS VEGAS STRIP

Las Vegas is an easy town to navigate. There's not a lot to it, actually: casinos and hotels along a few main corridors, and residential areas dissolving into the desert. Most of the gambling activity is concentrated in two main areas: the famed **Las Vegas Strip Ⓐ** and the downtown area on Fremont Street, about 3 miles (5km) north of the Strip

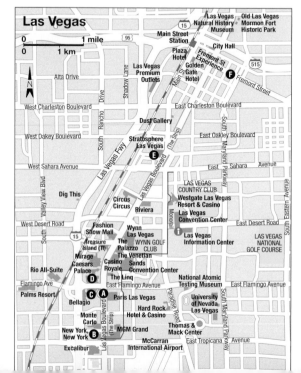

area. The Strip (properly known as Las Vegas Boulevard South) begins at Sahara Avenue and runs south as far as the airport. Most of the newer mega-hotels are in this southern part of the Strip. The Strip is a Hollywood back lot made reality. Where else would you find a Roman palace and a circus-topped casino – both of the "old school" of Vegas casino-hotel and the "new school" of Venetian canals and Eiffel Tower sharing the same stretch of highway?

In fact, most of the newer Strip hotels are self-contained attractions, increasingly shifting the emphasis from gambling to shopping and amusement. And in the past few years, there's been a determined effort to change, or at least broaden, the city's appeal. Now that gambling is legal in Atlantic City and in many other states, including Indian reservations, the state of Nevada has been forced to rethink its prime attraction and main source of revenue. In the background are the high rollers, in the foreground are families who spend, spend, spend.

The newer buildings are themselves the stars of the show. At **New York, New York** ❸ (tel: 702-740-6969; www.newyorknewyork.com), visitors can stroll in "Central Park," walk along the "Brooklyn Bridge," or ride a Coney Island-style rollercoaster looping around the hotel towers. The 30-story pyramid at the glass-paneled **Luxor** has an atrium big enough to hold nine Boeing 747s. The 3,000-room **Bellagio** ❸ (tel: 888-987-7111; www.bellagio.com), opened in 1998 at a cost of $1.6 billion, is geared for the upscale consumer with stores that include Prada, Armani, and Tiffany & Co. and comes complete with an 8-acre (3-hectare) artificial lake. In 1999, the equally large-scale **Venetian** opened nearby at a cost of $1.5 billion, also with upscale stores like Movado and Davidoff – accessible by gondola or on foot. Gilded ceilings with Renaissance-style frescoes hover over the hotel's interior.

At night, the magnificent and more traditional **Caesars Palace** ❸ (tel: 866-227-5938; www.caesars.com/caesars-palace) is theatrically bathed in

The bright lights of the Strip, with Caesars Palace and Paris Las Vegas Hotel in the foreground.

Slots at Paris Las Vegas.

blue-green light, with an arcaded auto-matic "people mover" and a geodesic-domed Omnimax Theater. **Treasure Island** (tel: 702-894-7111; www.treasure island.com) stages a sea battle in its own lagoon. The megalithic **MGM Grand** (tel: 877-860-0880; www.mgmgrand.com) has a casino bigger than a football field, as well as three adjoining non-gaming, non-smoking towers for guests who want a calmer experience.

Las Vegas is constantly reinventing itself. A number of venerable casinos have now, quite literally, bitten the dust (watching old casinos being blown up to make new ones is a popular local spectator sport. Famed as much for their distinctive neon signs as their somewhat louche history, the casinos live on in the memory of those who came here back in the day.

Fortunately, many of the neon signs have been rescued by enthusiasts and are now on display in the not-to-be-missed **Neon Museum** (770 N Las Vegas Boulevard; tel: 702-387-6366; www.neonmuseum.org; daily guided tours 8.30am–10pm; charge) on the

Tourists at the Neon Museum.

north end of the Strip. This nonprofit museum dedicated to the Strip's most iconic art form opened in 2012. Its nearly 2-acre (0.8-hectare) campus features the Boneyard, an outdoor space where more than 200 neon signs are on show, including signs from some of Las Vegas's most famous casinos – Caesars Palace, Binion's Horseshoe, the Golden Nugget, and the Stardust.

The museum visitor center is located in the lobby of the 1961 **La Concha Motel**, a striking example of Mid-Century Modern design, or Googie, characterized by Atomic and Space-Age shapes and motifs and still to be found in Sixties-era coffee shops, motels, and other buildings through-out the West. The Boneyard may be visited by guided tour only, but the Museum includes nine restored signs that can be viewed as public art and visited on a self-guided tour 24 hours a day, seven days a week. The gallery includes the Lucky Cuss Motel, the Bow & Arrow Motel, The Silver Slipper, Society Cleaners, Binion's Horseshoe, the Normandie Motel, the Hacienda horse and rider, the Landmark, and 5th Street Liquors.

On October 1 2017, tragedy hit the Strip when gunman Stephen Paddock shot dead 58 people and injured a further 546 from his 32nd floor hotel room overlooking the open-air Route 91 Harvest music festival, where the victims were enjoying the final per-formance of the event. It is the dead-liest mass shooting by an individual in American history and to date, the motive remains unknown.

DOWNTOWN AND FREMONT STREET

Just a mile north of the Strip – and where Downtown is said officially to begin – is **Stratosphere Las Vegas** Ⓔ (tel: 702-380-7777; www.stratosphere hotel.com; charge). Soaring to 1,149ft (350 meters), this casino-hotel and tower is the tallest freestanding observation tower in the United States. In 30 seconds, elevators whisk visitors to a revolving restaurant, observation decks, and thrilling rides. Those with romantic inclinations and little fear of heights can get married near the top.

Unlike the Strip, which had miles of empty desert on which to build sprawling resort hotels, the downtown gambling area was always limited to just a few blocks of **Fremont Street**  in the commercial center. The refurbishment of a pedestrian-only mall called the **Fremont Street Experience** gave the area a new lease on life. Years ago, the downtown area was known to one and all as Glitter Gulch. The merchants ran a contest to find a more sophisticated name for the district and "Casino Center" was the winner. Nonetheless, the old names are still in everyday use – Downtown, Glitter Gulch, or simply Fremont Street. Visitors stroll a five-block, casino-lined mall, attracting huge crowds every hour to enjoy a computer-generated high-tech sound-and-light show projected onto a screen.

In recent years, much of the downtown has been bought up by the young Taiwanese CEO of the popular online shoe retailer Zappos, Tony Hsieh, who has relocated his internet business to Las Vegas and created a less hierachical form of doing business that is dubbed "holocracy." He has invested $350 million of his own money in real estate, redevelopment, small businesses, and venture capital funds. A former casino became a hangout for Zappos employees, stocked with board games instead of slot machines. A vacant lot is now a trailer park crammed with shiny silver Airstreams that are rented out to visiting computer coders. Hsieh himself moved into one trailer and keeps a pet alpaca there. He calls the community "Llamalopolis."

It is a strange vision – sort of the anti Las Vegas – but absolutely fascinating, and very 21st century in its goals. To find out more about the unusual company vision, you can make a reservation to tour the campus on a **Zappo's Tour Experience** (tel: 877-513-7424; www.zappos.com/tours; reserved guided

Crowds pack the Fremont Street Experience.

⊘ WATER ATTRACTIONS

In an arid desert, Las Vegas's fast growth and the importance to tourism of water attractions such as huge, elaborate pools, and the Bellagio's fountains have created a water crisis. The Vegas Springs Preserve (333 S Valley View Boulevard; tel: 702-822-7700 www.springspreserve.org; daily 9am–5pm, individual attractions vary) is a multimillion-dollar effort to educate the public about water conservation with interactive exhibits, demonstration gardens, and even a simulated flash flood. It also features a re-creation of the original springs that brought explorers and ranchers to the valley, as well as an arboretum of plants from the various North American deserts and 2 miles (3km) of hiking trails through the natural Mojave landscape.

⊙ Tip

The sheer number of shows and concerts in Las Vegas is staggering. There's something here for everyone, from the Folies Bergère to lounge acts, the antics of the Blue Men, or concerts by headliners such as Elton John and Celine Dion. Tickets usually go on sale three months in advance for the most popular shows. For the best seats, call the day these go on sale – they sell out very fast – and expect to pay $150–$220 per person.

tours; charge). Interesting immersive 2.5-hour custom guided tours of the revitalized downtown Las Vegas are also offered by advance reservation. Accompanied by the company's own art and urban historian, you'll glimpse a hidden Las Vegas, then and now.

As a rule, it costs less to gamble downtown than on the Strip. Stakes are lower, and it is still possible to find inexpensive craps tables. Some people think downtown dealers are friendlier and more tolerant, too. Downtown casinos are said to have "loose" slots – slot machines that have been adjusted to pay out up to 90 percent of the money deposited in them. The volume of slot enthusiasts is so high that frequent payoffs are good promotions for the casinos.

AN OFFER YOU CAN'T REFUSE

Las Vegas casinos were initially family-run enterprises associated, of course, with Mob activity after World War II, when feared but charismatic gangster Bugsy Siegel and fellow mobster Meyer Lansky laundered money

Entering Red Rock Canyon.

through Mormon banks in Las Vegas and built the Flamingo Hotel in 1946. The Mormon-Teamster-mobster relationship continued through the Forties, allowing the most famous of the Vegas casinos to be built: the Sahara, the Sands, the New Frontier, Binion's Horseshoe, and many others.

To find out more, wander over to the **Mob Museum** (300 Stewart Avenue; tel: 702-229-2734; www.themobmuseum. org; daily 9am–9pm; charge), located in the handsome 1930s former post office and courthouse in downtown Vegas. Officially named the National Museum of Organized Crime and Law Enforcement, this $42 million history museum was designed by the same creative team responsible for the Rock and Roll Hall of Fame and other museums.

BEYOND VEGAS

Two more north-to-south crossings of northern Arizona are possible along the state's boundaries. In the east, US 491 travels through little-populated high country where forestry is the leading industry. In the west, SR 95 parallels

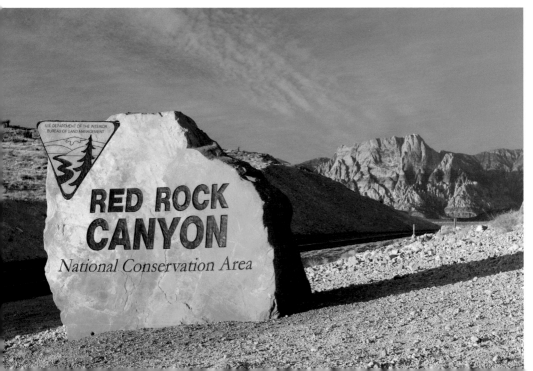

the **Colorado River** from Davis Dam to Parker, then heads straight south to Yuma. "River" no longer seems an honest word for the succession of reservoirs and wide sluices that this stretch of the Colorado has become, lined with resorts and trailer parks, converged upon during the summer by thousands of weekend revelers from Phoenix and Los Angeles.

Its most famous attraction is the 19th-century incarnation of **London Bridge**, purchased by the developer of **Lake Havasu City** ⓫ (www.golakehavasu.com) in 1967 and shipped over stone by stone from the UK, before being reassembled as a tourist attraction on Lake Havasu. That this commercialized, overheated lakefront in the Mojave Desert – a magnet for the rowdy spring break crowd – showcases an authentic piece of Victorian Britain (complete with World War II strafe marks on its stones) may seem absurd, but those who go to laugh at the bridge may be surprised.

Not far from Las Vegas, **Hoover Dam** ⓬ (tel: 702-293 8421; www.usbr.gov/lc/hooverdam; daily 9am–5pm for tours; charge), originally known as Boulder Dam when it was built in the 1930s, was one of the biggest projects of its time. It stands 726ft (221 meters) high, damming the Colorado River into Lake Mead, part of **Lake Mead National Recreation Area** (tel: 702-293-8990; www.nps.gov/lake; daily 24 hours, visitor center daily 9am–4.30pm; charge), popular with Las Vegas residents and visitors for boating. High plateaus and canyons define this desert; the lake itself is the largest – by volume – artificial reservoir in the US: 110 miles (177km) long, with over 500 miles (800km) of shoreline and 500ft (150 meters) deep in places.

Outdoor pursuits are, in fact, abundant in the surrounding Mojave Desert, and when you grow tired of man-made attractions, you'll find numerous natural destinations to enjoy. Southwest of Las Vegas on SR 159 is popular **Red Rock National Conservation Area** (W Charleston Boulevard; tel: 702-513-5350; www.redrockcanyonlv.org/visitor-information; visitor center daily 8am–4.30pm, Scenic Drive Apr–Sept daily 6am–8pm, Mar and Oct daily 6am–7pm, Nov–Feb daily 6am–5pm), under BLM management, which offers incredible redrock scenery and enjoyable hiking amid distinctive rock formations. A little farther west are the Spring Mountains and 11,916ft (3,632-meter) -high **Charleston Peak**, a great place to cool down when the desert gets hot in summer.

Las Vegas also makes a great jumping-off point for the Southwest Grand Circle of national parks, an hour north on Interstate 15 through the Virgin River Gorge and into southern Utah, then on to Zion National Park, Bryce Canyon, Grand Canyon, and other spectacular parks. Information is available at the **St George Interagency Information Center** (345 E Riverside Drive, St George, UT; tel: 435-688-3246; Mon–Fri 7.45am–5pm).

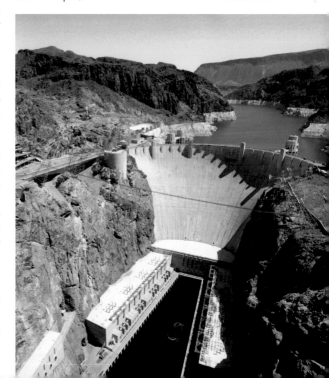

Hoover Dam.

Old Route 66 winds through the desert in Williams, Arizona.

USA SOUTHWEST

TRAVEL TIPS

TRANSPORTATION

GETTING THERE

By air

If driving to the Southwest from elsewhere in the country is impractical because of distance, the next best way to get there is to fly to a nearby city. The major hubs in the Southwest are:

Arizona: Phoenix Sky Harbor International, Tucson International, Flagstaff Airport.

Colorado: Denver International, Colorado Springs Airport.

Nevada: McCarran International (Las Vegas).

New Mexico: Albuquerque International Sunport and Santa Fe Airport.

Texas: El Paso International.

Utah: Salt Lake City International.

Among the domestic and international carriers serving these airports are:

Air Canada: tel: 888-247-2262; www.aircanada.com

American Airlines: tel: 800-433-7300; www.aa.com

British Airways: tel: 800-247-9297; www.britishairways.com

Delta: tel: 800-241-4141; www.delta.com

Frontier Airlines: tel: 800-432-1359; www.flyfrontier.com

JetBlue: tel: 800-538-2583; www.jetblue.com

Norwegian Airlines: tel: 800-357-4159; www.norwegian.com

United Airlines: tel: 800-864-8331; www.united.com

Virgin America: tel: 877-359-8474; www.virginamerica.com

WestJet: tel: 888-937-8538; www.westjet.com.

The following commuter airlines offer service within the region:

Allegiant Airlines: tel: 702-505-8888; www.allegiantair.com

Great Lakes: 800-554-5111; www.greatlakesav.com

Scenic: tel: 866-634-6801; www.scenic.com

Southwest: tel: 800-435-9792; www.southwest.com

Mesa Airlines: tel: 800-685-4000; www.mesa-air.com

Vision Airlines: tel: 800-256-8767; www.visionairlines.com.

Airport taxes

Domestic flights include up to 20 percent in additional taxes to cover US Excise Tax (7.5 percent), security costs, and airport and facility fees. Airlines include this in the final total for the plane fare.

Important Note: Expect delays departing US airports due to Homeland Security anti-terrorism rules. These are apt to change, so check before flying (www.dhs.gov). See also Visas and Passports, page 352.

Passengers may take one resealable 1-quart (1 liter) size clear plastic bag on board, which can contain liquids or gels in containers of 3 fluid ounces (100ml) or less. The contents of the plastic bag must fit comfortably and be completely closed/sealed and subjected to X-ray inspection separate from carry-on bag. Leave any gifts unwrapped, and take laptops out of bags for inspection by Transportation Security Administration (TSA; www.tsa.gov/travelers) personnel.

Note that footwear must be removed and scanned by X-ray machines. TSA Pre-certification programs such as TSA Precheck (www.tsa.gov/precheck) for domestic travel and Global Entry for international travel allow you to go through security faster and typically without removing clothing or electronics.

By train

Amtrak offers train service to more than 500 destinations across the US. The trains are comfortable, with lounges, restaurants, snack bars and, in some cases, movies and live entertainment. Most routes offer sleeper cars with private cabins in addition to regular seating. Delays can happen on long-distance trains, so build time into your schedule.

Amtrak's **Southwest Chief** runs from Chicago to Los Angeles. Stops include Kansas City, Missouri; Topeka, Kansas; Trinidad, Colorado; Raton, Lamy (Santa Fe), Albuquerque, and Gallup, New Mexico; Winslow, Flagstaff (bus service to Grand Canyon) and Kingman, Arizona.

The **Sunset Limited** runs from New Orleans, Louisiana to Los Angeles. Stops include San Antonio and El Paso, Texas; Deming and Lordsburg, New Mexico; Benson, Tucson, Phoenix, and Yuma, Arizona; and Los Angeles, California.

The **California Zephyr** runs from Chicago to San Francisco. Stops include Denver, Granby (for Rocky Mountain National Park), Glenwood Springs, and Grand Junction, Colorado; Green River, Utah (for Arches and Canyonlands and other Southern Utah national parks) and Salt Lake City (change for Las Vegas, Nevada); and San Francisco, California.

Ask about two- or three-stopover discounts, seniors, and children's discounts, and Amtrak's package tours. A USA Railpass is good for 15 days for eight travel segments, 30 days for 12 travel segments, or 45 days for 18 travel segments on the Amtrak system. **Amtrak**, tel: 800-USA-RAIL (872-7245) or log on to www.amtrak.com to purchase passes, train schedules, and other information. Note: Passholders must still make reservations for travel. Reserve well ahead, as seats for USA Railpass passengers are limited on each train.

In New Mexico, the **New Mexico Rail Runner Express** commuter train offers inexpensive regular daily service between Albuquerque's South Valley and downtown Santa Fe's historic train depot. Note: A shuttle bus runs between Albuquerque

International Sunport and the Rail Runner train station. For a schedule and more information, call 866-795-7245 or visit www.nmrailrunner.com.

By bus

One of the least expensive ways to travel in America is by Dallas-based **Greyhound Lines**, tel: 214-849-8966; www.greyhound.com, which offers interstate service to most major cities. Greyhound does not service remote areas, so you will either have to look into local shuttle bus service to your destination (available to national parks such as Grand Canyon), or rent a car.

Grand Canyon, Bryce Canyon, and Zion national parks all have free shuttle buses from adjoining gateway towns to visitor centers and destinations within the parks, which means you can park and ride. Many cities and towns in the Southwest also now offer free trolleys and streetcars and shuttle pickups in historic downtown areas, as well as inexpensive light rail service to more far-flung destinations. See individual destination chapters for more details.

Airport shuttles typically run between the airport and city destinations and are your best bet to get

⊘ Maps and information

Your greatest asset as a driver is a detailed map. They can be obtained from tourism offices, gas stations, supermarkets, and convenience stores. If you're traveling across the Indian reservations of the Four Corners, purchase the top-rated *Indian Country* road map from AAA, which is so detailed it is used by local residents.

Maps of national parks, forests, and other natural areas are offered as part of your entrance fee to the site. If you plan on hiking, purchase a good topographical map, such as those produced for various parks and other locations by Trails Illustrated (www.natgeomaps.com/trailsillustrated), now a division of National Geographic. They are available in most park bookstores and other outlets, along with detailed US Geological Survey government topographical maps. (www.store.usgs.gov).

to town on arrival and before picking up a rental car for touring. Costs are typically around $25 one way. It's usually not necessary to book shuttles from the airport ahead of time; if you are returning to the airport from a hotel, you will need to book ahead and be picked up at your hotel or a specific location in town.

By taxi

Taxi service is available at major airports and bus and train stations in most Southwest cities to hotels and other tourist destinations. Beyond major metro areas you may find it hard to find a cab; Santa Fe's only cab company went out of business in 2017, for example, a result of the popularity of ride-booking companies like Uber and Lyft, accessible via smartphone app.

The routes in this book are designed to be driven, so your best bet is to rent a car at the airport counter or take a shuttle to an outside location to pick one up, and then get on the road.

GETTING AROUND

On foot

Wherever possible, park your car and get outside and see the sights, either on foot or employing a combination of walking and shuttle bus, tram, or light rail, usually low cost or free. Historic downtown areas of Southwest cities such as Tucson, Bisbee, Santa Fe, Taos, Flagstaff, Sedona, Las Vegas, Moab, St George, and Albuquerque are compact enough to be walkable, and most produce free historic walking tour booklets that are available at visitor centers and at hotels. Visitors to city, state, or national parks will find numerous hiking trails geared toward hikers of differing abilities, including accessible trails for those with disabilities.

By bicycle

Mountain and road biking are very popular throughout the Southwest, particularly among the lovely red rocks of Sedona, Arizona, and Moab, Utah, the mountain biking capital of the world. Beyond the highways, mountain biking is permitted on most public lands, including forest trails,

but only on paved roads in national parks and not on park or wilderness trails. The main travel routes covered in this guide can be biked, if you are up for the challenge of long distances, changing elevations, and rough road surfaces, extreme weather conditions, few services, remote locations, and unexpected dangers, from cattle being rounded up on forest backroads in the Four Corners in spring and fall to rattlesnakes on the road in summer to icy roads in winter throughout the high desert. Most bicyclists average little more than 10–15mph (16–24kph), so your best bet is to cover a short scenic segment of any of the routes in this book, if you choose the bicycle option, and stick to areas with clustered attractions, scenery, and lodging/food services.

By motorcycle

For those with *Easy Rider* dreams, touring by motorcycle may be an inspiring option. Harley-Davidson and other major motorcycle vendors also offer rentals in some locations in the US.

If you do decide to ride a motorcycle on any of the routes in this book, be conservative; you won't be able to cover as much ground as in a car in a day (around 250 miles/320km) to allow plenty of time for visiting attractions. And inevitably, you'll be riding on scenic highways and backroads off the interstate, so factor that in, too (Route 66 travel is particularly popular in the Southwest, but there are so many scenic possibilities). Vital clothing includes a helmet, stiff boots, and, in cool weather, leather chaps to cut down on road abrasion, should you take a spill. There are several organizations for enthusiasts of particular motorcycle makes, from Harley-Davidson to Triumph to BMW. Several homegrown websites offer ideas on US motorcycle traveling.

By car

Driving is by far the most flexible and convenient way to travel in the Southwest, especially for outside the major cities. Major roads are well-maintained, although backcountry roads may be unpaved. If you plan on driving into remote areas or in heavy snow, mud, or severe weather, it's a good idea to use a four-wheel-drive vehicle with high clearance.

Safety tips for motorists

When you arrive, ask for advice from the car rental agent about the best route from the airport to your hotel. (Better still, arrange to pick up your rental car from an agency near your hotel on the morning after you arrive, rather than tackle unfamiliar routes when very tired.)

Plan your route before you begin a journey, to avoid getting lost. Don't take shortcuts in urban areas. If you get lost, drive to a well-lit and preferably busy area before stopping to look at a map. Ignore any pedestrian or motorist who tries to stop you, for example by indicating some supposed fault on your vehicle or even by ramming your car from behind.

Contact the police (tel: 911) and your rental car agency if an accident occurs. Always keep your car doors locked, windows closed, and valuables out of sight while driving.

Although roads are maintained, even in remote areas, it is advisable to listen to local radio stations and to check with local tourism offices for the latest information about weather and road conditions, especially in winter or if planning to leave paved roads. Departments of transportation in each state offer the 511 Traveler Information Service, allowing you to get information about closures, construction, delays, public transit, weather, and more by dialing 511.

Driving in remote areas

If you plan on driving in uninhabited areas, you will need to be self-sufficient. Carry a spare tire, nutritious snacks, first aid kit, and some kind of signaling device, such as a mirror, CD, or flares. Most importantly, be sure that you have plenty of water – carry and drink at least a gallon (4 liters) of water per person per day, if you are outdoors, and have more in the car. Three-gallon bottles of water with tap dispensers are available in grocery stores and are a good idea to keep in the back when you are traveling in the desert. Carry a cell phone, if only for emergencies; some areas, particularly those in canyons, will be out of range, but it's often possible to get service in wild areas. Gas stations can be few and far between. Not every town will have one, and many close early. It's always better to have more fuel than you think you'll need, and to carry a gallon gas can with extra.

A word of caution: If your car breaks down on a back road, do not strike out on foot. A car is easier to spot than a person and provides shelter. If you don't have a cell phone or your phone doesn't work, sit tight and wait to be found. Keep cool, do not exert yourself, ration water prudently, and be sure to eat something to avoid hyponatremia (electrolyte imbalance from water washing out salt and other minerals in the body). One tip: dissolve a little raw sea salt in your water to avoid any problems, particularly during the hottest times of year. It's surprisingly effective at maintaining balance in the body.

Car rental

Most rental agencies require you to be 21 years old or over (25 at some locations) and hold a valid driver's license and a major credit card. Most take debit cards these days, and some will take cash in lieu of a credit card, but this might require a cost as high as $500. Non-English speaking travelers must produce an international driver's license from their own country.

You will find rental car companies in most cities and airports. Rental vehicles range from economy cars to luxury convertibles, vans, and 4WD vehicles. Rates are generally quite low and usually include unlimited mileage. But you should still shop around, preferably online, for the best rates. Local rental firms outside the airport are often less expensive because they don't charge high airport fees.

It's cheaper to arrange car rental in advance. Look out for package deals that include a car: rental rates can be reduced by up to 50 percent if you buy a "fly-drive" deal.

Go over the insurance coverage provisions carefully with the agent before signing the rental agreement. Loss Damage Waiver, or Collision Damage Waiver, can be expensive, but is essential if your credit card or personal car insurance does not already include it. Without it, you'll be liable for any damage done to your vehicle in the event of an accident. You are advised to pay for supplementary Liability Insurance on top of standard third-party insurance. Insurance and tax charges can add a lot to an otherwise inexpensive rental – assume about $25–35 per day.

Major rental car companies are:
Alamo: tel: 855-533-1196; www.alamo.com
Avis: tel: 800-352-7900; www.avis.com
Budget: tel: 800-404-8033; www.budget.com
Dollar: tel: 800-800-4000; www.dollar.com
Enterprise: tel: 800-264-6350; www.enterprise.com
Hertz: tel: 800-654-4173; www.hertz.com
National: tel: 800-468-3334; www.nationalcar.com
Thrifty: tel: 888-400-8877; www.thrifty.com

RV rental

No special license is necessary to operate a recreational vehicle – RV for short (or motor home), but they aren't cheap. When you add up the cost of rental fees, insurance, gas, and campground fees, renting a car and staying in motels or camping may be less expensive. Cruise America (tel: 800-671-8042; www.cruiseamerica.com) has RVs for rent in a variety of sizes (from 19–30ft/6–9 meters). For additional information, call the Recreational Vehicle Industry Association (tel: 888-467-8464; www.rvia.org).

Distances and driving times

The routes in this book cover a lot of miles through the Four Corners states and are designed to take in the main sights, with some side trips to places off the beaten track. How long you take to drive the different routes is entirely up to you – preferably the slower the better. Driving no more than 200 miles (320km)/day or 3–4 hours allows you to get the driving done in the morning, when it's cooler and there is more contrast in the landscape for taking photographs, leaving the afternoon for sightseeing or resting. Two to three nights in each major destination, with single nights in between, is the suggested minimum, particularly if you are a late riser (not recommended if you are driving across the desert in summer, when temperatures soar to 100°F). It will allow you to arrive later in the day, check into lodging, get oriented, and enjoy a stroll, have dinner, and get a good night's sleep to be ready for a full day at your destination the next day.

Slowing down and getting a feel for the local rhythms is an essential component of travel in the culturally rich Southwest. On cross-country routes out West, it's easy to pile up some long travel days on empty highways to reach the next destination. Do a bit of planning and try to find a way of breaking up the journey to avoid burning out and having roads and towns blurring one into the other.

A

Accommodations

The Southwest offers a great variety of lodgings for every budget and inclination, from reliable mid-priced chains, rustic cabins, budget vintage motels, and scenic national park campgrounds and lodges to elegant vacation casitas, unique art-filled boutique hotels in converted downtown buildings, bed-and-breakfast inns, and intimate home stays through AirB&B, to full-service destination dude ranches and resorts, some run by Indian tribes, catering to outdoors and cultural activities, relaxation, and fun. Make reservations well in advance for lodging at popular destinations like the Grand Canyon and Santa Fe, which tend to be busy year-round with events and international visitors. Note that low-elevation cities like Tucson and Phoenix are busiest when temperatures cool down in winter, and offer deals during the low season in summer. Be flexible, and you will find a lot of deals.

Chains offer a clean, comfortable room at a reasonable cost and are a good bet for 1–2 nights – longer and you may prefer more of a character property. Motel prices are in the $50–$150 range, depending on location and additional amenities, such as a pool, exercise room, and restaurant. Some offer one- or two-bedroom suites (some with kitchenettes) suitable for longer stays or families. Note: several former budget chains are now clustered under the umbrella of larger hotel groups, such as Wyndham or Starwood, and prices have gone up somewhat; however, they offer frequent-stay reward programs that can be used for future stays.

Bed-and-breakfasts tend to be more homey and personal than hotels. In many cases, you're a guest at the innkeeper's home. Some are historic homes or inns decorated with antiques, quilts, art, and other period furnishings; others offer simple but comfortable accommodations. Before booking, ask whether rooms have telephones or televisions and whether bathrooms are private. Ask about breakfast, too. The meal is included in the price but may be anything from a few muffins to a multi-course feast. Guests may be served at a common table, a private table, or in their rooms.

Guest, or dude, ranches range from working cattle operations with basic lodging to full-fledged "resorts with horses" that have swimming pools, tennis courts, and other amenities. Most ranches offer horseback riding lessons; guided pack trips; entertainment like rodeos, square dances, and storytellers; and plenty of hearty chuckwagon-style food. Prices for guest ranches are often all-inclusive, known as "American Plan." If traveling with kids, ask about a children's program.

Most campgrounds in national and state parks and forests are now on a central reservation system (essential during peak summer season), with just a few campsites available on a first-come, first-served basis. Both www.recreation.gov and www.reserveamerica.com offer online campsite reservations at public lands managed by 12 federal participating partners, including the USDA Forest Service, Army Corps of Engineers, National Park Service, Bureau of Land Management (BLM), Bureau of Reclamation, Boundary Waters Canoe Area Wilderness, US Fish and Wildlife Service, and National Archives & Records Administration. Fees are charged for developed campsites; free dispersed camping is allowed in national forests. Permits are required for backcountry camping in parks.

There are hundreds of private campgrounds, too, some with swimming pools, RV hookups, showers, and other amenities. The largest network is Kampgrounds of America (KOA; tel: 888-562-0000; www.koa.com).

Admission charges

Entrance fees at most attractions and museums typically range from $5–20/person, with discounts often available for children aged 12 or younger, seniors aged 65 and older, and families of four or more. Check out www.visitarizona.com, www.newmexico.org, www.colorado.com, www.ttia.org (Texas Travel Industry Association), www.utah.com, and www.lasvegas.com, to find regularly updated deals on food, attractions, activities, lodging, and more.

B

Budgeting for your trip

The Southwest is a pretty affordable US destination, especially if you enjoy the outdoors, but as always it depends on what type of experience you are seeking and how much you have to spend. As a rough guide, in peak season in the Arizona low desert (December–April, when the temperatures are cool), good-quality hotels will cost $100–150 a night; for really memorable hotels, resorts, and bed-and-breakfasts, expect to pay in the $200–300 range. In the low season (May–October), resorts in Phoenix and Tucson drastically cut their rates, so if you can tolerate heat in the 100-plus-degree range, you will save.

Major destinations in the high desert of the Four Corners, such as Albuquerque, Santa Fe, Taos, and Flagstaff, are cool mountain escapes in summer and popular ski areas in winter. Typically, summer rates are high and winter rates are low from January to March, however.

At the other end of the spectrum, hostels and basic motel lodging in such chains as Motel 6 can be found for less than $50. The Southwest is known for its attractive national park, national forest, and state park campgrounds in desert, forest, and lakeside environments, and staying in these will help you stretch your dollars as well as offer a wonderful nature experience. Developed tent and RV sites with hookups run $15–50 per night; cabins, if available, $35–75 per night. If you are adventurous and self-sufficient, you may camp for free (dispersed camping) in national forests. Remember to pack it in, pack it out, and leave no trace.

You can probably get away with $40 per day per person for basic meals if you stick to diners, food carts, cafés, markets, and inexpensive world cuisine restaurants and don't drink alcohol. Meals in better restaurants cost a lot more, but if you're determined to visit that famous high-end establishment, one insider trick is to eat lunch there: you'll find many of the items on the dinner menu at much lower prices and still get to say you've eaten at a hip eatery.

At normal gas prices, you can budget around $2.50 per gallon to fuel your rental car; most economy vehicles get approximately 30 miles (48km) per gallon. Light rail, buses, and other public transit in cities like Phoenix and Tucson are just a few dollars per ride, or even free, allowing you to get around for much less.

C

Children

The Grand Canyon can turn us all into wide-eyed youngsters, but it is just one of many sites that appeals to kids. Cowboy towns with staged shootouts, water parks, chuck wagons, powwows, horseback riding, and rafting trips are all sure to please. Reduced admission rates at many museums and attractions (usually for those under 12) make budgeting a little easier. Still, parents might need some time to themselves. Many higher-end hotels and resorts can arrange babysitters. Some even provide the occasional "Parents' Night Out," where children are entertained with group activities while Mom and Dad hit the town.

Climate

The Southwest spans half a dozen climate and life zones, but by and large you will find sunny skies, low humidity, and limited precipitation. Climate varies widely with elevation. Climbing 1,000ft (300 meters) is equivalent to traveling 300 miles (500km) north. In temperature, traveling from the lowest to the highest points of Arizona is like traveling from Mexico to the north of Hudson Bay in Canada.

Arizona

Arizona gets 80 percent of available sunshine annually. Annual rainfall averages 12.5ins (30cm), much of it falling as torrential downpours in summer monsoon season and in winter precipitation. Northern regions average around 73 percent sunshine; southern areas average around 90 percent.

Average temperatures in Phoenix reach well above 100°F (38°C) in summer and fall to 30°F (-1°C) in winter. Phoenix gets about 7ins (18cm) of rain per year. In Flagstaff, 145 miles (230 km) to the north, temperatures range 75–80°F (24–27°C) in summer and fall to around 15°F (-10°C) in winter. Annual precipitation in Flagstaff averages 84ins (210cm), most of it falling in July, August, and December.

At its hottest, the south rim of the Grand Canyon reaches 90°F (32°C) rising to 100°F (38°C) or more at the bottom of the gorge. Flash thunderstorms are common. Generally, the weather is more comfortable in the spring and fall. Always bring a sweater and rain jacket when visiting the Grand Canyon and other high country sites, and dress in layers.

Colorado

Colorado is a popular four-season state for tourism. It spans a wide range of climate and life zones, but generally has sunny skies, low humidity, and limited precipitation. Climate varies widely with elevation.

Colorado enjoys 295 days of sunshine annually. The climate is semi-arid. Yearly precipitation ranges from 16ins (41cm) on the eastern plains and 14ins (36cm) in the Front Range to less than 10ins (25cm) on the Western Slope. Most rain falls in brief, intense thunderstorms during the summer season, when small streams, dry washes, and narrow canyons are prone to flash floods. Violent electrical storms are common on mountain peaks during summer

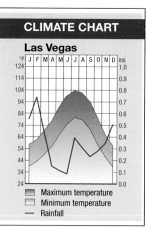

CLIMATE CHART

Phoenix

- Maximum temperature
- Minimum temperature
- — Rainfall

CLIMATE CHART

Las Vegas

- Maximum temperature
- Minimum temperature
- — Rainfall

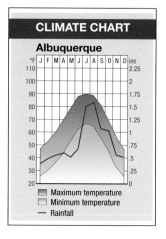

CLIMATE CHART

Albuquerque

- Maximum temperature
- Minimum temperature
- — Rainfall

afternoons. Nights in the mountains can be chilly even in July and August, and winds are often brisk, so bring a sweater or jacket. Snow, hail, and sleet are possible at the highest elevations at any time of year.

The spring thaw usually begins in March, though snow lingers well into July on the highest peaks and passes. Summer weather begins in late June or early July. Fall begins in September, a lovely period of sunny days, chilly nights, and spectacular colors on the Rockies' forested slopes. Winter sets in by late November, though ski areas such as Arapahoe Basin and Loveland sometimes open as early as late October (with the aid of snow-making machines) and close in June.

Average high temperatures in summer reach 88°F (31°C) in Denver (elev. 5,280ft/1,609 meters), 94°F (34°C) in Grand Junction (elev. 4,586ft/1,398 meters), and 80°F (27°C) in Aspen (7,773ft/2,369m). Nights are crisp and pleasant, usually ranging from 45°F (7°C) to 65°F (18°C).

Winter is very chilly but often sunny, with average lows of 16°F (-9°C) in Denver and Grand Junction, and 6°F (-14°C) in Aspen. Annual snowfall in Denver is typically 45–65ins (114–65cm), though warm spells between storms reduce large accumulations. Annual snowfall in excess of 300ins (760cm) is common in the ski areas around Aspen. Winter storms roll into Colorado from the Pacific, lose moisture over the desert Southwest, and then dump piles of the light, dry powder for which the Rocky Mountains are famous.

Nevada

Las Vegas is in the low-elevation Mojave Desert, and from June through September, daytime temperatures rarely register below 100°F (38°C). Spring and fall seasons are short, with temperatures around 75°F (24°C).

Daytime winter temperatures are generally 50–70°F (10–20°C) with January and February nights near freezing point.

New Mexico

New Mexico enjoys at least 70 percent sunshine year round, with July and August monsoon thunderstorms providing most of the precipitation.

From December to March, snowfalls vary from 2ins (5cm) in North-Central New Mexico's Middle Rio Grande Valley to 300ins (750cm)

or more in the mountains. Mile-high Albuquerque (5,000ft/1,524 meters) registers highs from the mid to high 90s°F to 100s (low to high 30s°C) in summer; winter lows are below 30°F (-1°C) in January. Northern New Mexico begins just above Albuquerque's North Valley, above the La Bajada escarpment on Interstate 25 that takes you onto the Colorado Plateau, at 7,000ft elevation (2,134 meters). Santa Fe and Taos report hotter summer temperatures these days, as the climate warms in general, with June highs in the low 90s°F (30s°C) and winter lows typically very cold, in the teens and 20s°F (-7°C to -2°C).

Utah

Southern Utah is on the Colorado Plateau and has sunny days, cool nights, and precipitation that sweeps through as fast rain storms in summer and snow storms in winter. Summer days warm up past 100°F (38°C), which makes hiking inadvisable during the day. Arches National Park, Zion, and the Needles District of Canyonlands national parks are at 4,000ft (1,220 meters), the warmest places in southern Utah, with consistent summer temperatures of 110–115°F (43–46°C). Bryce Canyon is much higher in elevation (8,000ft/2,440 meters) and therefore much cooler, with June, July, and August temperatures of 70–90°F (21–32°C) falling to a deliciously cool camping temperature of 45°F (7°C) overnight. Summer thunderstorms are usually brief, although they do sometimes go on all night, and occur in all the parks. They tend to arrive in the afternoon after huge thunderheads have built up. In summer, be prepared for a major desert temperature difference, with hot days and cooler nights.

What to wear

Think cool and comfortable. With few exceptions, Western dress is informal – jeans or pants, a polo or button-down shirt, and boots or shoes are appropriate at all but the fanciest places and events. Shorts or capris and light shirts are suitable for most situations in the warmer months, although it's a good idea to have a sweater or jacket for evenings, high elevations, or air-conditioned stores and restaurants.

Hot, jagged, uneven desert paths will quickly make mincemeat out of

light sandals and tennis shoes. Be sure to bring well-fitting, comfortable, and sturdy hiking shoes or boots or outdoor sandals for outdoor activities. Try to break them in before a big hike. Lightweight, wicking fabrics will make walks and hikes much more enjoyable. During the "monsoon" season in summer, temperatures can plummet with the rains, and waterproof parkas and pants should be on hand if you plan to be away from shelter.

In the high country summer, and in fall and spring elsewhere, layering is the name of the game. Mornings and nights are chilly enough to necessitate long pants and jackets, sweaters, or fleeces. As the sun comes out, the layers come off. Backpackers may want to consider purchasing convertible pants with zippered legs. Rain gear, thin gloves, and a wool or fleece hat can be handy for quick shift in weather.

Prepare for winters in the mountains to be cold and snowy, though sunny with dry air. Again, layering is highly recommended. Polyester or micro-fiber base layers, fleece, merino wool, rain shells, and down jackets are all good choices for active outdoors activities. A single thick coat may not be enough for the range of temperatures. Those layers will also come in handy (though fewer will be necessary) during the cold winter nights and mornings at low altitude.

Crime and safety

A few common-sense precautions will help keep you safe while traveling in the Southwest. For starters, know where you are and where you're going. Whether traveling on foot or by car, bring a map and plan your route in advance. Ask for directions. Most people are happy to help. Carry a cellphone for emergencies. Inexpensive pay-as-you-go phones are available and come in useful on long-distance drives, although reception may be spotty.

Don't carry large sums of cash or wear flashy or expensive jewelry. Lock unattended cars, and keep your belongings in the trunk. If possible, travel with a companion, especially after dark.

If you are involved in a traffic accident, remain with your vehicle. It is illegal to leave the scene of an accident. Call the police, and wait for emergency vehicles to arrive. Driving under the influence of alcohol (DUI) or drugs (illegal and some prescription) carries stiff penalties, including fines and jail. Wearing seatbelts is required in all states. Children under four must be in a child's safety seat.

Customs regulations

Everyone entering the United States must go through US Customs and Border Protection, a time-consuming process. To speed things up, be prepared to open your luggage for inspection.

You can bring into the US the following duty-free items: one liter of alcohol, if over 21 years of age; 200 cigarettes, 50 cigars for personal use, or 2kg of tobacco, if you're over 18; and gifts worth up to $100 ($800 for US citizens). Travelers with more than $10,000 in US or foreign currency, travelers' checks, or money orders must declare these upon entry. Meat, cheese, fruits, vegetables, seeds, or plants (and, note, even sealed prepared foods from them) are not permitted and must be disposed of in the receptacles provided before entering. For more information, contact US Customs and Border Protection (tel: 877-227-5511; www.cbp.gov).

Disabled travelers

Under the Americans with Disabilities Act (ADA), accommodations built after January 26, 1995, and containing more than five rooms must be usable by persons with disabilities. Older and smaller hotels are exempt, so be sure to inquire before booking. For the sight-impaired, many hotels provide special alarm clocks, voice-over television services, and security measures. To comply with ADA hearing-impaired requirements, hotels have begun to follow special procedures; local agencies may provide TTY and interpretation services. Check with the front desk when you make reservations to ascertain to what degree the hotel complies with ADA guidelines. Ask specific questions regarding bathrooms, bed height, wheelchair space, and availability of services. Restaurants and attractions are required to build ramps for those with limited mobility. Many major attractions have wheelchairs for loan or rent. Some provide menus, visitors' guides, and interpreters for hearing- and sight-impaired guests.

The Society for Accessible Travel & Hospitality (tel: 212-447-7284; www.sath.org) publishes a quarterly magazine on travel for the disabled.

Eating out

All-American
All-American mainstays (really German) like hot dogs, hamburgers, and pretzels are associated with ballparks, corner stands, bars, and fast food outlets and are available almost everywhere, accompanied by yellow American mustard, ketchup, onions, and sauerkraut (homemade raw fermented sauerkraut is more readily available in the Southwest these days, but you won't find it in mainstream outlets). Jewish deli favorites such as bagels, lox, and cream cheese can be found in most towns, as well as pizza joints serving everything from deep-dish Chicago-style to thin-crust New York–style pizza more reminiscent of Naples.

Barbecue
Slow-cooked barbecue in the West is typically beef. Most often, particularly in Texas, the state where it is an art form, you'll find dry barbecue – aged beef dry-rubbed with spices and served with a smoky tomato sauce. An increasing number of barbecue joints now specialize in Southern (wet) barbecue, too – "pulled" (shredded) pork in vinegar-based sauces.

Farm-to-table
The Four Corners states are agriculturally rich regions that are increasingly embracing organic food production and healthy food is available almost everywhere. In stores, at farmers' markets, and locavore restaurants and cafés – sometimes in the most remote and unlikely of places – you'll find dishes centered on fresh produce; meat, eggs, and cheese from free-range livestock living on pastures; fresh-harvested olive oil and aged balsamic vinegar from local producers; baked goods from locally milled wheat and traditional sourdough breads; nationally recognized vineyards producing excellent wine and Champagne and local distilleries in places like Santa Fe that produce unique spirits.

⊘ Environmental ethics

The old saw is good advice: "Take nothing but pictures, leave nothing but footprints." And in the fragile soils of the Southwestern deserts, you should not even leave footprints. The goal of low-impact/no-impact backpacking is to leave the area in the same condition as you found it, if not better. If you're camping in the backcountry, don't break branches, level the ground, or alter the landscape in any way. Make fires in designated places only. Otherwise, use a portable stove. When nature calls, dig a cat hole 6ins (15cm) deep and at least 100ft (30 meters) from water, campsites, and trails. Pack out all trash, including toilet paper.

Mexican and Southwestern
Mexican food is ubiquitous – fresh and authentic in Mexican-owned restaurants and food trucks but frequently Americanized in mainstream Mexican restaurants. Tex-Mex versions of Mexican food are heavy on the meat, beans, and cheese, and often served with mild chile sauces – a far cry from homemade tortillas, beans, tamales, burritos, and enchiladas accompanied by freshly prepared roasted salsas that are a mainstay of the fresher cuisine of Mexico.

New Mexican cuisine is a variant on Mexican food, but quite distinct. It involves traditional, generations-old recipes centered on the Three Sisters – corn, beans, and squash – grown by New Mexico's Pueblo farmers since prehistoric times and combined with meat and red and green chile introduced by the Spaniards during colonization. New Mexico is the Chile Capital of the World, and most people visiting the state want to eat chile with everything: the state obliges, and you'll find everything from green chile burgers to chile-infused beer to ice cream – even apple pie. The state question "Red or Green?" allows you to choose green (fresh) or red (dried) chile sauce to accompany your meal (smothered or on the side); ask for "Christmas," and you'll get both red and green. Chile is grown locally in Hatch and Chimayo, New Mexico; Tucson and Phoenix, Arizona; and Pueblo in southeastern Colorado, and used in both fresh and dried form to make varied sauces and fresh salsas. Time your visit for late summer or early fall, and you will smell the enticing aroma of chile being roasted everywhere.

Native

At high-end tribal-owned resort restaurants on Indian reservations and elsewhere in the Southwest, look for creative and Native-inspired heritage cuisine by professionally trained Indian chefs, drawing on traditional low-fat game, such as grass-fed bison, venison, boar, and elk, and wild-caught fish like Pacific salmon, mountain trout, and shrimp, accompanied by wild greens, pinyon nuts, wild berries, and locally grown produce. Kai, the 5-star dinner restaurant at Sheraton Wild Horse Pass Resort on the Gila River Indian Reservation near Phoenix, focuses on spectacular renditions of classics drawing on Native-raised foods and is worth saving up for.

Road food

Road food is a subject unto itself. Never pass up a slice of homemade pie made from local fruit. When you're traveling long distances, the most important meal of the day is breakfast. Even the lowliest truck stop or diner can fuel you properly for your travels with pancakes, waffles, and creative egg dishes for under $10. You'll find cafes in many places in the Southwest serving Modern Comfort Food, a lighter, healthier, more creative approach to the basics, such as corn cakes with shrimp, green chile mac n' cheese, and eggs in a variety of guises.

Western/ranch

Western dishes focus heavily on meat and potatoes, the kind of food that sustained pioneer ranchers during long days and are a mainstay of working people today. In Cowboy Country, blowout steak dinners are accompanied by the fixings – baked potato with butter and sour cream, corn on the cob, and coleslaw. In high country areas, such as Greer, Arizona, you'll also find locally caught trout on the menu. In southern Arizona's border country, ranchero/Norteño cuisine offers a Mexican variant on traditional western ranch cuisine. In urban foodie spots like Phoenix, Tucson, and Santa Fe, you will find restaurants serving New Western cuisine, often alongside Southwestern, which dials up the basics a notch with creative, modern renditions of meat- and

fish-based dishes using rubs and marinades and lighter pureed vegetable accompaniments leaning on cultural fusion techniques.

Electricity

Standard electricity in North America is 110–115 volts, 60 cycles AC. An adapter and sometimes a transformer is necessary for most appliances from overseas, with the exception of Canada and Japan.

Embassies and consulates

Foreign embassies are all located in Washington, DC. They include:
UK (tel: 202-588-6500; www.gov.uk/world/organisations/british-embassy-washington)
Germany (tel: 202-298-4000; www.germany.info/embassy)
France (tel: 202-944-6000; www.franceintheus.org)
Australia (tel: 202-797-3000; www.us.embassy.gov.au)
New Zealand (tel: 202-328-4800; www.mfat.govt.nz)
Canada (tel: 202-682-1740; www.cic.gc.ca/english/information/offices/missions/washington.asp)
Ireland (tel: 202-462-3939; www.embassyofireland.org)
South Africa (tel: 202-232-4400; www.saembassy.org).

Contact the US State Department for street addresses and other countries' embassy and consulate information (tel: 202-647-4000; www.state.gov/s/cpr/rls).

Emergencies

In case of emergency (police/fire), dial 911.

Etiquette

Visitors often associate the US with relaxed manners. While that may be true up to a point, particularly in dress and table manners, you should be prepared for many Americans, particularly those in traditional rural areas, to be surprisingly polite and formal in speech, dress, and the intricate dance of social interactions.

Americans as a rule are positive, curious about others, generally accepting of differences, warm, effusive, and tactile. This being a nation of immigrants, care is generally taken in polite society not to give offense to any one group, and chauvinism and

racism, though evident, are not tolerated in most social situations, so be careful about making off-color jokes or making assumptions about different regions of the country.

Be open to learning about the traditional cultures of the Southwest and willing to meet others on their own terms. In northern New Mexico, for example, the Hispanic population varies widely in its cultural origins. Many families in the Santa Fe area, for example, can trace their history back to Spanish Colonial times and consider themselves Spanish and natural heirs to a four-century tradition of governance, whereas other Hispanics may be recent arrivals from the adjoining Mexican provinces of Chihuahua or Sonora, or as far as El Salvador and Guatemala in Central America, who come here to work and have family back home. In southern Arizona, close to the US-Mexico border, however you'll

⊙ Film

Even in this era of instant-view digital cameras and smartphones, film is still widely available throughout the US. Business centers and discount chains often offer rapid development or conversion of digital to paper prints. The American Southwest is, of course, spectacularly photogenic. Some of the most rewarding photography is of cultural events, such as costume parades, American Indian dances, and wildlife.

If you plan on photographing in the desert, avoid the flat, washed-out light in the middle of the day and shoot in the early morning or evening instead; cloudy days will offer better contrast than bright sunny days.

Observe appropriate etiquette when photographing Indian tribes. Pueblos in New Mexico usually require you to pay a fee to photograph within the pueblos and during dances. Indian people will usually be happy to pose for you for a small fee. Always ask permission, and get a photo release if it's for commercial purposes, before taking a photo of anyone. Posting someone's photo on social media or a blog, for example, is an intrusion of privacy unless you have permission.

find families whose Mexican roots go back generations.

Visiting American Indian reservations, which are sovereign lands within the US with their own laws and moral code, calls for unique sensitivity and cultural awareness. Make an effort to blend in, dress conservatively (minimum bare skin), behave modestly – particularly at Indian dances, which are religious rituals – and never enter a home without being invited. Try never to refuse a meal if invited on a feast day, as that is considered rude, and when you have eaten, leave promptly, as many others will eat that day too. Many tribes rely on tourism for their income and have developed luxury resorts on their scenic lands to rival any in Las Vegas. In remote areas and at famous tourist spots such as Monument Valley, you will usually be asked to pay a small fee to take photos of family members.

H

Health and medical care

Health coverage and pharmacies

It's vital to have medical insurance when traveling in the US. Although hospitals are obligated to provide emergency treatment to anyone who needs it, whether or not they have insurance, you may have to prove you can pay for treatment of anything less than a life-threatening condition. Know what your policy covers and have proof of the policy with you at all times, or be prepared to pay at the time service is rendered.

Popular drugstore chain CVS Pharmacy has branches throughout the Southwest and several 24-hour locations in Phoenix and one in Tucson (www.cvs.com).

Health hazards

Altitude sickness

This is not a serious consideration in most parts of the state, although people traveling from sea level may feel uncharacteristically winded at elevations as low as 6,000–7,000ft (1,800–2,100 meters). The sensation usually passes after a few days. Symptoms, including nausea, headache, vomiting, extreme fatigue, light-headedness, and shortness of breath, intensify over 10,000ft (3,000

meters). Although the symptoms may be mild at first, they can develop into a serious illness. It's best to acclimatize gradually when you are coming from sea level. Spend a few days at a lower elevation, then move higher.

Cactus

To avoid being pricked, stay on trails and wear long pants and sturdy boots. Some people may have allergies to the prickly varieties of these beautiful desert plants.

Dehydration

Drink plenty of fluids and, if outdoors, carry bottles of water and a high-energy salty snack to eat. The rule of thumb is one gallon (four liters) of water per person per day, and at least one quart (one liter) for shorter walks. Don't wait to get thirsty; start drinking as soon as you set out. Dehydration and salt deficiency can lead to heat exhaustion. It's best to moderate or avoid alcohol and caffeine, drink plenty of water, and take time to acclimate to the heat if you are not accustomed to it. Also avoid the sun at its hottest: 2–5pm.

Drinking water

All water from natural sources must be purified before drinking. Giardia is found throughout the West, even in crystal-clear water, and it can cause severe cramps and diarrhea. The most popular purification methods are tablets or filters or by boiling water for at least five minutes.

Flash floods

Sudden downpours – even those falling miles away from your location – can fill canyons and dry riverbeds with a deadly roaring torrent of water and mud that will sweep away everything in its path. Travelers should be especially careful during the summer "monsoon" season (July to September). Avoid hiking or driving in *arroyos* (gulches) or narrow canyons, and never try to wade or drive across a flooded stream. If rain begins to fall, or you see rain clouds in the distance, move to higher ground. It's impossible to outrun or even outdrive a flash flood. Take action before water levels begin to rise.

Frostbite

Symptoms of frostbite occur when living tissue freezes and include

numbness, pain, blistering, and whitening of the skin. The most immediate remedy is to put frostbitten skin against warm skin. Simply holding your hands for several minutes over another person's frostbitten cheeks or nose may suffice. Otherwise, immerse frostbitten skin in warm (not hot) water. Refreezing will cause even more damage, so get the victim into a warm environment as quickly as possible. If one person is frostbitten, others may be too.

Heat stroke

Long, uninterrupted periods of exposure to high temperatures can lead to heat stroke, which means that the body's core temperature rises to a dangerous level and its normal cooling system – reddening and sweating – is overwhelmed. To head off problems, keep major arteries in your neck cool by wearing a wet bandanna or cotton shirt with a collar. If you start to feel dizzy and fuzzy-brained, feel muscle weakness and start to stumble, and your skin has become pale and dry rather than red and sweaty, immediately begin spraying yourself with water or, better yet, pour it on you. This creates evaporative cooling and is the fastest way to recover. You can also lie down in a dark room with a wet sheet over you and the air conditioning on. Whatever you do, don't jump into cold water in a pool: it can send your body into shock. Heat stroke is a common problem for light-eyed, light-haired Europeans from northern climates and is a potentially serious condition, so don't ignore the telltale signs.

Hypothermia

This occurs when the core body temperature falls below 95°F (35°C). At altitude, combinations of alcohol, cold, and thin air can produce hypothermia. Watch for drowsiness, disorientation, and sometimes increased urination. If possible, get to a hospital; otherwise blankets and extra clothing should be piled on for warmth. If necessary, skin-to-skin contact is effective. Don't use hot water or electric heaters and don't rub the skin. The elderly should be careful in extremely cold weather.

Sunburn

Even a few minutes outdoors in desert sun can result in sunburn, so protect yourself with a high-SPF sunscreen (be sure to put it on 15

⚲ Hiking advice

Avoid solitary hiking. The best situation is to hike with at least two other partners. If one person is injured, one member of the party can seek help while the other two remain behind. If you must hike alone, be sure to tell someone your intended route and time of return; you can also leave an itinerary in a parked car. Backcountry hiking and overnight backpacking trips on public lands usually require a permit. Ask a ranger before setting out.

Use common sense on the trail. Don't attempt routes that are too strenuous for your level of fitness. Concentrate on what you're doing and where you're going. Even well trodden and well-marked trails can be dangerous. Be careful near cliffs, rocky slopes, ravines, rivers, and other hazards. Don't attempt anything you're not comfortable with, or anything that's beyond your level of skill.

Carry the Ten Essentials for outdoor survival in your pack, even if you are only day hiking. These include: navigation (map & compass); sun protection (sunglasses & sunscreen); insulation (extra clothing); illumination (headlamp/flashlight); first-aid supplies; fire (waterproof matches/lighter/candle); repair kit and tools; nutrition (extra food); hydration (extra water); emergency shelter (tent/plastic tube tent/garbage bag).

---

minutes or so before going out in the sun), polarized sunglasses, and a broad-brimmed hat. The elderly and the ill, small children, and people with fair skin should be especially careful. Excessive pain, redness, blistering, or numbness are indications that you need professional attention. Minor sunburn can be soothed by taking a cool bath or using aloe vera gel.

Insects and animals

Gila monsters
North America's only venomous lizard, found in the Sonoran Desert, looks menacing but is easily recognized and rarely encountered.

Insects and arachnids
Bees are abundant, which should concern only those allergic to bee stings. Carry an Epi pen to be safe when traveling. The kissing bug is an unusual-looking black insect with an unpleasant bite. There are fire ants and some varieties of wasp. Their sting can be painful but isn't dangerous unless you're allergic to their venom. Cedar gnats, or no-see-ums, are one of the most annoying of bugs, starting in May when they, like many bugs, begin to hatch. They get into eyes, ears, noses, mouths, and hair and deliver a nasty bite that can swell and give flu-like symptoms. If camping or hiking among junipers (cedars, in pioneer slang), use fine-mesh netting and a tent with no-see-um-proof windows. Deer flies, a particularly large biting fly, may also be found in

Four Corners locations and will present an annoyance to hikers.

The bite of a black widow spider and tarantula and the sting of a pale-colored desert scorpion's tail can pack a punch, but are rarely a serious health threat to adults. Scorpions are nocturnal, so use flashlights and never walk barefoot in the desert. They often hide in recesses, dark corners, and old wood piles and like to crawl into protected places, so shake out clothes or sleeping bags that have been on the ground and check your shoes before slipping into them in the morning.

Snakes
The Southwest has two venomous snakes: rattlesnakes and coral snakes. Only about 3 percent of people bitten by a rattlesnake die, and these are mainly very small children. Walk in the open, proceed with caution among rocks, avoid dark and overgrown places where snakes lurk, shake out bedding or clothing that has been lying on the ground, and wear sturdy hiking boots. Snakes often lie on roads at night because of the residual heat radiating from the pavement, so use a flashlight if walking on a paved road after dark. Most important: Keep your hands and feet where you can see them, and don't let children poke under rocks or logs.

Snakebite kits are good psychological protection, but there is controversy over how effective they are. If bitten, stay calm, to avoid circulating the venom through your body more rapidly. Then apply a tourniquet lightly above the bite toward the heart. Try to identify the species and go immediately to a doctor.

I

Internet

Most public libraries, copy centers, cafés/coffee houses, hotels, and airports offer high-speed or wireless internet access. Some (but not libraries) charge a fee for access, either on their computer or your own device. Surprisingly, lower-priced chain hotels are less likely to charge than high-end hotels. In big cities, public Wi-Fi spots are plentiful. You won't have difficulty getting online in most rural locations these days, but in some very remote locations you may be out of luck. Check www.wifispc.com for updated maps of free Wi-Fi locations throughout the US.

L

LGBTQ travelers

On the whole, urban areas in the US are safer places to visit for gay and lesbian travelers than rural destinations away from the cities. Keep a low profile in such areas to avoid problems. Having said that, the lucrative LGBTQ market is one of the hottest targeted markets in the US, and most states now offer information on gay-friendly travel within their communities. Large metro areas in the Southwest, such as Phoenix, Tucson, Houston, Dallas, San Antonio, and Denver, roll out the red carpet. Smaller arts and university cities, such as Santa Fe, Austin, and Flagstaff, also have surprisingly large gay communities.

For more information, check out Arizona-based Pride Guides, available for Arizona (www.gogayarizona.com), Colorado (www.gogaycolorado.com), New Mexico (www.gogaynewmexico.com), and Nevada (www.gogaynevada.com), and the *Gay and Lesbian Yellow Pages* (tel: 713-942-0084, 800-697-2812 in the US; www.glyp.com. Damron Company (www.damron.com) also publishes city guides aimed at gay travelers.

M

Maps

A detailed road map is essential for any road trip, but particularly in the Southwest. They are widely available at state welcome center and city visitor centers, large bookstores such as Barnes and Noble, outdoor stores, filling stations, supermarkets, and convenience stores. Regional travelers may find it useful to purchase a road-map book with maps of all 50 states, such as the one published by Rand McNally. The American Automobile Association (AAA or "triple A") provides excellent maps for free to members. Free maps of national parks, forests, and other public lands are offered by the managing government agency at entrance stations and visitor centers. Extremely detailed topographical maps of states are available from the US Geological Survey (tel: 800-ASK-USGS; www.usgs.gov/pubprod). Topographic maps are usually available in high-end bookstores and stores that sell outdoor gear. "Topo" maps by Trails Illustrated are available for national parks and other outdoor desinations and are sold through *National Geographic* magazine (www.natgeomaps.com), which also helpfully offers a free online PDF printing service of individual 7.5-minute USGS maps.

Media

Newspapers

Most Southwest towns and cities still support a local newspaper, despite the major downturn in print media, and reading the hometown newspaper is a great way to get to know the community you are in. The *New York Times, Los Angeles Times, Washington Post,* and *the Wall Street Journal* are your best bet for national news. In the Internet era, all newspapers now have online editions and most allow you to read a few articles for free before subscribing, or, like the *Guardian* (UK and US editions), remain free to users.

Albuquerque Journal
7777 Jefferson NE, Albuquerque, NM 87109
Tel: 505-823-4400
www.abqjournal.com
Arizona Daily Star (online only)
4850 S Park Avenue, Tucson, AZ
Tel: 520-573-4142
www.tucson.com

Arizona Daily Sun
111 W Birch, Flagstaff, AZ
Tel: 928-774-4545
www.azdailysun.com
Arizona Republic
200 E Van Buren, Phoenix, AZ
Tel: 602-444-8000
www.azcentral.com
Denver Post
101 W Colfax Avenue, Suite. 800, Denver, CO
Tel: 303-954-1010
www.denverpost.com
Las Cruces Sun News
256 W Las Cruces Avenue, Las Cruces, NM
Tel: 575-541-5400
www.lcsun-news.com
Las Vegas Sun
2275 Corporate Circle, Las Vegas, NV
Tel: 702-385-3111
www.lasvegassun.com
Las Vegas Review-Journal
1111 W Bonanza Road, Las Vegas, NV
Tel: 702-383-0211
www.reviewjournal.com
Santa Fe New Mexican
202 E Marcy, Santa Fe, NM 87501
Tel: 505-983-3303
www.santafenewmexican.com
Salt Lake Tribune
143 S Main Street, Salt Lake City, UT
Tel: 801-204-6100
www.sltrib.com
Spectrum
St George, UT
Tel: 800-748-5489
www.thespectrum.com
Taos News
226 Albright Street, Taos, NM
Tel: 575-758-2241
www.taosnews.com

Television

All major cities have channels affiliated with major networks and local stations, as well as a vast number of cable hookups and satellite offerings. Hotel rooms usually have cable TV, and many have movie channels such as HBO and Showtime; you usually have to pay to watch movies (Pay Per View). Newspapers give daily and weekly information on TV and radio programs, and satellite TV programming (such as Dish and DirectTV) has a program guide through the remote.

Money

Credit cards are very much part of life in the Southwest, as in other parts of the US. They can be used to pay for pretty much anything, and it is common for car rental firms and hotels

to place a temporary deposit on your card. Rental companies may oblige you to pay a large deposit in cash if you do not have a card, although most will accept debit cards now.

You can also use your credit card/debit card to withdraw cash from ATMs. Before you leave home, check which ATM system will accept your card and what conversion charges you will incur (usually a small percentage of each purchase). Before leaving on your trip, be sure to contact your issuing bank and inform them of your travel plans so they do not freeze your account due to unusual activity in a different location. The most widely accepted cards in the US are Visa, American Express, MasterCard, followed by Discover Card, Diners Club, and Japanese Credit Bureau.

Foreign visitors may wish to take US dollar travelers' checks to the Southwest since exchanging foreign currency – whether as cash or checks – can prove problematic if you are not in a major city. An increasing number of banks offer foreign exchange services, but this practice is not universal. Some department store chains offer foreign currency exchange. Many, but not all, stores, restaurants, and other establishments accept travelers' checks in US dollars and will give change in cash. Alternatively, checks can be converted into cash at the bank.

American dollars come in bills of $1, $5, $10, $20, $50, and $100. The dollar is divided into 100 cents. Coins come in 1 cent (penny), 5 cents (nickel), 10 cents (dime), 25 cents (quarter), 50 cents (half-dollar), and $1 denominations.

Money may be sent or received by wire via any Western Union office (tel: 800-325-6000; www.westernunion.com) and online through Moneygram (tel: 800-666-3947; www.moneygram.com) or Pay Pal (tel: 888-221-1161; www.paypal.com).

O

Opening hours

Standard business hours for offices are Mon–Fri 9am–5pm, although in the desert Southwest, public lands management offices and other state and federal government offices typically open earlier, at 8am, to beat the heat and close by 4pm. Banks may also open a little earlier, usually 8.30am, with most open Saturday mornings from 8am to noon. Post offices are usually open Mon–Fri 8am–5pm and Saturdays until 4pm. Most stores and shopping centers are open late on weekends and evenings, with many opening at noon on Sunday.

P

Postal services

Even the most remote towns are served by the US Postal Service. Smaller post offices tend to be limited to business hours (Mon–Fri 9am–5pm), although central, big-city branches may open on Saturday too.

Stamps are sold at all post offices. They are also sold at some convenience stores, gas stations, hotels, and transportation terminals, usually from vending machines, and online.

For two-day national delivery that includes tracking and basic insurance, use **USPS Priority Mail**; flat-rate envelopes and small, medium, and large boxes are an economical way to mail packages safely. For overnight deliveries that include tracking and basic insurance, use **USPS Express Mail**. Global Priority and Global Express Mail are now also available for fast international delivery – at a price. All envelopes and packages shipped overseas must now be sent by first class mail, with prices calculated per ounce.

There are several domestic and international courier services: **FedEx,** tel: 800-463-3339; www.fedex. com; **DHL**, tel: 800-225-5345; www.dhl. com; **United Parcel Service (UPS)**, tel: 800-742-5877; www.ups.com.

Poste restante
Visitors can receive mail at post offices if it is addressed to them, care of "General Delivery', followed by the city name and (very important) the zip code. You must pick up this mail in person within a week or two of its arrival and will be asked to show some form of valid personal identification.

Public holidays

On public holidays, post offices, banks, most government offices, and a large number of stores and restaurants are closed. Public transportation usually runs less frequently.
New Year's Day: January 1
Martin Luther King, Jr.'s Birthday: January 15
Presidents Day: The third Monday in February
Good Friday: March/April – date varies
Easter Sunday: March/ April – date varies
Cinco de Mayo: May 5
Memorial Day: Last Monday in May
Independence Day: July 4
Pioneer Day: July 24 (Utah)
Labor Day: First Monday in September
Columbus Day: Second Monday in October
Veterans Day: November 11
Thanksgiving Day: Fourth Thursday in November
Christmas Day: December 25

R

Religious services

There is no official state religion in the United States, but the Southwest has always attracted spiritual seekers and you will find a great many churches, retreat centers, monasteries, mosques, synagogues, stupas, temples, zen-dos, meeting houses, and other religious/spiritual congregations.

In the heavily Hispanic Southwest, the major religion is quite visibly Catholic, particularly in northern New Mexico, where Christmas and Easter are major religious holidays in both Hispanic villages and Christianized Indian pueblos. Popular Christmas festivals include Las Posadas and Midnight Mass on Christmas Eve, Christmas Day and New Year's Day masses and Indian dances, and Epiphany (Los Reyes) on January 6. At Easter, you'll find many residents making a pilgrimage to the Santuario de Chimayo late Easter Week and offices and businesses closing early in Santa Fe on Good Friday.

Southern Utah/Northern Arizona communities are visibly Mormon, or LDS, and in some remote areas of the Arizona Strip, north of the Grand Canyon, such as Cedar City, you will encounter Fundamentalist Mormons (FLDS), who still practice polygamy and do not encourage visits from outsiders. After Utah, Arizona has the largest concentration of Mormons,

particularly in the White Mountains and the US-Mexico border region along the San Pedro River around St David.

Anglo followers of the late Yogi Bhajan make up the largest Sikh community in the US, the majority living in Santa Cruz outside Española in northern New Mexico. Sikhs are very visible in the Santa Fe area, where they run many successful businesses focusing on yoga, health, and security services.

S

Smoking

Smoking is increasingly frowned on in public places in Southwest cities due to the anti-social nature of smoking for the growing numbers of non-smokers and the known dangers of second-hand smoke. It is no longer permitted in most public buildings and many accommodations, restaurants, and businesses, unless specific rooms are set aside for smoking. Since 2006, Santa Fe has had a city-wide smoke-free ordinance in place prohibiting smoking inside public buildings (including businesses, lodgings, and restaurants, and also on Santa Fe Plaza). Posted signs advise smokers that smoking is not permitted within 25ft (7.62 meters) of entrances and exits to public buildings. Some hotels offer smoking rooms and provide special smoking areas for guests who require them. Other cities are following suit, but you'll still find many smokers in the rural Southwest.

T

Taxes

Most cities raise revenue by adding sales tax to purchases (groceries may be exempt), which is usually 7–9 percent of the sale, and by requiring hotels to charge a lodger's tax, which typically runs 11–12 percent of the room rate. Car rental companies charge both sales tax and service fees.

Telephones

In this era of cell phones, public pay phones have largely disappeared from transportation hubs, gas stations, shopping malls, and outside convenience stores. If you do find one, the cost of making a local call from a pay phone for three minutes is 50 cents. To make a long-distance call from a pay phone, use either a prepaid calling card or your credit card: dial 1-800-CALLATT, key in your credit card number, and wait to be connected. In most areas, local calls have now changed to a 10-digit calling system, using the area code.

Cell phones: American cell phones use GSM 1900, a different frequency from other countries. Only foreign phones operating on GSM 1900 will work in the US. You may be able to take the SIM card from your home phone, install it in a rented cell phone in the US, and use it as if it's your own cell phone. Ask your wireless provider about this before leaving. Cell phones can be rented for about $50 a week in the US, but it makes more sense to buy a cheap pay-as-you-go cell phone and either use it next time or give it away. Also available are GSM 1900-compatible phones with prepaid calling time, such as those offered by T-Mobile (www.t-mobile.com). Be aware that you probably won't be able to pick up a signal in many rural areas, although you may be able to in remote Canyonlands you can always get a signal if you are within sight of the La Sal Mountains. Check coverage before starting out.

Dialing abroad

To dial abroad (Canada follows the US system), first dial the international access code 011, then the country code. If using a US phone credit card, dial the company's access number below, then 01, then the country code.
Sprint, tel: 10333
AT&T, tel: 10288.

Country codes

Australia: 61
Ireland: 353
New Zealand: 64
South Africa: 27
United Kingdom: 44

Tipping

Service workers in restaurants and hotels depend on tips for a significant portion of their income. With few exceptions, tipping is left to your discretion and gratuities are not automatically added to the bill, but in the US, tips are expected. In most cases, 15–20 percent of the before-sales-tax

⊘ Time zones

New Mexico, Utah, Arizona, and Colorado are all in the Mountain Time Zone (GMT -7); Texas is in the Central Time Zone (GMT -6); and Nevada is in the Pacific Time Zone (GMT -8).

All Southwest states, except Arizona, follow Daylight Savings Time, which begins on the second Sunday in March and ends the first Sunday of November. Note: The Navajo Nation, which spans both Arizona and New Mexico, does observe daylight savings time; other Arizona Indian reservations, however, do not.

total is typical for tipping waiters, taxi drivers, bartenders, and hairdressers. Porters and bellboys usually get $1 per bag.

Tourist information

State tourism offices

Arizona
Arizona Office of Tourism
Tel: 866-275-5816
www.visitarizona.com
Bisbee Chamber of Commerce
Tel: 520-432-3554
www.discoverbisbee.com
Flagstaff Visitors Bureau
One E Route 66, Flagstaff
Tel: 928-774-9541 or 800-842-7293
www.flagstaffarizona.org
Grand Canyon Chamber of Commerce
Tel: 928-638-2901
www.grandcanyoncvb.org
Lake Havasu City Convention and Visitors Bureau
420 English Village, Lake Havasu City
Tel: 800-242-8278
www.golakehavasu.com
Navajoland Tourism Office
Tel: 928-871-6436
www.discovernavajo.com
Nogales–Santa Cruz County Chamber of Commerce
123 W Kino Park Way, Nogales
Tel: 520-287-3685
www.thenogaleschamber.org
Page–Lake Powell Chamber of Commerce
34 S Lake Powell Boulevard, Page
Tel: 928-645-2741
www.pagechamber.com
Phoenix Visitors Information Center
125 N Second Street, Suite 120, Phoenix
Tel: 602-254-6500 or 877-CALLPHX

(225-5149)
www.visitphoenix.com
Pinetop–Lakeside Chamber of Commerce
Tel: 928-367-4290 or 800-573-4031
www.pinetoplakesidechamber.com
Prescott Chamber of Commerce
Tel: 928-445-2000
www.prescott.org
Rim Country Chamber of Commerce
100 W Main Street, Payson
Tel: 928-474-4515 or 800-672-9766
www.rimcountrychamber.com
Scottsdale Convention and Visitors Bureau
Tel: 800-782-1117
www.experiencescottsdale.com
Sedona–Oak Creek Canyon Chamber of Commerce
331 Forest Road, Sedona
Tel: 928-282-7722 or 800-288-7336
www.visitsedona.com
Sierra Vista Convention and Visitors Bureau
21 E Wilcox Drive, Sierra Vista
Tel: 520-417-6980 or 800-288-3861
www.visitsierravista.com
Sonoita–Elgin Chamber of Commerce
Tel: 520-455-5498
www.sonoitaelginchamber.org
Tempe Convention and Visitors Bureau
Tel: 866-914-1052
www.tempetourism.com
Tombstone Chamber of Commerce
Tel: 520-457-9317
www.tombstonechamber.com
Tonto Basin Chamber of Commerce
Tel: 928-479-2839 or 800-404-8923
www.tontobasinchamber.org
Tucson Convention and Visitors Bureau
100 S Church Avenue, Tucson
Tel: 520-624-1817 or 800-638-8350
www.visittucson.org
Williams–Grand Canyon Chamber of Commerce
200 W Railroad Avenue, Williams
Tel: 928-635-1418
www.experiencewilliams.com
Yuma Convention and Visitors Bureau
202 N Fourth Avenue, Yuma
Tel: 928-783-1897 or 800-293-0071

Colorado
Colorado Tourism
1672 Pennsylvania Street, Denver, CO 80203; tel: 303-832-6171 or 800-265-6723;
www.colorado.com
Alamosa Visitor Information Center
Cole Park, Alamosa, CO 81101;
tel: 800-BLU-SKYS;
www.alamosa.org

Cortez Chamber of Commerce
928 E Main Street, Cortez, CO 81321; tel: 970-565-3414; www.cortezchamber.com

Durango Chamber of Commerce
111 S Camino del Rio, Durango, CO 81302; tel: 970-247-0312 or 800-463-8726;
www.durango.org

Mesa Verde Country Visitor Information Bureau
928 E Main Street, Cortez, CO 81321; tel: 970-565-8227 or 800-530-2998;
www.colorado.com/official-colorado/mesa-verde-country-visitor-information-bureau.com

Nevada
Nevada Tourism
401 N Carson Street, Carson City 89701
Tel: (800) NEVADA8
www.travelnevada.com

Las Vegas Metro Chamber of Commerce
575 Symphony Park Avenue, Las Vegas 89106
Tel: (702) 641-5822
www.lvchamber.com

Las Vegas Convention and Visitors Authority
3150 Paradise Road, Las Vegas 89109
Tel: 702-892-0711
www.lvcva.com

New Mexico
New Mexico Dept. of Tourism,
491 Old Santa Fe Trail, Santa Fe, NM 87501
Tel: 505-827-7400
www.newmexico.org

Alamogordo Chamber of Commerce
1301 N White Sands Boulevard., Alamogordo, NM 88310
Tel: 575-437-6120
www.alamogordo.com

Albuquerque Convention and Visitors Bureau
20 First Plaza Center NW, #601, Albuquerque, NM 87102
Tel: 505-842-9918
www.visitalbuquerque.com

Fort Sumner Chamber of Commerce
707 N 4th Street, Fort Sumner, NM 88119
Tel: 505-355-7705
www.fortsumnerchamber.com

Gallup-McKinley County Chamber of Commerce
106 Route 66, Gallup, NM 87301
Tel: 505-722-2228
www.thegallupchamber.com

Silver City–Grant County Chamber of Commerce
500 E 18th Street # 214, Silver City, NM 88061
Tel: 800-548-9378
www.silvercity.org

Taos County Chamber of Commerce
1139 Paseo del Pueblo Sur, Taos 87571
Tel: 575-751-8800
www.taoschamber.com

TOURISM Santa Fe
201 W Marcy Street, Santa Fe 87501
Tel: 505-955-6200
www.santafe.org

Texas
Texas Tourism
1100 San Jacinto, Austin, TX 78701
Tel: 512-463-2000
www.traveltexas.com

El Paso Convention and Visitors Bureau
1 Civic Center Plaza, El Paso, TX 79901
Tel: 915-534-0600
www.visitelpaso.com

Utah
Utah Office of Tourism
Council Hall/Capitol Hill, 300 N State Street, Salt Lake City, UT 84114
Tel: 801-538-1900 or toll free 800-200-1160
www.utah.gov

Utah's Canyon Country
P.O. Box 490, Monticello, UT 84535
Tel: 435-587-3235 x 5006 or toll free 800-574-4386
www.utahscanyoncountry.com/northern-region

St George & Zion Area Convention and Visitors Bureau
20 N Main Street, Suite. 105, St George, UT 84770
Tel: 435-634-5747 or toll free 800-869-6635
www.visitstgeorge.com

National parks and wilderness areas
Arizona State Parks Office
23751 N 23rd Street #190, Phoenix, AZ 85085
Tel: 877-MYPARKS
www.azstateparks.com

Bureau of Land Management Arizona
1 N Central Avenue #800, Phoenix, AZ 85004
Tel: 602-417-9200
www.blm.gov/contact/arizona

Bureau of Land Management New Mexico
301 Dinosaur Trail, Santa Fe, NM 87508
Tel: 505-954-2000
www.blm.gov/contact/newmexico

Bureau of Land Management Utah
440 W 200 South, Suite. 500, Salt Lake City, UT 84101
Tel: 801-539-4001
www.blm.gov/contact/utah

USDA Forest Service – Southwestern Region
333 Broadway Boulevard. SE, Albuquerque, NM 87102
Tel: 505-842-3292
www.fs.usda.gov/r5

National Park Service Intermountain Regional Office
12795 Alameda Parkway, Denver, CO 80225
Tel: 303-969-2500
www.nps.gov

New Mexico Energy, Minerals, and Natural Resources Department
State Parks Division, 1220 South St Francis Drive, Santa Fe, NM 87505
Tel: 888-667-2757
www.emnrd.state.nm.us

Utah Division of Parks and Recreation
1594 W North Temple, Suite 116, Salt Lake City, UT 84116
Tel: 801-538-7220
www.stateparks.utah.gov

Tour operators and travel agents

The US has a huge variety of travel agents and tour operators to assist with both general and specialty travel packages. Even if you are planning on doing the driving yourself you may want to hook up with a local tour operator to let someone else show you around for a few days. You can locate a US tour operator by

⊙ America the Beautiful Federal Lands Pass

If you plan to visit more than a couple of US national parks, national forests, national wildlife refuges, BLM, or Army Corps of Engineers/Bureau of Reclamation dam sites in a given year, be sure to buy the America the Beautiful Federal Lands Pass, which offers week-long admission for one vehicle containing four passengers to over 2,000 federal recreational sites across the country for $80. Passes are available online and from all park entrance fee booths (a portion of the purchase will go back into that specific park, so choose wisely). For more information and to buy a pass online, visit www.recreation.gov.

checking listings on the websites of the **US Tour Operator Assocation** (www.ustoa.com) and the **National Tour Association** (www.ntaonline.com). It is an excellent idea to contact the visitor center at your destination for officially sanctioned local listings, particularly for designated concessioners for river rafting and other activities in national parks.

Recommended tour operators serving all of the US, and throughout the Southwest, include top-rated **Tauck Tours** (tel: 800-788-7885; www.tauck.com) a family-run company that has been in business since 1924, and **Abercrombie and Kent** (tel: 800-554-7016; www.abercrombiekent.com), which specializes in small-group luxury tours. **The Smithsonian Institution** (tel: 855-330-1542; www.smithsonianjourneys.org) offers educational study tours to sites of archeological, historical, and scientific interest in the US, such as the Ancestral Puebloan ruins of the Southwest, guided by authorities in the field. National park concessioners offer bus tours, mule rides, and other guided tours; some, such as **Fred Harvey Detours** at the Grand Canyon, can trace their history with the park to its very founding. Park staff maintains listings of individual outfitters. **Gray Line** (tel: 303-394-6920, toll free: 800-472-9546; www.grayline.com) runs guided bus tours in most large US cities.

Specialty tour operators offer guided trips tailored to your interests, from tours of ghost towns in Arizona to historic walking tours in cities like Santa Fe, Taos, Tucson, and Flagstaff. Outfitters offer guided trips of the outdoors. You can enjoy hiking, wildlife watching, hunting, fishing, river rafting, horseback riding, rock climbing, canyoneering, skiing, and camping with outdoor outfitters in the Southwest.

One national company running popular outdoor tours in Southwest parks is **REI** (tel: 800-622-2236; www.rei.com/adventures/trips/signature-camping), the outdoor retailer, whose Signature Camping trips include guided hiking, kayaking, and "glamping" in small groups in large, comfortable tents with every comfort taken care of, including meals. REI offers camping itineraries in Zion, Bryce Canyon, Canyonlands, Capitol Reef, Grand Canyon, and Arches national parks. Children (age 8 and older) can take part in any of the itineraries. **Backroads Tours** (tel: 800-462-2848; www.backroads.com), another well-considered national outfitter, specializes in nature tours of national parks and other natural areas that involve kayaking, river rafting, hiking, wildlife watching, and mountain biking and deluxe camping.

Throughout the Southwest, you'll find specialty tour companies offering Jeep tours in Canyonlands and Sedona; winery tours in central and southern Arizona; elegant sunrise balloon trips in Sedona and Albuquerque; heritage tours on private ranches in southwestern Colorado; archeological and paleontological tours (sometimes involving participating in digs) throughout the Southwest; Native-guided tours of Monument Valley and other tribal parks; and tribal outfitters on many Indian reservations (contact the tribe for information). Tours exist aimed at those with special needs, health issues, disabilities, singles, women only, the LGBTQ community, and others.

Visas and passports

Entry requirements

Foreign travelers to the United States (including those from Canada and Mexico) must carry a valid passport; a return plane ticket is also normally required. A visa is required for visits of more than 90 days. Visitors needing a visa should apply to the American Embassy or Consulate in the city or country where they live permanently. As part of the application process, travelers may need to schedule an interview and fingerprint scan. Application fees start at $160.

Tourists or business travelers from countries participating in the Visa Waiver Program, such as the UK, can stay up to 90 days in the US without a visa. Travelers eligible for the program must register online via the website of the Electronic System for Travel Authorization, or ESTA (tel: 703-526-4200; https://esta.cbp.dhs.gov) at least three days before they travel. An approved application remains valid for up to two years, or until the traveler's passport expires. It also entitles the holder to multiple entries into the US during this period.

Note: An Executive Order signed by President Trump on 6 March 2017 has been partially introduced following a Supreme Court ruling on 26 June 2017. The Executive Order temporarily suspends entry into the United States of certain foreign nationals from six countries: Syria, Sudan, Iran, Somalia, Libya, and Yemen. For the most current information, contact the US Department of Homeland Security at www.dhs.gov.

Extensions of stay

Visas are usually granted for six months. If you wish to remain in the country longer than six months, you must apply for an extension of stay at the **US Immigration and Customs Enforcement (ICE)**, 500 12th Street SW, Washington, DC 20536, tel: 202-732-4242; www.ice.gov.

Weights and measures

Despite efforts to convert to metric, the US still uses the Imperial System of weights and measures.

☉ Wildlife

Did you know that the most dangerous animal at the Grand Canyon is the ubiquitous rock squirrel? That's because people find these little rodents cute and try to feed them and frequently get a nasty bite in the process. Rodents carry plague and other diseases such as hanta virus, which annually cause deaths in the Southwest, particularly New Mexico. Some animals, such as bison, may seem placid and slow-moving but will charge if irritated. In recent years, several visitors in national parks have been seriously injured or killed by bison after approaching to get a better photograph. If you want close-ups, buy a telephoto lens. In Bear Country, be careful to keep a clean camp and hang food or store it in bear lockers to avoid problems.

NONFICTION

Ancient Ruins of the Southwest: An Archaeological Guide by David Grant Noble. A detailed guide to major archeological finds throughout the deserts of the Southwest, with ample coverage of Arizona.

The Architecture of the Southwest by Trent Elwood Sanford. A look at the classic adobe architecture found throughout the Southwest.

Arizona's Ghost Towns and Mining Camps: A Travel Guide to History by Philip Varney. The second edition of the popular illustrated *Arizona Highways* guide to what remains from the old West.

The Hour of Land: A Personal Topography of America's National Parks by Terry Tempest Williams. This intensely personal and poetic look at national parks by the award-winning Utah naturalist was published in 2016, the centennial year of the National Park Service.

Best of the West: An Anthology of Classic Writing from the American West edited by Tony Hillerman, author of the Leaphorn/Chee mysteries set on the Navajo Nation.

Book of the Hopi by Frank Waters. A pioneering work on the culture, spiritualism, stories, and traditions of the Hopi by a novelist.

Book of the Navajo by Raymond Locke. The sixth edition of a scholarly cultural history of the Navajo, first published in the 1970s.

Buckaroo edited by Hal Cannon and Thomas West. Cowboy folklore specialists investigate the culture of the cowboy.

Desert Solitaire: A Season in the Wilderness by Edward Abbey. This classic ode to the desert, written by Abbey during his season as a park ranger in Arches National Park in the Fifties, should be in every backpack.

The Exploration of the Colorado River and its Canyons by John Wesley Powell. Major Powell's own recounting of his 1869 and 1872 voyages down the Colorado.

Roadside Geology of Arizona by Halka Chronic. One of an excellent series of state geology guides that introduce the geological wonders of the Southwest as seen through the car window.

The People: Indians of the American Southwest by Stephen Trimble. An engaging celebration of the Southwest's native people by this writer/photographer.

Santa Fe Style by Christine Mather, photographs by Jack Parsons, Rizzoli. A coffee-table book offering inspiration on the architecture, clothing, and aesthetic style that has come to be associated with Santa Fe.

FICTION

The Bean Trees by Barbara Kingsolver. Kingsolver's 1988 debut novel about a young woman who flees her home and finds herself working in a garage in Tucson.

All the Pretty Horses by Cormac McCarthy. A gritty tale of the border country and its realities by the El Paso-born author.

Call of the Canyon by Zane Grey. This classic Western novel is about a returning veteran who is nursed back to health by an Arizona gal.

Death Comes for the Archbishop by Willa Cather. Cather's fictionalized account of Archbishop Lamy in 1800s Santa Fe.

Ceremony by Leslie Marmon Silko. Silko's moving novel concerns a World War II veteran of mixed ancestry who returns to Laguna Pueblo deeply scarred by his experience as a Japanese POW and must "call back his spirit" in order to heal.

Judgment Call by J.A. Jance. A part-time resident of Bisbee, J.A. Jance's best-selling Arizona detective novels follow the exploits of Cochise County Sheriff Joanna Brady. This 2013 novel is considered by many to be her best.

The Milagro Beanfield War by John Nichols. The first novel in the Taos-based author's New Mexico Trilogy pits a small traditional village against a developer in a struggle for water rights in northern New Mexico.

Spider Woman's Daughter by Anne Hillerman. Tony Hillerman's daughter Anne picks up the reins of the beloved Leaphorn/Chee Navajo Police mystery series with a gripping yarn.

The Tennis Partner by Abraham Verghese. Written by the well-known AIDS researcher (and author of the best-seller *Cutting for Stone*), this memoir poignantly captures his experiences caring for AIDS patients as a young doctor in El Paso in the 80s.

Thief of Time by Tony Hillerman. One of the engaging Leaphorn/Chee mysteries set on the Navajo Nation by the late New Mexico journalist, *Thief of Time* delves into Southwest archeology.

⟳ Send Us Your Thoughts

We do our best to ensure the information in our books is as accurate and up-to-date as possible. The books are updated on a regular basis using local contacts, who painstakingly add, amend and correct as required. However, some details (such as telephone numbers and opening times) are liable to change, and we are ultimately reliant on our readers to put us in the picture.

We welcome your feedback, especially your experience of using the book "on the road".

We will acknowledge all contributions, and we'll offer an Insight Guide to the best letters received.

Please write to us at:
Insight Guides
PO Box 7910
London SE1 1WE
Or email us at:
hello@insightguides.com

OTHER INSIGHT GUIDES

Other titles focusing on the south and west of the US include Insight Guides to *US National Parks West*, *Arizona & the Grand Canyon*, *USA on the Road*, *Texas*, and *California*.

CREDITS

PHOTO CREDITS

123RF 205B
20th Century Fox/Kobal/REX/ Shutterstock 123
Al Argueta/Apa Publications 6ML, 21, 283B, 304, 307, 312B
Alamy 36, 37, 42, 43, 46, 47, 60BR, 61BR, 81, 92, 95TR, 118, 121, 141, 188, 200, 211, 212/213, 215, 218/219, 222, 226, 233, 236, 247, 256, 261, 291
AP/REX/Shutterstock 58
Arizona Office of Tourism 189
Bill Manns/REX/Shutterstock 49
Carol M. Highsmith/Library of Congress 29, 204, 205T, 277
Christopher Okula/U.S. Air Force 61BL
Design Pics Inc/REX/Shutterstock 262
Elliott Marks/Universal/Kobal/REX/ Shutterstock 120
Felicia Fonseca/AP/REX/ Shutterstock 88
FLPA 216BR, 217ML, 217BR, 217BL
Getty Images 0/1, 4, 10/11, 16, 26/27, 28, 30, 33, 34, 39, 41, 45, 50, 51, 52, 53, 54, 55, 56, 61TR, 62/63, 64/65, 66, 70, 71, 73, 74, 75, 76, 77, 78, 79, 80, 82, 83, 84, 85, 89, 90, 94/95T, 94BR, 94BL, 95BR, 97, 101, 103, 112, 119, 125, 132, 133, 134, 137, 146/147, 148/149, 150/151, 152, 187, 195, 201, 203, 206, 216/217T, 223, 227, 230, 237, 238, 240,
241, 242, 248, 249, 252, 257, 258, 263B, 274, 280/281, 284, 290, 292, 297, 315, 316/317T, 316BL, 317ML, 317BR, 317BL, 326, 328, 330/331
Glasshouse Images/REX/ Shutterstock 40
Granger/REX/Shutterstock 44, 124, 267
iStock 6MR, 6BL, 6BR, 7TR, 7ML, 7BR, 22, 95BL, 131, 143, 145, 167, 183, 202, 212, 216BL, 217TR, 225, 228, 234, 243, 245, 246, 259, 264, 265, 269, 270, 278, 279, 283T, 286/287, 288, 289, 293, 296, 298, 300, 301, 305, 308/309, 314, 319, 335, 353
Jeff Schultes/REX/Shutterstock 91
Joe Sohm/REX/Shutterstock 272
John Locher/AP/REX/Shutterstock 68
Julie Jacobson/AP/REX/Shutterstock 332B
Lenny Ignelzi/AP/REX/Shutterstock 69
Library of Congress 93
mtnmichelle 271
Ned Scott/United Artists/Kobal/REX/ Shutterstock 122
Nowitz Photography/Apa Publications 7MR, 7TL, 8, 14/15, 18, 19, 20, 23, 25, 31, 32, 35, 57, 59, 67, 96, 98, 100, 102, 104, 105, 106, 107, 108, 109, 110, 111, 113, 114, 115, 116, 117, 129, 130, 136,
138, 139, 142, 144, 153T, 153B, 156, 157T, 158, 159, 162, 163, 164, 166T, 166B, 168, 169, 170, 171, 172, 173, 174, 175, 176, 177, 178, 179T, 180, 181, 186, 190, 191, 192, 193, 194, 196, 235, 239, 244B, 244T, 250, 251, 253T, 253B, 254, 255, 268, 276B, 276T, 294/295, 302, 303, 310, 312T, 313, 317TR, 318, 321, 322B, 322T, 323, 324, 325, 327, 329, 332T, 334, 336, 338, 340/341
Orion/Kobal/REX/Shutterstock 128
P.E.A/Kobal/REX/Shutterstock 127
Photoshot 316BR
Public domain 61ML, 197
Robert Harding 38, 266
Ross D. Franklin/AP/REX/ Shutterstock 86
Shutterstock 7ML, 9, 24, 72, 95ML, 99, 135, 140, 157B, 161, 179B, 198, 199, 207, 208, 209, 210, 214, 229, 232, 260B, 260T, 263T, 273, 275, 285, 299, 311, 333
Sipa Press/REX/Shutterstock 182
Sipa USA/REX/Shutterstock 60/61T
SuperStock 12/13
The Art Archive/REX/Shutterstock 48, 60BL
United Artists/Kobal/REX/ Shutterstock 126
University of Southern California. Libraries/California Historical Society 87

COVER CREDITS

Front cover: Horseshoe Bend, Arizona *Shutterstock*
Back cover: Double O Arch in Arches National Park, Utah *iStock*
Front flap: (from top) Museum of Indian Arts and Culture, Santa Fe
iStock; Zion National Park *Shutterstock*; Sonoran Desert *iStock*; Arches National Park *iStock*
Back flap: Road in White Sands National Monument *Shutterstock*

INSIGHT GUIDE CREDITS

Distribution
UK, Ireland and Europe
Apa Publications (UK) Ltd;
sales@insightguides.com
United States and Canada
Ingram Publisher Services;
ips@ingramcontent.com
Australia and New Zealand
Woodslane; info@woodslane.com.au
Southeast Asia
Apa Publications (SN) Pte;
singaporeoffice@insightguides.com
Worldwide
Apa Publications (UK) Ltd;
sales@insightguides.com
Special Sales, Content Licensing and CoPublishing
Insight Guides can be purchased in bulk quantities at discounted prices. We can create special editions, personalised jackets and corporate imprints tailored to your needs.
sales@insightguides.com
www.insightguides.biz

Printed in China by CTPS

First Edition 1984
Sixth Edition 2018

Every effort has been made to provide accurate information in this publication, but changes are inevitable. The publisher cannot be responsible for any resulting loss, inconvenience or injury. We would appreciate it if readers would call our attention to any errors or outdated information. We also welcome your suggestions; please contact us at:
hello@insightguides.com

www.insightguides.com

Editor: Sarah Clark
Author: Nicky Leach
Head of Production: Rebeka Davies
Update Production: Apa Digital
Picture Editor: Tom Smyth
Cartography: original cartography Polyglott Kartographie, updated by Carte

CONTRIBUTORS

The natural choice to write this comprehensively updated new edition of *Insight Guide USA Southwest* was veteran writer/editor **Nicky Leach**, who has worked with Insight Guides since 1995 and is author of Insight Guides to *Arizona*, *Colorado*, *Utah*, *New Mexico*, *Texas*, and *Florida*, among others. A longtime resident of Santa Fe, Nicky contributed chapters to the last edition of this classic guide in 2000, and enjoyed updating it for the 21st century with extensive new material reflecting the stunning diversity of the contemporary Southwest.

Original contributors to the book included well known Southwest authors: **Tony Hillerman**, **Leslie Marmon Silko**, and **Rudolfo Anaya**.

The book was commissioned and edited by Managing Editor **Sarah Clark**. Thanks go to **Penny Phenix** for proofreading and indexing.

ABOUT INSIGHT GUIDES

Insight Guides have more than 45 years' experience of publishing high-quality, visual travel guides. We produce 400 full-colour titles, in both print and digital form, covering more than 200 destinations across the globe, in a variety of formats to meet your different needs.

Insight Guides are written by local authors, whose expertise is evident in the extensive historical and cultural background features. Each destination is carefully researched by regional experts to ensure our guides provide the very latest information. All the reviews in **Insight Guides** are independent; we strive to maintain an impartial view. Our reviews are carefully selected to guide you to the best places to eat, go out and shop, so you can be confident that when we say a place is special, we really mean it.

Legend

City maps

Freeway/Highway/Motorway
Divided Highway
Main Roads
Minor Roads
Pedestrian Roads
Steps
Footpath
Railway
Funicular Railway
Cable Car
Tunnel
City Wall
Important Building
Built Up Area
Other Land
Transport Hub
Park
Pedestrian Area
Bus Station
Tourist Information
Main Post Office
Cathedral/Church
Mosque
Synagogue
Statue/Monument
Beach
Airport

Regional maps

Freeway/Highway/Motorway (with junction)
Freeway/Highway/Motorway (under construction)
Divided Highway
Main Road
Secondary Road
Minor Road
Track
Footpath
International Boundary
State/Province Boundary
National Park/Reserve
Marine Park
Ferry Route
Marshland/Swamp
Glacier   Salt Lake
Airport/Airfield
Ancient Site
Border Control
Cable Car
Castle/Castle Ruins
Cave
Chateau/Stately Home
Church/Church Ruins
Crater
Lighthouse
Mountain Peak
Place of Interest
Viewpoint

INDEX

MAIN REFERENCES ARE IN BOLD TYPE

INSIGHT ⊙ GUIDES

OFF THE SHELF

Since 1970, INSIGHT GUIDES has provided a unique perspective on the world's best travel destinations by using specially commissioned photography and illuminating text written by local authors.

Whether you're planning a city break, a walking tour or the journey of a lifetime, our superb range of guidebooks and phrasebooks will inspire you to discover more about your chosen destination.

INSIGHT GUIDES

offer a unique combination of stunning photos, absorbing narrative and detailed maps, providing all the inspiration and information you need.

PHRASEBOOKS & DICTIONARIES

help users to feel at home, when away. Pocket-sized with a free app to download, they go where you do.

CITY GUIDES

pack hundreds of great photos into a smaller format with detailed practical information, so you can navigate the world's top cities with confidence.

EXPLORE GUIDES

feature easy-to-follow walks and itineraries in the world's most exciting destinations, with our choice of the best places to eat and drink along the way.

POCKET GUIDES

combine concise information on where to go and what to do in a handy compact format, ideal on the ground. Includes a full-colour, fold-out map.

EXPERIENCE GUIDES

feature offbeat perspectives and secret gems for experienced travellers, with a collection of over 100 ideas for a memorable stay in a city.

www.insightguides.com

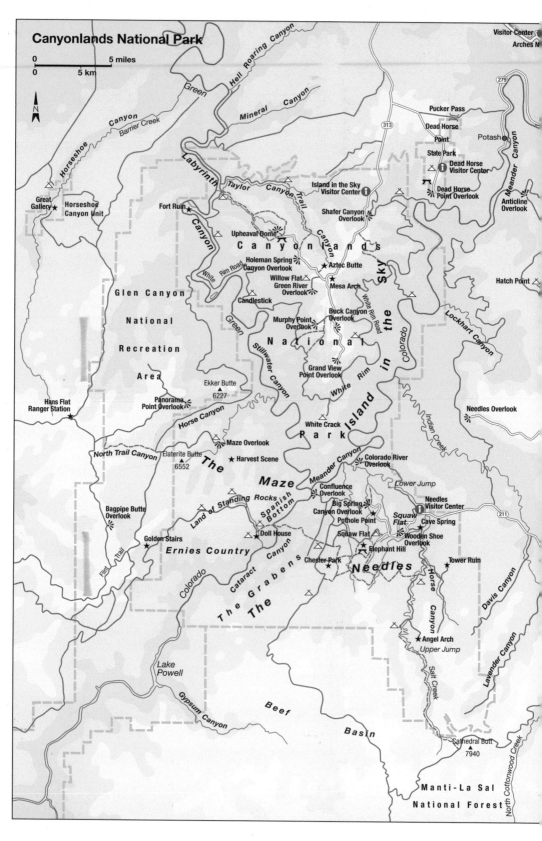